AT THE EDGE OF

SPACE

AT THE EDGE OF
SPACE

MILTON O. THOMPSON

Foreword by Neil A. Armstrong

THE X-15 FLIGHT PROGRAM

Smithsonian Books
Washington and London

Editor: Martha J. King
Designer: Janice Wheeler

Library of Congress Cataloging-in-Publication Data
Thompson, Milton O.
    At the edge of space : the X-15 flight program / Milton O. Thompson
        p.   cm.
    Includes index.
    ISBN 1-56098-107-5 (alk. paper)
    1. X-15 (Rocket aircraft). 2. Airplanes—California—Edwards Air Force Base—Flight
testing—History. I. Title.
TL789.8.U6X578 1992
629.134'53'0973—dc20   91-23701

British Library Cataloguing-in-Publication Data is available

A paperback reissue (ISBN 1-58834-078-3) of the original cloth edition

Manufactured in the United States of America
10 09 08 07 06 05 04 03   5 4 3 2 1

∞ The paper used in this publication meets the minimum requirements of the American
National Standard for Permanence of Paper for Printed Library Materials Z39.48-1984

The photographs appearing in this book are National Aeronautics and Space
Administration and U.S. Air Force photographs from the archives of the Dryden Flight
Research Facility and Air Force Flight Test Center. Smithsonian Books does not retain
reproduction rights for these illustrations individually, or maintain a file of addresses for
photo sources.

Publisher's note: The description of otherwise undocumented personal incidents and the
recollections of episodes and persons are entirely the author's. Every effort has been made
to verify details and ensure correctness; inaccuracy, if it occurs, is regretted.

Dedicated to my wife Therese,
who courageously supported my participation
in this program.
Take care of her, God.

Contents

Foreword

From time to time in the world of flight, a flying machine is produced that has no commercial or military purpose. The 1903 Wright Flyer was such a machine. Indeed, many of the early flying machines were crafted just to investigate an idea or prove a concept. In an airplane, the proof is in the flying. Craft built to demonstrate a concept, or to pave the way for a commercial or military derivative, were termed "experimental." In some countries, experimental airplanes were so licensed and prohibited from commercial activity.

World War II provided an enormous impetus for rapid aircraft development. Bombers needed more speed to reduce their chances of being shot down by enemy interceptors. Fighters needed more power to improve rate of climb and speed to permit them to intercept enemy bombers. Pilots of these new faster fighters soon noticed that their steeds sometimes became cantankerous in steep dives. At maximum speed, the aircraft buffeted and controls became sluggish and ineffective. These compressibility effects were believed to be the cause of a number of catastrophic accidents. When jet-powered fighters entered the scene late in the war, they could fly fast enough in level flight to encounter such difficulties and it became imperative to understand these and other phenomena associated with high-speed flight.

Aircraft designers depend on testing models in wind tunnels for predicting aircraft behavior. Wind tunnel results were generally reliable at speeds up to a Mach number of .75 (subsonic) and greater than 1.2 (supersonic). Airflow around an airplane, however, is characterized by wide variations in speed at various positions around it. Consequently, when an aircraft is flying near the speed of sound, some airflow around the craft is subsonic while the flow at other locations is supersonic. Wind tunnel testing was notoriously poor in this "transonic" region, partly because shock waves would form and be reflected off the tunnel walls onto the model, thus negating an accurate representation of the actual flow.

A number of researchers came to the conclusion that the best method for investigating this region was with a full-scale aircraft in actual flight. The U.S. Navy and the National Advisory Committee for Aeronautics (NACA) sponsored a turbojet-powered transonic research aircraft (the Douglas D-558-I), and the U.S. Army Air Force and the NACA sponsored a rocket-powered supersonic aircraft (the Bell XS-1). The Bell XS-1 became famous as the first manned aircraft to fly (in 1947) faster than sound. It was followed by a variety of other research aircraft: the Douglas X-3 (stubby, thin wing); the Northrop X-4 (tailless); the Bell X-5 (variable sweep wing); the Douglas D-558-II (swept wing, jet and/or rocket powered); and the Bell X-2 (swept wing, rocket powered). This stable of flying research tools made significant contributions to the understanding of the transonic and supersonic regimes and engendered wide support for the research airplane concept.

The German development of large rocket engines invited new advanced flight concepts. Among the most mind-boggling were the proposals of German scientists Eugene Sanger and Irene Bredt. They suggested the possibility of a rocket boosting a winged glider to very high speeds above the atmosphere. By skipping across the top of the atmosphere like a flat stone skipped across a pond, the glider could fly unpowered across the ocean!

Such heady ideas, whether practical or not, inspired substantial creative thinking on the possibilities of very high-speed flight. During the summer of 1952, the NACA Committee on Aerodynamics called for the NACA to increase its flight research at Mach numbers between four and ten and altitudes between twelve and fifty miles.

At about the same time, a number of proposals emerged for a piloted, rocket powered hypersonic (five or more times the speed of sound) research airplane. Max Hunter of Douglas Aircraft, Walter Dornberger of Bell Aircraft, and Hubert Drake and Robert Carman of the NACA generated preliminary designs. By the mid-1950s, enthusiasm had grown to the point where key policymaking groups at the NACA, the U.S. Air Force, and the U.S. Navy were supporting manned hypersonic flight. The X-1 and D-558-II rocket aircraft had been operated in a relatively successful manner over a number of years, and their launching from a "mother aircraft" was performed with confidence.

The problems would be substantial. It was well known that aircraft stability decreased as Mach number increased. The X-1A, flown by Chuck Yeager, went out of control at a Mach number of 2.44. The X-2, flown by Milburn Apt, similarly went out of control at a Mach number of 3.2. Unfortunately, both the X-2 and its pilot were lost. Clearly, finding a design configuration and developing techniques to maintain safe, controlled flight at high Mach number would be a major objective of any hypersonic airplane effort.

The second major challenge dealt with heating. When any object passes through air at high speed, the air molecules are heated, and the heat is transferred to the object. The effect is generally unnoticeable at subsonic speeds. At the speed of the Concorde supersonic transport, however, the passengers can easily feel the warming of the window panes. A craft at hypersonic speeds reaches temperatures at which aluminum would melt, and the temperature differences between different parts of the craft would create enormous stresses. A hypersonic airplane would require new materials, new fabricating techniques, and new methods for predicting the thermally induced stresses.

A rocket craft with hypersonic performance would have the ability to climb above the atmosphere where conventional control systems, airspeed indicators, and altimeters would not be functional. Clearly such a machine would need alternative instruments and methods of control.

These difficulties were not the reason why the hypersonic airplane was not built. They were, in fact, the very reason for its existence. Interest continued to grow, and the NACA conducted numerous studies during 1954 to refine the performance goals, configuration, and structural concepts. The results were encouraging. Inconel-X, a nickel-based alloy, could maintain structural strength to a temperature of 1,200° F. This would permit maximum Mach numbers of about 7. And a craft with a Mach number of 7 could reach altitudes well above 50 miles.

Late in 1954, the air force, navy, and the NACA agreed to go forward with the project, identified as the X-15, and established a joint committee responsible for its technical direction with Dr. Hugh Dryden of the NACA as chairman. The aeronautical industry was invited to compete on the program early in 1955. The companies who completed proposals were the Douglas Aircraft Company, the Bell Aircraft Company, the Republic Aviation Corporation, and the North American Aviation, Inc. After a tight competition, the contract was awarded to North American late in 1955.

The X-15 was to be capable of a speed of 6,600 feet per second and an altitude of 250,000 feet. It was to carry a pilot and a payload of 800 pounds of research instruments and recorders. At the time it seemed audacious. It had taken half a century for aircraft to reach Mach 2 and 80,000 feet. Now one new design would attempt to triple those achievements.

The X-15 would accomplish all its goals and more. In 199 flights over nearly a decade, it would become the most successful research airplane in history. But there is much more than numbers to that story.

Milt Thompson tells that "much more" in At the Edge of Space. And he is well qualified to spin the yarn. He was a participant in the program throughout the X-15's career: as engineer, research scientist, and X-15 pilot. He brings vitality and vibrancy to a tale that bears retelling. He tells of the people, the triumphs, and the tragedies as observed from the inside of the project.

The X-15 no longer carves giant trajectories over southwestern deserts; no longer plunges earthward and slides to a stop on the dry lakebed at Edwards, California. The X-15 is long retired to museum status, a primitive pathfinder in the conquest of space. But history will record its legacy: a large ring of keys for unlocking the mysteries of future flight.

Neil A. Armstrong

Acknowledgments

This book was successfully completed primarily as a result of the moral support, encouragement and inspiration offered by Jack and June Kolf and their lovely daughter, Kathy. Their further assistance in the actual preparation and editing of the manuscript was an added bonus and an indication of the sincerity of their friendship. I cannot thank them enough for all the help that they provided.

I owe special thanks to Dick Hallion, my favorite author, who reviewed my first rough handwritten chapter and encouraged me to continue. His encouragement was crucial in convincing me that I could write a credible account of the flight program.

Paul Bikle read and reread several early versions of the book and provided many critical comments and recommendations. After several painstaking reviews, he finally began to like the book. Bob Rushworth and Neil Armstrong added their blessings. Johnny Armstrong, an X-15 flight planner, and Ed Saltzman, a research engineer, verified the authenticity of the book and offered suggestions for additional humor.

Tim Horton and Roy Bryant searched through their extensive personal accumulation of photos and other memorabilia to provide material that does not officially exist. Jim Young, the Air Force Flight Test Center Historian, loaned me his collection of X-15 photos for duplication. NASA Dryden provided additional photographic material, flight reports, and maps. Ted Ayers, Dryden's deputy director, and Nancy Lovato, Dryden's public affairs officer, provided good critiques.

And finally, my sons and daughter—Eric, Milt Jr., Peter, Kye, and Brett—as well as their spouses Dale, Cherri, and Gregg provided outstanding support and encouragement during the lengthy writing process. They were my cheering section. I am deeply indebted to them.

AT THE EDGE OF
SPACE

Introduction: The Men

The twelve X-15 pilots were a rather low-key bunch of pilots. None were celebrities or national heroes prior to being designated as X-15 pilots. They were known only in the flight test community. They were typical of the many highly capable but relatively unknown NACA and military test pilots who had been routinely testing airplanes since World War I. (The National Advisory Committee for Aeronautics [NACA] was the predecessor of NASA. The NACA was established by Congress in 1915 to conduct aeronautical research. When NASA was established in 1958, the NACA was used as the nucleus of the newly established space agency.) The X-15 pilots were all military or former military pilots. Five of them were combat pilots in World War II and three were combat pilots in Korea. They were all college graduates with engineering or physics degrees. Each of the career military pilots was a graduate of his respective test pilot school, while the NASA pilots were trained in-house. Five of the pilots were career USAF pilots, one was a career navy pilot, and five were NASA pilots. Crossfield was a contractor pilot for North American Aviation but also a former NACA pilot. Four of the pilots, (Crossfield, Walker, McKay, and Armstrong) had previous rocket airplane experience. Crossfield had the greatest number of rocket flights—eighty-one—followed by McKay with forty-eight, Walker with twenty-eight, and Armstrong with four. Ivan Kinchloe, the original prime USAF X-15 pilot, had rocket aircraft experience in the X-2, however, he was killed in an F-104 accident before the X-15 flew.

Based on this rocket airplane experience, NACA/NASA had a substantial advantage in experience going into the X-15 program, but it really was not evident in the relative performance of the pilots once they completed their checkout in the X-15. White and Rushworth were just as competent as Crossfield, Walker, and McKay. Forrest Petersen did not get a chance to demonstrate his full potential in the X-15 since he was recalled to squadron duty after only five flights. Although Neil Armstrong had only four rocket flights prior to his X-15 assignment, he was possibly the most technically capable of the early pilots, but he also left the program early, going on to Gemini, Apollo—and the history books. The later X-15 pilots performed as well as, or in some cases better than the original pilots. The biographies of the individual pilots prior to joining the X-15 program provide a little more information on their background. Some of my personal recollections of each pilot are included to provide some additional insight into their personalities and characters. The biographies are arranged chronologically according to involvement in the X-15 program.

A. SCOTT CROSSFIELD

Scott was a navy fighter pilot during World War II serving in the South Pacific. Following the war, he attended the University of Washington under the GI bill. He joined the naval air reserve unit at the Sand Point Naval Air Station and flew fighter aircraft on weekends while attending the university. He was a member of the navy acrobatic team flying FG-1D Corsairs at various exhibitions and airshows in the Pacific Northwest.

Scott graduated as an aeronautical engineer and went on to earn a master's degree in aeronautics. He left Seattle in 1950 to work as a research pilot for the NACA at Edwards. As a research pilot, he flew almost all of the early research aircraft, including the X-1, X-4, X-5, XF-92, and D-558-I and -II, accumulating eighty-one rocket flights in the X-1s and the D-558-II aircraft. Scott left the NACA in the fall of 1955 to work for North American Aviation which had just been awarded the contract to design and build the X-15 aircraft. He was hired as a pilot and a design consultant for the X-15 program.

I have conflicting views of Scott's role as an X-15 pilot. On the one hand, he did not participate in the high-speed exploratory flights of the aircraft. He flew the low-speed checkout and demonstration flights. In a sense, he tested the race car prior to someone else actually driving the race. On the other hand, he was intimately involved in the design of the aircraft and contributed immensely to the success of the design, as a result of his extensive rocket airplane experience. The X-15 had some outstanding features which significantly enhanced the safety of flight operations. For example, it had very effective speed brakes. Good speed brakes are essential in an unpowered aircraft to adjust energy and ensure that a pilot gets to his intended destination. The more effective they are, the more precise the control of the energy and the more accurate the landing.

The X-15 had excellent landing characteristics for an unpowered aircraft. Once the main gear skids touched down, the nose of the aircraft came down and the aircraft stayed on the ground. There was absolutely no tendency for the aircraft to bounce back in the air. (Bouncing back in the air on an unpowered landing can spoil your whole day. You can run out of airspeed during the bounce and then stall and crash on the next impact.) The X-1s had this bad characteristic and many nose gears were busted as a result. The X-15 could be planted on the ground at almost any speed if we were high on energy and really wanted to set it down before running out of runway. It was also very stable during slideout due to the extreme aft mounted skids. The aircraft slid out straight without any tendency to weave or oscillate.

Scott was responsible for a number of other excellent operational and safety features built into the aircraft. Thus, one might give Scott credit for much of the success of the flight program. In Scott's opinion, the high-speed exploratory flight program was somewhat superfluous since all of the serious potential problems had been addressed in the design and the contractor demonstration tests. The high-speed flight program simply validated the soundness of the design. I can empathize with Scott to some extent. I spent a couple of years supporting the development of the lifting bodies. I contributed to the design of every system in those vehicles. I spent hundreds of hours in the simulator assisting in the development of the flight control system. As the prime lifting body pilot, I greatly influenced the design of those vehicles. If someone else had made the first flight, I would very likely have felt that the first flight simply validated my design inputs. However, if unanticipated problems were encountered, it was a new ball game.

A number of problems were encountered in the exploratory flight program of the X-15. Thus, the X-15 pilots were not just validating North American and Scott's design. They were probing the unknown. Scott did, however, make the first flight of the X-15, an extremely significant accomplishment. Anyone who makes a first flight deserves a lot of respect. Prior to the flight program,

Scott had assumed that he would participate in the entire flight program. He was eminently qualified with over eighty previous rocket flights in the X-1 and D-558-II aircraft. Paul Bikle, Dryden's director, had the unpleasant task of informing Scott that his participation would end once the aircraft were delivered to the government.

Scott is an extremely intelligent individual. He is a good engineer, a good pilot and when all of this was combined, he made an excellent research pilot.

JOSEPH WALKER

Joe was my boss during the ten years that I flew as a NASA research pilot. He was NASA Dryden's chief pilot. Joe had a bachelor's degree in physics from Washington & Jefferson College in Pennsylvania and was a fighter pilot in World War II flying P-38s out of North Africa. Joe began his NASA/NACA career following World War II at the Lewis Research Center in Cleveland, Ohio. He was involved in aircraft icing research at Lewis and spent many hours droning around in the crappiest winter weather that they could find in the Great Lakes region. He transferred to the NACA at Dryden in 1951 and became chief pilot in 1955.

Joe was, in my opinion, the most competent of all the government X-15 pilots. He had extensive test experience in the early X-series aircraft and twenty-seven flights in rocket aircraft. As the chief X-15 pilot, he combined this experience with good sound engineering judgment to direct the X-15 flight program through its most crucial phases. He was not necessarily the best X-15 stick and rudder pilot, but he was a good test pilot. He was a very demanding boss who was prone to temper tantrums, but he gave his pilots plenty of freedom to conduct their own individual flight programs.

Joe's major flight programs prior to the X-15 included the X-3, X-4, X-5, the X1A, and the X1E. Joe received an NACA medal for heroism in 1955 for his efforts to save the B-29 and X-1A during an in-flight emergency. Joe was in the cockpit of the X-1A in the B-29 bomb bay preparing for a launch on a research mission. As Joe initiated propellant tank pressurization in the X-1A, an explosion occurred which caused Joe to lose consciousness. The explosion also blew the landing gear of the X-1A out of the wheel wells to the extended position.

The B-29 crew opened the canopy of the X-1A and pulled Joe out of the cockpit, but by this time Joe had regained consciousness and realized that he had to deactivate the X-1A to prevent any additional damage to it or the

B-29. He crawled back into the X-1A, depressurized the remaining tanks, and inerted all the other systems. This action provided the launch crew a temporary respite, but then the problem of what to do next had to be addressed. The X-1A was still a smoldering bomb, so they had to do something immediately. They had to either land right away or jettison the X-1A and let it crash. The choice of actions was biased considerably by the fact that, due to the explosion, the X-1A gear was now extended. The gear in that position was lower than the extended gear of the B-29, which meant that at landing the X-1A gear would touch down first.

No one knew for sure what the implications of that would be. It could potentially result in a catastrophic structural failure on landing. While the flight crew and the control room crew were discussing the possible options and courses of action, one of the B-29 crew members reported that he smelled hot peroxide. That report terminated any further discussion. They could not ignore hot hydrogen peroxide. The decision was made to jettison the X-1A. The B-29 headed for the bombing range and unloaded its volatile cargo. The X-1 entered a spin after launch and crashed into the desert. The B-29 made a successful landing on the lakebed with a very dejected crew.

Just prior to the X-15 flight program, Joe did some pioneering work in reaction controls, flying an F-104 that had been modified to include a reaction control system. A zoom maneuver was developed to test these controls at very low dynamic pressures. The zoom maneuver starting from Mach 2 at 35,000 feet would result in a peak altitude of 85,000 to 90,000 feet. The indicated airspeed going over the top of this maneuver would be less than 30 knots. At that speed, aerodynamic stability was almost nonexistent and the aircraft behaved as though it were in space. Reaction controls could be readily evaluated under these conditions. The results of these tests were used in the design of the X-15 reaction control system.

An incident occurred just prior to the first flight of this system that demonstrated the volatility of the hydrogen peroxide used as the energy source for the reaction controls. Joe Walker had completed his walk around inspection of the aircraft and was in the process of strapping in to the aircraft when he smelled what he thought was hot peroxide. He decided to get out of the airplane and do another visual inspection. As he started around the aircraft, the peroxide tank located behind the cockpit exploded. That explosion produced the first coke bottle F-104 with exaggerated area ruling. It took several months to repair the damage but our mechanics and sheet metal technicians did a beautiful job. You can see the results of their efforts if you examine the F-104 hanging in the Smithsonian Institution's National Air and Space Museum.

This reaction control system design was later incorporated into two rocket powered F-104 trainer aircraft developed by Lockheed for the USAF Aerospace Research Pilot School. Chuck Yeager lost control of one of these aircraft during a record altitude attempt and had to eject.

In his book, *The Right Stuff,* Tom Wolfe mentions the argument between Joe Walker and Gus Grissom about who would fly the highest and the fastest. I am surprised that Tom knew about that argument since both Joe and Gus were dead long before the book was published. I happened to be with Joe and Gus when they had that argument. Joe and I had traveled to the Cape to watch Grissom's flight. We sat around for over a week waiting for the flight to launch because of the many delays and aborts. In that discussion, Joe pointed out that the X-15 engine had almost as much thrust as the Redstone booster engine— 60,000 pounds of thrust in the X-15 versus 76,000 pounds in the Redstone, and the X-15 engine had a throttle. He also pointed out that the X-15 pilot was flying the boost profile, while Gus was just along for the ride. In terms of actual performance, the X-15 and the Mercury-Redstone were comparable. Al Shepard reached a maximum speed of 5,180 MPH and a maximum altitude of 116 miles on his Mercury Redstone flight. The X-15 achieved a maximum speed of 4,100 MPH without tanks, 4,520 MPH with tanks, and a maximum altitude of 67 miles. Not a huge difference between the performance of the two vehicles. The X-15 theoretically had the performance to reach an altitude of 100 miles, but it could not safely reenter from that altitude.

Joe was not really arguing seriously. He knew the astronauts were ultimately going to go much faster and higher. He was just giving Gus a bad time, but Joe was a little irritated by the special treatment that the astronauts were receiving. They were allowed to accept gratuities and sign a contract with *Life* magazine for their exclusive stories. Joe, as a civil servant, was not allowed to accept any kind of gratuity and yet, he and the astronauts both worked for NASA. Joe was also upset that his salary as a NASA pilot was approximately half that of an airline pilot. Joe did a lot of this type of griping, but he would not have traded jobs with anyone. He loved his job and it was a sad day for American aerospace when he perished in a midair collision in 1966.

ROBERT M. WHITE

Bob White became the prime USAF X-15 pilot following the death of Ivan Kinchloe. Bob was a fighter pilot in World War II, flying P-51s in Europe.

He was shot down on his fifty-second mission in February of 1945 and remained a prisoner of war until his release in April of 1945. Following World War II, Bob joined the air force reserve at Mitchel Air Force Base in New York, and attended New York University. He graduated in 1951 as an electrical engineer. He was recalled to active duty during the Korean War and remained on active duty following the war.

He transferred to Edwards AFB in 1954 and attended the Experimental Test Pilot School. He then served as a test pilot, deputy chief of the flight test operations division, and later, as assistant chief of the manned spacecraft operations branch, all while flying the X-15. Bob flew a number of test programs prior to flying the X-15, the most notable of which was the F-107 program.

I did not know Bob very well because he left the X-15 program before I began flying it. Bob seemed to be very bright and very capable as a test pilot. To me he seemed to be very formal and somewhat aloof. He seemed to be less formal and much friendlier when he returned to Edwards many years later as the center commander.

FORREST S. PETERSEN

Forrest "Pete" Petersen served as a naval officer during World War II. Pete attended the Naval Academy at Annapolis and initially served as a member of the "black shoe" surface navy. He later went through flight training and became a fighter pilot in the "brown shoe" carrier navy. He was selected by the navy to participate as the navy pilot representative in the X-15 program. The navy was a partner in the X-15 program although a very small one in terms of financial contributions. I believe the navy only invested ten million dollars in the program compared to the three or four hundred million that the USAF invested, and yet the navy was allowed one pilot slot. That was a tremendous return on their investment.

Forrest Petersen was a real breath of fresh air for the pilot's office when he came to NASA to participate in the X-15 program. He came about a year before he flew his first X-15 flight. Joe Walker and Pete became good friends immediately. Joe treated Pete exactly as he did his own pilots. He assigned him to NASA research programs to keep him current while he was waiting to fly the X-15.

Pete and I served as coproject pilots on the ALSOR (Air Launched Sounding Rocket) program, his first NASA program. The intent of that program was to release a balloon from an air launched rocket at over 1,000,000 feet altitude (approximately 190 miles) and then measure its rate of descent to determine air density. Pete made the first rocket launch from our F-104 launcher aircraft. We tracked the rocket up to about 700,000 feet altitude, but we could not detect the balloon that should have been released at peak altitude. We assumed that the release mechanism had malfunctioned, so Pete and I decided to try and find the rocket to verify this.

Our radar had tracked the rocket during its descent all the way to impact. The rocket had impacted in the Camp Irwin restricted area in the vicinity of the Three Sisters Lakes. Pete and I flew the C-47 up to that area on a Saturday morning and landed on the lake closest to the impact point. We both had hangovers from a party the night before. We began trudging through the desert sagebrush looking for the rocket.

We had the radar map to pinpoint the impact location, but the accuracy of that radar plot at that distance was questionable. What made the entire situation even more ridiculous was that the rocket had impacted after descending from 700,000 feet altitude. To think that there would be any recognizable piece of that rocket was idiotic to say the least. That did not deter us though.

We spent all morning wandering around the desert stirring up the lizards and the sidewinders. We finally came upon a Basque sheepherder with his flock and his dogs. We tried to ask him by words and gestures if he had seen a rocket fall from the sky and hit the ground, but he could not understand a thing we were saying. In retrospect that was an amusing adventure. Two dumb pilots out in the middle of the desert looking for a lost rocket, trying to converse with a Basque sheepherder while his dogs were nipping at our ass—that is one of the ways I remember Pete.

Pete was a world-class drinker in those days, as many of us were. Pete, Jack McKay, Joe Vensel, the chief of flight operations, and I decided to stop for a drink one day after work. Pete introduced us to Baltics: a shot of gin and a shot of vodka mixed with a lemon twist. We each had three or four of those at Juanita's in Rosamond and then decided to head for home. As we approached the County Line Bar, we decided to stop for another drink. We had three or four more Baltics there and then ran out of money. Pete suggested that we move to the Desert Inn in Lancaster since he had a credit card that they would honor.

By the time we got to the Desert Inn, it was after eight o'clock. Joe Vensel wanted to go home, but we wanted him to stay and, since he was riding with us, he was stuck. We had a couple more drinks when Pete suggested we all go over to his house to meet his wife, who had just moved to Lancaster to join

Pete. After meeting Pete's wife, we had a drink and then decided to go back to the Desert Inn.

Joe Vensel again tried to convince us to take him home, but we would have none of that. After all, the evening was young. About nine o'clock, we noticed that Joe Vensel had disappeared. It turned out he had called his wife and she had come to pick him up. Jack had flown an early flight that morning, so about 9:30 P.M. he finally asked to be taken home. Pete suggested that we have just one more, which we did and Jack finally gave up and went to sleep on the bar. Pete and I closed the bar. We woke Jack up, took him home, and then I decided it would be nice to introduce Pete to my wife. You can imagine the reception that we got when we showed up at my house about 2:30 A.M.

The next morning, Jack was scheduled to fly the X-1E. I was scheduled to be the copilot on the B-29 mothership. We all got to work on time and went down to the locker room to change into flight gear. While we were dressing, Walt Williams, the first director of Dryden and an early proponent of the X-15, burst into the locker room with Joe Vensel in tow. Joe Vensel had told Walt about our drinking bout the night before. Walt and Joe had decided to cancel the flight. Pete and I argued and convinced them that Jack had gone to sleep at 9:30 and was okay to fly. We did not tell them *where* he had gone to sleep. They reluctantly agreed to go ahead with the flight, but they did decide to put Pete instead of me in the B-29 as copilot. Pete appeared to be in better shape. The flight went off without a hitch.

Petersen also served as a project pilot on an F-107 that we acquired from the USAF. The F-107 was a prototype with several advanced technology features. It had some unusual features also, such as an engine inlet located above and behind the cockpit. The wags said that this was a backup pilot escape system. The pilot only had to open the canopy and he would be sucked into the inlet and spit out the tailpipe. Another unusual feature was an all moving vertical tail. The advanced technology features included a variable geometry inlet and a command augmentation control system. We had modified the aircraft to incorporate an X-15 sidearm controller to evaluate the controller prior to the first flight of the X-15.

I was chasing Pete on one of those evaluation flights. The flight plan called for some evaluation maneuvers at 1.7 Mach number. Pete accelerated out to the desired Mach number and began his handling quality maneuvers. I was chasing him in an F-100A and fell way behind because my maximum speed was only about 1.4 Mach. He had almost disappeared from sight when all of a sudden I saw a series of light flashes from the sun reflecting off a gyrating airplane. For a second I thought Pete was doing some unplanned acrobatics. Then I heard Pete say, "Son-of-a-bitch!" The huge vertical tail had momentarily deflected all the way over to one side. That had caused the airplane to do a couple of quick snap rolls which then stalled the engine. Pete heard a tremendous bang and thought the back end of the airplane had blown off. He finally recovered and we went back home to see what damage had been done. For some reason, Pete never thought much of that airplane.

The airplane had another bad characteristic that gave us some problems. The wheels and brakes tended to heat up excessively during ground operations. Some of this was due to the high-idle thrust which in turn required continuous braking to keep the taxi speed down. But some of the heating was due to just rolling friction without braking. This excessive heating would cause the tires to blow out and the wheels to disintegrate. It became standard procedure when the aircraft taxied back to our ramp to wait until the tires blew before approaching the aircraft. The crew stood by with firebottles and nitrogen bottles to extinguish any fire that might result.

On one occasion when the tires blew, pieces of the wheel went swishing over the X-1E and its crew, about 100 yards away on the ramp. We finally gave up taxiing it altogether. We would tow it to and from the runway for each flight—even then the wheels got hot.

This wheel heating problem finally crippled the airplane. Scott Crossfield requested a checkout in the aircraft to evaluate the X-15 sidearm controller. He attempted a takeoff on the north lakebed but aborted because of a problem. By the time he got the airplane stopped, the wheels had overheated and ignited a wheel fire. Scott called for a fire truck, but before it could get there and extinguish the fire, the fire had damaged the wing structure. The airplane never flew again.

JOHN B. "JACK" McKAY

Jack was a navy fighter pilot who had served in the South Pacific during World War II. Jack did not tell many war stories, but he did tell me about an accident that he had while in the navy that really made my hair stand on end.

Jack was flying as a wingman in a flight of four F6F Hellcats on a cross-country flight into Houston, Texas. When they arrived at Houston, the weather was overcast with rain and some fog. In that day and age, very few fighter pilots flew instruments, let alone instrument approaches. The flight leader decided to go out over the water and let down through the overcast to get under the clouds and make a visual approach into Houston. As the flight descended in the clouds, it became obvious that the bottom of the overcast was very low. They were at 300 feet and had not reached the bottom of the clouds.

The leader started a descending turn back toward the shore, with Jack on the inside of the turn. All of a sudden, Jack's wing tip hit the water. The aircraft were flying at about 250 knots at the time. Jack's aircraft cartwheeled a number of times before finally slamming into the water. Within an instant, Jack's aircraft turned into a submarine. Jack managed to get out of the aircraft and then was amazed to find that he could stand up in the water. It was only chest deep. It's hard to believe anyone could survive such an accident. Maybe Jack was allowed to survive so he could go back and beat the crap out of that stupid flight leader.

Following the war, Jack went back to Virginia Polytechnic Institute and graduated in 1950 with a degree in aeronautical engineering. Jack worked at the NACA Langley Research Center as an engineer for a brief period before transferring to Dryden to work as an engineer and subsequently as a research pilot. Jack flew a variety of research programs in the F-100, YF-102, F-102A, F-104, D-558-I, D-558-II, X-1B, and the X-1E. Jack accumulated more rocket flights than any U.S. pilot other than Crossfield. Jack had a total of forty-six rocket flights before flying the X-15. Jack was an excellent stick and rudder pilot, possibly the best of the X-15 pilots. He was one of the few pilots who did not break a nose gear during landing of the X-1. Jack was an expert at dead sticking an airplane to a landing.

Jack also was involved in some humorous incidents. He picked up a brand new F-102A aircraft from the manufacturer to ferry back to the NACA at Edwards. Jack landed without incident and then taxied back to the NACA ramp. The ground crew parked him and then signaled him to shut the engine down, which Jack did. He unstrapped and then tried to open the canopy. It would not budge. Jack strained and strained but with no luck. The canopy would not move.

By this time, he was getting hot. It was summer and the temperature on the ramp was well over 100° F and Jack was effectively sitting in a small greenhouse. The ground crew got some stands up next to the cockpit to try to open the canopy from the outside. No luck. They began to get frantic because it looked like Jack was going to collapse from heat exhaustion. Someone finally suggested that they pull the aircraft into the hangar, which they did. They continued to work on that canopy for another half hour in the hangar before someone else suggested that we try to get a Convair rep to help us. The ground crew finally got the canopy open an hour and a half after Jack had shut the engine down. He came out of that cockpit like a steamed clam.

A couple of years later Jack was flying the F-107 that we acquired from the flight test center. As mentioned earlier, the engine inlet on the F-107 was above and immediately behind the cockpit. The pilot definitely had to shut the engine down on that airplane before he opened the canopy or it would vacuum out the cockpit, including the pilot if he was not strapped in. As Jack taxied the F-107 back to the NACA, one of his wheel brakes caught fire. The base firefighters in the substation near the NACA saw the fire as Jack taxied by. They immediately pulled in behind him as he taxied up to the NACA ramp. The ground crew began waving frantically to Jack to stop and shut the engine down. He did as he was directed and then noticed the firetrucks pulling in beside him and unlimbering their fire hoses. He quickly realized that he must have a serious problem, and decided to open the canopy and get out.

The canopy started to open and then it stopped. It was a big, heavy canopy that was hydraulically powered. When it stopped, it stopped for good. It would not move. The fire was getting bigger and Jack was trapped. He finally squeezed under the edge of the canopy and fell out on the roof of one of the carryall vehicles that had pulled up next to the aircraft. This whole incident would have been a keystone comedy if it had not been so damn serious. Luckily no one got hurt and the aircraft was repairable.

Jack had a pretty good sense of humor. He originated several very good one-liners that have been quoted at Dryden for the last 25 years. One of my favorites was a comment Jack made during a weather flight. He was flying the weather flight and the weather was very marginal all along the planned X-15 track. Jack described the weather and cloud cover to NASA-1 at each of the emergency lakes and at the launch lake as he flew up range. The weather did not appear to be adequate for an X-15 flight, but NASA-1 could not get Jack to state that unequivocally. Finally in exasperation NASA-1 asked Jack for a bottom-line assessment. His response was, "Any improvement will be for the better."

Jack was one of my best friends. We did a lot of hunting and fishing together, when we could get some rare time off. It was really tough getting any time off as a NASA pilot. We were somewhat shorthanded and whenever the X-15 flew, all the pilots were needed to support the flight operation, either as the pilot, the controller, or chase pilot. The weather was good most of the year, so the X-15 operation kept going year round. We did manage to get away occasionally on long holiday weekends. Several times Joe Walker, Forrest

Petersen, Jack, and I hiked into high country over Whitney Portal to fish. That is a hell of a lot of effort for just a weekend of fishing, though.

Jack was a true southern gentleman. I miss him.

ROBERT A. RUSHWORTH

Bob was the backup X-15 pilot to Bob White. Bob was a C-46 and C-47 pilot during World War II, flying in the China, India, Burma theater of operations. Bob participated in the famous flights over the hump from India to China during this time. After the war, he became a member of the air force reserve and attended the University of Maine. He graduated in 1951 as a mechanical engineer and later received a degree in aeronautical engineering from the Air Force Institute of Technology at Wright Patterson AFB. Bob was recalled to active duty in 1951 during the Korean War and remained on active duty following the war.

Bob began his test-flying career at Wright Patterson AFB testing automatic flight control systems. He transferred to Edwards AFB in 1956 and attended the Experimental Test Pilot School. Following graduation, Bob was assigned as a test pilot to the fighter operations branch at Edwards and later as operations officer in the manned spacecraft operations branch while flying the X-15. Prior to flying the X-15, Bob flew test programs on the F-101, TF-102, F-104, F-105, and F-106 aircraft.

Bob also served as a mentor to the Dyna-Soar pilots in his role as operations officer in the manned spacecraft operations branch. He spent quite a bit of time in Seattle during the early development phase of Dyna-Soar. Bob also played a key role in NASA Dryden's dealings with the U.S. Air Force Flight Test Center. He worked hard to assure flight test center support for the X-15 program. The X-15 had a surprisingly low priority within DOD programs and it was primarily a result of Bob's efforts that the X-15 was able to maintain reasonable schedules.

I vividly remember one incident that involved Bob. He had been flying a chase mission in an F-104 and on completion of the mission had returned for landing. When he lowered the landing gear he did not get a successful deployment. He recycled the gear in an attempt to get three green lights but no luck. He recycled the gear several more times, but on each cycle he got a different result. One of the three gear would stay up while the other two came down. He tried the emergency gear extension system and violent maneuvering to free the stuck landing gear but had no success. It finally became obvious that Bob was going to have to eject. You do not attempt to land F-104s with one gear retracted. This scenario is, in some respects, the worst ejection scenario since you have time to sit and think about it. I also had to eject from an F-104 but in my ejection, I really did not have time to think about it. I had to go. I personally preferred that scenario. In Bob's case, he did have more time to prepare for the ejection, and pick the ideal location, but I personally would not have traded places with him.

When all the possible options had been exhausted and the gear still came down asymmetrically, Bob turned out over the bombing range and initiated the ejection. The ejection was completely successful and the aircraft impacted in the bombing range. Bob's name is now permanently on the list of pilots in the parachute packing facility who have successfully parachuted from an aircraft in an emergency. That's a hell of a way to qualify for celebrity status.

I really like Bob. He is a down-to-earth type person and an extremely capable research pilot.

NEIL A. ARMSTRONG

Neil was a navy fighter pilot during the Korean War. He lost a wing tip from his F9F-2 fighter during one mission due to a collision with an anti-aircraft cable and had to eject. Following the war, Neil attended Purdue University, graduating in 1955 with a degree in aeronautical engineering. He went to work for the NACA in 1955 as a test pilot at the Lewis Research Center in Cleveland, Ohio. He transferred to the Dryden Flight Research Center that same year and began flying research programs on the F-100, F-104, X-1B, and X-5.

In 1959, Neil was assigned to the Dyna-Soar program as the lead NASA pilot-consultant. He served as a pilot-consultant on Dyna-Soar until his selection as a NASA astronaut in 1962. Neil did some outstanding work developing an abort maneuver for the Dyna-Soar spacecraft to save the aircraft in the case of a booster malfunction.

Neil was the copilot of the B-29 on a mission to launch Jack McKay in one of the D-558-II rocket aircraft. Just prior to launch, Jack called an abort because he was having trouble pressurizing his propellant tanks. Shortly after the abort call, the propeller on the number four engine of the B-29 began to overspeed. Stan Butchart, who was the pilot of the B-29, attempted to regain control of the prop, but quickly realized he was losing the battle. He informed Jack McKay that he was going to have to launch him even though Jack had called an abort and deactivated the systems in his aircraft.

Butch launched Jack and within seconds, the propellor oversped and came off the number four engine. The propellor cut through the bottom of the number three engine as it came off, cutting the main oil line of that engine. The propellor continued on and cut through the lower fuselage of the B-29 at the exact location where the D-558-II cockpit had been just seconds before. In cutting through the fuselage, the propellor also severed some flight control cables which resulted in a partial loss of control on both control columns. Butch lost his roll control and Neil lost his pitch control. Between the two of them, they managed to get the B-29 back to Edwards for a safe landing with both engines inoperative on the right wing.

In the meantime, Jack McKay was fighting to activate the D-558 aircraft so that he could jettison the propellants and try to glide to one of the lakebeds for a landing. Jack had been launched a long way from Edwards and really had to stretch his glide to make it to a lakebed. He finally made it to Edwards and made a great landing.

Neil lived in a small house on a couple of acres in Juniper Hills on the southern edge of the Antelope Valley. Neil had several cars, none of which were in good mechanical condition. Neil worked out a pretty good procedure to compensate for the questionable condition of his automobiles. His home was up in the hills above the Pearblossom Highway. He would simply start rolling down the hill in one of his cars on the way to his job at Edwards. If the car started running and sounded good, he would continue on across Pearblossom Highway and head for Edwards. If it did not start, or if it sounded bad, he would simply make a left turn at the highway and coast on down to an automotive repair shop. He would then walk back up and try another car. Later that day after work, he would stop at the shop to pick up the other car. He really had a car repair production line going. The mechanic at the repair shop knew him well. Neil tends to disclaim this story by saying that he would never walk 6 miles back up the hill to get another car. I do remember him saying on a number of occasions that God gave man a fixed number of heartbeats and that he was not going to use his up by overexerting himself.

Neil was a pretty good piano player. After a few beers at a flight party, he could usually be coaxed into playing some songs. Neil also had a rather dry sense of humor. During one flight party Neil combined these two talents to confound an air force officer who requested that Neil play a song. Neil looked at the officer and noted that he was wearing a missile commander's badge. He then nonchalantly responded, "I don't know any old missileer songs" and immediately struck up a chorus of "The Wild Blue Yonder."

In my opinion, Neil was probably the most intelligent of all the X-15 pilots, in a technical sense. He was extremely well qualified to fly the X-15. I worked and flew with Neil for over six years. I knew Neil, but I did not know him.

JOSEPH H. ENGLE

Joe was a member of the USAF ROTC at the University of Kansas at Lawrence in the early 1950s. After graduation in 1955, he worked at Cessna Aircraft as a flight test engineer before beginning active duty in 1956. Joe flew F-100 Super Sabres with the 309th Tactical Fighter Squadron at George AFB for 4 years before being selected to attend the Experimental Test Pilot School at Edwards. Joe served as a fighter test pilot at Edwards after graduation until his assignment to the X-15 program in 1963.

Joe and I were assigned to the X-15 program at the same time. We went through ground school together and participated in all of the other checkout activities during the summer and early fall of 1963. Joe and I worked together on the simulator for many, many hours before our first flights. We continued to work together during our subsequent flights alternating as pilot and ground controller. We worked hard trying to improve the accuracy of control of each flight. It was quite common to miss the intended altitude on a given flight by 5,000 to 10,000 feet and the speed by 100 or 200 knots. We managed to reduce those errors significantly by working many extra hours together on the simulator.

Joe was an excellent pilot. He really took the job as a test pilot seriously except occasionally when his exuberance overcame him. That happened on his first X-15 flight. After he had completed the familiarization maneuvers, he slow rolled the X-15. That maneuver really shocked the engineers in the control room. They did not immediately recognize it as a slow roll. They assumed the worst and thought Joe had a control problem. In a research program, the pilot simply did not add an extemporaneous maneuver to the flight plan. Joe was thoroughly chastised by Bob Rushworth after the flight.

Joe went on to become a straight arrow after that incident. In fact he became one of the best X-15 chase pilots in addition to being one of the better X-15 pilots. As a chase pilot for one X-15 flight, he saved Bob Rushworth from a potentially serious accident by a timely call just before touchdown.

Joe was also a very resourceful individual according to this fish story. Joe had planned to go fishing in the high Sierras with some other pilots but had to cancel due to a change in his X-15 flight date. He subsequently decided to surprise his fishing buddies with some fresh supplies. He bought some steaks, froze them, and then brought them in to work one morning. He was scheduled to fly a proficiency flight in an F-104 that morning. He took the frozen steaks out to the airplane, opened the speed brakes, put the steaks in the speed brake well, and then closed the speed brakes. Joe knew where his friends had planned to camp. He flew up to the camp site, made a reconnaissance pass, and then returned and dropped the steaks by opening the speed brakes. It is a good thing that Joe was not an accurate bomber pilot. He could have killed someone if he had hit them with 10 pounds of frozen steaks traveling at 300 MPH.

Joe was, and still is, an avid sportsman.

MILTON O. THOMPSON

I had been in flight training in the navy for a year and a half prior to the end of World War II. I remained in the navy to complete my flight training and then served in the fleet for another three years as an attack pilot and later a fighter pilot, flying off carriers in the Pacific and Atlantic Fleets. I was released from active duty in November of 1949 and then enrolled at the University of Washington in Seattle to complete my engineering studies. Following graduation, I worked at the Boeing Aircraft Company as a structural test and flight test engineer for two and a half years and then went to work for the NACA at Edwards in March 1956 as a research engineer.

As an engineer, I worked on the early X-airplanes and watched apprehensively as these programs wound down and were terminated. By the time I began flying as a research pilot in 1958, I felt that the glory days of the X-airplanes were over and I had missed it all. In the next few years I realized that I was wrong. The golden years were still to come.

Prior to being assigned to the X-15, I had gone through a research pilot apprenticeship program at the NACA. I was assigned to relatively minor research programs initially and then graduated to more complex programs as I gained experience. I also did a lot of support flying, as did each of the other NACA pilots. When I first began flying for the NACA we had only five pilots: Joe Walker, Stan Butchart, Jack McKay, Neil Armstrong, and myself.

Among the five of us, we flew a total of fourteen airplanes. These included a P-51, a T-33, an F-100A, an F-100C, an F-102A, two F-104s, two F-107s, the X-1B, the X-1E, the B-29 mothership, a KC-135, and a C-47. Before I began flying, we had just cleaned out our hangars, getting rid of older research aircraft such as the D-558-II Skyrockets, the X-3, the YF-102, an F-101A, and a B-47. We had cleared the hangars in anticipation of acquiring the X-2 and eventually the X-15s. We never acquired the X-2 since it crashed on its last flight prior to being transferred to the NACA. We finally acquired the X-15s beginning in 1960.

My first flight as an NACA pilot was in the C-47. Within the first year I also qualified in the P-51, the T-33, the F-102A, and the B-29. The P-51, T-33, and C-47 were support aircraft. The B-29 was the X-1 mothership. I flew as copilot and pilot on several X-1 launch flights before we grounded the last X-1.

The C-47 was our real workhorse aircraft. We used it as an administrative aircraft, as a program support aircraft and on occasion as a research aircraft. We hauled engineers to meetings at various locations around the country. We hauled engineers, technicians and parts up the X-15 high range to build the tracking stations for the X-15. We used the C-47 to explore for usable emergency landing lakes for the X-15, and then we used it during the flight program to check the hardness of the lakes after the rainy season by making landings on the lakes and hoping that we could get airborne again. We used it as a tow plane to tow the first lifting body, the M2-F1. We used the C-47 in every way that it was qualified to be used and possibly in ways that it was not qualified to be used. It was truly a remarkable airplane. I enjoyed flying it and we all had more than enough opportunities to fly it.

I subsequently qualified and flew research programs in the F-102A, the F-100C, and then, the F-104A. We had no limits on the number of aircraft that we could fly at any given time, and it was not uncommon to jump from one aircraft into another on any given day. I was current in as many as eight different aircraft during a couple of years and averaged five a year during my career at Dryden. During my nine years as a research pilot, I flew twenty-three different types and several models of various types of aircraft on research and support flights.

I participated in the X-20 Dyna-Soar program and flew the first Rogallo Wing hang glider and the first manned lifting body prior to being assigned as an X-15 pilot.

WILLIAM J. "PETE" KNIGHT

Pete joined the air force in 1951. Following flight training, he was assigned to the air defense command as a jet fighter pilot. During this tour of duty, Pete won the Allison Jet Trophy at the National Air Show in Dayton, Ohio in 1954. Pete attended the Air Force Institute of Technology, graduating in 1958 with a degree in aeronautical engineering. He transferred to Edwards to attend the Experimental Test Pilot School and graduated in 1959. He stayed at Edwards following graduation serving as a test pilot in fighter operations. In 1960 he was assigned to the Dyna-Soar program as a pilot-consultant and was ultimately designated as a Dyna-Soar pilot prior to program cancellation in 1963. After Dyna-Soar was cancelled, Pete returned to Edwards and entered the Aerospace Research Pilot School. He graduated in 1964, and was finally assigned to the X-15 program in the summer of 1965. Pete flew a number of test programs in various fighter aircraft in between his various schools and his Dyna-Soar assignment.

Pete was an excellent and aggressive pilot. He demonstrated this on numerous occasions during his X-15 assignment. The flight test center was very selective in assigning pilots to joint NASA-USAF research programs. They were putting their best foot (pilot) forward, so it was not unusual for each of the air force pilots to be outstanding in all respects.

Pete and I became close friends during the Dyna-Soar program. We suffered through the same stupid qualifying physical examinations that the Mercury astronauts did and then went through additional stress tests at Wright Field and Brooks AFB. Pete and I also spent many weeks at Johnsville undergoing centrifuge tests simulating the Dyna-Soar boost profile. After all of that qualifying testing for Dyna-Soar, Pete and I deserved something more than a cancelled program as a reward. The X-15 program turned out to be our real reward.

WILLIAM H. DANA

Bill graduated from West Point in 1952 and elected to become an air force officer. After flight training he served as a fighter pilot flying F-84s in Korea. Following the war, Bill resigned his commission and returned to school, graduating from the University of Southern California in 1958 with a master's degree in aeronautical engineering. Bill joined NASA in 1958 and began flying as a research pilot in 1959. One of Bill's first assignments was the Dyna-Soar program. He worked with Neil and me as pilot-consultants on Dyna-Soar for almost 3 years. During that assignment, he and I spent a lot of time in Seattle, individually and occasionally together.

On one trip, I had driven up to Seattle in my Jaguar roadster and Bill had flown up. He asked to borrow my car one evening to tour the town. I gave him the keys and told him to check the gas. He stopped at the nearest gas station and had the attendant fill it up. The attendant checked the oil and told Bill that nothing showed on the dipstick. Bill told him to put in a quart. He did and checked it again. Nothing. Bill told him to put in another quart, which he did. Another check still showed nothing on the dipstick. After 2 more quarts the dipstick finally showed a trace of oil on the bottom tip. Bill said that was enough.

The next day, he was complaining to me about paying two dollars for gas and four dollars for oil. I realized that I had forgotten to tell him that the car held 13 quarts of oil and that I routinely ran it 5 or 6 quarts low before I refilled it. He accused me of intentionally setting him up to get a free oil change.

Bill met his future wife in Seattle while assigned to Dyna-Soar. As they prepared to leave Seattle for Edwards, Bill decided to get rid of her car since he felt she would not need it after they were married. The night before Bill was to leave Seattle, Boeing hosted a dinner for the Dyna-Soar pilots. Several Boeing VPs and their wives attended and Bill sat near one of them. He was telling the VP about his desire to sell his wife's car. The VP asked what kind of car it was. Bill informed him that it was an MG roadster. The VP said that he might be interested in buying it for his wife and that he would like to see it. The VP's wife was sitting between the two men. Bill looked at her and said, "Oh, no, she's too old for this car." The VP almost fell off his chair laughing but when he calmed down, he wrote out a check on the spot for the car without even looking at it. Bill has always been brutally honest.

One of Bill's first flights as a NASA pilot was with Jack and me in the C-47 on a trip to Ely, Nevada. We hauled some radar technicians up to check out the radar at the Ely tracking site. Jack, Bill, and I stayed in Ely while the technicians went on up to the site. Jack and I had a few beers and played the slot machines while we waited. When the technicians returned, we headed back to the airplane, cranked it up, and took off. Jack was flying as pilot and I was copilot. Bill had not checked out in the airplane yet. He was just along for the ride.

Shortly after takeoff, Jack decided to go in the back to get some rest since he had been up late the night before. I had Dana come up to take over as copilot. After about an hour, I decided to go back and get some rest too and I left Dana as pilot in command. We left Dana in the cockpit alone for almost two hours. Jack and I both returned to the cockpit before we got to Edwards, but Dana told me later that he could not believe how casual we were about flying that airplane. He had just come out of the military and he was flabbergasted by our informality.

While still a bachelor, Bill Dana would quite often make cross-country flights on weekends to build up his flight time. He preferred flying the F-104 on these trips but we had only three F-104s for use as proficiency and support aircraft and we needed all of them to support each X-15 flight. Walker was reluctant to let one go on a weekend. He would usually suggest that Bill take our T-33 or lesser aircraft. After many refusals of his requests for an F-104, Bill walked into Joe Walker's office one day and asked if he could take an X-15 on a cross-country flight. Joe glared at him and then slowly the scowl turned into a grin. Bill finally got his F-104.

I found a chink in Bill's armor when I checked him out in an L-19. We were using an L-19 to tow the paraglider research vehicle to altitude for its research flights. We decided to check Dana out as a tow pilot in the L-19 to have a backup tow pilot. I put Dana in the front seat and I climbed in back. We took off on the north lakebed and headed for Tehachapi. I had to deliver a package to the airport operator there. I let Bill fly most of the way and then landed it at Tehachapi while I followed him through on the controls.

On departure, Bill made the takeoff and then flew the return trip to Edwards. As we approached Edwards, I got a call that I was to attend a meeting as soon as I could get on the ground. Bill landed the aircraft on the lakebed, while I followed through on the controls. We taxied up to NASA and I got out.

The paraglider project engineer was there to meet us and I told him to climb in the back seat and go with Bill to show him our flight pattern. Bill taxied out and took off. I went to my meeting and came back to the pilot's office about a half hour later. Within a few minutes, Bill came walking in from the lakebed. He had flown around the pattern and had then come in for a landing. The instant he touched down, the airplane ground looped. He bent the right main gear under the aircraft, but fortunately did not damage anything else. He tried to contact NASA by radio, but could not raise anyone. He finally had to walk in from about a mile offshore.

He later informed me that he had never flown a tail wheel airplane. All of his pilot training had been in tricycle gear aircraft. I had probably unintentionally assisted him in his landings by following on the controls, thus preventing him from sensing the ground loop tendency of a tail wheel aircraft.

The accident was potentially very embarrassing to NASA. We had borrowed that L-19 from an army reserve unit in Long Beach. We did not tell them what we were going to use it for. We would fly the airplane to Edwards and then install a glider tow hook and release system and use it to tow the Parasev. We would use it during the week and, after removing the tow hook, return it before the weekends so the reserves could fly it. We had been doing this for months at the suggestion of an army pilot who was temporarily assigned to our office. Now we had a dilemma. We had a damaged landing gear and no spare parts.

Someone finally realized that the civilian version of the L-19 used the same landing gear. We located and bought a landing gear strut for the civilian version. We painted it olive drab and installed it on the aircraft in time to return it to the army for the weekend. Bill Dana was formally presented the damaged landing gear strut. It adorned his desk for years before it finally disappeared.

I checked Bill out in another vehicle some time later. It was the M2-F1, the wooden lifting body. I had flown the first flights on this vehicle and then checked out some other NASA pilots and an air force pilot, Chuck Yeager. Dana was to be the third NASA pilot and Jerry Gentry was to be the second air force pilot. Dana, Gentry, and I got out on the lakebed early one morning and after waiting for some rain showers to pass over, I made a quick flight to check the vehicle. We then put Bill in it and sent him off on his checkout flight. He did fine, but he had a little trouble with the rainwater that had leaked into the aircraft, since it pooled on the nose window during descent. That was the window that we used to determine when to flare. The rainwater turned that window into a big magnifying glass. Bill landed safely and then it was Jerry's turn.

We got Jerry strapped in, then lowered the canopy and hooked him up to the C-47 tow plane. When Jerry called to let everyone know he was ready, the C-47 started its takeoff roll. At 75 knots, Jerry raised the nose of the M2-F1 just as I had instructed him to and shortly thereafter, he lifted off the ground. He climbed up to a position slightly above the tow plane and stabilized in that position for the climb to altitude. Then, slowly, the M2-F1 began to oscillate on the towline from side to side while simultaneously rolling back and forth.

The amplitude of the oscillation began to increase rapidly. I called out on the radio for Jerry to steady his wings and hold them level. The oscillations became more violent. The tow plane was only a couple hundred feet off the ground and struggling to climb higher. I began to panic. The oscillations had increased to the point where the M2-F1 was rolling up almost inverted as it swung from side to side. I was screaming over the radio for Jerry to try to level the wings and as it got worse to "Release! Release!" and finally as he rolled completely over the top I hollered "Eject! Eject!" At this same instant, Jerry released the towline while simultaneously the observer in the tow plane released the towline from his end. Jerry was only about 400 feet in the air. We normally started the landing flare at that altitude, but Jerry was inverted. He somehow simultaneously rolled back to wings level while he flared to land. He essentially landed on the bottom of a slow roll. He touched down hard, but the vehicle appeared to be intact. Dana and I were in total shock.

The ground crew picked us up in the carryall and we drove out to the M2-F1. Jerry was out of the cockpit when we arrived and he immediately began telling us what the problem was. He had, in his own mind, convinced himself that he knew exactly what he had done wrong and he wanted to try again immediately. Bill and I were in such a state of shock that we agreed to try it again.

We began towing the vehicle back to the takeoff spot, when we noticed that the vehicle was listing slightly. When we stopped at the takeoff position, our crew chief began to inspect the landing gear. While we were waiting for his report, we got a call over the radio from Joe Walker. He did not mince any words. He said, "Get that thing back in the hangar, NOW!" Someone had told him what had happened and that we were thinking about making another flight. Thank God someone had retained his sanity. When we got the vehicle back in the hangar, we found some severe damage to the hull structure at the landing gear attach point. If we had tried another flight, the landing gear may have simply fallen off. We decided to delay any further checkout flights in the M2-F1. It was not until a year later that we decided to try again.

During that year I had checked Jerry out in sailplanes to give him some experience on the towline. He did quite well. I felt confident that he would do a great job in the M2-F1 on his upcoming checkout flight. We had the same cast of characters on this second attempt. We got him in the cockpit and closed the canopy. After a final check, Jerry instructed the tow plane to begin the takeoff. Again Jerry made a perfect takeoff and climbed immediately to a position just above the tow plane. He stabilized there and I finally began breathing again.

As Bill and I watched the tow plane begin the climb, we noticed a slight motion of the M2-F1 from side to side on the towline. As we continued to watch, the amplitude of that motion began to increase. The motion became hypnotic. We stood there and watched an exact repeat of the flight the year before. I finally broke out of the trance long enough to scream, "Eject! Eject!" as Jerry rolled up on his back above the tow plane. This time, Jerry simply released the towline, fired the landing rocket and continued the roll to a wings level position while flaring for a landing. This time he made a perfect landing.

Neither Bill nor I could talk when the ground crew came to pick us up. We were in total shock. Years later when I was asked to take over as chief pilot, I remembered those two incidents and decided that I never wanted to be responsible for the actions of other pilots. I was more terrified watching those two incidents than at any other time in my life. Bill felt exactly the same way. Jerry Gentry went on to become one of the more capable lifting body pilots, distinguishing himself while flying the M2-F2, the X-24A, the HL-10, and the M2-F3. Bill and I still shudder, however, when we reminisce about those early M2-F1 flights.

Bill Dana is one of my better friends. He is an excellent pilot and a person of high moral character and integrity.

MICHAEL J. ADAMS

Mike joined the air force in 1950 and received his wings and commission in 1952. He served as a fighter-bomber pilot during the Korean War. Mike attended Oklahoma University while in the air force and graduated in 1958 with a degree in aeronautical engineering. In 1962 Mike attended the Experimental Test Pilot School and won the Honts Trophy as the best scholar and pilot in his class. He subsequently attended the Aerospace Research Pilot School, graduating in 1963. Mike was designated as a MOL (Manned Orbital Laboratory) astronaut on completion of this school. Mike served as both a MOL astronaut and a test pilot at Edwards until he became impatient waiting for the MOL to launch. He applied for an assignment to the X-15 program. He was accepted and designated as an X-15 pilot in the summer of 1966.

While attending the Aerospace Research Pilot School, Mike survived a harrowing accident in an F-104 aircraft. Mike was in the back seat of the F-104 which was being flown by Dave Scott, another student who later became an Apollo astronaut. Dave was making a simulated X-15 unpowered landing for training and evaluating purposes. As he approached the runway, the aircraft suddenly lost power and the rate of descent began to rapidly increase. Dave rotated the aircraft and advanced the throttle in an attempt to arrest the rate of descent, but the engine failed to respond. Both pilots quickly realized that the aircraft was going to hit the runway hard. Dave decided to ride it out, Mike decided to eject. The aircraft slammed into the runway with sufficient force to break off the landing gear. Mike ejected just as the aircraft impacted the runway—an optimum time for a successful ejection. If he had ejected before impact, Mike's ejection would have been unsuccessful due to the high rate of descent. The chute would not have had time to deploy. If Mike had delayed a fraction of a second after impact, he would have been crushed since the engine slammed forward into the rear cockpit within milliseconds after impact.

Dave Scott stayed with the aircraft as it slid down and off the side of the runway and began to burn. As soon as it stopped he attempted to evacuate the aircraft, but his ejection seat had partially sequenced due to the impact and his feet were locked in the stirrups. He finally had to pull the emergency cable cutter handle to release his feet. As he was climbing out of the burning aircraft, he noticed Mike standing several hundred feet down the runway waving at him. Mike's parachute had successfully deployed just seconds before impact. According to observers, Mike swung through just one oscillation after chute deployment before touching down. Mike was lucky that time.

Mike was an outstanding pilot, as he so aptly demonstrated on his first X-15 flight. Mike appeared to be a very laid-back, easygoing individual. He and Jack McKay—a man of similar nature—quickly became good friends. I went deer hunting with Mike and Jack one time, but other than that I had very little personal contact with Mike. I really did not know him very well. I had left the X-15 program before he was assigned.

Flight 3-65-97

10:29:06	NASA-1:	"One minute now, Mike, one minute."
	Adams:	"Rog."
:09	Adams:	"Experiment, camera. Give me a 45-second call."
:22	B-52:	"Forty-five seconds now, zero-eight."
:26	Adams:	"Rog."
:30	Adams:	"Prime, igniter ready."
:36	Adams:	"And precool, igniter, and tape. And give me 15 seconds Joe, will you? I missed that."
:51	B-52:	"Fifteen seconds, zero-eight."
:54	Adams:	"Pump—good igniter."
10:30:02	B-52:	"Five seconds, zero-zero-eight."
:03	NASA-1:	"Looks good here, Mike."
:07	Adams:	"Rog, two, one, launch."
:11	NASA-1:	"Rog, we got a good light here, Mike. Check your alpha and your heading."
:21	NASA-1:	"Right on track, Mike, you're coming up on profile."
:29	NASA-1:	"Standby for theta."
:33	NASA-1:	"How do you read, Mike?"
:39	NASA-1:	"Check your boost guidance null, Mike, and how do you read?"
– –		[squelch break]
:44	NASA-1:	"OK, Mike, we have you right on the track, on the profile."
:45	B-52:	"You're on track and profile, Mike."
:52	Adams:	"Roger."

27

:54	B-52:	"I'll relay, Pete."
	NASA-1:	"OK."
10:31:01	NASA-1:	"Standby for 83,000, Mike."
:04	B-52:	"Standby for 83,000."
:09	NASA-1:	"Do you read us at all, Mike?"
:12	NASA-1:	"OK, you're right on the track."
	B-52:	"Right on the track, Mike."
:19	NASA-1:	"Coming up on 110,000."
	B-52:	"Coming up on 110,000. "
:22	NASA-1:	"On the profile, on the heading."
:24	B-52:	"On profile, on heading."
:26	NASA-1:	"Standby for shutdown."
:27	B-52:	"Standby for shutdown."
:33	NASA-1:	"Precision attitudes, Mike."
:35	B-52:	"Precision attitudes, Mike."
:39	NASA-1:	"Alpha to 0."
:40	B-52:	"Alpha to 0."
:42	NASA-1:	"And rock your wings and extend your experiment, Mike."
:45	B-52:	"Extend your experiment, Mike."
:50	NASA-1:	"On the heading, on the profile."
:52	NASA-1:	"Have you going a little bit high, that's all right."
:54	B-52:	"On the heading, on the profile, maybe a little bit high."
:58	Adams:	"I am reading him now. I got a computer and instrument light now."
10:32:03	NASA-1:	"OK, Mike."
:08	NASA-1:	"We'll go ahead and try computed alpha at 230, Mike."
:14	NASA-1:	"Check your computed alpha now."
:18	NASA-1:	"And you're right on track, Mike."
:27	Adams:	"I lost my pitch and roll dampers."
:31	NASA-1:	"OK, Mike, let's try and get them on."
:32	Adams:	"They reset."
:34	NASA-1:	"Did they reset?"
:35	Adams:	"Yep."
:36	NASA-1:	"OK."
:37	NASA-1:	"And I'll give you a peak altitude, Mike."
:42	NASA-1:	"Have you coming over the top. You're looking real good. Right on the heading, Mike."
:51	NASA-1:	"Over the top at about 261, Mike."
:54	NASA-1:	"Check your attitudes."
10:33:02	NASA-1:	"You're a little bit hot, but your heading is going in the right direction, Mike."
:09	NASA-1:	"Real good."
:11	NASA-1:	"Check your attitudes. How do you read, Mike?"
:14	NASA-1:	"OK, let's check your dampers, Mike."

:17	Adams:	"They're still on."
:18	NASA1:	"OK."
:24	NASA-1:	"A little bit high, Mike, but real good shape."
:33	NASA-1:	"And we got you coming downhill now. Are your dampers still on?"
:37	Chase-1:	"Dampers still on, Mike?"
:39	Adams:	"Yeah, and it seems squirrely."
– –		[squelch break]
:44	NASA-1:	"OK, have you coming back through 230, ball nose, Mike."
:50	NASA-1:	"Let's watch your alpha, Mike."
:58	NASA-1:	"Let's not keep it as high as normal with this damper problem. Have you at 210. Alpha, beta, and check your alpha, Mike."
10:34:02	Adams:	"I'm in a spin, Pete."
:05	NASA-1:	"Let's get your experiment in and the camera on."
:13	NASA-1:	"Let's watch your theta, Mike."
:16	Adams:	"I'm in a spin."
:18	NASA-1:	"Say again."
:19	Adams:	"I'm in a spin."
:21	NASA-1:	"Say again."
:27	NASA-1:	"OK, Mike, you're coming through about 135 now."
:34	NASA-1:	"Let's get it straightened out."
:37	– –	[two squelch breaks]
:42	NASA-1:	"OK, you got theta 0 now."
:44	NASA-1:	"Get some angle of attack up."
:50	NASA-1:	"Coming up to 80,000, Mike."
:53	NASA-1:	"Let's get some alpha on it."
:57	NASA-1:	"Get some *g* on it, Mike."
:59	NASA-1:	"Let's get some *g* on it."
10:35:02	NASA-1:	"We got it now. Let's keep it there. Coming around."
:09	NASA-1:	"OK, let's keep it up, Mike."
:14	NASA-1:	"Keep pulling up. Do you read, Mike?"
:20	NASA-1:	"Let's keep pulling it up, Mike."
:27	NASA-1:	"OK, 130 let's head down that way."
:37	NASA-1:	"He was abeam Cuddeback, 130, three-five-eight."
:42	NASA-1:	"Chase-4, do you have anything on him?"
:44	Chase-4:	"Chase-4, negative."
:47	NASA-1:	"OK, Mike, do you read?"
:52	Chase-4:	"Pete, I got dust on the lake down there."
:55	NASA-1:	"What lake?"

PART 1 . . . .

THE INGREDIENTS

Chapter 1 . . . .

The Machine

The X-15 was the third aircraft type in a series of higher-speed experimental aircraft. The first was the X-1, the second the X-2, the third the X-15. A fourth was to be the Dyna-Soar X-20. The X-1 was developed to break the sound barrier and to explore the low supersonic flight region. The X-2 was intended to investigate aerodynamic heating phenomena up to speeds of Mach 3. The X-15 was designed to explore the hypersonic speed regime and the fringes of the upper atmosphere. The original design speed and altitude of the X-15 were Mach 6.6 and 250,000 feet respectively. The design Mach number was later reduced to Mach 6.0. The X-20 Dyna-Soar was intended to be the follow-on to the X-15 to explore the high-hypersonic flight region up to Mach numbers near 18. Dyna-Soar was subsequently upgraded and designed to go into orbit on the new Titan III booster, but the program was cancelled shortly after production of the spaceplane began.

To provide some perspective, the hypersonic-speed regime starts at Mach 5 or roughly 5,000 feet per second (3,300 MPH) and it extends on up to orbital speeds of roughly 24,000 feet per second (18,000 MPH). The modified X-15 (X-15A-2) achieved a maximum speed of Mach 6.7 or approximately 6,700 feet per second (4,520 MPH). To more fully appreciate what this means, the speed of a bullet fired from a high-performance hunting rifle is approximately 3,000 feet per second. The X-15 could fly over twice as fast as that rifle bullet.

Tank cannons have a higher muzzle velocity than most any other gun. Those muzzle velocities average about 5,500 feet per second. The X-15 could fly 1,200 feet per second faster than those shells. A Mach number of 6 is roughly equivalent to 4,000 miles per hour. This equates to more than one mile per second. The X-15 was pretty damn fast!

There were a number of other early research aircraft in the X-series which were not high-speed airplanes. The X-3, the X-4, the X-5, and the XF-92 were unique configurations, rather than high-speed aircraft. The D-558-I and the D-558-II type aircraft were high-speed aircraft, but they were funded by the U.S. Navy and thus, were not recognized by the air force as real X-type aircraft. The air force controlled the X-number designation. Both the D-558-I and the D-558-II established speed records, but their records were short-lived.

The original X-1 type had a follow-on version which included the X-1A, the X-1B, the X-1C, and the X-1D. These vehicles were somewhat larger, carried more propellant, and expanded the maximum speed of the X-1s to Mach 2.5. The X-15 also had a follow-on version in the rebuilt number two aircraft which ultimately achieved a maximum speed of Mach 6.7. For a more detailed description and discussion of these earlier research aircraft, I would refer you to several books written by Richard P. Hallion, an excellent aviation historian. He is also a pilot historian. He writes about old pilots like me.

The early X-airplanes were rather simple airplanes with purely mechanical systems, reminiscent of World War II fighter aircraft. The control systems were cable and pulley type systems with some power boost. There were no stability augmentation systems nor were there any other avionics systems. Thrust-to-weight ratios were less than one even on the rocket aircraft.

The X-15, by comparison, was a much more state of the art airplane. It had a high gain, high authority, stability augmentation system and an advanced command augmentation type control system in the number three aircraft. It utilized an inertial platform for attitude and velocity information and a special ball nose for air data. The X-15 was part spacecraft with a reaction control system and a thermal protection system to withstand the heat of reentry. Thrust to weight ratio of the X-15 was more typical of missiles and space boosters with a maximum T/W of four just prior to burnout. The empty weight of the airplane was approximately 15,000 pounds. Engine thrust was roughly 60,000 pounds.

The X-15 was the first aircraft designed for flight above the atmosphere. Some may quibble about whether the X-15 flew above the atmosphere since there are some air molecules above 100 miles altitude. In actuality, the major portion of the atmosphere is below 100,000 feet. The edge of the sensible atmosphere is very visually obvious as you climb through 100,000 feet. The sky changes from blue to black and there is no apparent atmospheric haze above that altitude. The space shuttle people consider 400,000 feet to be the edge of the atmosphere, since that is where they first sense some atmospheric effects at orbital speeds, but no airplane will ever cruise at that altitude. A hypersonic transport or the "Orient Express" as the Reagan administration referred to it, will not cruise much above 100,000 feet.

Why was the X-15 built? The glib answer was "to explore the hypersonic-flight regime." The real answer was to find out if we were smart enough to design an airplane that could fly and survive at hypersonic speeds. We knew much about hypersonic flight from theory and subscale wind tunnel testing, but there were still some real basic questions that needed answers. Could we design an airplane that was stable and controllable at hypersonic speeds? Could we design a structure that would survive the high heating rates associated with hypersonic speeds? Could we design an airplane that would be controllable outside the atmosphere and one that could successfully reenter the atmosphere at high speed and steep entry angles? More important, could a pilot survive and function adequately in this high-energy environment?

The only way to answer these questions was to design and build an airplane and then attempt to fly it at hypersonic speeds. If it survived, we were right. If it didn't, we had more to learn.

To me, the X-15 was a big propellant tank with a cockpit on the front end and an engine on the back end. It was 50 feet long, but the propellant tanks constituted approximately 25 of those 50 feet. The X-15 weighed roughly 15,000 pounds without propellants and 33,000 pounds with them. The propellants consisted of approximately 1,000 gallons of liquid oxygen and 1,400 gallons of anhydrous ammonia. The tanks for these propellants made up the major portion of the fuselage. The outer skin of the aircraft fuselage was the exterior wall of the tank.

All of the hydraulic and electrical lines from the front to the back of the aircraft were housed in the fairings along the sides of the tanks. The tanks were made in a toroidal shape, like a doughnut in cross section with a void in the middle. In essence, they were a long cylindrical tank with a hole going through the core of the cylinder. In that core of the liquid oxygen tank, there was a long, skinny cylindrical tank that contained the high pressure helium gas used to pressurize the propellant tanks to get the propellant moving to the engine pump.

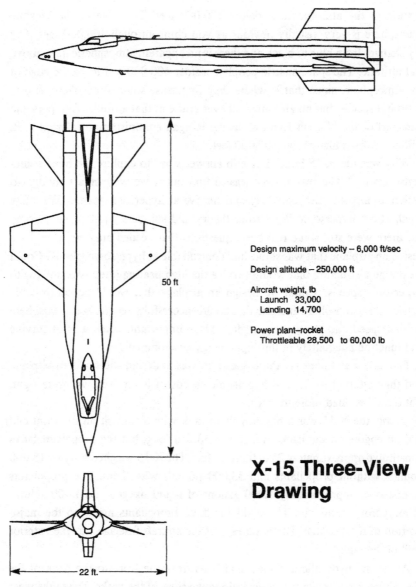

Design maximum velocity – 6,000 ft/sec

Design altitude – 250,000 ft

Aircraft weight, lb
  Launch   33,000
  Landing 14,700

Power plant–rocket
  Throttleable 28,500 to 60,000 lb

X-15 Three-View Drawing

Figure 1. Three-view drawing of X-15 aircraft.

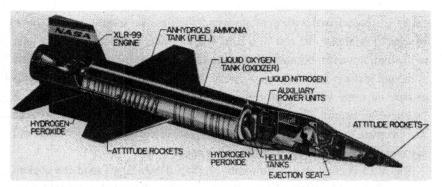

Figure 2. Cutaway drawing of X-15, showing location of components.

On the nose of the airplane was the airflow sensor which determined the airflow direction and the airflow impact pressure. This sensor was referred to as the ball nose. It was servo-driven to align with the airflow impacting the nose of the aircraft. From this, we obtained angle of attack, angle of sideslip, and impact pressure of the air flowing over the aircraft. The ball nose was cooled with liquid nitrogen to prevent it from melting during high-speed flight.

Behind the ball nose were the pitch and yaw reaction control jet nozzles. There were two nozzles on top of the nose pointing up and two on the bottom of the nose pointing down. There were two yaw rockets on each side of the nose. The twin jets in each direction were part of separate, redundant systems, one jet on each system. Thus, if one system failed for any reason, you still had the jet in the other system for control. The roll rockets were in the outboard wing panels, two on each wing. Redundant or duplicate systems are common on aircraft for safety reasons and are beginning to show up in automobiles for the same reasons. Dual brake systems on cars, for example, are the norm in this day and age and have been for some time. They were used in aircraft over 40 years ago. The nose landing gear compartment was located just behind the reaction control jet compartment.

The cockpit forward bulkhead was located just aft of the nose gear compartment. The cockpit compartment was an aluminum structure suspended inside the Inconel-X outer aircraft structure. The aluminum cabin, isolated from the outer structure to keep it cool, was sealed and pressurized to keep the cabin at a maximum 35,000 feet pressure altitude regardless of how high the aircraft flew. This level of pressurization prevented the pilot's pressure suit from inflating during a normal flight. It was difficult to fly the aircraft with an inflated pressure suit, but it obviously could be done under emergency conditions. The cabin was pressurized with pure nitrogen. Nitrogen was used instead of air or oxygen to minimize the risk of a fire. The nitrogen environment was a pain in the butt, however, because we did not dare open our pressure suit faceplate. Although it is not toxic, nitrogen gas can be very deadly. One or two breaths of pure nitrogen will start an irreversible process of asphyxiation over which you have no control. I would occasionally tempt fate by opening my pressure suit faceplate to scratch my nose or wipe sweat off my brow, but I would hold my breath until I had closed my faceplate again.

The X-15 cockpit was quite roomy. In fact it was larger than the cockpit of most fighter planes that I have flown. The only feature that made it seem small was the raised portion of the canopy which contained the windows. The pilot's head was enclosed rather snugly by the raised portion of the canopy. The pilot had good visibility straight ahead or laterally, since the windows were right next to his head but the wider fuselage below the windows restricted the downward vision. In order to see the runway during the unpowered approach it was necessary to roll over to a 60- or 70-degree bank. One very unusual thing about the visibility out of the X-15 windows was that the pilot could not see any part of the airplane. He could not see the nose, he could not see the wings—nothing. Normally, in an aircraft, pilots use the nose and the wings for attitude reference. In the X-15, all we had for a reference was the window frame—very disconcerting.

In addition to all the normal gauges, switches, levers, and controls, the X-15 cockpit contained an enormous ejection seat. The seat weighed 270 pounds. It had two large stabilizing fins that deployed after ejection, and two large telescopic booms that also extended for seat stabilization. The ejection handles were large, beefy handles that pivoted out from the arm rests and locked the pilot's arms and body firmly in place prior to ejection. Some metal leg restraints also clamped down on his legs during the ejection sequence to prevent the legs from flailing. In some ways that seat reminded me of a throne and in other ways of an electric chair or a chair designed for torture. The pilot was strapped in tight initially, but enveloped even further in case of ejection. I never did trust that seat to work properly. It was too complicated. It was designed to operate at speeds up to Mach 4 and up to 120,000 feet altitude, but few of the pilots really believed that. In case of an emergency, most of the pilots would have stayed with the airplane until it slowed down to lower speeds before ejecting. No pilot had to make that decision except perhaps Mike Adams. He may have tried to eject but we will never know. The evidence was inconclusive.

Behind the cockpit, there was a fairly large bay for instrumentation. We carried approximately 1,200 pounds of instrumentation for measuring things like airspeed, altitude, pitch rate, roll rate, yaw rate, control surface positions, tank pressures, wing bending loads, landing gear loads, wing leading edge temperatures. If it moved, we measured it. And if it did not move, we measured it to find out why not. The instrument compartment was big enough to hold a man. A couple of our flight planning engineers were almost serious about volunteering to ride in that compartment just to get a ride. It was pressurized, but other than that it was very inhospitable. However, I really think they might have tried it if they had ever had the opportunity.

The auxiliary power units (APU) supplied hydraulic and electrical power for the airplane. The APU compartment was behind the instrument compartment. In a conventional jet aircraft, hydraulic and electrical power would normally be provided by pumps and generators on the jet engine. The X-15 did not have an engine to generate this power, so auxiliary power units were required. These units were small steam turbine units. Highly concentrated (90 percent) hydrogen peroxide was forced through a silver catalyst bed to cause the peroxide to decompose into steam and oxygen. This steam was then directed through the turbines to drive the hydraulic pumps and generators.

The X-15 had redundant (two) APUs since hydraulic and electrical power were essential to control and to fly the aircraft. The APUs were started about 12 minutes before launch to provide power during checkout of the various systems in the X-15 prior to launch. Prior to starting the APUs, the B-52 supplied electrical power to the X-15. This external power from the B-52 allowed certain X-15 systems to be active at all times during captive flight. The APUs ran continuously from 12 minutes prior to launch until the pilot shut them down after landing. Each APU had its own peroxide tank which could also be replenished with any leftover peroxide from the main engine turbo pump tank. We had enough peroxide for 45 minutes of APU operation under normal circumstances. During the X-15 flight program, we had many problems with the APUs, but we did not lose an airplane due to APU problems. We came close, however, on at least two occasions.

The liquid oxygen (LOX) tank was located behind the APU compartment. Liquid oxygen is quite cold, as you may remember from demonstrations in high school. We could always tell how much liquid oxygen was in the tank by the frost on the outer skin of the fuselage. It was always comforting to know that if we crashed in the X-15, we would not suffer very long. The liquid oxygen from a ruptured tank would freeze dry us in seconds.

Behind the LOX tank there was a small equipment compartment that also contained a large spherical helium tank. This helium was used for tank pressurization and pneumatic valve operation.

The ammonia tank was behind this compartment. Behind the ammonia tank there was a compartment for the large engine peroxide tank. This tank contained about 800 pounds (about 80 gallons) of peroxide to run the engine turbopump which pumped both LOX and ammonia into the rocket engine. The engine turbopump was similar in concept to the APU—a steam turbine driven by decomposed peroxide. It pumped roughly 30 gallons of LOX and ammonia every second into the rocket engine combustion chamber at 600 psi. It was a pretty potent pump.

Behind the engine peroxide tank compartment was the engine compartment. The LR-99 engine was approximately 7 feet long, 2 feet of that being the nozzle. The engine weighed approximately 910 pounds. It produced 60,000 pounds of thrust which gave the airplane an impressive thrust-to-weight ratio. Liquid ammonia running through tubes on the inner surface cooled the engine nozzle. This inner surface was also coated with a ceramic material that protected the metal from the searing heat of combustion. This ceramic coating had to be repaired quite often due to the erosion caused by the tremendous heat and gas velocities in the rocket plume.

The landing gear on the aircraft was unusual. The nose gear was rather conventional with a strut and dual wheels. It folded forward and was stowed internally forward of the cockpit. The main gear was unconventional. It consisted of metal skids mounted on struts at the rear of the aircraft. The main gear struts also folded forward, but they were stowed externally along the lower side of the fuselage. Both gears depended on gravity and air loads for proper deployment.

The combination of a wheeled nose gear and aft mounted main gear skids was a very stable configuration during slideout after landing. This landing gear configuration and orientation eliminated any tendency to bounce back in the air on touchdown since the drag of the aft mounted skids forced the nose down once they contacted the ground.

The X-15 landing gear configuration was not readily steerable on the ground. There was no nose wheel steering and, with skids for main gear, it did not have conventional asymmetric braking to steer the aircraft. Applying rudder only resulted in the vehicle sliding sideways without turning. The only way to turn the vehicle was to apply roll control to load up the skid in the desired turn direction. Right roll resulted in a right turn. This was only effective, however, above 100 knots. Below 100 knots the pilot was just along for the ride. The airplane went where it wanted to. That is why we landed on the lakebed. You had a lot of room to deviate during slideout on a lakebed.

The aircraft had a rather conventional wing, although it was relatively small with only a 22-foot span and roughly 200 square feet of area. The empennage of the aircraft was unusual with two canted horizontal surfaces and two vertical surfaces. These tail surfaces resembled the feathers on an arrow and served the same purpose by keeping the aircraft stable and pointed in the right direction. The upper and lower vertical tail surfaces were quite large and thick compared to those found on conventional airplanes. They were wedge-shaped in cross section with the sharp edge in front and the thick blunt base at the rear. This shape provided additional stability to prevent the aircraft from swapping ends at very high speeds. The lower half of the lower vertical had to be jettisoned before landing because it protruded below the landing gear.

The aerodynamic control surfaces on the aircraft consisted of an upper and lower rudder and two canted horizontal stabilizers. The rudder surfaces were the outer half of the upper and lower vertical fins. These surfaces pivoted about an axis at about midspan. They were large surfaces and quite effective. The canted horizontal surfaces served as pitch and roll control surfaces. They moved symmetrically for pitch and asymmetrically for roll. We referred to the horizontal surfaces as a rolling tail. There were no ailerons or other roll control surfaces on the wings. The only movable surfaces on the wing were trailing edge landing flaps.

Speed brakes, spoilers, or other drag devices are commonly used on unpowered aircraft, as an inverse throttle, for energy control. The X-15 had four speed brake segments located on the rear portions of the upper and lower vertical fins. These surfaces opened in a V shape to produce drag. They were very effective, particularly at high dynamic pressure, and were normally used to kill off excess energy. When they were used in this manner, the approach to landing was always made with excess energy. The speed brake was then used to kill off the excess energy just prior to landing, when we knew we had enough energy to make it to our intended landing location.

Speed brakes can also be used to modulate energy by deploying them to a midposition and then opening or closing them to increase or decrease drag. Used in this manner, they work almost as a conventional throttle. Good speed brakes are essential on an unpowered aircraft to ensure that the pilot can consistently and routinely land the aircraft at the desired landing location. We could routinely land the X-15 within 1,500 feet of our desired touchdown point, mainly due to the good effective speed brakes. That is as good as some pilots can do with an engine.

The aerodynamic flight control system was a fairly conventional, hydraulically powered system with dual hydraulic systems. The control system included a high-gain, high-authority stability augmentation system to provide dynamic stability. The X-15 was one of the first aircraft to use such a system. Aerodynamic control was accomplished either through a conventional center stick and rudder pedals or a side stick and rudder pedals. The center stick was seldom used during powered flight due to the high g forces. It could be used for landing, but the pilots found that they could land the aircraft successfully using the side stick and they did not bother to revert to the center stick for landing. It also became a macho thing to fly the entire flight using the side stick. I always felt that I could fly more precisely using the center stick, but I was not about to admit that to anyone. My ego would not let me use the center stick, even in an emergency.

The reaction control system, or ballistic control system as it was occasionally referred to, was a dual hydrogen peroxide rocket system with two rockets in each control direction. Each rocket was fired by manually opening a valve using the reaction control hand controller. When the valve opened it allowed liquid peroxide to flow over a silver screen catalyst bed. As mentioned previously, the silver screen causes peroxide to decompose into water and oxygen. The heat of decomposition turned the water into steam. Thus, we basically used steam rockets to control the aircraft outside the atmosphere.

The pilot operated the manual reaction controls through a side stick controller located on the left-hand instrument panel. It was a three axis controller for pitch, roll, and yaw control. It was not a very precise controller and we ended up using it in a so-called bang-bang mode, where it was momentarily displaced to fire a rocket and then returned to neutral—kind of a blip-type control input. If we did not get the response we wanted, we put in another blip or two. It actually was a proportional controller, whereby the more you displaced the control stick, the more thrust you got. The pilots did not like to use it in that manner though, because we did not want to get any large aircraft motions started when we were outside the atmosphere.

Liquid nitrogen was used as the primary cooling medium in the X-15. Liquid nitrogen circulated through the ball nose and also cooled the APU bearings. Liquid nitrogen converted to gaseous nitrogen cooled the avionics and instrumentation units. The cockpit was pressurized and cooled with gaseous nitrogen and the pilot was cooled in his pressure suit by evaporated liquid nitrogen. There were provisions for ram air cooling of the cockpit, however this mode could not be used supersonic.

The X-15 was one of the first aircraft to utilize an inertial platform for attitude reference and guidance information and a computer to calculate inertial quantities. Standard barometric instruments were almost useless in the X-15. We had them on the instrument panel, but the only time we used them was in the landing pattern because they did not work at high altitudes or outside the atmosphere. For the major portion of the flight, we used inertial data for control and guidance.

On my second X-15 flight, the computer failed and I lost my inertial data. It is quite a shock to be without any speed, altitude, or rate of climb information when you are moving at more than 3,000 MPH and cannot see the ground or a horizon. Following this experience, I really took my emergency simulation practice seriously. I practiced each of my flights with all kinds of simulated failures. For example, I practiced my flights with all my flight instruments failed using only the stopwatch, attitude indicator, and the horizontal stabilizer position indicator. That obviously was an extreme case, but I could successfully fly a flight that way. I practiced my flights with many other combinations of instrument failures. This definitely paid off in my ability to handle emergencies. The one quantity that was essential was time.

All the flights were planned on the basis of total energy which was directly related to engine burn time. All the events during a flight were initiated at a precise combination of time and energy. If our clock stopped, we were in trouble. The ground controller could help us out by calling time over the radio, but it was not uncommon to have radio failures or momentary loss of communications. The cockpit timer was a critical instrument. Because of its importance, one might expect the timer to be a very sophisticated high technology electronic device. In fact it was a simple stopwatch with a 100-second sweep that started automatically with main chamber ignition. We had a backup stopwatch that we started at one minute to launch since we were too busy to start it at launch.

To fly at Mach 6, or 4,000 MPH, one must have an airplane that will survive temperatures as high as 1,200° F. The X-15 was built of steel to withstand these temperatures. The steel used was Inconel-X, a tough high-strength nickel-steel alloy that retained most of its strength up to 1,200° F. I first encountered this material while working as an engineer at Boeing Airplane Company. I was trying to find some bearing material that could be utilized in an engine thrust reverser. I ordered a number of high-temperature steels to make bearings and test them under high-temperature load conditions. One of the materials I ordered was Inconel-X. I received a 3-inch diameter cylindrical billet of the material and took it to the machine shop to have a 3-inch piece cut off to make a bearing. The shop foreman fired up a band saw and started to cut the billet. He only managed to make a small groove in the billet before the cutting action stopped. The Inconel-X had destroyed the sawteeth in just a few seconds. The foreman then tried a large power hacksaw. Those sawteeth also disappeared. I then foolishly suggested that he try cutting a chunk off with a cutting torch. He fired up his cutting torch and within a couple of minutes we had a billet of metal that looked like taffy. It would not cut; it would just soften up as it got white hot. We tried pulling off a chunk, but it was too tough to pull apart. It was indeed a piece of steel taffy when we finished. Looking back on it, the entire process was hilarious, but I really developed tremendous respect for the strength of that material. I was impressed.

The major structure of the X-15 was made of this material. Most of the skin was also made of Inconel-X. During a flight to Mach 6, some parts of the airplane would be heated to 1,300° F, but only momentarily. As soon as the engine burned out, the speed and the heating rate decreased. In addition, the heat tended to redistribute throughout the structure over a period of time and stabilize out at a lower overall temperature. As a result, the average maximum structural temperature during a flight was less than 1,000° F. Inconel-X could easily tolerate that temperature and we could therefore fly up to Mach 6 and pull 6 g without overstressing the aircraft. The X-15 was a tough old bird. It did pop and bang as it accelerated above Mach 5, but it all hung together and got us back home.

A rocket airplane sounds pretty exotic, but in many ways it is rather simple. A rocket engine has almost no moving parts other than valves. Fuel and oxidizer are forced into a combustion chamber at the right mixture ratio and are burned in a controlled explosion. Getting the fuel and oxidizer into the engine is the tricky part. The early rocket airplanes used pressure feed systems to force the fuel from the tanks into the engine. This was a simple system, but the tanks and all the propellant lines had to be designed for high pressure to equal the pressure in the combustion chamber. Later rocket airplanes, including the X-15, utilized turbopumps to build up the propellant pressure to force the fluids into the combustion chamber. This allowed the tanks and propellant lines to be designed for much lower pressures. Tank pressures in the X-15 were only 45 to 50 psi for example. The 50 psi pressure in the tank was used to force the propellant from the tank into the turbopump. Combustion chamber pressure was 600 psi. The turbopump raised the propellant pressures from 50 psi in the tanks and propellant lines to 600 psi going into the combustion chamber.

In the X-15, an igniter was required to light the propellants. The igniter in the X-15 engine was similar to a spark plug. The igniter was used in the engine to light a small stream of propellants in a small combustion chamber attached to the main combustion chamber. This small chamber acted like a blow torch. Once it was lit, it served as the igniter for the main combustion chamber. We referred to this starting ignition sequence as igniter idle. We had this small chamber firing before we launched from the B-52. We lit the main chamber after launch.

Because a rocket engine involves a controlled explosion, it is quite temperamental. The controlled explosion can sometimes blow itself out and quit producing thrust. Or, at the other extreme, it can become an uncontrolled explosion. Fortunately, most of our flights took place between these two extremes.

Throttling a rocket engine is one way to precipitate a problem. We had a throttle in the X-15, but we used it cautiously since it was not uncommon to lose the engine completely by throttling it back. The X-15 rocket engine was one of the first rocket engines to have a throttling capability. The engine initially had a throttling capability from 30 percent power to 100 percent power. The throttling worked surprisingly well, however the lower limit of 30 percent finally had to be increased because the engine did not want to run reliably at that power setting. The minimum throttle setting was increased to 40 percent power which solved most of our engine problems.

The LR-99 rocket engine in the X-15 had another unique feature. It had a restart capability. If the engine failed to light the first time, you could recycle the starting process and try again. This feature saved a number of missions since it was not uncommon early in the program to fail to get a light on the first try after launch. Most of the failures to light in the early part of the flight program were primarily due to the fact that we were starting the engine at the minimum throttle position of 30 percent power. We later changed our starting procedure to start the engine with the throttle at 100 percent power and then throttle back if required to reduce thrust. This cured most of the failure to light problems. A failure of the engine to light after launch or a "no light" callout over the radio could cause a few missed heartbeats both in the air and on the ground.

The engine relight capability was theoretically useful only when the tanks were mostly full. If the tanks were not full, the propellant feed line could be unported and you could not get propellants to the engine. The only relights that were made with partial fuel were those made by Scott in the LR-99 demonstration flights. I tried an engine relight once when the engine quit after forty-one seconds of burn time. I didn't get a relight, but we later found that the engine had been damaged before I had attempted the relight. There had been a small explosion in the engine when it shutdown prematurely. That explosion prevented the engine from recycling properly. I may have gotten a relight if that had not happened.

I really wanted to try an engine relight just before landing. Quite often we shut the engine down 5 or 10 seconds before all the fuel was burned. That few seconds of burn time would be adequate to make a go-around since the aircraft weight would be down to about 16,000 pounds and the engine would produce 60,000 pounds. One could get back up to high key damn fast with that kind of acceleration. I know it would have been a spectacular maneuver if I could have pulled it off. I also know I would have been fired if I had done it, but I think it would have been worth it. It would have stunned a lot of people since half the people on the base were outside watching the X-15 land after each flight. Even the commanding general of the flight test center came out to watch each X-15 landing. General Branch, an outstanding center commander, would have loved it. Paul Bikle, our director at Dryden would also have loved it, but he would have fired me to make a point. He did not tolerate foolishness during business hours. After hours, he was a pretty regular guy. Another person who really would have been impressed with a go-around would have been the chase pilot who would have been "left in the dust."

The X-15 had a propellant jettison capability if all engine light attempts failed. The pilot could jettison a full load of propellants in two minutes. This was extremely crucial since the aircraft would not survive a landing with any significant amount of propellants on-board.

The LR-11 engine was used in the X-15 on an interim basis while we waited for the LR-99 to complete its demonstration tests. The LR-11 engine had been previously used in the X-1 and the D-558-II rocket airplanes. It consisted of four separate barrels or chambers that developed 1,500 pounds of thrust in each barrel or a total of 6,000 pounds of thrust. Each barrel could be operated independently, and as a result the pilot had an incremental throttling capability. Two engines were installed in each X-15 to provide a total of 12,000 pounds of thrust. The engines burned a combination of water and alcohol using liquid oxygen as the oxidizer. The relatively low level of thrust developed by these engines severely limited the performance of the X-15, but use of these engines allowed the flight program to begin on schedule.

Three X-15 aircraft were constructed. Two were delivered to the government on completion of the contractor demonstration phase. The third aircraft blew up during a ground run prior to its first flight. It was subsequently rebuilt and delivered to the government almost a year later. The number two aircraft was severely damaged in November 1962 and was later rebuilt as the X-15A-2— a highly modified version of the X-15.

A. Scott Crossfield

Joseph A. Walker

Robert M. White

Forrest S. "Pete" Petersen

John B. "Jack" McKay

Neil A. Armstrong

Robert A. Rushworth

Joseph H. Engle

Milton O. Thompson

William H. Dana

Michael J. Adams

William J. "Pete" Knight

Left to right: Pete Knight, Bob Rushworth, Joe Engle, Milt Thompson, Bill Dana, and Jack McKay.

View from the X-15 during an altitude flight. Las Vegas is in the lower left.
The Colorado River runs through the center of the photograph from left to right.

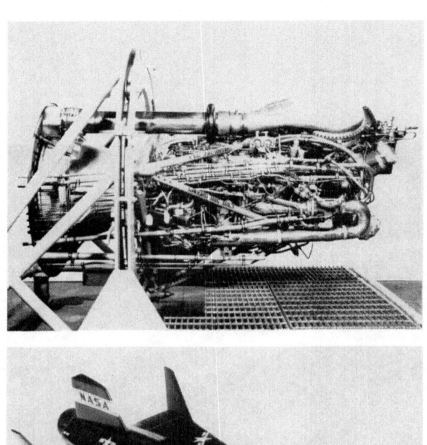

Top: The LR-99 rocket engine. Bottom: Model of the proposed delta-wing X-15

Top: Aerial view of the Dryden Flight Research Center, circa 1953. Short taxiway onto lakebed is at center top. Bottom: X-15 being hoisted up to pylon on B-52 wing. Hoists were located in X-15 servicing, fueling, and mating areas.

Top: Preparing to start B-52 engines prior to taxi for takeoff. Bottom: X-15 servicing area during an attempt to fly two X-15s on the same day. Although several attempts were made, we never succeeded in launching two X-15s during one day. Both X-15s got airborne, but only one launched.

X-15 on B-52 in servicing area during preflight fueling operations. LOX vapor surrounds the aircraft.

Rear view of X-15 mated to the B-52 mothership during preflight fueling operations. Large hole in nozzle flange is engine turbopump exhaust duct.

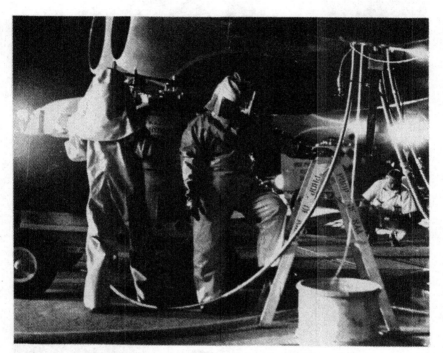

Servicing crew loads hydrogen peroxide aboard the X-15.

Top: Frost coats the exterior skin of the propellant tanks during fueling operations prior to flight. Bottom: X-15 being towed into position for mating to the B-52 pylon. Note rear-wheeled dolly used during ground towing operations. Nose boom was used prior to delivery of the ball nose that was used for all high-speed flights.

Dual LR-11 engines used prior to delivery of the LR-99 engine. Each rocket
chamber produced 1,500 pounds of thrust.

Top: LR-11 engine run in engine test stand. Bottom: X-15A-2 with ablative coating. Ablative charring can be seen on the canopy leading edge, the wing, horizontal and vertical tail leading edges, and the upper and lower speed brakes.

Top: The number three X-15 on the Edwards lakebed. North Base hangars are visible above the horizontal stabilizer. Bottom: X-15 with F-104 landing chase aircraft approaching touchdown. Smoke from pyrotechnic flare provides pilot an indication of surface wind. North Base hangars are in background.

Top: X-15A-2 engine light follows launch on maximum-speed flight. External tanks and dummy scramjet are visible. Vapor trail above X-15 fuselage is APU exhaust. Bottom: X-15A-2 with dummy scramjet installed accelerates and climbs after launch.

Chapter 2 . . . .

The Operation

Transport he only practical way to reach hypersonic speeds in a manned airplane in the late 1950s was to use rocket power. The largest jet engine available produced less than 30,000 pounds of thrust whereas rocket engines with over 200,000 pounds of thrust had been developed to power ballistic missiles. A rocket engine developing almost 60,000 pounds of thrust was designed for the X-15.

A rocket propulsion system has the advantages of being powerful and relatively simple. It does not require air inlets, compressors, turbines, or other airflow and pressure control components. It provides its own oxidizer for combustion of the fuel. It makes a nice, neat propulsion system. It has its disadvantages, however. It burns horrendous amounts of fuel and oxidizer. Thus, you have to use this fuel in the most effective manner possible. The operational concept of air launch and unpowered landings was developed to optimize the use of the available rocket fuel. In this concept, the rocket powered airplane is carried up to altitude by a mothership and then launched to make its own flight on rocket power. All of the rocket fuel can then be used to accelerate to the desired speed or to climb to much higher altitudes. No fuel needs to be retained for landing, because the airplane is designed for a power off or deadstick landing.

This operating concept had been used very successfully for each of the early rocket airplanes. B-29s or B-50s were used as motherships to carry these early rocket aircraft to a launch altitude of 35,000 feet. These early rocket aircraft would generally be launched within 30 to 40 miles of the Edwards lakebed, heading toward the lakebed. After launch, the pilot would light the rocket engine and then accelerate to the desired speed or climb to the planned altitude. The flights were generally planned so that fuel exhaustion occurred as the aircraft passed over the Edwards lakebed.

After engine burnout, the pilot would decelerate and descend while turning back to land. Using this procedure, the aircraft were never beyond gliding distance of the Edwards or Rosamond lakebeds. It was essential that the aircraft remain within gliding distance at all times during free flight to ensure that it could be recovered at any time if the rocket engine failed to light or if it quit prematurely. This same operating procedure was used for the first fourteen X-15 flights and for all of the pilot checkout flights using the LR-11 engine. A B-52 was used as a mothership for the X-15. Two early production B-52s (AF serial numbers 52-003 and 52-008) were modified to carry the X-15s.

As flights to higher speed and altitude were planned, it became obvious that more distance was required to allow for acceleration, deceleration, climb, and descent. Circling flights around Edwards were impractical to acquire stabilized flight conditions. At maximum speed, for example, the X-15 would have to be turning continuously at 6 g to stay within gliding distance of Edwards. This was totally impractical. The solution was to move the launch point farther away from Edwards to allow more straight line distance to conduct the higher-speed and higher-altitude flights.

A constraint on moving the launch point was the requirement to be within gliding distance of a landing site at launch, in case the rocket engine failed to light. The solution to this problem was to locate some lakes at various distances from Edwards that could be used as launch sites. These lakes would then be available for emergency landings if the engine failed to light after launch. Initially only four lakebeds were used as launch lakes: Silver, Hidden Hills, Delamar, and Mud. Two others, Smith Ranch and Railroad Valley, were used during the latter portion of the program for very high altitude flights. Wendover was originally designated as a launch lake, but was never used.

Silver Lake was 105 miles from Edwards, Hidden Hills was 130 miles, Mud Lake was 200 miles, Delamar was 220 miles, Smith Ranch was 280 miles, and Railroad Valley was 230 miles. This combination of launch lakes gave us a great deal of flexibility in planning flights to various speeds and altitudes, because the ground distances to Edwards varied from 100 miles to almost 300 miles among these six lakebeds.

The X-15 would be launched at these remote launch lakes on a heading back to Edwards. We always planned our flights to land at Edwards in order to minimize recovery and turnaround operations. Edwards was the only landing site that had all the facilities to conduct an X-15 operation. If we landed at any other lakebed, we had to bring the airplane back on a flatbed truck since there were no facilities to load it on the B-52 to fly it out. We could have installed facilities for X-15 operations at some other lakebeds, but it made more sense to plan to recover at Edwards on every flight. The only problem using Edwards as the recovery site was that there were no lakebeds to the south or west of it. Thus, if you overshot Edwards coming from the north or northeast where most of the launch lakes were, you had a problem.

After launch at one of these remote launch lakes, the X-15 would climb and accelerate to build up enough speed and altitude to allow it to glide back to Edwards following engine shutdown or burnout. The X-15 could glide over 400 miles once it achieved its maximum speed, although we never attempted to fly that far. There was a potential problem, however, if the X-15 did not build up enough energy to get back to Edwards. This might be the case if, for example, the engine quit prematurely. If that happened, the X-15 would need an intermediate landing site. This requirement had to be considered in the selection of suitable launch lakes. Each launch lake had to have one to three usable lakebeds located between it and Edwards to accommodate these potential emergency situations. Luckily, the southern California desert region is liberally sprinkled with dry lakebeds. Suitable combinations of launch and intermediate lakebeds were found to accommodate all of our needs.

In all, we examined 40 or 50 lakebeds in the southern California and western Nevada deserts and selected fifteen or so that were suitable for X-15 emergency use. We preferred lakes that were at least 3 miles long, but reluctantly accepted some as small as 2 miles, hoping that we would never have to use them.

These launch lakes and intermediate lakes had to be carefully inspected for adequate hardness and smoothness. They were marked with tar strips to define the best landing area or areas if the lake was large enough for more than one runway. The runways that were marked off were standardized at 300 feet wide. The tar strips outlining the edge of the runway were also standardized at 8 feet wide. The width of the strips was quite critical because it was our only good reference measurement to judge height. Many of the lakebeds were very smooth with no surface texture. Looking down on a lakebed of that type was like looking down on smooth water. We could not judge height, thus the need for a known reference dimension such as the tar strips.

The Edwards Flight Test Center devoted a lot of effort to marking out the runways on each of the lakebeds. These runways had to be re-marked at least once a year, and sometimes more frequently if we had heavy rain or snow. The rain and melting snow tended to cover the tar strips with mud which made them almost invisible. Over the years, the thickness of the tar strips increased with each new marking until they exceeded 3 or 4 inches in height above the lakebed surface.

The rain and snow caused other problems on these lakes. It softened the lakebed surface and, in the case of heavy rain or snow, it created a gooey mud or even a shallow lake full of water. I have seen some of the lakebeds covered with as much as a foot of water. If that happened, we could not use the lake for 3 or 4 months. It took that long for it to dry up and regain its hardness.

NASA took on the responsibility of checking the lakebeds for hardness throughout the year. We used our Gooney Bird to fly up to each of the lakebeds with a small team of people to survey the marked runways for soft spots and sinkholes. We had a 6-inch-diameter lead ball that we dropped from a height of 5 feet on the lakebed surface. We would measure the diameter of the depression and then compare that to some reference measurements on a hard useable lakebed to determine whether the runway would support the weight of the X-15. It was a crude but effective means of verifying the usability of the lakebeds.

Prior to landing on the lakebed to inspect it, we would make a low pass or two to visually look for wet spots or standing water. If the lakebed appeared to be damp, we would make another pass and roll the Gooney Bird wheels on the lakebed and then come around to check the depth of the tracks. That could be a tricky maneuver if the lakebed was softer than it appeared to be, because we could be sucked down into the mud. That happened on a couple of occasions. In his book, Chuck Yeager described one such occasion during an inspection of a lakebed using a T-33. Neil Armstrong was flying the T-33 and he and Yeager ended up stuck in the mud and stranded on the lakebed. It took a lot of effort to salvage that airplane.

We carried a motorcycle on the Gooney Bird to ride up and down the runways to inspect them. Walter Whiteside, a retired air force maintenance officer and veteran dirt bike rider, was among other things, our primary lakebed inspector. He really loved to get out on those big lakebeds with that motorcycle. Whenever I went out in an F-104 to practice X-15 landings, I would look for him if he were uprange inspecting a lakebed. I would try to catch him out on the lakebed on his motorcycle and sneak up behind him at 600 knots so he could not hear me coming and then try to blow him off the motorcycle by buzzing him at 10 to 15 feet above his head. To make it even more dramatic, I would light the burner as I passed over him. He admitted that he nearly lost control a few times during these buzz jobs. It really is a terrifying experience to be buzzed like that if you cannot see the airplane coming. You cannot hear it coming, at that speed, until it is just a fraction of a second away. Then the noise hits you like a bomb blast. You can really get someone's attention like that.

We had three primary launch lakes, Hidden Hills, Mud, and Delamar. Each of these launch lakes had a separate set of intermediate lakes on a line leading back to Edwards in case we could not make it all the way home. We also used Smith Ranch and Railroad Valley as launch lakes for the very high energy flights.

Perhaps surprisingly, altitude flights required the greatest distance from launch to landing. We covered a lot of ground while we were outside the atmosphere, and we could not kill off any energy while we were in space. Speed brakes do not provide any drag in a vacuum. The maximum altitude flight of 354,200 feet made by Joe Walker, required a ground distance of 305 miles to climb out of the atmosphere coast to peak altitude, descend, make the pullout, and then slow down before reaching Edwards. The maximum speed flight of 4,520 MPH required a ground distance of only 225 miles since on a speed flight, we stayed within the atmosphere and we could slow down relatively quickly.

One of the major reasons for utilizing longer distances on each flight was to allow time to accomplish test maneuvers or to conduct various experiments. During the early X-15 test flights, for example, we performed maneuvers to determine the stability of the aircraft at various speeds, the control effectiveness at various speeds, the aerodynamic performance or lift/drag ratio, the loads and the stress imposed on various parts of the aircraft.

All of these maneuvers required a finite amount of time to set up a quasi-steady state airspeed and altitude condition and then perform the maneuver. This is the kind of thing a research pilot is required to do to earn his money— accomplishing good maneuvers for data purposes. Flying the airplane is just something the pilot does to get the desired test maneuver. He can be the greatest stick and rudder pilot in the world, but if he cannot do the required data maneuvers, he is worthless as a research pilot.

Where the X-15 would land during any given flight was precomputed on the basis of planned versus actual engine burn time. If the engine did not light in two attempts after launch, we made an emergency landing at the launch lake. If the engine did light, but only burned for a short period of time, we would

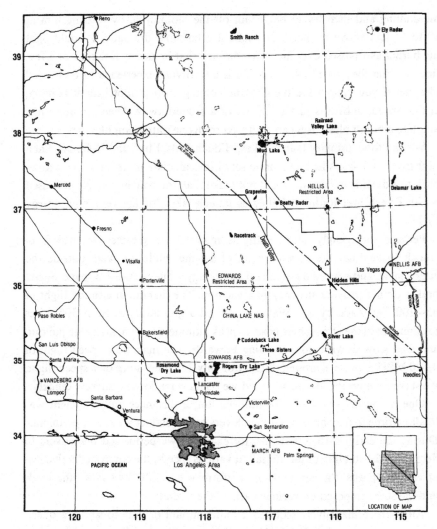

Figure 3. Map of X-15 operating area and all X-15 lakebeds.

end up making a landing at the launch lake since we could still turn around and make it back. If the engine burned over half of the available burn time, which was approximately 82 seconds, but less than 80 percent, for example, we would very likely end up at one of the intermediate lakebeds since we could not make it to Edwards nor could we get back to the launch lake. If the engine burned longer than 80 percent of the planned burn time, we could make it home to Edwards. These percentages quoted are representative and vary with each launch lake and type of flight. Some representative decision times for a typical flight out of Delamar Lake are: 0 to 40 seconds—land at Delamar, 40 to 46 seconds—land at an unnamed lakebed in a highly classified restricted area, 46 to 64 seconds—land at Hidden Hills, 64 to 68.5 seconds—land at Cuddeback, and 68.5 seconds or longer—land at Edwards.

Hidden Hills was used as a launch lake on many flights, but it also served as an intermediate lakebed for flights from Delamar Lake since these flights passed almost directly over Hidden Hills. Mud Lake, another launch lake, also served as an intermediate lakebed for flights out of Smith Ranch.

The precomputation of landing sites was part of a process called energy management. In an unpowered aircraft, the distance you fly depends on how much initial energy you have. Speed and altitude are the primary components of energy. With plenty of speed and altitude, it is possible to glide a long distance. With a minimal amount of speed and altitude, you can only glide a short distance. With the optimum combination of speed and altitude, in the X-15, we could glide over 400 miles. This was not a slow speed glide either. We normally averaged over 2,000 MPH during gliding flight after engine burnout. If we needed to maximize our gliding distance we flew at the airspeed that gave us the maximum lift-drag ratio. Using a combination of these techniques, we could vary our gliding distance from over 400 miles to less than 50 miles, starting from Mach 6 at 100,000 feet altitude.

We always planned our flights to have more than enough energy to get home. Thus, our primary energy management task was to dissipate the excess energy that we had before we arrived at Edwards, to ensure that we did not go whizzing on by, unable to get back home. Our primary means of dissipating energy was to use our speed brakes. This is the same technique used in gliders or sailplanes to make precise landings during gliding flight.

The pilot of the X-15 was unable to accomplish this energy management task at high speed and altitude on his own due to the high levels of energy involved. He could not simply look out the window and decide if he could glide another 100 or 200 miles. He had to rely on the control room to provide that information. The pilot could successfully judge energy at the lower energy levels. The unpowered landing approach is an exercise in energy management. In order to make a precise landing on a preselected runway, the pilot would look out the window while turning and using speed brakes as necessary.

In a normal flight operation, the X-15 would be carried out to the selected launch lake and then launched in the direction of Edwards. Normal launch conditions were 0.8 Mach at 45,000 feet altitude. The X-15 pilot would light the rocket engine and then climb and accelerate up to the desired test conditions. Depending on the specific flight plan, he would either shut the engine down or let it burn until the fuel was exhausted. After engine shutdown, the pilot would maneuver the airplane back to Edwards in gliding flight and then make an unpowered or deadstick landing. During the flight the pilot would perform various research maneuvers as called for in the flight plan or he would activate various experiments that were being carried on the airplane.

There were two basic types of flights made in the X-15, atmospheric flights and altitude flights. The atmospheric flights were made within the atmosphere generally below 100,000 feet altitude. In these flights, the X-15 was flying much like a normal airplane. The wings were developing lift and we could turn and maneuver like we could in a conventional airplane. On these flights, after launch, the pilot would establish a moderate climb angle and then begin a pushover at 60,000 to 70,000 feet altitude to come level below 100,000 feet altitude. The final portion of the flight, before engine burnout, would be in level flight either at a stabilized speed to gather data or in accelerating flight to achieve a high speed. The maximum speed flights were typical of these flights. After engine burnout, the pilot would glide back to Edwards in a shallow descent.

Altitude flights involved a steep climb out of the atmosphere, followed by a ballistic trajectory up to peak altitude, then a steep descent back into the atmosphere, a pullout to level flight after entering the atmosphere, and then a glide back to Edwards in a shallow descent. An altitude flight was a short duration space flight. We left the atmosphere and for 2 to 5 minutes, depending on peak altitude, we were weightless in a 0 g space environment. We could not turn or change our flight path outside the atmosphere. We could only control aircraft attitude through the use of reaction controls. We made an exit of the earth's atmosphere and a reentry just like any other spacecraft.

The big difference between the X-15 and a spacecraft is that we did not have enough velocity to stay outside the atmosphere. That would have required speeds of 18,000 MPH. Our maximum speed was 4,500 MPH. Our space flights were up and down, much like Al Shepard's first suborbital flight. Our space flights were also like the flight of a ballistic missile, except that we could make a pullout when we reentered the atmosphere and glide down to a landing.

Early in the development of the X-15, it became obvious that the X-15 would require a long test range to conduct its high-speed and high-altitude flights. A tracking and telemetry range was set up with three sites, one at Edwards, one at Beatty, Nevada, and one at Ely, Nevada. Each of these sites had an FPS-16 radar installation, telemetry receiving antennas and two way voice

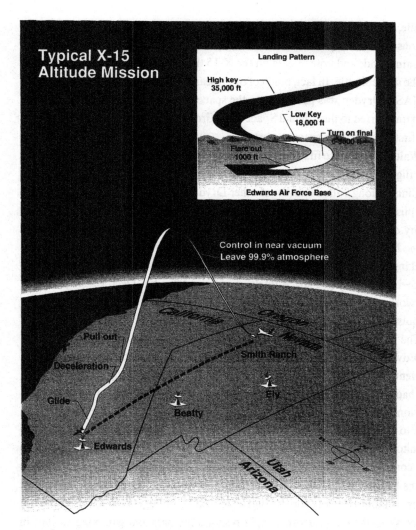

Typical X-15 Altitude Mission

Landing Pattern

High key 35,000 ft

Low Key 18,000 ft

Turn on final

Flare out 1000 ft

Edwards Air Force Base

Control in near vacuum
Leave 99.9% atmosphere

California　Oregon　Nevada　Idaho

Pull out

Deceleration

Smith Ranch

Glide

Ely

Beatty

Edwards

Utah

Arizona

Figure 4. Typical X-15 altitude mission.

communications. These sites were initially autonomous, but subsequently linked via microwave to transmit radar and telemetry data in real time between sites. The three sites were spaced roughly 200 miles apart and spanned a total distance of almost 400 miles. From these three sites, we could track the X-15 anywhere in the state of Nevada and the lower portion of the state of California.

The radar data from these tracking stations was used to monitor the track, profile, and total energy of the X-15. The telemetry data was used to monitor various systems in the aircraft and safety of flight data. We were monitoring the same kinds and type of data on the X-15 that NASA is currently monitoring on the space shuttle. In fact, much of our research aircraft operational experience at NASA Dryden was passed on to the space program through key individuals who transferred to the original Space Task Group, planning for Project Mercury, the first American in space venture.

Walt Williams, the first chief of the NASA Dryden Center became the deputy for flight operations to Bob Gilruth who headed the Space Task Group. Williams, along with a number of other Dryden personnel who also transferred, established a space version of Dryden's experimental aircraft test complex. Many of the flight test procedures developed at Dryden were applied directly to the Mercury spacecraft flight operation. The man who developed the X-15 tracking range, Gerry Truszynski, transferred to NASA headquarters and proceeded to develop the space tracking net and later the Deep Space Tracking Network. He subsequently became NASA's Chief of Tracking and Data Acquisition.

The data received at the X-15 tracking sites was used to vector the X-15 to Edwards or to an alternate landing site, if a problem developed which prevented the X-15 from making it home to Edwards. Early in the program, we had a control room at each site because we were unable to transfer information in real time between sites. That, of course, meant that each control room had to be manned on each flight by a controller and a team of engineers to monitor safety of flight data in real time. This requirement further added to the complexity of the support operation for each flight. These control room teams had to fly up to the sites the night before to be able to check the control room out and be ready for the flight the next morning. These teams rarely got much sleep the night before a flight because the bars and gambling casinos in Beatty and Ely stayed open most of the night. The bordellos stayed open all night. Pilots were used as controllers at these uprange sites, so we all spent plenty of time in Beatty and Ely, Nevada.

The NASA pilots also piloted the Gooney Bird that we used to haul the teams back and forth. I logged a lot of flight time in our R4D (the navy version of a C-47) flying up and down the X-15 tracking range. The NASA pilots also had to fly range checkout flights to exercise the radar and telemetry tracking systems. On these flights, we simply flew uprange and then flew back down the intended track of the upcoming X-15 flight to allow the individual sites to track the aircraft and exercise the total X-15 Hi Range System.

We used our support airplanes, T-33, F-100, or F-104 aircraft, to make these flights. We would simulate emergency approaches into each of the intermediate lakes to give the radar technicians some practice tracking a simulated X-15 flight. The radar people would lose us on radar a few thousand feet above the lakebed due to curvature of the earth or intervening mountains. I used to love to stay low after a simulated emergency approach to a lakebed and then sneak back up on the tracking site. I would stay below 50 feet and would be traveling at close to 600 knots as I approached the site. As I passed over the site, I would light the afterburner and do a roll. When I used that technique, they could not see or hear me coming. As I passed over, the noise was like a bomb going off. Even though the crews manning these sites knew I liked to do this and were expecting it, it still scared the hell out of them when I went over. They claimed that I shook the radar loose in its mount over a period of time because of those low passes. These stunts did relieve the boredom for the crews that were permanently stationed at these sites. These sites were located on some of the most desolate terrain in the inland desert. Even the lizards would avoid the Beatty site. One might see an occasional sidewinder, but not much else.

There was a small lakebed just west of the Beatty tracking site that we used as an airstrip to haul people and supplies to the site. It was less than a mile in diameter, but it was adequate to get the Gooney Bird in and out. We occasionally used our Aero Commander to make this same trip, however, it was a little dicier to maneuver that airplane particularly with a full load of passengers on a hot day. The Beatty site was less than 20 miles from Death Valley, so it did get hot. My favorite trick to get airborne under those conditions was to start accelerating around the edge of the lake and then turn in toward the center for the final takeoff.

On one trip, prior to takeoff out of that lakebed, I could not get the left engine started on the Aero Commander. I asked Ron Waite, one of the X-15 operations engineers, to get out and pull the prop through backwards. That was an old trick that I had learned as a crop duster pilot. Ron Waite had worked previously as an engineer for Pratt & Whitney. He had never heard of such a procedure. He thought I was kidding. When he realized that I meant it, he insisted that I shut all the switches off for that engine and then hold my hands out the window so that he could see them while he was pulling the prop through. I guess he did not trust me.

Ron had never propped an engine in his entire career. While in college I flew crop dusters. We used to routinely prop the 450 HP engine on our duster aircraft. I did not necessarily like to do it, but it came with the job. Propellers could be scary. I will never forget moving around among the airplanes on an aircraft carrier deck in the late 1940s when the aircraft were all fired up and the propellers were turning prior to takeoff. That was scary.

But back to the desert, I used to enjoy the trips up to the Beatty and Ely sites. I made most of the trips at treetop level, even though there were not a lot of trees. I enjoyed buzzing the desert looking for coyotes and other animal life. There were no traffic rules or regulations up in that desert region. We did what we pleased while flying in that area. We felt that we owned that desert territory, even though much of it was outside the Edwards restricted area. We owned it by the right of eminent domain. We lived in that airspace. The only area that we avoided was the atomic energy test area and a restricted test site dubbed "The Ranch." The remainder of the inland desert was our territory.

It was really fun to fly in that time period. Just before I quit flying, the FAA and the military began tightening the rules in the Edwards test area. The joy slowly went out of flying for me as they began to control all traffic, even though I refused to comply with their regulations on local proficiency flights. I just would not tell them where I was going or what I was going to do. I am glad I quit test flying when I did. I would hate to have someone monitoring my every move during a proficiency flight. Flying should be fun. I had always managed to enjoy my flying career before that time.

A minimum of three and a maximum of five chase planes were used on X-15 flights. Three chase were used on the early low-speed X-15 flights that were launched in the immediate Edwards area. Four chase were used for the major portion of the flights and five were used for the longer range flights out of Smith Ranch.

Chase-1 was the prelaunch chase. This chase took off with the B-52 and stayed with it throughout the entire prelaunch checkout procedure. An F-100 aircraft was used during the first few years of the program and later a T-38. Chase-1 was normally flown by a USAF pilot. This chase flew tight formation on the B-52/X-15 combination to monitor various checklist procedures which involved visible X-15 activities such as control surface movements, propellant jettison checks, ballistic control system checks, APU start, engine start cycle, and control surface trim checks. This chase also provided independent airspeed, altitude, and heading checks, and served as a lookout for conflicting traffic.

Chase-2 was the launch chase. It took over as the prime chase at 1 minute to launch. An F-104 aircraft was used and it was normally flown by a NASA pilot. This chase took off as the B-52 was departing the Edwards area on its outbound leg to the launch point. The chase served as the landing chase for any emergency landings that might be required either before or shortly after launch. This chase trailed the B-52 out to the launch point. After launch it chased the X-15 until the plane left the launch lake area or followed the X-15 down to a launch lake landing if the engine failed to light or shut down prematurely.

Chase-1 and -2 were somewhat redundant in coverage of the flight, however, we did not have one kind of aircraft that could do both missions well. Neither the F-100 or the T-38 could follow the X-15 down to a landing. They could not produce enough drag to reduce their lift-drag ratio to match that of the X-15. Only the F-104 could do that. The F-104, conversely, could not fly formation on the B-52 throughout the flight up to launch. The F-104 would not cruise at 45,000 feet due to its high-wing loading.

Chase-2 normally trailed the B-52 outbound at 35,000 feet. Then about 3 minutes to launch, the pilot would light the afterburner and begin a climb to arrive at 45,000 feet in formation with the B-52 at 1 minute to launch. To maintain formation, the F-104 pilot had to use minimum afterburner and partial speed brakes—an ungodly way to fly. If he timed it just right, he did not have to fly formation for more than a minute. If he did not, he used up a lot of gas.

Chase-2 was almost always low on fuel at launch and usually landed back at Edwards with the low-fuel light on. It was especially bad if some problem caused a ten minute hold. Then the pilot was lucky to get home on a straight-in approach to the North lakebed. Sometimes we resorted to riding the vortex off the B-52 wing tip as a fuel saving maneuver. This could save the chase a lot of gas. It was almost like surfing. The tip vortex was quite strong and when the chase pilot positioned the F-104 in the proper location relative to the wing tip, he could maintain position with about half the power normally required. Ducks and geese have utilized this vortex riding technique for millions of years but never with a B-52.

Chase-3 was the intermediate chase that covered any emergency landings at intermediate lakebeds. An F-104 was used and a NASA pilot usually flew this chase position. This chase took off about 30 minutes prior to launch and orbited over the intermediate lake or between the intermediate lakes if there were more than one. It would attempt to join up with the X-15 and escort it to a landing on the designated emergency lake.

Chase-4 was the chase that covered the Edwards landing. An F-104 was used and the pilot was usually a USAF pilot. This chase also took off about 30 minutes prior to launch. It orbited 30 to 40 miles up the X-15 track from Edwards. The pilot usually began accelerating and climbing along the X-15 track back toward Edwards to rendezvous with the X-15 at the maximum possible speed and altitude as the X-15 descended into the Edwards area. It was a tricky task. Chase-4 was vectored in for rendezvous by radar. Because the X-15 was hard to see due to its small size and dark color, quite often the chase relied on the contrail caused by the jettison of propellant to acquire the X-15. Once rendezvoused, Chase-4 would visually inspect the X-15 and advise the X-15 pilot of any abnormalities. Chase-4 would then provide airspeed, altitude, and position information during the approach as requested by the X-15 pilot. Chase-4 would verify flap and gear extension and call out height above the lakebed during the last few seconds prior to touchdown.

A second intermediate chase was required on the flights out of Smith Ranch to cover all of the intermediate lakes. The maximum distance between intermediate lakes was over 150 miles and the F-104 could not accelerate fast enough to cover a landing at both lakebeds.

We occasionally had sufficient aircraft to have the luxury of a roving chase. This chase served as a backup for Chase-2, -3, -4, or -5. It was usually orbiting about halfway between Edwards and the launch lake.

In all of my years as a research pilot for NASA, I always accepted the fact that a chase was essential for any risky test flight. This was the accepted way of doing business for ourselves and for the entire test community throughout the country. I was very surprised to have Deke Slayton challenge the practice when we became a part of the test team to support the air launch tests of the space shuttle. I think he challenged the need for chase aircraft just to force everyone to reexamine and rejustify the requirement. Before becoming an astronaut, he apparently had a bad experience with a chase aircraft while flying as a test pilot at Edwards. We reviewed our chase experience to determine what benefits the chase actually provided.

Surprisingly, we could only remember one incident in a 20-year-period where the chase had definitely saved an aircraft. This was a real shock. Before we did the study, I would have guessed that there were 50 or 100 incidents wherein the chase saved an aircraft or at least provided crucial information. Not so. We may have forgotten one or two other incidents, but the occurrences of clear-cut saves by the chase were infinitely small. The chase provided helpful information on almost every test flight of every research aircraft, but surprisingly few critical bits of information.

The one major thing that a chase does provide is verification type information which can be psychologically important to the test aircraft pilot. It is damn nice to have a chase with you in an emergency, if for nothing else than to hold your hand. He also makes a good witness during an accident investigation.

During the X-15 program, everyone accepted the need for chase aircraft and we did not fly without them. Thank God for that, although when I did have emergencies in the X-15, I personally did not get that much help from the chase.

The ground support required for an X-15 flight was quite extensive. At the launch lake, we had a rescue helicopter, a fire truck, and a NASA emergency vehicle with X-15 crew members aboard. At the intermediate lakebeds, we had a fire truck and a NASA emergency vehicle with X-15 crew members. At Edwards, we had the works. After landing at Edwards, the pilot was greeted by a convoy of vehicles that converged on him almost before he stopped. The Edwards fire chief led the pack in his bright red pickup. He was not officially the leader of the convoy, but he had the fastest vehicle. He would simply outrun everyone. There was no rigid convoy formation or speed limit.

Everyone was on his own once the mobile control van started moving. The fire chief routinely hit speeds approaching 100 MPH as he drove across the lakebed. There were at least ten or twenty vehicles plus a helicopter that roared across the lakebed to rescue the X-15 pilot whether he wanted to be rescued or not. Ironically, if we made it home to Edwards we usually did not have a problem. We normally needed the most help if we did not make it home to Edwards. It was, however, a spectacular show with all those vehicles racing across the lakebed raising a dust cloud that rose 1,000 feet into the air. Sitting in the X-15, it was somewhat frightening to see all these vehicles converge on us. We really hoped and prayed that their brakes worked properly. On routine flights, this was the most dangerous part.

All of this emergency ground support equipment was supplied by NASA and the Edwards Flight Test Center. This obviously involved a lot of logistics to get the support vehicles to their appropriate locations prior to each flight. The launch lake rescue helicopter normally flew up to the launch lake early on the morning of the scheduled flight. They normally had to be on station at 8:00 A.M., which required that they leave Edwards at four or five in the morning to get to a launch lake 200 to 300 miles from Edwards. The fire trucks and the NASA emergency vehicle were flown up to the launch lake in a C-130.

Edwards had two C-130s dedicated to X-15 support, and they were obviously critical to the operation. They were sometimes late accomplishing their support mission, but we did not often cancel a flight because of lack of support. The C-130s would deliver the launch lake vehicles and then fly back to Edwards to pick up another rescue vehicle and a paramedic team. They would then fly back up range to assume a position about halfway between the launch lake and Edwards. From that orbit position, they could react and cover an emergency landing at the intermediate lakebeds. If a call came over the air indicating an emergency landing at one of the intermediate lakebeds, the C-130 headed to the designated lakebed. The C-130, with its paramedics, would also cover any crash or ejection anywhere along the ground track.

This total ground support system was tied together through VHF and UHF radio communications, as well as single side band radios. The ground support vehicles and crews were completely dependent on radio communications to alert them to an emergency landing at their particular location because they normally could not see the X-15. They waited to hear the call that the X-15 was going to make it home or make an emergency landing. That decision was made in the first minute and a half after launch.

Everyone was happy when the call came that Edwards was the landing destination. When any other landing destination was called out, everyone immediately tensed up. An emergency landing in the X-15 was an honest-to-God emergency. The call for a landing at an intermediate lakebed was the call that the emergency lakebed crews dreaded. They knew they could have a potential disaster on their hands in the next few minutes. But of course that is the reason they were on station in the first place. That is when they really earned their pay.

The final phases of the flight involved an unpowered approach and landing. The unpowered approach ideally involved a 360 degree spiraling descent. The starting position was directly over the desired touchdown point at 35,000 feet altitude on the runway heading, at 250 to 300 knots airspeed. This position was referred to as high-key. From this position, we began a turn using a nominal thirty-five degree bank while maintaining 250 to 300 knots airspeed. The turn was usually made to the left, although it could be made in either direction. At the completion of 180 degrees of turn, we were approximately 4 miles abeam of the intended touchdown point at 18,000 to 20,000 feet altitude headed in the opposite direction of the landing runway. This position was referred to as the low-key position. The turn was continued from this position through another 180 degrees to line up with the landing runway about 5 miles short of the runway. At this point we were set up for the landing.

The X-15 simulator initially established the geometry of the approach pattern. The pattern was then verified in flight using other aircraft such as the F-104 configured to match the X-15 gliding performance. The rate of descent in the landing pattern averaged about 12,000 feet per minute which meant that the landing approach averaged about 3 minutes in duration.

The nominal approach described had many variations to compensate for off nominal initial energy conditions at the high-key position or starting point. If we were high on energy at high key, we could widen the pattern by using a shallow bank angle or conversely, we could tighten the pattern if we were low on initial energy. We could also adjust our energy in the pattern by using a higher or lower airspeed, or by using speed brakes to kill off excess energy. The approach pattern could also be abbreviated if we were very low on initial energy. We could use a 180-degree approach or a straight-in approach. If there were multiple runways, we could use 270-degree or 90-degree approaches. We normally planned all of our flights to have a lot of excess energy so that we always had enough to make the preferred 360-degree approach. We did on occasion have to make other approaches due to unanticipated problems.

The possible variations in the approach seemed limitless. Successful approaches were made starting from speeds as high as Mach 3 at high key and altitudes as high as 70,000 feet. A successful approach was also made from an altitude as low as 25,000 feet at high key. It is amazing how much versatility there is in an unpowered approach. We ultimately achieved consistent high-key energy conditions by initiating energy adjustments 50 miles before reaching high key.

Very precise pinpoint landings can be made in aircraft that are unpowered as demonstrated for many years in gliders and sailplanes. The X-15 and the other early rocket aircraft pilots utilized these same basic approach techniques to make over 500 successful landings with a high degree of accuracy. Overall landing accuracy in the X-15 was within 2,000 feet of the intended touchdown point. Not bad for a hypersonic glider. We did miss by as much as 4,000 to 5,000 feet on some emergency landings. Now I understand where that old statement, "missed by a mile," came from.

The culmination of an X-15 flight was the unpowered landing. Unpowered landings were routine in the early rocket aircraft. Prior to the X-15 program, there were over 250 unpowered landings made in the X-1s, the X-2 and the D-558-II rocket aircraft. Unpowered landings were a way of life at Edwards. The X-15 just happened to be the latest of the series.

Even before the X-15 aircraft was constructed, it was obvious that a special unpowered landing technique had to be developed. Some preliminary inflight simulations of an X-15 using an F-104 to duplicate the subsonic lift/drag ratio revealed that the old power off landing techniques were not adequate. Landing flare initiation was hard to judge due to the steep approach angle and the high rate of descent. The ensuing landings were not consistently successful in the flight simulations and many wave offs were initiated prior to touch-down. The Lockheed test pilots were having similar problems demonstrating a flame out approach technique for the F-104. It also had a very low subsonic lift/drag ratio and came down like a streamlined brick without power. The Lockheed pilots crumped at least two airplanes trying to demonstrate power off landings.

A proposed landing technique was developed by a NASA Ames pilot, Fred Drinkwater. He developed the technique using an F-104 aircraft. He varied lift/drag ratio using flaps and speed brakes to investigate a range of low lift/drag ratio unpowered approaches. He simulated the X-15 with a lift/drag ratio of 4 as well as simulating other more inefficient unpowered aircraft. He found that unpowered landings of very low lift/drag ratio (L/D as low as 2.5) vehicles could be made successfully using a high-speed approach and two different aim points short of the runway to assure touchdown accuracy.

Using Fred's technique, the pilot literally dove at the first aim point at an angle that would result in a 300 knot stabilized airspeed. On reaching a pre-computed altitude, he would initiate a programmed flare maneuver and pick up the second aim point on a much shallower 3-degree glide slope. He maintained this glide angle until he descended through a height of 100 feet above the runway, at which time he made the final flare maneuver. This technique produced some very accurate touchdown locations but somewhat inconsistent touchdown sink rates, when the NASA pilots at Edwards evaluated it.

As a result of these evaluations, the Edwards pilots modified the technique to eliminate the second aim point and reduce the inner glide slope to a degree or less. This produced both accurate touchdown locations and very acceptable sink rates of less than 1 foot per second. The X-15 landing flare was initiated at about 1,000 feet above the ground at an airspeed of 300 knots. We attempted to come level 50 to 100 feet above the runway. We lowered the landing flaps as soon as we came level and then deployed the landing gear as we decelerated through 230 knots. During this float period, after the flare, we were adjusting height above the runway and rate of sink to touchdown at a low-sink rate as the airspeed decreased through 200 knots.

This modified technique became the accepted approach and landing technique for all the early pilots in the program except Crossfield. He developed his own technique using ground simulation and flight simulation in an F-100 aircraft. Scott had to use a drogue chute on the F-100, in addition to speed brakes to simulate the low lift/drag ratio of the X-15. Scott's approach and landing technique utilized lower airspeeds, which made the landing flare maneuver more difficult to execute properly.

With the higher-speed approach, the pilot could make the landing flare maneuver and come level to the runway with a lot of excess airspeed. For example, by starting the flare at 300 knots, the pilot could complete the flare and come level with more than 260 knots of airspeed. After flare, the pilot had 60 to 70 knots of airspeed to lose before touching down at 190 to 200 knots. We were decelerating at about 4 knots per second, so we had between 15 and 18 seconds to adjust height and rate of sink for a smooth landing. This does not seem like much time but it was completely adequate. The sink rates at touchdown using the high-speed approach averaged less than 2 feet per second. Crossfield's technique provided very little float time after flare and his average sink rate was substantially higher using his lower speed approach. He later began using the high-speed approach and his sink rates decreased significantly.

The landing and slideout completed an X-15 flight operation. The aircraft slid 1.5 to 2 miles before it finally came to a stop. As the aircraft slid to a stop, the recovery convoy converged on it to assist in getting the pilot out and in deactivating the aircraft. Residual propellants and peroxide were jettisoned on the lakebed and the aircraft was then towed on a dolly, back to the hangar to be inspected prior to starting over a whole new flight operation.

One of the more risky jobs during an X-15 operation was to set out the landing smoke flares. These were used to provide information for the X-15 pilot on the direction and relative velocity of the surface wind on the lakebed runway. The smoke flares spewed colored smoke for approximately 1 minute after they were ignited.

Some flares were normally ignited at least 1 minute before landing to enable the pilot to set up his approach and landing to compensate for the wind. Additional flares were ignited within a half minute of landing to ensure that smoke would still be visible during final touchdown. These flares were positioned on the edge of the runway about halfway down the lakebed runway. The critical nature of this task was to position and ignite the flares at the proper time and then get the hell out of the way since the X-15 could not be accurately steered on the ground, particularly in a crosswind, and thus, we were not certain where it was going to end up. Nothing is more frightening than to see the X-15 bearing down on you at over 200 MPH throwing up a 200-feet-high rooster tail of dust.

The usual procedure was to drive a carryall vehicle out to the proper location about 10 minutes prior to landing and then begin tossing flares out 1 minute or so prior to landing. You tossed the last flare at about 20 seconds to touchdown and then headed out at full throttle perpendicular to the landing runway. This usually provided reasonable clearance. Every once in a while though, someone would panic and stall the engine while attempting to accelerate away from the runway. That could result in some world-class record hundred-yard dashes by the vehicle occupants.

In summary, the unique features of an X-15 rocket aircraft operation were the air launch several hundred miles from Edwards, the tremendous acceleration during the short engine burn time, the unpowered hypersonic glide to the landing site, and the deadstick landing. The flights seldom exceeded 10 minutes in duration from launch to landing. This meant that on a pilot's first flight, he had to learn to fly the X-15 sufficiently well enough in 10 minutes to make a deadstick landing on his first try. There was no go-around capability. It had to be done right the first time or no cigar.

In preparation for a flight, we flew the X-15 ground simulator and we flew F-104s. The ground based simulator was used to practice the major portion of the flight, beginning with launch and proceeding through boost, hypersonic flight, and energy management maneuvering to arrive at the landing site. The F-104s were used for in-flight simulation of the landing approach.

The ground simulator was a replica of the X-15 cockpit with all of the instruments, gages, switches, and controls. This cockpit was connected to a computer that translated the pilot's control actions into meaningful instrument readings, simulating what the aircraft would do in-flight in response to these control inputs. Flying on instruments in the simulator was essentially doing just as you might do if you were flying in the clouds. We used this simulator to practice each flight. But before the pilot could practice a flight, someone had to plan it or lay it out in minute detail. This was the job of the flight planner.

The research engineer would first request certain maneuvers at a specific flight condition of speed and altitude. He might want a maneuver to measure the stability and control characteristics, or he might ask for a maneuver to apply g loads to the airplane in order to measure the stresses induced in the structure of the airplane. The flight planner would take all of these requirements and lay out a flight plan to obtain these maneuvers at the desired flight condition. This flight plan would define the distance in miles required to reach the desired flight conditions for each maneuver and to obtain the desired data. Based on this distance, the flight planner would select a suitable launch lake from those which we had available. The flight planner would then select the intermediate lakes to be used for emergency landings, and then begin finalizing the flight plan in great detail.

Flight planners spent their entire working day in the simulator. In fact, they spent their entire life in the simulator. We would occasionally find a flight planner who had died a natural death in the simulator. Because they lived in the simulator, they were the experts on the airplane. They knew all of its innermost secrets. They would determine what thrust level to set the engine at after launch. They determined the climb angle, the pushover time, the throttle back time, the engine shutdown time. They would define the maneuvers to be accomplished after engine burnout and the maneuvers required to decelerate into the approach pattern at Edwards. They would also define the cutoff times or decision points for the various emergency lakebeds.

Once they had defined all of this, they took the pilot under their wing and taught him to fly the desired flight plan. They worked with the pilot for days and weeks practicing for a particular flight. The pilot would fly the flight over and over again getting the timing down to the second. During these training sessions, the pilots memorized the flight conditions second by second. At any given second during the boost phase, the pilot knew what the altitude, velocity, and rate of climb should be. He also knew what the g level should be, the angle of attack, the pitch attitude, the heading, the roll attitude, the dynamic pressure, and so on.

Once the pilot knew the basic flight plan by heart, the flight planner would simulate emergencies for the pilot. Hours and hours were spent practicing emergency responses. Typically, the pilot spent a minimum of 15 to 20 hours on the simulator practicing for an 8 to 10 minute flight. A pilot could conservatively practice each flight six to ten times an hour, so over a 20-hour practice session, he could fly the mission 120 to 200 times. The pilot was almost jaded by the time he finally got in the airplane, but that training saved his butt on many occasions. He could fly the flight completely on his own if, for example, he lost radio communications. In fact, we did lose radio communications quite often. Mike Adams added something new to the simulation routine. He would occasionally get bored and start practicing the mission while flying upside down.

The simulator was continually updated with data obtained on previous flights to ensure the validity of the simulator. The original simulator was created using predicted data obtained in the wind tunnel. As the flight program progressed, various maneuvers were performed to obtain aerodynamic derivatives. These flight determined derivatives may or may not have agreed with the original predictions obtained from wind tunnel tests. If the wind tunnel and flight data disagreed, we would attempt to determine which data was correct by repeating the flight maneuvers and in some cases asking for a rerun of the wind tunnel tests. In many cases, the pilot influenced the final decision by comparing the simulator responses, using both old and new sets of data, with the actual aircraft responses. The data that created the best match between the simulator responses and the actual aircraft response was normally selected to update the simulator and ensure its continuing validity. By continually updating the simulator, we were able to more accurately predict potential problems as we continued to expand the flight envelope.

Prior to initiation of the flight program, a simulation was conducted on the human centrifuge at Johnsville to assess the pilot's ability to control the X-15 while being subjected to the large acceleration forces involved in a typical flight. This was the first use of the human centrifuge in a closed loop simulation. After many simulated flights, and occasional wild rides due to electrical glitches, it was determined that the pilots could cope with the highly unusual acceleration environment.

One other unique simulator was used to evaluate a particularly vexing control problem, an in-flight simulator. The Cornell Aeronautical Laboratory had recently developed a variable stability aircraft which could be programmed to simulate the flight characteristics of almost any other aircraft. This in-flight simulator was used to simulate a marginally controllable atmospheric entry maneuver to determine whether the pilots could successfully complete a reentry. The results of this simulation indicated that it was unlikely that the pilot could make a successful reentry without stability augmentation. This in-flight simulator was considered to be a very good simulator since it provided much more realistic cues to the pilot. It was, in fact, so realistic that Neil got carried away in his struggle to salvage a deteriorating entry maneuver and broke the handle off the reaction controller.

The X-15 was the first research aircraft program to make extensive use of simulation for flight planning and pilot training. The simulation was particularly useful during envelope expansion. We were able to avoid many pitfalls because of the simulation. It really paid off. I personally do not believe we could have successfully flown the aircraft without a simulation, particularly in regard to managing energy. There was no way that a pilot could manage energy in the X-15 by simply looking out the window. For example, at speeds of Mach 5 and greater, there was no way that a pilot could land at a field or a lakebed that was directly under him. He had too much energy. He would continue along his flight path, regardless of how hard he was trying to turn. The landing site starting from Mach 5 or greater had to be at least 50 miles down range (preferably farther) to allow him to dissipate his speed in a reasonable manner. Simulation was essential for high-speed flight. The simulation was initially created using wind tunnel data, however the simulation was updated with flight data as the program progressed.

Regardless of how much practice we had on the simulator, we always seemed to be behind the airplane when flying the real flight. We could not easily keep up with the flight plan. One of our brighter flight planners, Jack Kolf, came up with the idea of a fast time simulation, wherein we compressed the time in the simulator to attempt to represent the actual flight. This technique seemed to make the simulation more realistic. Simulation is now used routinely and extensively in training for test flights for military missions, for airline operations, and for many other applications. Simulation technology was given a big boost by research and experimental aircraft test programs such as the X-15, for we had to develop good simulators to survive.

The team morale was excellent throughout the entire program. There was a lot of competition among the three aircraft crews to outdo the other crews in any endeavor imaginable. The crews competed in minimizing the time to turn the aircraft around after a flight and prepare it for the next flight. They competed in minimizing the time to mate the aircraft with the B-52. They compared actual flights versus attempted flights for the three aircraft. They competed for the next available B-52 launch opportunity. Many of the team members contributed numerous hours of unpaid overtime just to ensure that they were not responsible for a delayed or aborted flight.

Paul Bikle, the Dryden director, aided and abetted this competition by betting money against the various crews on any schedule, or other event that the crew was attempting to achieve. He stimulated competition among the different crews in numerous ways, in a continuous effort to maximize the morale and productivity of the project team. To keep morale high, he supported the postflight parties.

Parties were the final act of a flight operation. These parties were not organized or planned, but rather, were a spontaneous celebration following the massive team effort to accomplish a successful flight operation. Parties were an extremely successful mechanism for boosting team spirit. They characteristically began immediately after working hours at the biggest bar in Rosamond—Juanita's. This was the favorite watering hole on the way home to

Lancaster and Palmdale. The normal clientele at Juanita's included local farmers, prospectors, gamblers, and house players for the neverending poker games. These people were engulfed by the X-15 team on the occasion of a flight party. What a strange mix of the past and the future among the patrons on those nights, prospectors looking for the end of the rainbow and rocket pilots looking for the top of the rainbow.

The parties were almost exclusively stag and free of any animosity. They would continue on for four or five hours at Juanita's and then gradually transition to various bars in Lancaster. Quite often, the transition would include a race down Sierra Highway to Lancaster (15 miles away) with no holds barred.

One memorable race involved about twenty different high-performance vehicles with multiple occupants. I had started out in the race, but dropped out to assist Ralph Jackson, our public relations officer. He was limping along at 70 MPH in his old MG roadster with Jack McKay as a passenger. I decided to help him out. I was driving a '57 Jaguar roadster. As I came up behind him, I downshifted to third gear and then pulled up to begin pushing him. I managed to push them up to 90 MPH before I finally backed off due to some frantic waving by Ralph and Jack. I later learned that the steering on Ralph's MG locked up at speeds over 80 MPH. We had a ready excuse if the California Highway Patrol had observed this operation. We planned to tell them we were trying to get Ralph's car started.

Otherwise, the race was proceeding in an orderly fashion until the participants overtook a large semi truck just outside of Lancaster. The racers chose to pass the truck at extreme speeds in a random fashion on the left or right as the oncoming traffic might allow, while creating tremendous confusion and huge clouds of dust. As this stream of speeding cars entered the outskirts of Lancaster, a deputy sheriff observed the race and immediately pursued and stopped the leaders and subsequently the entire line of drunken race car drivers. He proceeded to write tickets from the first to the last car, including one team member's car who was not racing but just happened to be overtaken as the deputy sheriff apprehended the racers.

The truck driver, who had been terrorized by the racers, pulled up as the deputy sheriff wrote out the speeding tickets. He was almost incoherent as he explained to the deputy sheriff what had transpired. He insisted that the deputy arrest every one of the drivers and passengers and offered to transport them to jail in his semi truck trailer. The deputy would not buy any part of the proposition. He realized he was pushing his luck by simply passing out speeding tickets to that supercharged group of revelers.

No drunk-driving tickets were issued. The sheriffs in those days were very tolerant of drunk drivers, in many cases giving them a ride home rather than a ticket or a ride to the drunk tank. If today's laws had been in effect, we would have had a lot of people in jail after each flight.

Throughout most of the flight program, the rocket engine was tested in the aircraft on the ground prior to each launch. The engine was sequenced through its normal starting cycle in a step-by-step fashion to allow various checks and inspections to be made during each phase of the starting cycle. When all this was accomplished, the main chamber was lit off and the engine was throttled from minimum thrust up to maximum for a few seconds and then back to minimum thrust before being shut down. We then went through a restart sequence and again ran up to full thrust and back to minimum thrust up to maximum and then shut it down for a post-engine-run inspection.

When an X-15 engine was being tested, it was obvious to everyone on the base. The engine could be heard very distinctly anywhere on the sprawling test center complex, regardless of how many other aircraft were flying or taxiing or running up their own engines. The X-15 engine had a very distinct banshee-type sound that was instantly recognizable. The X-15 made 199 flights, resulting in hundreds of post-engine-runs preparing for these flights.

I am not sure that anyone knows exactly how many total engine runs were made, because we made extra engine runs if there were any anomalies. We also made extra engine runs if there was an excessive delay in getting a flight off after an initial qualifying engine run. I remember making at least four engine runs in preparation for just one flight, due to a series of malfunctions during each of the first three runs. We also had a separate engine test stand to test engines after engine repairs or overhauls. A conservative guess of the total number of X-15 engine runs would be roughly 400.

The X-15 engine runs were conducted in the same sequence each time and for about the same duration. As a result, everyone at Edwards became familiar with the sequence of events and the sound pattern. They subconsciously realized that there was a problem if the sequence or the timing was interrupted. It seemed that regardless of what we happened to be doing when we heard an X-15 engine start, we subconsciously listened to the sequence and timing of the run to ascertain whether the run would be successful.

One of the X-15 operations engineers, Ron Waite, could imitate the sound of the entire sequence of the rocket engine run from the rumbling of the ignition sequence, through the main chamber light off to the peculiar hog calling like noise of the shutdown. It was a real joy to hear him go through the sequence. He can still go through the routine almost 20 years after the last X-15 flight.

I was always impressed by an X-15 engine run, whether I was in the cockpit making the run or just observing it. I loved to watch a run and see and hear the raw power of that engine. In those days, we could get as close to the aircraft during a run as we dared. No one really kept us away from the aircraft, however, everyone was aware of the potential danger. Most of the rational people took cover during the run in the blockhouse or in one of the pillboxes around the test stand or at least got behind something solid in case of an explosion. I was different than most. I was fascinated by the sound and fury of the engine. I would get as close as possible and watch the whole sequence. Kind of like intentionally standing out in the fury of a tremendous storm.

I have always loved to hear the sound of a powerful engine, whether it was a rocket, a jet, or an automobile engine. After the X-15 program ended, we acquired two YF-12 (SR-71 prototype) aircraft to do flight research. I thoroughly loved to listen to those aircraft starting up because there was a double treat. Those aircraft used Buick automobile engines as starter engines for the jet engines. So I was first treated to the sound of the powerful automobile engines revving up to 7,000 or 8,000 RPM and then the sound of the jet engines winding up and lighting off and creating their own overpowering symphony of sound. I really wish now that I had a recording of both the X-15 and the YF-12 engines runs so that I could play them when I needed a psychological boost. Maybe I will ask the X-15 operations engineer to make a recording of his imitation of the X-15 engine run. I wonder if he can do Buick engines?

This love of engine noise is undoubtedly a result of my engineering background. I believe engineers would rather listen to an engine or a machine running than listen to a symphony orchestra. They particularly appreciate a smooth running engine. I drive an old Mercedes that has a lot of miles on it. It is getting a little tired, but it is so incredibly smooth that it is pure pleasure driving it. I also like smooth running airplanes. The smoothest airplane I ever flew was the F-106. To me, it was the Mercedes of airplanes. The X-15 also ran smoothly because the engine had no rotating parts.

My fascination with X-15 engine runs was somewhat diminished when I was scheduled to make the run. Part of this was due to the fact that I could not really see or hear the run as well from the cockpit, and part of it was due to the realization that I would now be sitting in the midst of all that sound and fury, while everyone else was safely tucked away behind the reinforced concrete walls and steel doors of the blockhouse and the pillboxes.

Surprisingly, I really did not think about the danger associated with the rocket engine operation during a flight, but I was very aware of it during a ground run. Part of this may have been due to the fact that during a flight I had many things to think about and do. I was busy and did not have the time to dwell on unpleasant thoughts. During an engine run, I was not that busy. The test sequence was slower than real time and I had time to think about what might happen if something went wrong or a leak developed or a component malfunctioned. I was very aware of sitting in front of an extremely volatile mixture of exotic liquids and gases.

Immediately behind the pilot there was a big 1,000 gallon liquid oxygen tank, almost 5 tons of liquid oxygen. Behind that, there was another huge tank filled with 1,400 gallons of liquid anhydrous ammonia. The ammonia was similar to that used for household cleaning purposes, but it was much more highly concentrated. One whiff of that ammonia would clean your sinuses out for at least 3 months. In addition to those propellants, there were other tanks filled with hydrogen peroxide. Again, this substance was similar to the hydrogen peroxide that you might find in any medicine cabinet, however the concentration of our peroxide was 50 times that of the peroxide for household use. That stuff was really volatile. It was comparable to nitroglycerine in terms of instability.

The older mechanics used to impress the new mechanics by throwing a cup full of that peroxide on a sagebush. The bush would explode in flames. One good quality of hydrogen peroxide is that it gives a warning before it explodes. It gets hot and gives off a very pungent odor. When we smelled hot peroxide, we got the hell out of there.

In addition to these volatile substances, the aircraft was filled with numerous tanks of high pressure helium. These gases pressurized the liquid oxygen and ammonia tanks and the hydrogen peroxide tanks to force the liquids out of the tanks into the feed lines to the engine. These gases also operated various pneumatic valves in the propellant system to initiate the pressurizing of the tank, to open the feed valves to the engine, to open the jettison valves in case we had to jettison fuel in an emergency, and so on. These high-pressure tanks of gaseous helium were latent bombs in and of themselves. If one of those tanks failed, the whole airplane would disintegrate.

I do not know why it seems more dangerous sitting on top of thousands of gallons of highly explosive propellants when only a few gallons will blow a person to bits. Maybe it's because all the extra gallons will spread the pieces over a wider area and make them harder to find. Maybe that is what worries us psychologically. We kind of hate to end up scattered all over the landscape.

Getting back to my personal thoughts during an engine run, I may have been apprehensive because one of the X-15s had blown up during an engine run with Scott Crossfield in the cockpit. The explosion destroyed the entire rear half of the aircraft and blew the front part of the aircraft out of the test stand. Scott was not injured, thanks to the rugged steel structure of the aircraft, but the explosion really got his attention.

In his book, *The Right Stuff,* Tom Wolfe discusses the psychological impact of "our rockets blowing up" on the astronauts. The fact that there were numerous rocket booster explosions had to cause some concern among the astronauts even though no one had been riding them when it happened. At that time no one had been killed as a result of those rocket booster explosions. Everyone was safely hunkered down in the blockhouses when they blew.

Tom Wolfe failed to mention that rocket airplanes also frequently exploded. The difference was that there were pilots in the rocket airplanes when they blew up. The X-1D exploded and caught fire in the bomb bay of the B-29 mothership as it was returning to Edwards following an aborted flight. The aircraft had to be jettisoned to save the B-29 and its crew. Luckily, no one was injured since the X-1D pilot had climbed out of the airplane into the mothership after the abort. The number three X-1 blew up in the bomb bay of its B-50 mothership on the ground following a captive flight. The pilot was seriously injured. The number two X-2 exploded in flight in the bomb bay of its B-50 mothership killing the pilot and a crewman and severely damaging the B-50. The X-2 disappeared in the explosion. The X-1A exploded in the bomb bay of the B-29 mothership during flight with Joe Walker in the cockpit. Joe was pulled from the cockpit and the aircraft was jettisoned. These prior rocket aircraft explosions were food for thought as the crew helped us into the cockpit for an engine run.

The crew was always very helpful, making sure that we were securely strapped in so that we could successfully ride out an explosion. The crew hooked up to the radio, the intercom, cooling air, oxygen, and then they shut the canopy and gave a final thumbs up and a wave through the window. Then, they all retreated to the blockhouse and the pillboxes to await the beginning of the engine run sequence. It was very comforting to the pilot in the aircraft to know that the crew was all comfy and cozy in their blastproof shelters. It really eased the pilot's mind. Personally, I felt that the crew should stay out there with me, so that we could participate in the engine run as a close knit team. Unfortunately, I was not able to convince the crew of that. They preferred the remote teamwork concept.

Occasionally the pilots got a chance to scare the hell out of the crew during an engine run. Normally, the crew came out of their pillboxes to inspect the aircraft and the engine only during stabilized periods of the engine start sequence. They came out the first time to check for leaks after the pilot had pressurized the main propellant tanks. Once that inspection was complete, they would go back into their holes and wait for the next sequence. The next sequence was a jettison check of first, the liquid oxygen and then, the liquid ammonia. When that was completed, they would come out again and check for leaks or any other anomaly. This procedure was followed for each step of the engine start sequence. The crew would only come out after everything was stabilized because the chances of an explosion were much less after things had stabilized. The crew was very cautious about getting under cover before the next event was initiated. Knowing this, the pilot would occasionally pretend that he heard a call to begin the next sequence while the crew was still climbing around the aircraft. The pilot might say, over the radio and intercom net, "Did you say go to prime?" or "Go to pump idle?" This would create an absolute panic with crew members jumping off the aircraft and running for their pillbox.

The rocket engine startup procedure sounds quite complex but it really is not. In the X-15, we first had to pressurize the propellant tanks (the liquid oxygen and liquid ammonia tanks) with gaseous helium. This pressure was used to force the propellant out of the tanks into the main feed lines to the turbopump and the engine.

The next sequence was a precool sequence to cool down the oxygen system to ensure that the liquid oxygen would not be heated up and vaporized before it got to the turbopump. Vaporized LOX would cause the turbopump to cavitate and go into an overspeed condition which could cause an automatic shutdown or pump failure. It required 10 minutes to chill the oxygen system down to operating temperature. Once it was chilled down, we went to the engine prime sequence which allowed a low flow of liquid oxygen and ammonia to circulate through the propellant lines and into the turbopump. The igniter-ready light came on when the prime sequence commenced and we then selected the precool cycle to increase the flow of LOX to the engine turbopump. Once this flow was established we turned the igniter switch on to prepare the engine for the ignition cycle.

The ignition cycle was initiated by pressing the pump-idle button to start the turbopump. The turbopump came up to idle speed quickly and forced propellants into the first-stage igniter. These propellants were ignited by the spark plug in the first-stage igniter. Propellant was next forced into the second-stage igniter chamber where it was ignited by the flame of the first stage. The second-stage igniter itself produced 1,500 pounds of thrust. That is a pretty impressive pilot light.

The main chamber was lit by advancing the throttle. This action forced propellant at a rate of 30 gallons a second into the main chamber where it was ignited by the second-stage igniter. Main chamber ignition produced a real kick in the pants, 60,000 pounds of thrust in one big bang.

During ground runs, we would light the main chamber at 100 percent thrust and stabilize for 8 seconds. We would retard the throttle to idle for 5 seconds and then shut the engine down. Next we would go through an emergency restart sequence and relight the main chamber at 75 percent thrust. We would stabilize at 75 percent thrust for 5 seconds, reduce throttle to idle for a second or 2 and then, shut the engine down. This completed the engine run.

Each pilot normally made his own engine run prior to a flight, however, on occasion, another pilot made the engine run. I made an engine run for Bob Rushworth one time when he had a scheduling conflict. His upcoming flight called for the engine to be throttled back to obtain some stabilized speed data. During the engine run we attempted to duplicate the proposed thrust reduction, but when the throttle was retarded, the engine quit. We tried it again with the same results. Since it was essential to reduce thrust to get the desired flight data, a decision was made to delay the flight and fix the engine. Rocket engines are very temperamental. They seem to either work properly or they do not work at all. There does not seem to be any middle ground.

The X-15 engine was one of the few rocket engines that had a throttling capability. The throttling capability was designed to allow the pilot to achieve stabilized test points, but it complicated the reliability of the engine. It required the engine to run at a nonoptimum condition. The engine did not like to run at a nonoptimum condition and occasionally, it would refuse to cooperate and just quit. Many adjustments and fine tuning were required to make it operate satisfactorily at reduced power settings.

Before the next engine run, a number of adjustments were made and some components were changed. We attempted another engine run a couple of days after the first run. The results were the same. When the throttle was retarded, the engine quit.

Following that engine run, the engine was removed from the aircraft and checked thoroughly. A number of components were replaced and some more adjustments were made before the engine was reinstalled and prepared for another run. The results of that run were the same. We tried two more times to fix the engine and get a successful run, but no luck. Every time we pulled the throttle back, the engine quit. By this time, the entire maintenance crew was really frustrated. I finally suggested that we give up trying to fix the engine and just not bother to tell Rushworth that the engine would quit when he throttled back. After all, if a pilot cannot make his own engine run, he should not be too picky about the results.

During the X-15 program I was asked to serve as a technical advisor to the producers of the movie "X-15." On one occasion, I escorted a number of the film crew to the X-15 engine run-up and test area to observe an engine run. We watched the operation from a vantage point about 100 yards in front of the aircraft. I was explaining the engine run process as it progressed from one sequence to another. I described the aircraft crew actions as they entered and exited their pillboxes during the various stages of the engine firing sequence, making a special point of the danger involved and the need to be in the pillbox during the actual engine run. The engine run sequence proceeded smoothly and finally the command was issued to fire the engine. The main chamber lit off with its characteristic explosive boom and then all of a sudden the hatch on one of the pillboxes flew open and the two occupants came out in a dead run.

Their pillbox was almost directly behind the X-15 and within 50 feet of it. It was almost within the flame pattern of the engine. That did not seem to deter the two occupants one bit as they ran directly across the exhaust of the engine. They ran like terrorized wild African antelope fleeing from an attacking lion. They would run three or four strides and then leap into the air as though they were looking for the pursuing lion. It was an amazing sight to behold.

One of the occupants, Wayne Ottinger, had failed to remove his radio headphones. As he reached the end of the headphone extension cord, the cord snapped taut and stopped his head in midflight. His legs and body continued on until he was stretched out flat in midair. We could hear the thump as he hit the ground over the deafening banshee wail of the rocket engine. He seemed to bounce immediately back into the air on his feet and he continued running without missing a stride. It was the most hilarious scene that I had ever witnessed. It was as humorous as any Charlie Chaplin or Marx Brothers routine that I had ever seen.

We subsequently learned that the hatch on that pillbox would not seal properly that day. During the engine start-up sequence, some ammonia vapors had drifted over the pillbox and had seeped in. Those vapors were so pungent that you had to run to escape them. The pillbox occupants were so panicked by the ammonia vapors that they ran directly through the exhaust of the rocket engine. Their graceful leaps into the air were desperate attempts to get above the ammonia cloud and get a breath of fresh air. That ammonia vapor was a real Olympic-class athletic stimulant. It could make a world-class runner out of any poor slob who got a whiff of it.

PART 2...............

THE PROGRAM

Chapter 3 ....

Program Phases

T he X-15 program was a joint effort of NASA, the USAF, and the U.S. Navy. NASA had technical control of the program and did the conceptual design of the aircraft. The USAF and the Navy funded the design and construction and managed those phases of the program. The program involved the design and construction of the aircraft and its rocket engine. Three aircraft were constructed. The program also included the modification of two B-52 aircraft to carry the X-15 aircraft.

The flight program was under NASA management with NASA and the air force both providing people and support. NASA maintained and operated the X-15 aircraft, the Hi-Range, the X-15 simulator, and half of the chase aircraft. NASA also maintained the APUs, the inertial platform, the ball nose, and the instrumentation system. The USAF operated and maintained the B-52 motherships, the C-130 support aircraft, the rescue helicopters, half of the chase aircraft, the X-15 servicing area, and the rocket engine test stand. The USAF also maintained the rocket engines, the pilot's pressure suits, the ejection seats, and provided the standard base support such as fire trucks, crash and rescue vehicles, and ambulances. Both organizations provided X-15 pilots, chase pilots, and engineering support.

The primary objective of the flight program was to explore the hypersonic-flight region by using the X-15 as the means to get to that region of flight. The

X-15 aircraft configuration was only of passing interest. We could have used any of a number of different aircraft configurations to probe the hypersonic-speed region as evidenced by the different configurations proposed by the various contractors. The real interest was in the reaction of the air to a large-scale winged object traveling at hypersonic speeds. Did the air react as theory would predict or as the wind tunnel indicated that it would? This is where the X-15 configuration became important. The configuration had been analyzed and tested at small scale in the wind tunnel. By flying the X-15 airplane, we would obtain flight data to compare to these predictions. In this manner we would determine, for example, what the real boundary layer characteristics were, what the actual stagnation temperatures were, and what the true heating rates were. We could then update our analytical tools and our wind tunnels to improve our predictive capability for future aircraft.

The flight program consisted of a number of phases, some distinct and some not so distinct. Several of these phases were not foreseen in the original program plan. They evolved during the program as a result of unanticipated problems or developments. As an example, the airplane initially flew with an interim engine, the LR-11, due to development problems with the LR-99 engine. This resulted in the addition of an LR-11 checkout and demonstration phase.

The number three aircraft blew up during a ground run of the new LR-99 engine. During the rebuilding of the aircraft, a new flight control system (the MH-96 system) was installed, which then required a separate flight demonstration phase.

The number two aircraft was seriously damaged in a landing accident on its thirty-first flight. The program planners decided to modify the aircraft during rebuilding to carry an experimental scramjet engine to test at hypersonic speeds. This dictated another new demonstration phase. The flight program ultimately involved nine identifiable phases rather than the four or five originally envisioned. These nine phases are not officially designated in the records of the flight program, but are instead my own postflight definitions.

PHASE I

The first phase was the contractor demonstration phase using the LR-11 engine. The purpose of this phase was to check out and demonstrate the proper operation of all of the various systems in the aircraft and to demonstrate the structural integrity of the aircraft. During this phase, the number one and two aircraft were tested and demonstrated. The number three aircraft was also scheduled to be demonstrated in this phase, but as mentioned previously, it blew up during a ground run and its checkout and demonstration was delayed and eventually completed by the government. The low level of thrust developed by the LR-11 engines severely limited the performance of the X-15, but their use did allow the flight program to begin on schedule.

This phase consisted of eleven flights—one through eight, ten, eleven, and seventeen. This phase began on June 8, 1959, and concluded on May 26, 1960. Scott Crossfield made all of these flights. The airplanes involved were the number one and two aircraft. The maximum speed and altitude achieved during these flights were Mach 2.53 and 88,116 feet, respectively. These flights were all made in the immediate vicinity of the Rogers lakebed at Edwards Air Force Base. A number of significant problems were encountered during this phase. These included a severe PIO problem during a landing approach, a failure of the fuselage structure following an emergency landing, and several rocket engine fires.

PHASE II

The second phase of the program was the government envelope expansion phase using the LR-11 engine. During this phase, the aircraft flight envelope was expanded incrementally to the maximum attainable Mach and altitude to demonstrate the airworthiness of the aircraft. This phase consisted of ten flights—numbers nine, twelve through sixteen, and eighteen through twenty-one. These flights began on March 25, 1960, and ended on September 10, 1960. This phase commenced before the conclusion of Phase I.

Walker and White, the prime government pilots, split these flights, each making five flights. These flights were all made in the number one aircraft. The maximum speed and altitude achieved during this phase were Mach 3.31 and 136,500 feet respectively. These maximums were achieved on separate flights. Four of these flights were made in the immediate vicinity of Edwards, while the other six were made starting from Silver Lake. This was the first use of a remote launch lake by a rocket aircraft.

One additional LR-11 envelope expansion flight (Flight 33) was made following the completion of the pilot checkout phase (Phase III). This flight was made by Bob White to a maximum speed of Mach 3.50. This was the last flight using the LR-11 engine. No significant problems were encountered during this phase.

PHASE III

This phase was the pilot checkout phase using the LR-11 engine. The purpose
of this phase was to check out the four backup government pilots. Each of the
four pilots received two flights for a total of eight flights in this phase—flights
twenty-two through twenty-five, twenty-seven, twenty-nine, thirty-one and
thirty-two.

This phase began on September 23, 1960, and ended on February 1, 1961.
The pilots involved were Forrest Petersen, Jack McKay, Bob Rushworth, and
Neil Armstrong. The number one aircraft was used for all of these flights. The
flights were all made in the immediate vicinity of Edwards. The planned nominal
maximum speed and altitude for these flights were Mach 2.0 and 50,000 feet.
No significant problems were encountered during this phase.

PHASE IV

This phase was the contractor demonstration phase using the LR-99 engine.
During this phase, the contractor demonstrated the various capabilities of the
LR-99 engine including normal airstart and operation, throttling from 50 to
100 percent power and restart capability. This phase consisted of only three
flights, numbers twenty-six, twenty-eight, and thirty. These flights began on
November 15, 1960, and ended on December 6, 1960. This phase was accomplished within the same time frame as Phase III.

Scott Crossfield made these three flights using the number two aircraft, which
was the first aircraft to fly using the LR-99 engine. The maximum speed and
altitude achieved were Mach 2.97 and 81,200 feet. These flights were made
in the immediate vicinity of Edwards. No significant problems occurred during
these flights.

PHASE V

This phase was the government envelope expansion phase using the LR-99
engine. The purpose of this phase was to demonstrate the airworthiness of the
X-15 up to its design speed and altitude—the primary objective of the flight
program. The flight envelope was expanded in incremental steps to the design
speed of Mach 6 and the design altitude of 250,000 feet. This was accomplished
in ten flights—numbers thirty-four through thirty-eight, forty, forty-three

through forty-five, and fifty-two. These flights began on March 7, 1961, and concluded on April 30, 1962.

Walker and White alternated flights, each making five. White achieved the design Mach number of 6 with an actual Mach number of 6.04 and Walker achieved the design altitude of 250,000 feet with an actual altitude of 247,000 feet. Eight of these flights were made using the number two aircraft and two using the number one aircraft. These flights were all made using remote launch lakes.

We were to fly faster and much higher on subsequent flights, but these flights concluded the basic design envelope expansion phase. Surprisingly, there were no major problems encountered on these flights.

PHASE VI

This phase was the Minneapolis-Honeywell (MH-96) flight control system checkout and demonstration phase. The purpose of this phase was to demonstrate the capabilities of the MH-96 system, an advanced command augmentation type control system. This system offered a number of potential advantages over the original X-15 flight control system, particularly during exoatmospheric flights.

This phase consisted of four flights—numbers forty-six, forty-eight, forty-nine, and fifty-one. These flights were the first four flights in the number three aircraft and they were all made by Neil Armstrong. The flights began on December 20, 1961, and ended on April 20, 1962. The flights were accomplished within the same time period as Phase V. The maximum speed and altitude achieved during these flights were Mach 5.51 and 207,500 feet. All of these flights were made from remote launch lakes. No major problems were encountered during this phase, however an operational hazard was highlighted, namely, bouncing back out of the atmosphere during a pullout fom high altitude. This created major energy management problems

This flight control system was later flown to higher speeds and much higher altitudes. The system was subsequently utilized for all planned altitude flights above 270,000 feet.

PHASE VII

This phase was the basic aircraft research phase. During this phase we were attempting to determine the flight characteristics of the basic airplane. We were measuring its performance characteristics, its stability and control characteristics, its handling qualities, or flying qualities, and the loads acting on the structure of the aircraft. We were measuring the aerodynamic pressures acting on various parts of the airplane, the temperatures of the structure at points of interest, and calculating the aerodynamic heating rates at various flight conditions. At the completion of this phase, we would know the characteristics of the aircraft thoroughly and would be able to compare its actual characteristics with those predicted by wind tunnel tests or theory. This comparison would reveal any errors in the predictive techniques and ultimately allow the engineers to revise and improve these techniques for use on future aircraft. This is a primary reason for building and flying research aircraft, to investigate a new configuration or probe a new flight region and bring back data that will help to design the next aircraft better.

During this phase we were expanding the flight envelope to higher dynamic pressures and to higher heating regions. We were intentionally flying fast at lower and lower altitudes to load and heat the aircraft up to its design limits.

This phase began with Flight 53 and continued through Flight 100. The time span for this phase was roughly from April 1962 through January 1964. The primary pilots participating in this phase were Walker, White, McKay, and Rushworth. All three aircraft were utilized during this phase. The maximum speed and altitude achieved during this phase was Mach 6.06 and 354,200 feet. The maximum dynamic pressure recorded was 2,027 pounds per square foot and the maximum temperature measured on the aircraft was 1,323° F.

All of these flights were made from remote launch lakes. One accident occurred during this phase—a landing accident in the number two aircraft. We began carrying some generic research and scientific experiments in the latter half of this phase.

PHASE VIII

This phase was the generic research and scientific experiment phase. Generic research involved aerodynamic experiments that were independent of the aircraft. The X-15 was simply used as a testbed to get the experiment to a desired flight condition. As an example of one of these generic research experiments, we installed a sharp leading edge on the upper vertical stabilizer. We measured the skin friction and heating rates behind this leading edge and then compared that data to theory and to data obtained behind the original blunt leading edge. Another generic experiment involved measurement of the standoff distance of the bow shock in front of a blunt conical nose shape. There were a number of generic experiments flown during this phase.

Other experiments flown during this phase were scientific experiments that were completely unrelated to aircraft. These were nonaerodynamic experiments that again utilized the X-15 as a testbed. Examples of these experiments were experiments to collect micrometeorites; measure the ultraviolet stellar radiation; measure sky brightness; measure the high-altitude infrared background of the earth, horizon, and sky; and measure optical degradation at hypersonic speeds by using standard and infrared cameras to photograph targets on the ground.

The X-15 carried more than thirty experiments at various times, some aerodynamic, some space-related. The X-15 was an excellent testbed since an experiment could be carried into space and then returned to be adjusted if necessary and flown again. Many potential satellite payloads and experiments were developed using the X-15 as a testbed.

This phase began on the seventy-fifth flight and continued on through the duration of the program. This phase overlapped the latter half of Phase VII, the basic aircraft research phase. It began in December 1962 and ended in December 1968 at the conclusion of the program. The primary pilots involved in this phase were Rushworth, McKay, Engle, Thompson, Knight, Dana, and Adams.

The major portion of the generic research experiments were flown on the number three aircraft, although all three aircraft carried scientific experiments. In general, the generic research experiments involved flights at the lower altitudes while most of the scientific experiments involved high-altitude flights up to 300,000 feet. There were a number of problems encountered during this phase as well as the loss of Mike Adams and the number three aircraft.

PHASE IX

This phase was the X-15A-2 envelope expansion phase. This phase was intended to demonstrate the capability of the X-15A-2 aircraft to carry a scramjet experiment to a speed in excess of Mach 7.0. It involved the expansion of the flight envelope of the modified airplane in incremental steps up to Mach 6.7. This phase began on the 109th flight, the first flight of the modified X-15A-2, and concluded on the 188th flight after a total of twenty-one flights on the X-15A-2 airplane. This phase started on June 25, 1964, and ended on October 3, 1967.

Bob Rushworth, Jack McKay, and Pete Knight flew all the flights in this phase. During Phase IX, a maximum speed of Mach 6.7 was achieved. There were a number of problems encountered during the envelope expansion flight culminating with major damage to the aircraft on its last maximum-speed flight. Bob Rushworth encountered landing gear extension problems while Pete Knight experienced unanticipated heating problems. The aircraft was repaired, but it never flew again. The program officials decided to terminate the X-15 program before the repairs were completed.

Chapter 4

Demonstration Phase
(1959–1962)

S cott Crossfield had a couple of exciting flights during the initial contractor demonstration phase. Scott launched on the first flight with an inoperable pitch damper even though mission rules dictated an abort. He elected to launch since it was a very benign glide flight to a landing on the extra long lakebed runway three-five. The flight went well until Scott began the landing flare. As he attempted to decrease the steep glide path, he unintentionally initiated a longitudinal oscillation which quickly became divergent as he attempted to dampen the oscillation. It was a classic PIO (pilot-induced oscillation) maneuver, which was potentially catastrophic because he was rapidly approaching the ground. Scott's plane was losing airspeed and the oscillation was increasing in amplitude.

Scott somehow managed to touchdown safely on the bottom of an oscillation. It was a terrifying sight, but he was able to salvage the airplane. The landing was firm enough, however, to damage the landing gear. The aircraft had to be returned to Los Angeles for repairs. Increasing the horizontal stabilizer actuator rate later resolved the PIO problem.

Shortly after launch on Scott's fourth flight, one of the rocket chambers exploded causing an engine bay fire. Scott shut down the engine and began jettisoning propellants while setting up for an emergency landing on Rosamond Lake. Due to the steep nose-down attitude during the landing approach, Scott was unable to jettison all of the propellants. He touched down at a low speed in a nose-high attitude with a considerable amount of propellant in the tanks. When the nose slammed down the fuselage buckled just behind the cockpit. The airplane slid out on its nose gear, belly, and main gear skids. Scott's only injury was to his pride. It definitely was not his best landing.

Scott still tells the story about his tug-of-war with the flight surgeon after the aircraft came to a stop. The flight surgeon aboard the rescue helicopter overheard someone say something about a broken back. The comment actually referred to the aircraft, but he assumed that Scott's back was broken as a result of the landing accident. When the rescue helicopter landed next to the X-15, the flight surgeon jumped out with a backboard and ran up to the X-15 cockpit to rescue Scott from the burning plane. Scott had partially opened the canopy in preparation for an evacuation of the aircraft. The flight surgeon decided that he had to get the canopy out of the way to get the backboard on Scott before moving him from the cockpit. The flight surgeon pushed the canopy up to open it further. When Scott realized what the flight surgeon was doing, he grabbed onto the canopy in a desperate attempt to hold it down since he knew that excessive canopy motion would arm the ejection seat. He did not want to be ejected accidentally after surviving an explosion, a fire, and an emergency landing. Scott could not talk to the flight surgeon since his faceplate was still closed. The two highly motivated individuals struggled mightily—one pushing, the other pulling on the canopy, both attempting to save Scott's life. After a minute or two of this Herculean effort, the flight surgeon finally gave up. He rationalized that Scott could not be seriously injured if he could pull that hard on the canopy.

The remainder of Scott's flights were uneventful, although he did have a couple more minor fires with the LR-11 engine. He completed the checkout and demonstration of the various aircraft systems using the LR-11 engine and then concluded his participation in the flight program by making three flights with the LR-99 engine. On these flights he demonstrated all of the unique features of the LR-99 engine, such as the restart and throttling capabilities.

At one point in the X-15 program, North American Aviation made a proposal to modify the X-15 to enable it to fly into orbit and then reenter and fly back to a landing. North American Aviation made the proposal during the early days of the space program as an alternative to Mercury and/or Dyna-Soar. The government did not take the proposal too seriously although it was a major topic of discussion for awhile among some of the X-15 program personnel.

Scott Crossfield touted the proposal on several occasions, thus prompting

Jack Allavie, one of the B-52 pilots, to come up with his own proposal for putting the X-15 into orbit. He said, "I'm going to get Scott up to the launch point and then I'm going to count down to the drop. (In that early phase of the program, the B-52 crew launched the X-15.) I'll say, 'Five, four, three, two, one, drop,' but I won't drop him. Crossfield will think that I launched him and he will light his big rocket engine. That rocket engine of his will start the B-52 spinning like a top and as a result, the B-52 will climb on up to 100,000 feet, and then I'll drop him and Crossfield will go into orbit hollering, 'Bonus, bonus, bonus!'"

Jack Allavie was a real colorful character and an excellent B-52 pilot even if he did taxi the B-52 at 90 MPH. The gaggle of ground vehicles that were following the B-52 and X-15 out to the takeoff runway would be strung out for a mile, really straining to keep up. Allavie was a B-52 mothership pilot during the first 3 years of the program. He was the B-52 pilot on Bob White's record altitude flight to 314,750 feet. That was Jack's last B-52 drop flight.

Forrest Petersen was the first pilot to check out in the X-15 after Joe Walker and Bob White completed the envelope expansion phase with the LR-11 engine. Pete's first checkout flight called for a launch in the Palmdale area on a heading toward Boron. At Boron Pete was to make a left turn and fly toward Mojave. At Mojave he would make another left turn and head back toward the Edwards lakebed, for a landing on runway one-eight. These checkout flights were made at a nominal speed and altitude of Mach 2 at 50,000 feet.

Pete got both engines going after launch and headed out for Boron. On reaching Boron he started his left turn and immediately noticed a change in longitudinal acceleration. He was decelerating. Pete glanced down at his engine instruments and noted that both chamber and manifold pressures were dropping on the upper engine. Within seconds he also noted a pump overspeed light. The upper engine had shut down.

Pete immediately attempted to restart the chambers of the upper engine, but with no luck. He tried again with the same results. He then realized the lower engine had also shut down. This was confirmed by NASA-1, who advised Pete to continue the turnaround to head for a high-key position on runway one-eight. Pete did as he was advised and arrived at high key with 25,000 feet of altitude. This was lower than desired for a comfortable approach and Pete was not sure that he could make it around the pattern. Joe Walker, who was flying chase on Pete, quickly advised him that he had enough altitude and that he should continue on with the approach. With Joe flying a tight-wing position and coaching him along, Pete rolled into a tight turn and pulled it on around.

He actually ended up slightly high on energy on final approach and had to use some speed brakes to get the airplane on the runway at the desired touchdown location. Joe was right, as usual. Pete had had ample energy for the approach. Pete's first flight resulted in an emergency landing, but he handled the incident with his usual aplomb.

There had been a lot of chomping at the bit to get to the LR-99 envelope expansion phase. Joe Walker and Bob White were the primary pilots conducting this phase. Forrest Petersen made two flights and attempted a third, but had engine problems and had to abort. During the envelope expansion phase the aircraft was to be flown to its maximum design limits—the ultimate demonstration of the airplane. The flight envelope would be expanded to the design altitude of 250,000 feet and to the design speed of Mach 6.

Logic tells us that we would encounter our major problems during envelope expansion to the design speed and altitude. During expansion, we were probing the effects of higher speeds and higher altitudes on the airplane. The principal concerns were the maximum temperatures to be applied to the airplane and the effects of these temperatures on the structure of the aircraft. There was also a major concern about the stresses that would be introduced into the structure by the extreme temperature gradients that would be established between the hot external skin and the cool internal structure during the initial heating of the aircraft.

Would we have a structural failure or burn through or would a control surface bind up due to thermal expansion? These were new, unique concerns for the hypersonic speed regime. The standard concerns that accompany a new airplane were also not forgotten. Will the airplane be controllable? Will it be stable, or will it swap ends? Will the structure withstand the aerodynamic forces imposed on it by ramming through the air at over 4,000 MPH? Will the wings stay on during a 6 g pullout from 250,000 feet altitude after they have been heated to 1,200° F? Will the ballistic controls work properly outside the atmosphere or will we lose control and come back into the atmosphere backwards or sideways or upside down? These were just a few of our many concerns.

The X-15 Joint Operating Committee designated Joe Walker and Bob White to bring back the answers to these and many more questions. The pilots would probe higher and faster on each successive flight to address these concerns individually. They would prove the designers right and get a medal for doing so, or they would prove them wrong and get a street named after them on the base at Edwards. (Streets at Edwards are named after pilots killed during test missions.)

The flight program was laid out to expand speed and altitude concurrently. Normally speed was increased first to ensure that the aircraft was controllable at the speed needed to make the next higher-altitude flight. During the speed flights, the flight plan called for the pilot to pull up in angle of attack to simulate a pullout from high altitude. This allowed a relatively safe evaluation of the effects of a pullout. Expansion of the flight envelope to the maximum design conditions of Mach 6 and 250,000 feet altitude involved only ten flights. These flights began at the maximum flight conditions achieved with the LR-11 engine, Mach 3.50 and 136,500 feet altitude.

This phase began with Flight 34, a flight to Mach 4.43 by Bob White. Bob had previously flown to Mach 3.50 on Flight 33 with the LR-11 engine. Thus the envelope expansion with the LR-99 engine began with an increase of almost one Mach number on the first flight.

Joe Walker made the next flight, Flight 35, to an altitude of 169,600 feet, which was 30,000 feet higher than the previous maximum altitude. The planned altitude was only 150,000 feet. This flight also went off without any real problem. Joe made a couple of interesting observations on this flight. A fixed base simulator was adequate to prepare for this flight as long as the pilot had been exposed to centrifuge simulation training. Unfortunately, this centrifuge training procedure was not followed for the second group of pilots and it caused some surprises and problems due to the many unusual forces and accelerations involved in an altitude flight. The second observation was that 0 g flight was not a problem from the piloting standpoint. Joe commented, "One consciously appreciates the sensation of resting after the great physical effort while power is on." In other words, 0 g was quite pleasant.

Bob made the next flight, Flight 36, to a speed of Mach 4.62. The planned Mach number was 4.60. This was his first flight at 100 percent thrust. He commented, "That's quite a push," after lighting the engine. During the flight he noticed a few bangs and thumps after engine shutdown as well as wisping smoke in the cockpit.

Joe made the next flight, Flight 37, another speed flight to Mach 4.95. The planned Mach number was 5.00. Joe had several problems on this flight. He lost his stability augmentation at launch and was unable to reengage it. As a result, the airplane was very loose in pitch with the nose continually bobbing up and down. During engine burn, Joe initially held his head forward off the headrest. As the g force increased, he could no longer hold his head forward and he allowed it to move back onto the headrest. When he did so, he got the immediate sensation that the airplane had just gone over on its back. He had to have total faith in his instruments to convince himself otherwise. During a later pullup to higher angle of attack, he noted that the airplane wallowed in roll without stability augmentation.

Bob made Flight 38, another speed flight to Mach 5.27, just under the planned Mach 5.30. He had a couple of minor problems on this flight. Bob noted smoke in the cockpit and his pressure suit inflated due to a partial loss of cabin pressure. He had some minor controllability problems due to the loss of mobility with the inflated pressure suit. There was some wing skin buckling and a couple of popped rivets due to thermal expansion of the wing skin.

The next envelope expansion flight was Flight 40. Joe was scheduled to fly to Mach 5.60 on that flight, but only reached 5.21 due to a propulsion system problem. Joe also saw smoke curling up into the cockpit and heard creaks, pops, and bangs after engine shutdown. Joe again commented on the poor handling qualities of the aircraft at higher angles of attack without stability augmentation. He indicated that the aircraft was neutrally damped or even divergent at these conditions. Joe also complained about the big loss in pilot proficiency as a result of flying one flight every 4 to 6 months. Joe's last flight had been almost 4 months earlier. This was indeed a real problem for all the X-15 pilots. A pilot obviously could not stay proficient in the aircraft while only flying 10 to 12 minutes at a time once every few months. Each flight seemed like a first flight under those circumstances. He felt reasonably proficient if he could fly at least once a month. Throughout the program, however, the average time between flights for each pilot was twice that long.

Flight 43 was the next envelope expansion flight. (Flights 41 and 42 were research flights flown by Forrest Petersen and Bob Rushworth.) Bob White made this flight, which was an altitude flight to 217,000 feet. The planned altitude was 200,000 feet. The left-hand windshield shattered during reentry due to aerodynamic heating. Fortunately, only one pane of the dual-panel window broke. This flight was otherwise very uneventful and didn't stimulate any significant pilot comments.

Flight 44 was another speed flight by Joe to a Mach number of 5.74. The planned Mach number was 5.70. The only unusual thing about this flight was a severe aircraft vibration attributed to the flight control system. Joe again complained about the poor controllability at high angles of attack without stability augmentation. Joe's evaluation of the controllability at high angles of attack during these flights verified a predicted stability and control problem. As a result of his evaluation, an all out effort was initiated to find a solution since we could not make the pullout during entry from the design altitude without the ability to fly at high angles of attack.

Bob White made the last speed flight to a Mach number of 6.04 on Flight 45. On this flight, the right-hand windshield shattered and Bob commented, "Good Lord, I hope the other one doesn't go." The windshield was completely opaque. If the other one had shattered, Bob considered jettisoning the canopy and trying to land the airplane without a windscreen. The odds would have been against him though, due to the potentially severe buffeting at approach speeds. Luckily, the other windshield remained intact. Bob was not happy with the visibility during landing with only one windshield available. He had trouble lining up with the runway and judging height. This concluded the speed envelope expansion for the standard aircraft. He had achieved design speed.

The last envelope expansion flight was Flight 52, which was an altitude flight to 247,000 feet. Joe Walker made this flight. Previously, a backup stability augmentation system was added to the flight control system to ensure that stability augmentation would always be available to provide good controllability during entry from high altitude. This was a partial solution to the controllability problem that Joe had verified on previous flights. Flight 52 was very uneventful. Joe commented, "Up on top I thought that Los Angeles was already under me and I was mentally bracing myself for an unfortunate flight call. L.A. was really down under the nose and as a matter of fact, I seemed to be rapidly coming up on the shoreline." I, Milt Thompson, was not privy to these comments when I made my first altitude flight which resulted in similar anxious moments for me.

The maximum altitude was ultimately increased to 354,200 feet on Flight 91 by Joe Walker. The airplane had the power to fly to higher altitudes, but it was questionable whether a successful reentry could be made without exceeding a structural limit. The simulator predicted that altitudes as high as 450,000 feet could be achieved. Successful reentries could also be made from these altitudes on the simulator, but these simulator reentries were accomplished under ideal conditions. The slightest error in control technique under such conditions would result in the loss of the airplane. Wiser heads decided that it was not worth the risk to attempt higher altitudes. The maximum Mach number was ultimately increased to Mach 6.7 during the X-15A-2 flight program.

This phase went surprisingly fast, considering that we were flying into a totally new flight regime—the hypersonic flight region. This was the flight regime where theory predicted that a potential thermal barrier may exist. The most pessimistic predictions indicated that the expected heating rates would soften the best available structural steels. Any airplane entering this region would become a red hot limp noodle, according to some experts. The flight results proved them wrong.

As the results of these flights would indicate, there were no major problems encountered during this envelope expansion phase. The airplane stayed together and the pilots could control it throughout the design speed and altitude envelope. The airplane had survived flights into the hypersonic flight region to speeds more than twice as fast as any previous aircraft.

The airplane had also penetrated and survived the so-called thermal barrier. Amazingly, it had accomplished all this so effortlessly. On the other hand, the feat probably was not so amazing to the designers. They obviously anticipated the major problems and designed the airplane to cope with them. It did. It came through with flying colors—a little bit scorched but completely intact.

The more significant problems cropped up as we exceeded the design envelope. We also had problems with the aerodynamic heating expansion flights during which the airplane was flown at high speed at lower altitudes to intentionally heat the structure of the airplane. These flights were made during Phases VII and VIII. The airplane really did get hot on those flights. Temperatures in excess of 1,300° F were recorded. Parts of the airplane glowed cherry red and softened up a bit during those flights. The airplane got so damned hot that it popped and banged like an old iron stove. It spewed smoke out of its bowels and it twitched like frog legs in a skillet. But it survived.

Forrest Petersen's last flight occurred during this phase of the program. It was the forty-seventh flight of the program. Pete was scheduled to launch at Mud Lake on January 10, 1962. The engine failed to light after launch. Pete recycled the engine by retarding the throttle to the off position. He then pushed the engine reset button, primed the engine for 5 seconds until the igniter ready light came on and then advanced the throttle to the on position again. This procedure required about 10 seconds to accomplish, but it seemed more like 10 minutes or even 10 hours.

The pilot did not have much time to waste after launch. He either had to get the engine lit or abort the flight and make a landing at the launch lake. The problem was that he was losing altitude rapidly (about 12,000 feet per minute) while waiting for the engine to light. If he lost too much altitude before deciding to abort, he could not accomplish the normal approach pattern or finish jettisoning propellants before landing. Also, if he descended too far before getting an engine light, he negated all of the preplanned energy management calculations. This was not an airplane that could be flown on guesswork. The pilot would not know which emergency lake to head for if the engine quit prematurely. Another possible problem in descending too low was that the pilot might overstress the airplane by flying at high speed through the dense, lower altitude before he managed to get the plane pointed uphill. And finally, if he descended too low before getting an engine light, he may not regain enough energy to make it home. All of these considerations dictated that the pilot make a decision to abort the flight before descending through 30,000 feet altitude.

This cutoff altitude provided enough time to attempt two restarts. The engine failed to light on Pete's first restart attempt. He again recycled the engine and waited for that big kick in the butt. No luck. The engine failed to light again. That was it. Now, he had to turn toward Mud Lake and start to jettison the aircraft's unused propellants. Pete continued to jettison until he turned on final approach. Pete made a nice landing to conclude his participation in the X-15 program. His departure from the X-15 program was necessary for him to get back in the mainstream of naval life to advance his career. Pete began and ended his X-15 flight activity with an emergency landing.

When an X-15 landed at an emergency lake, the only way to get it home was to load it on a flatbed truck and bring it back on the highway. The airplane had a short wingspan, less than 25 feet, so it could be transported legally on the highway without removing the wing. A factor in our favor was the lack of traffic and obstructions along the highways in the remote desert regions where we were operating. We could load the airplane, put a wide load sign on the truck bumper and haul ass down the road. Our truck drivers did conscientiously try to pull way over to one side to avoid opposing traffic.

On one trip coming back from Mud Lake, our driver noticed a big camper coming at him at a high rate of speed. Our driver vainly attempted to warn the camper driver to slow down and stay over to the side of the road by blinking his lights. The camper driver went by our truck doing about 70 MPH. Our driver felt a jolt and slowed to a stop. The camper also came to a stop. A quick examination of the two vehicles revealed a huge gash through the side of the camper about a foot below the top, from the front to the rear of the camper. The wing of the X-15 had almost sliced the top off that camper. The X-15 was not damaged at all. Steel wings do have their advantages.

THE LONGEST FLIGHT

The MH-96 checkout phase was a brief phase involving the first four flights in the number three aircraft to check out the MH-96 adaptive flight control system. Neil Armstrong was the expert on this system and he flew all four flights. These flights were primarily altitude buildup flights starting at 81,000 feet and progressing to 133,000 feet, 180,000 feet, and finally to 207,000 feet. The benefits of the MH-96 system were predicted to be more obvious during altitude flights, and thus, altitude flights were used to check out the system.

The MH-96 system was the first command augmentation system with an adaptive gain feature. This type of system is intended to provide invariant aircraft response throughout the flight envelope of the aircraft. The MH-96 system utilized a rate command control mode wherein a given control stick deflection produced a specific rate response of the aircraft. For example a one-inch pitch stick deflection would result in a 5-degree-per-second pitch rate. This response would be the same regardless of airspeed within the normal flight envelope. In a more conventional aircraft, the pitch rate response would vary with airspeed. In an aircraft with a large speed envelope, and a conventional control system, a one-inch stick input could produce aircraft responses that varied from no response at low speed to a violent response at high speed; possibly violent enough to tear the wings off. Thus for a high-speed aircraft, it would seem desirable to have invariant response to prevent the pilot from inadvertently destroying the aircraft.

Nothing comes free however. With invariant response, you lose some of the cues that you may have depended on to warn you of impending disaster. The controls do not become sloppy or ineffective as you approach a stall, for example. Everything feels fine until the aircraft departs. With rate command, you also lose speed stability unless it is artificially provided. The aircraft nose does not tend to drop as airspeed decreases since the control system wants to maintain a zero pitch rate unless commanded otherwise. Without speed stability, it is quite easy to fly into a stall.

A good rate command system also eliminates trim or altitude changes as a result of configuration changes such as gear, flap, or speed brake deployment. The system also masks any shift in center of gravity. In one sense, these features are desirable. You do not have to retrim. You do, however, lose the cue that confirms that the gear or flaps deployed as commanded. You can also lose control due to an undetected center of gravity change. Overall, however, these systems are generally pleasant to fly and they do have some distinct advantages.

This system proved to be superior to the basic flight control system during altitude flights for a number of reasons. For example, it combined the aerodynamic and reaction control commands on one control stick. This eliminated the need to fly with both hands on an altitude flight. The system also offered several autopilot modes, such as roll hold, pitch attitude hold, and angle of attack hold. These modes could be used to reduce significantly the pilot workload during altitude flights.

This system also minimized any extraneously induced aircraft motions due to its much higher system gain. The pilots appreciated this feature particularly on altitude flights since extraneous motions were very undesirable and hard to damp out using manual control, particularly during reentry. This system was later used for all maximum altitude attempts.

The first flight was flown on December 20, 1961. The flight launched at Silver Lake. The flight plan called for a climb at 50 percent thrust to 62,000 feet altitude and then a pushover to come level at 75,000 feet. The engine was to be shut down at a speed of 3,500 feet per second after 104 seconds of burn time. Various control system pulses were to be performed throughout the flight to evaluate the performance of the MH-96 flight control system.

During the actual launch, the stability augmentation in all three axes disengaged and a severe right roll occurred with accompanying yaw and pitch excursions. Neil recovered from the rolloff, lit the engine, and then managed to successfully reengage all three axes of stability augmentation. The flight progressed as planned from that point on, with only minor flight control system problems and some severe radio problems.

The second flight was made on January 17, 1962. This flight launched at Mud Lake. NASA-2 at Beatty, Nevada controlled this flight until the X-15 passed China Lake en route to Edwards, at which time NASA-1 at Edwards took control. This transfer of control from Beatty to Edwards was normal during the early envelope expansion flights before telemetry and tracking data were transmitted in real time between tracking sites.

Nothing significant occurred on this flight. The flight plan called for numerous maneuvers to evaluate the flight control system and, as a result of pilot preoccupation with these maneuvers, the planned speed and altitude were substantially exceeded. The aircraft landed without incident after it obtained all the desired data.

The third flight occurred on April 5, 1962. The aircraft was launched at Hidden Hills and the flight plan called for a peak altitude of 170,000 feet. When Neil attempted to light the engine after launch, he said he saw the igniter pressure go to zero and then failed to hear the engine start. Neil checked the engine instruments noting that everything looked good, so he attempted a relight. The engine restarted successfully, but he noted that it seemed like an awful long time for the engine to light.

By the time the engine came up on thrust, Neil had lost almost 10,000 feet altitude. He had to mentally recompute his climb schedule to get back on his desired climb profile. At 25 seconds after launch when finally back on profile, he advanced the throttle to 100 percent thrust. Neil reached the desired climb attitude of 35 degrees and then noted as he maintained that attitude, that he felt the airplane was continuing to rotate upward. He thought that he was going straight up or even going over on his back. He attempted to crosscheck his attitude by referring to his backup attitude indicator, but it was on the stop at 35 degrees. He said he asked NASA-1 (Joe Walker), "How is my trajectory?" in a casual, offhand way, not wanting to admit that he thought he was climbing straight up. Joe indicated that his climb angle was good.

In the postflight debriefing, someone asked Neil, "Did it occur to you that since you thought you were going straight up that you would be coming straight down?" Neil admitted that the thought had occurred to him and that is why he had asked Joe about his trajectory. He was very happy to hear that his trajectory was normal.

Neil peaked at 180,000 feet altitude and then set up for the entry. For some reason he could only command 11 degrees angle of attack, instead of the planned 15 degrees, but he felt that it was adequate to make the reentry. As the normal acceleration began to rise during the entry, several engine malfunction lights came on. For a moment Neil thought the engine was trying to light up. He commented that, "it seemed like an awful lot of stuff was going on at the same time and it was difficult to evaluate something like the engine trying to light up. This could get you in trouble if it really did. If that engine lights up when you're going downhill, that's all." It would have been catastrophic. Neil finally cycled the throttle on and then off and the lights went out. Neil completed the entry without any further incidents and proceeded to a successful recovery at Edwards.

Neil's fourth flight in the number three aircraft occurred on April 20, 1962. He made the launch at Mud Lake. The plan called for a flight to a peak altitude of 205,000 feet, in which Neil would perform maneuvers during ascent and descent to evaluate the flight control system. The flight proceeded as planned with only minor deviations in speed and altitude. Neil commented, "In general, the aircraft control and damping during ballistic flight and entry were outstanding and considerably more smooth than had been expected. Unfortunately, this may be at the expense of excessive reaction control fuel consumption." The number one APU and BCS peroxide-low lights did light up at approximately 160,000 feet during the descent, verifying a higher than normal consumption of peroxide. The peroxide transfer system used to transfer unused engine turbo-pump peroxide was immediately energized and the light was extinguished as he descended through 115,000 feet altitude. Radio communications were intermittent during this period and a potential new problem surfaced as indicated in the radio communications.

NASA-1:   "OK, brakes out."

Neil: "Rog, and we're getting a little. . . oh, that head bumper."

NASA-1:   "OK, and a hard left turn, check the RCS off."

Neil: "Say again."

NASA-1:   "Hard left turn, check the RCS off."

Neil: "RCS off, brakes are out and I have the base in sight."

NASA-1:   "OK, lots more left there, retract the brakes, 25 degrees stabilizer, Neil." [NASA-1 is concerned because Neil is not turning the airplane toward Edwards.]

NASA-1:   "We show you ballooning, not turning, Neil. Six- seven-two, hard left turn." [Neil is beginning to bounce back out of the atmosphere, rather than descend into it. As a result, he is unable to pull *g* to turn.]

Neil: "Rog, I'm reading."

NASA-1:   "Hard left turn, Neil."

Chase: "He seems to be in position."

NASA-1:   "OK, you have 30 degrees stabilizer." [Thirty degrees nose up stabilizer.]

Neil: . . .

NASA-1:   "Your surfaces are bottomed out." [Stabilizer is full nose up in an attempt to pull *g* to turn.]

Neil: "I agree, 300 knots. They're coming down now."

NASA-1:   "You're heading toward the homebase at zero zero zero degrees now." [The aircraft has finally turned back toward Edwards.]

Neil: "I have the base in sight, Joe."

During the pullout portion of the entry, Neil was monitoring the *g* limiting feature of the flight control system. During this period the airplane completed the pullout and actually began a slight climb. Neil did not notice this ballooning or bounce tendency and when Joe first called for a hard left turn, Neil rolled into a 60-degree left bank and pulled up in angle of attack to start the turn. When he got the next hard left turn call, he realized that he was above the atmosphere and was not turning. He sailed right on by Edwards and Palmdale in a 90-degree bank with full nose up stabilizer trying to turn the aircraft around.

This situation typifies the problem of energy management in high-speed flight. Neil was traveling at approximately Mach 3 at 100,000 feet as he passed over Edwards. At this high altitude, it is not possible to pull enough g to change the flight path rapidly. The aircraft continues down the flight path until it slows down and descends enough to turn around. The only way Neil could have expedited the turn was to roll on over and pull down into the atmosphere to build up his g or turn capability. Neil finally realized this, but by that time he was 45 miles south of Edwards, over La Canada and the Rose Bowl. He now had a major problem facing him. Could he make it back to Edwards? Ironically, too much energy as he boomed by Edwards a few moments ago had now left him in a position of possibly not having enough energy to get back to Edwards.

NASA-1:	"What is your visual estimate of your location?"
Neil:	"Looks like I'm pretty . . . in pretty bad shape for the south lakebed."
NASA-1:	"You're at 8 degrees alpha?"
Neil:	"Affirmative, and I'm going to jettison now."
NASA-1:	"What altitude, Neil?"
Neil:	"Got 47,000."
NASA-1:	"Yes, we check that. Have you decided what your landing runway is yet?"

Neil was not sure that he could make it back to Edwards. In his postflight debriefing, he noted that, "the only other alternative at that point would have been Palmdale and I didn't want to get into their traffic pattern." If he had landed at Palmdale, it is doubtful that Neil could have kept the aircraft on the concrete runway due to the lack of steering capability in the X-15 during slideout.

Neil was not getting any help on energy management from the control room. This was partially due to the fact that our calculations were not accurate and that we never planned on the aircraft approaching from the south. We had no checkpoints marked on the map to the south of Edwards. All of the flights normally approached Edwards from the north or northeast. Neil had to decide if he could make it back to Edwards. No one else could offer much help at that instant.

Neil added, "Mirage Lake was about as far away as Rogers, and Rosamond (dry lake) wasn't much closer so I decided to head for the south lakebed at Edwards. It looked like we were in good shape." The radio communications continued.

Neil:	"Let me get up here a little closer. I can definitely make the base now."
NASA-1:	"Yep."
Neil:	"Check head bumper up, I'm 41,000."
NASA-1:	"We're 26 miles to the south lakebed and have you at 40,000." [NASA-1 is telling Neil that he is 26 miles from the south lakebed and that he is at 40,000 feet altitude.]
Neil:	"OK."
NASA-1:	"Stop jettison on peroxide."
Neil:	"Rog. OK, the landing will be on runway three-five south lake and will be [a] straight-in approach and I'm at 32,000, going to use some brakes to make it. OK, I'm about . . . approaching . . . pretty hard to tell from here."
Chase:	"OK, I've got you now. I'm one o'clock to you."
Neil:	"OK."
Chase:	"Don't know if I'll be with you though." [The chase had been in position to join up for a landing on the north lakebed. He had to quickly revise his flight path to attempt to rendezvous with Neil as he approached the south lakebed. He was not sure that he could rendezvous before Neil landed.]
Neil:	"OK, going to use some brakes to get in . . . OK, the ventral is armed and the brakes are in. I'm landing on three-five and I'm about 15 miles out from the end now. Peroxide-low light is out, on again, source is 1,600 pounds. I'm turning 290 knots."
Chase:	"Coming up on your left."
Neil:	"OK, I haven't got a hold of you yet. And a little brakes here. I'm back to pressurize. Going to land in sort of the middle of the south lakebed. Brakes are in again, 280."
Chase-4:	"Henry, I'll take the left side if you want me to."
Chase-3:	"Rog."
Neil:	"You want to call the ventral jettison, Harvey?"
Chase-4:	"OK."
Neil:	"Little shorter than I thought."
Chase-4:	"You can punch it out anytime you want to Neil for drag."
Neil:	"Oh, I should have done that before shouldn't I?"
Chase-4:	"Yep. Start your flaps down now . . . Off. OK, you're well in, go ahead and put her down. Very nice, Neil."
NASA-1:	"The posse [recovery convoy] will get there shortly."
Chase-4:	[Sarcastically] "In about 30 minutes." [The recovery vehicles were all

up on the north lakebed anticipating a landing there as originally
planned. They had to drive almost 10 miles to rendezvous with Neil
on the south lakebed.]

Helicopter: "We'll be there, Neil."

In the postflight debriefing, there was a discussion of the approach to landing
on the south lakebed. It was generally agreed that it was a rather close call
making it in to the runway. Someone asked how much clearance Neil had from
the Joshua trees on the edge of the lakebed. The chase pilot answered, "Oh,
at least 100 feet . . . on either side." Neil was right down among 'em.

This flight was the longest duration flight on record, 12 minutes, 28.7 seconds.
It was referred to as Neil's cross-country flight. It was also the largest miss
distance for a planned touchdown point (12 miles) but Neil later managed to
make a much more precise landing—"on the moon!"

THE DEPUTY'S BAD LANDING

One of the pilot's "other duties as assigned" was flying VIPs when necessary.
Our deputy director, De E. Beeler, called the pilot's office one day to request
a T-33 ride down to Los Angeles International Airport. This was rather unusual.
We did sometimes fly people down to LAX for various reasons, but we normally
flew them down in our C-47. On this occasion, the deputy director wanted
to be dropped off at the TWA terminal to catch a flight out to Washington,
D.C. He did not explain why he wanted the T-33 instead of the C-47, but we
assumed that he wanted to make a big impression as he climbed out of a military
jet in his business suit to board a passenger airliner.

I was chosen to make the flight. The weather at LAX was not very good,
so I had to be prepared to spend some time in the holding pattern. I did not
want to have to shut down and refuel at LAX. I had the airplane loaded with
enough fuel to spend some time in the holding pattern and to make the round-
trip plus some extra fuel for taxiing around the airport to drop off my passenger.
By the time I added a couple of extra gallons just to be safe, I had a pretty
good fuel load. I called Approach Control as I crossed the San Gabriel Mountains for an instrument approach into LAX.

I fully expected a long delay due to all the airline traffic. I was cleared to
descend immediately and given a vector to begin my approach. I broke out
of the overcast on final approach at 400 feet and prepared to land. I was slightly
long and fast and I was very heavy since I had only been airborne 20 minutes.

I touched down very gently, but I was in too big a hurry to start braking. I just barely touched the brakes when the right tire blew. The airplane began to swerve off the runway and I had to apply the left brake to stop the swerve. The left tire blew, and suddenly I had no brakes at all. I managed to keep the airplane on the runway, but I did take out a couple of runway lights before the airplane stopped. Our deputy director certainly made an impression on his arrival at LAX. It was not what he had in mind, but what the heck—he got some attention.

A vehicle and crew came out to assess the situation. It was obvious that the aircraft could not be easily moved, so they decided to close the runway and wait until the aircraft could be repaired. They notified NASA Edwards of the problem and NASA indicated they would send parts and a crew down to repair the aircraft. They hauled my passenger off to the TWA terminal and I was left with my airplane on the side of the left-hand runway.

It took over an hour for our NASA C-47 to arrive with spare wheels and a maintenance crew. It took another half hour to change the two wheels, reconnect the brake lines, and recharge the brake fluid. Both brake lines had come loose after the tires had blown during the landing rollout. We got the airplane started with a borrowed start cart and then the crew had to help me turn the aircraft back to the center of the runway because the brakes were soaked with brake fluid. We finally got the aircraft straightened out on the runway centerline and I added power for takeoff. Luckily, I was able to keep it headed down the runway and I got airborne without any real problem.

When I arrived at work the morning after the incident, I was told that Joe Walker had returned from Washington, D.C. the previous day on an airliner and had to spend an extra 45 minutes in a holding pattern because one of the runways was obstructed. When the airliner finally landed, Joe looked out the window and saw two of "his" aircraft sitting on the other runway. His aircraft had caused the 45-minute delay. I was damn glad he had not come to work that day and that he took the rest of the week off.

I was obviously very chagrined about the whole affair and I took a lot of ribbing for many years about that incident. I tried to convince the other pilots that it was the deputy director's fault. I told them that he had had his feet on the brakes when we had landed, and to add credence to that story I claimed to have broadcast over the air my admonition to the deputy to, "get his damn feet off the brakes." No one bought that story.

Chapter 5. . . . .

In the Contrails of Giants
(1962–1964)

Following Neil Armstrong's MH-96 evaluation flights in the number three X-15, Bob White made a checkout flight and then two flights for contractual demonstration of the MH-96 flight control system. Although Bob's flights were justified as contractual demonstration flights, there was another motive in making these flights. The USAF had arbitrarily designated an altitude of 50 miles as the altitude separating aerodynamic flight from space flight. To achieve an astronaut rating and wings, a pilot had to exceed 50 miles altitude, or 264,000 feet. These flights were utilized to build up in altitude to qualify Bob for astronaut wings.

Bob's checkout flight was routine except that he undershot his planned altitude by more than 20,000 feet. His explanation for the undershoot sounded vaguely familiar. He thought he was climbing much steeper than planned. Bob said, "The reason that we went low on the profile was because of me. When we got up to 32 degrees, and at about 60 seconds in time, I guess it was just a small case of disorientation. I say a small case because I didn't lose complete orientation but when I was up at this climb angle, and this is the first time that I've had this feeling, I looked at the ball. I had 32 degrees in pitch, but I had the darndest feeling that I was continuing to rotate. I couldn't resist the urge just to push on back down until the light blue of the sky showed up. I never did get to the horizon. Then I was satisfied that it wasn't happening. I pulled back up, but that's the reason for the lower altitude." Bob described the flight control system as "quite remarkably good. I like it and I'd like to try it again."

Bob's second flight was also routine. His actual maximum altitude was just 3,000 feet less than the planned altitude of 250,000 feet, a very accurate flight profile. Bob did note when he looked out the window at peak altitude, "When you're up there it feels like everything is right under the nose. It was reassuring again to hear ground saying, 'You're right on profile and track.' That eliminates any concern on the pilot's part for sure." The concern, of course, was the typical one on the altitude flights that you were going to substantially overshoot Edwards during the descent.

The third flight was planned to 282,000 feet altitude. Bob actually achieved 314,750 feet. There was a suspicion that Bob intentionally overshot his altitude to establish an unbeatable altitude record. This was never confirmed, however, subsequent experience indicated that substantial altitude overshoots were not uncommon. It was relatively easy to miss the desired altitude by 10,000 to 20,000 feet.

The third flight was flown on July 17, 1962. It was launched out of Delamar Lake, north of Las Vegas, Nevada. At 1 minute to launch Bob commented, "OK, my MH system has dropped out, completely dropped off the line." This meant that his primary flight control system was not working. The B-52 pilot asked NASA-1 if they wanted him to make a 360-degree turn while they sorted out the problem. Before NASA-1 could answer, Bob called again and said that he had reset his circuit breakers and he was ready for the 1- minute countdown call. The B-52 then called, "One minute now," and the countdown proceeded on to launch.

In retrospect, this seemed to be a rather cavalier response to a major problem. The entire electronic flight control system went belly up and the only reaction was to check the circuit breakers, reset, and then proceed with the flight. That was a rather risky action since the electronic flight control system was essential for a safe reentry, but things worked out satisfactorily. If that sort of thing happened today, we would cancel the flight and troubleshoot the flight control system for weeks, if necessary, to determine the cause of the momentary failure. We may be somewhat safer nowadays, but I am not sure we are much smarter.

The boost portion of the flight went well. Bob was late on engine shutdown and thus, high on energy. After the flight, someone asked Bob what his climb angle was. Bob replied, "I would say that it averaged just about 41 degrees.

I was darned if I was going to be low on this one." He commented that, "It seemed like a hell of a long time to get over the top." He peaked out at 314,000 feet altitude, 32,000 feet higher than planned. That kind of averaged out the three flights. He was 20,000 feet low on the first, almost perfect on the second, and 30,000 feet high on the third. Bob would have made a good artillery man. After the flight, Bob said, "This looked like I was quite a bit higher than the last flight because I could just look out and—you know what the pictures look like when the guy is flying around in orbit, well, that's what it looked like."

Someone asked him, "What were the limits on the horizon going over the top? How far could you see?" Bob's answer was, "You could see as far as you looked. I turned my head in both directions and you see nothing but the earth. It's just tremendous. You look off and the sky is real dark. I didn't think the impression would be much different than it was up around 250,000 feet, but I was impressed remarkably more than I was at 250,000 feet. It amazed me. I looked up and was able to pick out San Francisco Bay (about 400 miles away) and it looked like it was down over there off the right wing and I could look out, way out. It was just tremendous, absolutely tremendous!"

In a more technical vein, Bob said, "I'll tell you fellas, this is getting high, and I'd hate to lose stability augmentation. You can toss in the towel if you lose stability augmentation." In other words, if the flight control system was not working properly to damp out any vehicle motions, the pilot probably could not make a successful entry. This, of course, is the system that went belly up just before launch. During the entry, Bob commented on the severe eyeballs out *g* forces and the pain due to the blood pooling in his right arm.

Bob completed the pullout and came level much further down range than planned due to the overshoot in altitude. He, in fact, was almost over the north lakebed at Edwards when he completed the pullout. You might say that he hit the high-key position at Mach 3.5 and 80,000 feet altitude. He had the potential energy to go whizzing right by Edwards, just as Neil had done.

He commented, "I was mainly concerned at this time with the possibility of overshooting the landing point. When I went by the lake (Edwards) and turned it around and when I went around in the turn, I just pushed in on the bottom rudder, so I could get the nose down and stay in (the atmosphere) where I had some dynamic pressure. I didn't want any bounce in altitude. If I had gotten a bounce, I would never have gotten back."

Bob made a wide sweeping turn around the Edwards and Rosamond Lakes and came back in to a more normal high key at 28,000 feet at subsonic speed. He continued around for a perfect landing. Joe Walker in NASA-1 commented,

"Good shot, chief," and closed out the flight by saying, "This is your happy controller going off the air."

Bob had made a great flight and had also demonstrated the ability of the X-15 to handle an extreme amount of excess energy in the approach pattern and still recover successfully. This ability to handle large variations in energy was emphasized during the design of the space shuttle as a very desirable feature for unpowered vehicles .

This altitude (314,000 feet) is still an FAI record altitude for airplanes. It can only be surpassed one time because space begins at 100,000 meters (approximately 328,000 feet) according to the FAI definition. To surpass Bob's record, one must exceed it by 3 percent, which is roughly 10,000 feet. Thus there is only one opportunity to exceed Bob's altitude and still stay below 328,000 feet, the beginning of space. Walker's subsequent flight to 354,200 feet did not qualify as a record altitude. It will be some time before anyone beats Bob's official record in an airplane.

THE NELLIS AFFAIR

As the flight program progressed, there was a realization that another launch lake further removed from Edwards was needed to cope with the higher energy flights. On higher altitude flights more ground distance was required, to comfortably accomplish the climbout, the ballistic trajectory, the pullout, and the deceleration into Edwards. Several candidate lakes had been identified, and on May 21, 1962, Joe Vensel asked Neil to fly up to Delamar Lake, to check it out for use on some upcoming high-altitude flights. Neil took off in an F-104 and headed out for Delamar Lake.

Delamar was located approximately 90 miles north of Las Vegas. It took Neil about a half hour to get there. He immediately began a descent to the lakebed. As he descended, we lost radio contact. We normally monitored proficiency and program support flights on radio in case some kind of a problem developed. During these flights the pilot would try to check in by radio every 15 to 20 minutes to verify that everything was okay. Thirty minutes passed by and Neil did not check in. Della Mae, our secretary, tried to contact him by radio, but got no answer. Another 15 minutes passed and still no call from Neil. By this time, everyone was getting a little nervous. We began calling Neil every few minutes over the next half hour knowing that he should be on the way home due to a low fuel state. Still no luck. Della Mae called Edwards

Top: X-15 approaches touchdown on lakebed runway after landing gear deployment. Frost on lower fuselage indicates location of residual propellant in tanks during landing descent. Bottom: Number two X-15 on Mud Lake after landing gear failure on Flight 2-31-52. Dryden C-47 aircraft is in the background.

Top: F-100 chase monitors prelaunch operations during contractor demonstration flight. Bottom: X-15 drops away from the B-52 during a contractor demonstration flight of the number one X-15.

Top: Climbout after takeoff. Note B-52 gear doors cycling closed. X-15 has wing tip pods installed. Bottom: B-52 with X-15 departing Edwards area en route to launch lake.

Top: B-52 and X-15 en route to launch point. Note B-52 and X-15 flight history symbols under U.S. Air Force markings. Inclined aircraft symbols with rocket plumes symbolize successful powered flights. Bottom: X-15A-2 during launch countdown on maximum-speed flight.

Top: An aerial salute by the B-52 mothership and two of the F-104 chase aircraft.
Bottom: X-15 on Edwards lakebed after landing. Recovery crew is monitoring
postlanding shutdown activities.

Top: X-15 on Cuddeback Lake following emergency landing on Flight 3-29-48. Emergency recovery crew members are deactivating the aircraft's subsystems. Bottom: Edwards crash and rescue helicopter alongside X-15 after landing on lakebed.

Top: Recovery crew vehicles, Neil Armstrong, and personnel on lakebed after landing. Bottom: Left side of cockpit. Control stick on left console is manual reaction control system controller.

Top: Cockpit showing instrument panel and all three control sticks: the reaction control system controller on the left console, the center control stick, and the right-hand sidearm controller for aerodynamic controls. Bottom: Rear view of X-15 showing LR-99 engine nozzle. Upper and lower speed brakes are fully extended. Propellant jettison tubes are located on either side of the engine in the outer portion of the fuselage side fairings.

Top: Aircraft sitting in the sagebrush following Jack McKay's emergency landing at Delamar Lake. This event prompted Jack's statement that the runway on Delamar was "3 miles long with a 500-foot overrun." Bottom: Aircraft on Rosamond Lake following Scott Crossfield's emergency landing due to engine fire on Flight 2-3-9. The fuselage broke behind the cockpit.

Top: Forward fuselage of X-15 number three following in-flight breakup of aircraft on Flight 3-65-97. Accident investigation team is examining wreckage. Bottom: Aircraft sits in sagebrush off the end of the runway on Delamar Lake following emergency landing on Flight 1-63-104.

Top: X-15 on Cuddeback Lake following the author's emergency landing on Flight 3-29-48. Emergency recovery crew is deactivating the aircraft. C-130 rescue aircraft is in the background. Middle: Number one X-15 aircraft slides out after landing on lakebed. Bottom: B-52 with X-15 taxis out for takeoff.

X-15 separates from B-52 after launch. F-100 chase is in the background.

Top: Recovery crew personnel and program officials examine aircraft after first flight landing on south lakebed. Aircraft deviated from runway heading during final slideout and came to a stop off the runway. Bottom: Number three X-15 climbs out after launch.

X-15 contrail during climbout after launch. Photo taken from chase aircraft.

Close-up of X-15 canopy illustrating small cockpit window size. Note NASA meatball insignia on side of nose section. This insignia usually burned off during flight, requiring frequent replacement.

Top: Early morning view of preflight activity. Bottom: Front view of damage to lower ventral fin by shock impingement on Flight 2-53-97 to Mach 6.7.

tower to ask if they had heard from Neil. They had not. Worry turned to fear. We were missing an airplane, but more important, we were missing a pilot.

As we were discussing our next move, the hot line rang ominously. Della Mae was almost afraid to pick up the phone. She finally did, and within seconds, she was smiling. Neil had landed safely at Nellis AFB just north of Las Vegas.

Several minutes later, Neil called to talk to Joe Walker to brief him on the results of the flight. He indicated that his airplane had sustained some minor damage during the landing and that he needed a ride home. Joe told him we would send an airplane to pick him up.

We had a two-seat F-104B available and Joe instructed the maintenance people to prepare it for a flight to Las Vegas. Joe checked to see which pilots were available and I happened to be the only one without any other commitment. I got the nod for the flight. I was a little reluctant to take it and told Joe that I had not checked out in the two-seat F-104B, but Joe decided that I should go anyway. I had flown the F-104A, the single-seat model, and Joe said there was no significant difference between the A and the B models. I took his word for it and rushed out to strap in to the airplane.

The instant I broke ground, I knew that Joe had stretched the truth a bit. There was a big difference in the way this aircraft handled compared to the A models that I had been flying. The airplane was a lot looser. I was all over the sky for a few seconds after takeoff until I could reduce my own gain. I was to learn in the next few months that there could be a significant difference in the handling qualities among each of the early F-104 aircraft. They each had their own peculiarities.

I managed to get the aircraft headed uphill and off toward Las Vegas and then leveled off at low altitude to burn off fuel for a landing at Nellis. I called Nellis tower as I approached Las Vegas for landing instructions. The air traffic controller gave me clearance to land on runway zero-three. I came straight in for the break and pitched out in a snappy turn to downwind. I dropped the gear and began the approach to landing. I soon realized that I was not going to be able to crank it around tight enough to line up with the runway for a landing, so I initiated a go-around.

I widened my pattern considerably on the next approach, but I still could not turn tight enough to line up with the runway. I initiated another go-around. I really began to wonder about the turn performance of this airplane compared to the A model. I just could not seem to pull this thing around. I decided to try using landing flaps. Our A model did not have a landing flap position. We were limited to use of takeoff flaps for both takeoff and landing. Later model F-104s had a landing flap configuration with boundary layer control to reduce landing approach speeds. Our F-104B had this flap configuration. I soon found that the handling qualities were very poor in the landing flap configuration. I did, however, manage to get the airplane lined up with the runway. As I passed over the runway threshold, I noted that I was drifting across the runway due to a strong crosswind, but I decided to plunk it on the runway anyway. The strong crosswind, which was not reported by the tower, explained the problems I had had in the previous approaches.

The instant that I touched down, the left main tire blew. I managed to keep the airplane headed down the runway until it slowed down and then, I turned off at the center taxiway and parked the airplane. A fire truck and a base ops vehicle quickly joined me. After shutting the airplane down, I got a ride into base ops. The base operations officer introduced himself as I walked in. He was not very happy. He had to close down the runway to clean up the debris from my blown tire. He informed me that this was the second time that day that he had to shut the runway down. The previous time was after Neil's landing.

Neil had landed with his arresting hook down and had engaged the emergency arresting gear at the approach end of the runway. The arresting gear was not designed to be engaged in that manner. The arresting gear consisted of a cable attached to a length of ship's anchor chain. The chain was hooked up and laid out in an arrangement that, under normal engagements, would fold the chain back on itself as the cable was pulled out. This would result in a relatively smooth increase in drag as the cable pulled the chain along. If the cable is engaged in the wrong direction, the aircraft picks up the drag of all the chain instantaneously. When this happens, something has to give. In Neil's case, the airplane gave a little and the chain came apart. Links of anchor chain weighing 30 pounds were catapulted through the air for hundreds of feet. Needless to say, Neil's airplane stopped abruptly. It took 30 minutes to clear the runway and considerably longer to rig an interim arresting gear.

Previously, when Neil arrived at Delamar, he set up an X-15 type approach to descend down to the lakebed to inspect it. There was no runway marked out on the lakebed, but Neil picked the most likely location for a runway and continued his approach to touchdown. Just prior to touchdown, he extended the landing gear as he typically did during simulated X-15 landings. This time, the landing gear did not fully extend and lock before the aircraft touched down.

Neil had apparently misjudged his height and sink rate and extended his gear too late.

Judging height and rate of sink on these dry lakebeds was not easy. The surface texture on the different lakebeds varied tremendously as did the texture on various parts of the lake. The surface tended to have a crust of clay that cracked as it dried out. On some lakes, the crust was thick and the cracks were large. On other lakes, the crust was thin, and the cracks small. From the air, it was hard to judge whether the cracks were large or small and thus, you had no good reference to judge height. On some lakes, there was no visual texture at all. It was like trying to judge height above glassy smooth water. That is why we marked the lakebed runways with black lines of known width to use as a reference in judging height. Neil apparently touched down in an area with no visible surface texture, and was unable to judge his height accurately.

The tire tracks on the lakebed told the whole story. On initial touchdown, the distance between the two main gear tires was less than it should have been with the gear fully down and locked. As the aircraft continued to settle, the tire tracks began to merge. The weight of the aircraft was forcing the gear to retract. Neil realized that he was in trouble when he touched down before the landing gear green lights came on. He immediately applied power to abort the landing and get airborne. For what must have seemed like hours, the aircraft continued to settle before it began to rise. In this few seconds of actual time, the aircraft settled far enough to allow the ventral fin and landing gear doors to contact the lakebed. The ventral, which contained the radio antenna, was damaged and the door actuator was broken on one door. This allowed the utility hydraulic fluid to escape, deactivating that system. One other result of the ground contact, was the release of the emergency arresting gear hook.

Neil managed to get the airplane started uphill before the fuselage struck the lakebed. As Neil struggled into the air, he realized he had damaged the aircraft and was losing hydraulic fluid, so he headed for the nearest airfield, which happened to be Nellis. He attempted to contact Nellis to request landing instructions, but received no response due to the damaged radio antenna. He then entered the traffic pattern and made a pass down the runway wagging his wings to indicate a radio failure. He turned downwind and set up for his landing approach not realizing that his arresting hook was down and as a result, he engaged the arresting gear in an abnormal manner shortly after touchdown.

The base operations officer calmed down a bit after he got the runway open the second time. He then informed me that they had no F-104 parts at Nellis. Now, both Neil and I were stranded. This time, I had to make the call back to NASA. I knew that Joe Walker was going to be mad as hell, but I had to let him know what had happened. When Joe finally calmed down, he indicated that he would send another aircraft to pick us up. Our C-47 was out of commission so he could not send parts and mechanics to fix my aircraft. That would have to be done at a later date.

While we were waiting for the next NASA airplane to arrive, Neil and I chatted with the base ops officer trying to cheer him up. As we were talking, another USAF transient pilot joined the conversation and asked what our plans were for our F-104 aircraft. He happened to be the commanding officer of one of the last active F-104 squadrons in the U.S. and he needed spare parts. He believed he had stumbled on a fortune in spare parts in our damaged aircraft. The commanding officer rubbed his hands and danced around like Walter Huston after he and his partner had struck gold in the movie *Treasure of Sierra Madre.* We informed him, in no uncertain terms, that we intended to repair the airplanes. There would be no abandoned airships for him to claim salvage rights. We really had a hard time getting rid of him.

The ops officer was finally notified that another NASA aircraft was inbound for a landing. He and Neil and I went outside to watch the aircraft land. It was our T-33. Bill Dana was flying it. Bill made a nice approach, but he landed long and hot. After landing, the aircraft did not appear to decelerate. The airplane went by base ops at what appeared to be 100 knots ground speed. There were only a couple of thousand feet of runway remaining and it did not appear that the aircraft could stop in the remaining distance. The operations officer said something like, "Oh no, not again" and I saw Neil hide his head in his arm. I did not want to watch either, but I was transfixed.

Somehow, Bill got the airplane stopped before he ran off the end of the runway. The ops officer was a nervous wreck by this time and when Bill walked in later and told him that he would take Neil home and that NASA would send another airplane for me, he broke down. He said, "Please don't send another NASA airplane." He promised that he would personally find me transportation back to Edwards. I ended up riding back to Edwards that night in the back end of a USAF C-47 that happened to be passing through Nellis on the way to Los Angeles. I believe that ops officer gave them some free gas to haul me away from Nellis. The base ops officer related the tale of the three hot shot NASA test pilots for years after that. Neil, Bill, and I became infamous. Needless to say I did not go back to Nellis for a long time.

MY EJECTION

In December 1962, Joe Walker was scheduled to make an altitude buildup flight in the number three X-15. Bill Dana was originally scheduled to make the weather flight, but he wanted to take some time off and he asked if I would fill in for him. Based on the results of that flight, I still think he had a premonition of what would occur and decided to beg off. At least I accuse him of that.

The plane I was flying was a unique F-104 with a centerline displacement rack for a weapon such as a large bomb or a big missile. We had borrowed that unique airplane from the USAF to do several unusual tests. In one test program, we were dropping a dummy bomb that contained a Mercury capsule drogue chute system. The bomb simulated the weight of the Mercury capsule. The Mercury program manager wanted to test the deployment and stability of the drogue chute at supersonic speeds at 70,000 feet altitude or greater. We could achieve desired test conditions by accelerating to Mach 1.6 or more at 35,000 feet and then start a gentle climb while still accelerating to 60,000. Above 60,000 feet we were trading airspeed for altitude. We usually got to 70,000 feet with more than 1.2 Mach number before dropping the bomb, which was adequate for the test. Quite an interesting flight profile and test.

With this airplane, we also did the ALSOR program to launch a balloon to altitudes approaching 1,000,000 feet in order to measure air density. We needed to know air density to be able to calculate dynamic or impact pressure on the X-15. The balloon was in the nose of a large rocket that we fired vertically from the aircraft as we pulled up in a loop. We started the loop at Mach 2 at 35,000 feet. We were vertical at 50,000 feet still indicating about 1.5 Mach number, and we went over the top above 60,000 feet. It was quite a maneuver. Every once in a while, we would lose the engine or fall out of the loop, but we managed to get some rockets up to 600,000 feet or more. We never were able to determine whether the balloon came out of the rocket nose cone because we never detected it with radar. We finally gave up on that program, after impacting some errant rockets in some very sensitive areas.

On our last attempt, we went down to Point Mugu Naval Air Station to use their overwater test area. We had been politely evicted from the Edwards restricted area because we could not keep our rockets from impacting outside the area. The Edwards area was huge—30 miles wide by 50 miles long—but we missed once on the short side and once on the long side and impacted a rocket in Death Valley National Park. When we went to Point Mugu, we did not mention our minor impact error problem. Instead, we stressed the importance of the program and our competence to do the job. The Point Mugu personnel finally agreed to support us by letting us use their overwater range and their tracking facilities. The only proviso they had was that we impact our rocket well away from any of the channel islands.

The big day came. We flew down from Edwards, accelerating all the way, and pulled up and launched the rocket. Our engineers in the Point Mugu control room watched in horror as the rocket soared up to 600,000 feet and then came down headed right for San Nicolas Island. It impacted just offshore. The navy range safety officer was furious, but our engineers were smart enough not to stick around for a postflight debriefing. Those rockets seemed to have a mind of their own. They refused to go straight. We did not go back to Point Mugu for some time. We later partially redeemed ourselves when we fired a rocket for the navy at Point Mugu.

The weather flights were made very early in the morning. In fact, we usually got airborne before sunrise and were uprange over the launch area by daybreak. Weather information was critical since the massive flight preparation effort was initiated or cancelled based on real time observations.

The morning of my weather flight was a classic desert winter morning. It was cold, freezing in fact, but the sky was crystal clear and there was not a hint of a breeze—a beautiful morning for a flight. The launch lake was Mud Lake. I flew up to the launch area as the dawn lit up the rugged landscape. The desert is very pretty early in the morning with the pinkish glow of the dawn. I was really enjoying the sights. I could see over 30,000 square miles of desert from my cruise altitude and there was not a cloud in sight. I started a leisurely turn back toward Edwards as I passed over the launch lake.

As I rolled out on heading to Edwards, I lit the burner. I wanted to make some simulated X-15 approaches when I got back to Edwards and I had to burn up some fuel to get the weight down for the touch and go landings. I was supersonic by the time I arrived at the high-key position for my first simulated X-15 approach. I chopped the throttle, extended the speed brakes and started the turn to low key. As I decelerated through 0.9 Mach, I lowered the flaps to the takeoff position. I was now configured for a simulated X-15 unpowered approach.

In this configuration, the maximum lift/drag ratio of the F-104 was 4.5. The subsonic lift/drag ratio of the X-15 with landing flaps was also 4.5. This was a rather low lift/drag ratio for unpowered landings and special techniques had been developed to ensure consistently successful, smooth landings. I held 300 knots indicated airspeed around the pattern through low key and rolled out on final, right on speed. I picked up my aim point on the north edge of the lakebed and dove at it until I reached the flare altitude of roughly 800 feet. At that speed in the dirty F-104, you were coming downhill at about 18,000 feet a minute at a -18 to -20 degree flight path angle. The flare to come level was a rather gentle 1.5 *g* maneuver and I extended the gear and flew the airplane gently down to touchdown. Shortly after touchdown, I added power, retracted the speed brakes and lifted off for a go-around and another simulated X-15 approach.

I climbed back up to the high-key position and then started to dirty up the airplane for another approach. As I extended the speed brakes and lowered the flaps to the takeoff position, the aircraft started to roll off to the left. I applied aileron to counteract the roll off but I could not stop it. I added full rudder but it still kept rolling. I finally added throttle and lit the burner, hoping to get some more airspeed and some more control effectiveness. That worked. As I accelerated through 350 knots indicated, I could stop the roll rate. I managed to roll the aircraft upright and then began to troubleshoot the problem.

I knew I had an asymmetry problem. I either had an asymmetric speed brake or an asymmetric flap problem. I had retracted the speed brakes and the flaps simultaneously when I applied power to gain airspeed, but I was not sure whether everything had retracted. I checked the flaps in my rearview mirror and both leading edge flaps were up and locked. I could not see the trailing edge flaps. I recycled both the speed brake and flap switches to the closed and up position respectively, but nothing changed. I still needed full aileron and full rudder to keep the wings level. I tried a few other ideas, but nothing worked. I was now beginning to wonder how I was going to get that damn airplane on the ground. I could control it at 350 knots, but I could not land at that speed. If I slowed down, I could not stop the airplane from rolling off. The awful truth slowly confronted me. I would have to eject.

I really did not want to eject on such a pretty morning, but there was no way to get that thing on the ground safely. I called NASA-1 and asked if Joe Walker was on the radio. I told them I had a problem. They said they would try to get him on the air and I asked them to hurry because I was getting tired of holding full aileron and rudder. Even with full trim, the forces were quite high. Walker finally came on the air. He was in the pressure suit checkout van being suited up for his flight. I told him the symptoms of my problem and he decided that I had a split trailing edge flap situation with one down and one up.

He suggested I recycle the flap lever to the up position to attempt to get both flaps up and locked. I had already tried that, but I gave it another try. No luck. Joe asked if I had cycled the flap lever all the way from the up to the takeoff position and then back up again. I said no. I had only cycled the flap lever from the up position to a position just below it and then back to the up position. Joe suggested we try it his way. I moved the flap lever from the up position all the way to the takeoff position and then back to the up position. As soon as I moved the lever to the takeoff position, I knew I had done the wrong thing.

The airplane started rolling again, but this time I could not stop it. The roll rate quickly built up to the point where I was almost doing snap rolls. Simultaneously, the nose of the airplane started down. I was soon doing vertical rolls as the airspeed began rapidly increasing. I knew I had to get out quick because I did not want to eject supersonic and I was already passing through 0.9 Mach. I let go of the stick and reached for the ejection handle. I bent my head forward to see the handle and then I pulled it. Things were a blur from that point on.

I felt a terrible pain in my neck due to the seat acceleration while my head was bent forward. I felt the air hit me like a crashing wave in the ocean and I began to tumble violently. Then I noticed something flopping around in front of me. I focused on it and realized it was my ejection seat. I still had a death grip on the ejection handle which was attached to the seat by a cable. I knew I had to let go of that ejection handle and get rid of the seat or it could foul my chute. You cannot imagine how hard it is to let go of something when you are falling through the air like that. That handle was my security blanket. I could not let go but I finally did. Within a couple of seconds the chute streamed automatically toward my feet. Apparently, I had ejected inverted and I was falling upside down. When the chute blossomed, I had my neck snapped again. Luckily, it was in the other direction.

When I finally ended up hanging under the chute, I realized I was having trouble breathing. I checked to see if I had pulled the green apple for my bail out oxygen and, just for good measure, I pulled it again. Apparently I was getting oxygen, but I was not getting enough, so I finally loosened my oxygen mask. The flight surgeon and I later realized that when I was breathing rapidly after all that excitement, the metered flow from the emergency oxygen bottle did not supply enough gas volume to allow me to fill my lungs. I was getting sufficient oxygen but nothing else. I suggested that they modify the orifice on all bail out bottles to allow a higher flow rate since I was pretty sure everyone who ejected would be breathing rapidly. I am not sure if they ever modified them. I did not have the opportunity to eject again, so I will never know.

I watched the airplane as it snap rolled toward the ground. It hit the ground in the bombing range, near the road on the east shore of the lakebed. It exploded on impact and a huge column of black smoke rose from the crater created by the impact. At NASA they quickly spotted the black smoke and began looking for a parachute. They could not see one. I had not said much before I ejected. I told Joe that, "it was going," as the airplane began to roll off after cycling the flap lever. I did not tell them I was ejecting. They did not know where I was or what my altitude was when all this occurred. They just heard my last call to Joe and then nothing. They called a couple of times to try to reach me, but then Whitey Whiteside saw the ominous smoke cloud. They did not want to believe it but deep down they knew I was dead. They had not lost a pilot since Howard Lilly was killed in 1949. The gloom was pretty thick. The pilot's secretary, Della Mae, was crying and a number of other employees were visibly shocked. At that time we were a small, close-knit group at NASA and everyone really cared about his coworkers.

In the meantime, I was slowly descending in the parachute and drifting toward the south end of the lakebed. It was only 7:30 A.M. and still a beautiful morning. I was swinging back and forth under the parachute due to a slight bit of turbulence and I remembered a recent lecture on parachuting that recommended that you cut two riser lines at the rear of the chute. This would minimize the oscillations and also give you a forward velocity for maneuvering the chute. I looked up at that big orange and white chute and then down at the ground several thousand feet below me. I thought to myself, "Bull hockey." There was no way that I was going to cut two riser lines on that chute. The chute was fully blossomed and working fine. There was no way that I was going to "fix it" under those conditions. "Don't fix something if it ain't broke."

It took about 15 minutes to get to the ground and I had gotten pretty proficient in steering the chute and damping the oscillations by pulling on the shroud lines at the right times. As I approached the ground, I unbuckled all my straps to prepare to jump out of the harness just prior to touchdown. This procedure was recommended to ensure that I would not be dragged along the ground by the chute after landing. Again, I reconsidered. I knew it was possible to misjudge height coming down in the desert in a chute like that. There were instances of people jumping out of the harness 50 or 100 feet up in the air because they had misjudged their heights. I decided I did not want to do that, so I stayed in the harness until my feet hit the ground.

It was a gentle landing and I stood up quickly and gathered up my chute. I had landed near the road along the east shore of the lakebed. I walked over to the road about 100 yards away to hitch a ride up toward the crash site. I assumed that someone from NASA would be there. I did not make it to the crash site because I saw a NASA vehicle coming up to the road from the lakebed and I flagged it down. Joe Vensel, our chief of flight operations, was in the vehicle. He was on the way to the crash site. He almost cried when he saw me. He was convinced that I had been killed in the crash. We drove back to the base for a quick debriefing and an examination by the flight surgeon and then back to NASA for breakfast in our cafeteria.

Our director, Paul Bikle, was also very relieved to see me, but he was concerned that Joe Walker might have gotten emotionally upset by all the excitement. He went down to the mating area to talk to Joe and found him to be very relaxed and ready to go on his X-15 flight. Joe Vensel and I had previously stopped in to see him to assure him that I was all right. The X-15 flight proceeded as planned and Joe achieved an altitude of 160,000 feet. At the flight party that night I was the center of attention rather than Joe, since I had made the headlines in the local paper.

There was some humor associated with this ejection. When the crash and rescue team arrived at the crash sight, they noticed three main F-104 wheels in the wreckage. They immediately assumed there had been a midair collision between two F-104s, but they could not find any other extra parts. Joe Walker solved the mystery when he revealed that he had the crew store a spare main wheel in the gun bay in case of a flat tire on cross-country flights.

The following week I was sent back to the Lovelace Clinic in Albuquerque, New Mexico for a physical exam to see if I had any neck or back injuries from the ejection. I went to Old Town for dinner the night I arrived. As I was driving back to my motel, a young high school student pulled out of an intersection directly in front of me and I hit him broadside. I ended up in Lovelace Clinic that night with Dr. Randy Lovelace sewing up my lip and putting a cast on my broken hand. The car was totaled. I spent the next day undergoing various examinations to see if I had sustained any injuries from my F-104 ejection. They found no broken bones or spinal injuries so I was sent home. Dr. Lovelace was very upset about the fact that I had survived an ejection without injuries and had come to Albuquerque and sustained some very visible injuries. He somewhat seriously suggested that I tell the folks back home that my injuries were a result of the ejection and that they had been overlooked by the Edwards doctors.

The tail number on the F-104 that I ejected from was 749. The final epitaph to the ejection incident was a punchline by Bill Dana in response to my emergency call, "Roger 749, you are cleared straight in."

GOING FOR BROKE

As a final reward for his contributions to the X-15 program, Joe Walker was allowed to make the maximum altitude attempts in the X-15. As mentioned earlier, the simulator predicted that the X-15 could easily achieve altitudes in excess of 400,000 feet. It also predicted, however, that the aircraft could not consistently reenter safely from altitudes above 400,000 feet. The simulator also indicated that the reentry had to be precisely flown to preclude aircraft damage entering from 400,000 feet.

To provide some pad for potential problems or pilot error, it was decided to try for a maximum altitude of only 360,000 feet. This provided a 40,000 feet pad for cumulative errors. This sounds like a lot of pad, but it really was not based on previous experience. Bob White had overshot his intended altitude by 32,000 feet on his last altitude flight from a planned 282,000 to an actual 314,000 feet. It must be remembered that the X-15 was climbing at over 4,000 feet per second just prior to burnout or shutdown. Thus, if the pilot was 1 second late in shutting the engine down, he would go 4,000 feet higher than planned.

We also determined from calculations and past experience that an extra 1,000 pounds of thrust would add about 5,000 feet to the maximum altitude. The engine thrust varied from engine to engine and also varied somewhat from flight to flight. Engine thrust varied from a low of 57,000 pounds to a high of over 60,000 pounds among the various engines. This could not always be accurately predicted before a flight because thrust varied with atmospheric density. A 1-degree error in climb angle also resulted in roughly a 5,000 foot variation in peak altitude.

If you added up all these seemingly insignificant deviations from the planned values, it was very easy to deviate 15,000 feet in peak altitude from the planned value. We tried to compensate for these types of errors by cross-checking speed, altitude, and rate of climb at various points during the climb and adjusting the final shutdown conditions accordingly, but this did not always prevent large errors. To compound the problem, our inertial system was not always accurate and our backup radar information did not necessarily agree with our inertial data. The pilot quite often had to average out all the data in real time and adjust the planned flight using his best judgment.

To assist the pilot in this demanding task, the engineers finally developed a computer program to predict the maximum altitude on the basis of inertial data. This prediction was displayed to the pilot on a separate altitude display.

This prediction program became very accurate near the end of the program, but it had its growing pains during its early development.

Joe did not do a buildup series of flights prior to the maximum altitude flight. On his previous four flights in the last four months before his maximum altitude attempt, his maximum altitudes were: 209,000; 92,000; 111,000; and 220,000 feet, respectively. His previous maximum altitude was 271,000 feet, but he had made that flight six months earlier.

On his only altitude buildup flight, Joe reached an altitude of 347,800 feet. The flight plan called for an altitude of 315,000 feet. Joe overshot the planned altitude by almost 33,000 feet due to a higher-than-expected engine thrust, a longer-than-expected engine burn, and a one-and-a-half-degree error in climb angle. An error like that would be awfully tough to explain to the FAA Air Traffic Control. Luckily, we did not have to file a flight plan with the FAA. Of course, we did not have much conflicting traffic at that altitude either. Joe did not have the altitude predictor available on this buildup flight. It was available on the final altitude flight, but its performance had not been demonstrated. It was actually being checked out on that flight.

The final maximum altitude attempt was made on August 22, 1963. It was planned to a peak altitude of 360,000 feet. Joe was in excellent spirits before the flight. He had made the buildup flight a month earlier and there were numerous problems and delays getting the flight airborne, but Joe seemed to take it all in stride. In fact, I cannot remember him being happier at any other time.

An examination of the events leading up to the flight revealed an unusual amount of problems. The X-15 was first mated to the B-52 on August 5th for a flight attempt on the next day. This flight was aborted prior to launch due to bad weather conditions up range. Because of continuing bad weather, the aircraft preflight functional checks were rerun in preparation for another flight attempt the following week. During these checks, a problem was encountered requiring that the X-15 be demated from the B-52. It was mated again and another attempt to fly was made on August 13th.

This flight attempt was aborted after take off due to an APU problem. After some troubleshooting and repair, another flight attempt was made on August 15th. Bad weather up range caused the flight to be aborted. During the return to landing, the pilot attempted to start the number one APU in order to check its operation. It would not operate properly. Following this abort, the X-15 was again demated and all preflight checks were reaccomplished. Another engine ground run was made on August 19th.

The X-15 was mated to the B-52 for the fourth time and the flight was finally made on August 22nd As all this would indicate, it was occasionally tough to get a flight off. Every once in a while we went through a series of problems like this. Thank God for a patient and thorough maintenance crew.

The prelaunch activity went smoothly except for a loss of radar tracking by both Edwards and Beatty radars at 8 minutes to launch. Both radars reacquired track at 4 minutes to launch and the launch occurred on time. Joe got a good light and pulled back on the stick to increase angle of attack to 13 degrees. At 11 seconds after launch, he had reached the desired 2 *g* rotation rate and he maintained 2 *g* until 29 seconds after launch, when he should have reached his 48-degree climb attitude.

At 28 seconds he was only indicating about a 40-degree climb attitude, so he quickly pulled the nose up to 48 degrees where he stabilized. At 70,000 feet altitude his altitude predictor should have read 100,000 feet. Instead, it showed 135,000 feet. It appeared that he might be going higher than planned. Joe decided to reduce his climb attitude by 4 degrees to preclude another altitude overshoot.

At 90,000 feet altitude, his predictor was indicating 170,000 feet which again was higher than it should have been. Joe made a couple more corrections in pitch attitude and finally at 150,000 feet altitude, the prediction appeared to be agreeing with the planned forecast for that altitude. Joe planned to shut the engine down when the predictor passed through 360,000 feet, however, just before he could retard the throttle, the engine burned out. Joe checked the predictor immediately after burnout and saw that it indicated a maximum altitude of 362,000 feet.

At burnout, Joe was passing through 176,000 feet altitude traveling at 5,600 feet per second. He then began the long coast to peak altitude. It would take almost 2 minutes to reach peak altitude after burnout. Two minutes does not sound like a lot of time, but try timing it. Just sit back in your easy chair and count off the seconds. It is almost impossible to believe that you can continue to coast up in altitude for that length of time after the engine burns out. It gives you some feel for how much energy is involved at those speeds. For comparison, when you throw a ball up in the air as hard as you can, it only coasts upward a maximum of 4 or 5 seconds. The X-15 coasted up for 120 seconds.

The airplane would coast up another 178,000 feet during that time to peak out at 354,200 feet rather than the 362,000 feet predicted. On this flight, the engine burned an extra second, but Joe's average climb attitude was one and one-half degrees low, so the two errors tended to average out with a slightly low peak altitude. At 330,000 feet on the way up, Joe was supposed to roll into a 45-degree left bank and hold that bank until he reached peak altitude. However, the airplane began rolling off to the right. Joe attempted to correct the drift by applying left roll control, but he got no response. He finally resorted to the left-hand manual reaction controller and managed to level the wings and then roll into his desired left bank.

Postflight analysis indicated that one of his roll reaction control rocket lines had frozen up, preventing the rocket from firing. By going to the manual reaction controller, he commanded both left roll rockets and managed to get one to respond. He continued to use manual roll command until he reentered the atmosphere. At peak altitude, Joe pushed to a 20-degree nose-down pitch attitude to set up for the reentry. This attitude gave him an angle of attack during entry of about 25 degrees, since the flight path was about −45 degrees. Again, the automatic reaction controls failed to maintain this attitude, so Joe had to resort to manual reaction controls to keep the nose at this attitude.

The aircraft began its plunge back toward earth picking up speed and rate of sink as it descended. On altitude flights such as these, the airplane came down at the same angle that it went up, which on this flight was 45 degrees. The aircraft also entered the atmosphere at roughly the same speed that it left the atmosphere, so as it descended through 170,000 feet it was traveling at 5,500 feet per second and descending at over 4,000 feet per second or 240,000 feet per minute. The g forces began building up very gradually as the aircraft descended through 120,000 feet and finally peaked at just over 5 g at 95,000 feet.

By this time, the aerodynamic controls became effective and were used for control during the pullout. Joe maintained 5 g during the pullout until he came level at 70,000 feet altitude. The pullout, as Joe said, was, "One big squeeze." He was decelerating as he was pulling out, and as a result he was subjected to a combination of eyeballs-out and eyeballs-down g forces. This combined g vector could approach 7 g acting on the pilot which again does not sound like much, but he had to maintain this g level for about 25 seconds to complete the pullout. The blood tended to pool in the pilot's arms and legs regardless of the squeezing action of the g suit. It really hurt.

The glide back to Edwards was uneventful, and Joe made a beautiful landing right next to the smoke flare marking the desired touchdown location. He had traveled a ground distance of 294 miles starting from a launch at Smith's Ranch in Nevada. He had climbed almost 60 miles after launch to a peak height of 67 miles and had descended to make a perfect landing 11 minutes and 8 seconds after launch.

Joe did not say much about the view at peak altitude on this flight, but on his previous flight to 348,000 feet, he said, "The overhead aspect is just like one of these dark velvet photographer's cloths as far as the sky appearance, but there weren't any specks of light shining through that I could pick out." Joe did not necessarily wax eloquent about the view on either of these flights, but then Joe was pretty businesslike when he was flying airplanes. He would much prefer to talk about the airplane.

Joe was the fifth pilot to leave the program. White had left six months after his record altitude flight. Rushworth and McKay were the only remaining pilots of the original group. It was time to add some new pilots. Joe Engle and I were to be the replacement pilots. We two rookies were replacing five veterans— some very big shoes to fill. For my part, I was replacing Joe Walker and Neil Armstrong. Someone must have had a lot of confidence in my abilities. I was flattered. I would be following the contrails of giants.

THE GENESIS OF A RESEARCH PILOT

One might wonder how an unknown pilot became involved with a famous airplane. In my case, it was a result of being in the right place at the right time. I had become aware of the NACA (National Advisory Committee for Aeronautics) and its role in flight research through Scott Crossfield. He and I were in the same naval reserve squadron in Seattle, Washington, for a brief period of time in 1950. I joined the reserve fighter squadron about six months before Scott left the squadron to move to California to begin flying for the NACA at Edwards. Over the next few years I was really impressed with the stories I heard about Scott flying experimental aircraft, particularly the rocket aircraft.

I did not know Scott very well before he left, but I wrote to him anyway inquiring about a job as a test pilot for the NACA. Scott did not answer my letter. It was several years later that I found out Scott had a very low opinion of me. In fact, he considered me to be a dumb idiot. Scott was never one to mince words, especially in his younger days. He has mellowed over the years and I think he now considers me a friend. At least he has not called me an idiot lately. Since I did not get any encouragement from Scott, I kind of gave up trying to get a job with the NACA as a test pilot and instead worked at Boeing as an engineer after graduating from the University of Washington. I started working at Boeing as a structural test engineer, but was later transferred to flight test, since they needed flight test engineers to support tests of the new B-52 bomber.

I enjoyed flying as a flight test engineer on the B-52, but it was a terribly demanding job. The test flights varied in duration from 4 to 8 hours and the test engineer was working nonstop from takeoff to landing. Everyone on the test team except the flight test engineer, got a break or two during a test mission. The flight test engineer was always the one individual pacing the entire flight and thus, everyone had to wait for him at one time or another during the flight. I have never in my entire life worked so hard and so fast as I did then as a flight test engineer on the B-52. As a test engineer, if I was not taking data, I was reloading oscillographs, calculating weight and balance, managing fuel transfer, keeping a log on every event that occurred or strapping myself in and out of the damn ejection seat, because I was always having to move around that cramped cabin.

After about 6 months of flying as a test engineer, I decided that if I was going to fly for a living, I would rather fly up front. I went to see the chief pilot about a job as a pilot. He was nice to me, but he politely informed me that I did not have much chance of being a Boeing pilot since I was a former navy pilot. Boeing built and sold airplanes to the air force. A navy pilot was not the best salesman to sell airplanes to the air force. That was my first exposure to the politics of the military-industrial complex.

Something unusual happened next. Three engineers from the NACA at Edwards showed up at Boeing to obtain data on the structural loads being measured on the B-52. I felt this visit by the NACA engineers was strange, because I had tried to get a job with the NACA at Edwards and then had given up. Now, all of a sudden, the mountain had come to Mohammed.

I happened to be working on the structural loads B-52 aircraft that they were interested in. They spent a few days monitoring our test operations before gathering data to take back to Edwards. One of the NACA engineers, De Beeler, was the number two man in the NACA Edwards organization. He was impressed with my work as a flight test engineer and asked if I would like to work for the NACA at Edwards. I said, "Yes, if there is a chance to eventually fly as a test pilot." He said he could not promise anything, but he felt there was a chance. That was enough for me. I went home and told my wife that we were going to California. I made one last attempt to get a job as a Boeing pilot and, after being turned down again, I packed up and left for California.

I arrived in California in February of 1956. I worked for the NACA at Edwards for two years as an engineer. I began flying as a research pilot for the NACA in January of 1958, just a year and a half before the first X-15 flight. I became an X-15 pilot by the process of simple elimination and succession.

When I first began flying for the NACA, there were only five pilots at Dryden. Three were designated as X-15 pilots at the beginning of the program. That left only two of us who were not scheduled to fly it. At least two NASA pilots were needed to keep three X-15 aircraft flying. As the flight program progressed, Joe Walker moved out of the X-15 into the B-70 program and Neil Armstrong left the X-15 program to become an astronaut. That left two openings for an X-15 pilot and I was next in line. As I said previously, I was in the right place at the right time.

As a young kid, I was very interested in airplanes, but not overwhelmed by a desire to fly. I built model airplanes by the carload and had them hanging all over my room. I could not get them to fly properly because no one had ever told me how to ballast the model properly. I became so disgusted that I would build them and then take them up to my second floor bedroom, set them on fire, toss them out the window and watch them go down in flames.

I did talk my father into letting me fly in an open cockpit biplane and in a Ford Trimotor when I was 12 or 13. I also spent a lot of time hanging around my hometown airport at Pontiac, Michigan. I really loved to see the army airplanes that occasionally landed there, but I did not live for flying alone. I enjoyed a lot of the normal things that young boys do like hunting, fishing, and ice skating. I think the biggest adventure I had as a teenager growing up was working on my uncle's ranch in Colorado. So to me, flying was not every-thing, but I did get turned on by it.

Recruiters from the U.S. Army and the navy came to our high school in the spring of 1943 to talk to the boys in the senior class. They were looking for volunteers for aviation cadet training. About a third of the boys in the class volunteered, including a major share of the senior football players. The majority opted for the army aviation cadet program. I did too, but I was not old enough. You had to be 18. I was only 16 and would not turn 17 until just before graduation.

The navy, on the other hand, was willing to sign me up, so I joined the naval aviation cadet training program. At that time, they had a program designated as the V-5 program for aviation cadets, which involved one year of college before entering formal flight training. It was really a good deal for a youngster who wanted to fly. I went to Detroit to take my physical and I passed with flying colors even though I was kind of a runt at that time. Surprisingly, a number of the football players flunked their physicals.

I received orders to report for duty the following February. I had 7 months after graduation before I had to report, so I went to work on my uncle's ranch in Colorado. I really had a ball working on the ranch because we went hunting and fishing whenever we got the urge. I would love to have stayed there and worked as a cowboy, but the war would not wait. Instead of growing spurs, I was to grow wings.

I spent my first year in the navy at Milligan College in eastern Tennessee, cramming two years of college into one year of classes. Eastern Tennessee was beautiful, but racial segregation and hillbillies were a real shock to us midwesterners. I will never forget those hillpeople walking down from the hills in single file with the man in front and then the woman and all the kids following her. The man was usually carrying a rifle, and the woman was carrying a baby and chewing tobacco—a page out of the past.

I was finally transferred to preflight school at Chapel Hill, North Carolina in March 1945. Preflight school was normally a 3-month school, but the war seemed to be winding down, so they extended our preflight training to 6 months. The war ended just as I graduated from preflight school in September of 1945. Every cadet was given the opportunity to get out of the navy at that time and I decided to get out, along with 95 percent of the other cadets.

Separation processing was, however, painfully slow. After waiting two weeks to be processed, I changed my mind and decided to finish my flight training. I was immediately transferred to primary training at Norman, Oklahoma. At Norman, I learned to fly in Stearman biplanes. The navy designation for the Stearman was N2S. I will never forget taking off and landing in echelon, with a hundred other Stearmans on my wing, on those big square blacktop landing fields. The traffic congestion was unbelievable, and yet we had no midair collisions. God has to be protecting innocent fools.

I will also never forget how cold it was in those open cockpits during an Oklahoma winter. We prayed for a temperature inversion when we took off in the morning and if we encountered one, we stayed at altitude to keep from freezing to death. Even those bulky sheepskin flying suits would not keep a person warm.

From Norman, Oklahoma, I went to Corpus Christi, Texas, for instrument training. I flew SNJs, the navy version of the AT-6, at Cuddihy Field outside of Corpus Christi for 3 months, and was then transferred to Pensacola, Florida, for advanced training. My first training at Pensacola was in PBY flying boats. At that time, all cadets were given multiengine training in either PBYs or SNBs, the navy version of the C-45. I really enjoyed flying the PBY, although it was terribly slow and had enormous control forces. Maximum cruise speed, as I remember it, was 105 knots. In seaplanes, the real significant events are the takeoffs and the landings. Flying is just the boring interval between the takeoff and the landing. On takeoff, if we did not get the airplane up on the step, we could not get airborne. I watched PBYs ploughing through the water for miles trying to get airborne when the student had failed to yank the yoke back hard enough at the proper instant during the acceleration.

Landing techniques varied depending on the sea state. In calm weather with smooth glassy water, the pilot simply set up a rate of descent at a speed slightly above stall and flew the airplane into the water since he could not judge height. In rough seas, he stalled the airplane before he hit the water. The thing the pilot always feared in a landing was a bounce, because this could result in severe porpoising and structural failure if proper recovery procedures were not initiated immediately. My major impression from flying PBYs was that the water was hard and it was amazing how hard one of those airplanes could hit the water and still stay intact. They were fun to fly and taxi on the water, but the control forces were horrendous. Flying a PBY was like flying a seagoing ship. A throwback to the World War I navy.

From PBYs, I went to "Bloody Barin" Field for advanced training in SNJs. At Barin Field, we learned to fly formation, shoot gunnery, and drop bombs. This phase of training was the toughest in terms of the number of cadets washing out. The type of flying taught in this phase quickly separated the men from the boys. It also permanently separated out many of the marginal students. That is how "Bloody Barin" acquired its name.

From Barin Field, I was transferred to Saufley Field for carrier landing training. At Saufley, we learned to fly around the pattern for hours at speeds just 3 or 4 knots above stall. We also learned the rigid discipline associated with carrier landings, wherein you put your life in the hands of someone standing on the ground or on the ship—the LSO, or landing signal officer. When he signaled that we were going too fast, we slowed down regardless of what our airspeed indicator said or how close we were to stall.

Once the pilot was in the carrier landing pattern, he was under the LSO's command. The pilot's opinions or judgment were irrelevant. He obeyed the LSO's commands without the slightest hesitation. Carrier landing training must have been patterned after the same type of training given Custer's troopers or the cavalry in the Charge of the Light Brigade—totally rigid discipline. It worked though. That kind of training enabled a fledgling birdman to plant an airplane on what looked like a postage-stamp-size carrier deck that was bobbing around in the middle of an ocean.

The first carrier landing obviously was the toughest, but once the pilot was convinced that the LSO knew what he was doing the carrier landings became an exhilarating challenge. I successfully completed my carrier landing qualification by making six landings on the light carrier USS Saipan. Following an unusual side trip up the canal to Houston on the carrier, we returned to Pensacola to be commissioned as ensigns and presented our wings. After two and a half years of training I became a full-fledged navy pilot.

I spent three and a half more years in the navy, flying off carriers in the Pacific and later the Atlantic. I really enjoyed those years. I cannot think of a finer way for a young man to spend his early manhood, particularly as a bachelor. I made one major cruise around the world on a small jeep carrier and another to China and Japan on our air group's big carrier.

The round-the-world cruise involved a secret mission to photograph from the air the beaches around the entire Persian Gulf. I volunteered for this mission. We spent about a week completing the task because we had only nine airplanes. The cover for the mission involved ferrying a shipload of trainer aircraft to Turkey. Interspersed with the trainers on the ship were nine photographic aircraft that were subsequently used for the photo mission. Someone had a lot of foresight, since this mission took place in 1948. He must have known that area would eventually become a hot spot.

We were not very well received in the Arab world at that time. Israel had just been granted its sovereignty and Americans were blamed for giving the Jews Arab land. That trip to the Persian Gulf was like a trip back in time to the days of the "Arabian Nights." Slavery was still practiced in parts of that area. People were actually being sold. I spent some time ashore on Bahrain Island at the British airfield. It was a real education for an unsophisticated, young American. I was introduced to not only slavery but also child prostitution, totally veiled women, and thieves hanging by their thumbs or having their hands chopped off.

During our photographic missions, the aircrafts' guns were loaded in case we had to protect ourselves. We were issued .38 caliber revolvers and an ammunition belt in the event we had to crash land or ditch the aircraft. We were taught an Arabic phrase that we were to use in case we were captured by some Bedouin Arabs. The phrase theoretically was an Arabic plea for mercy that they had to honor for 24 hours. They, in effect, had to give us a 24-hour-head start.

The pilots quickly realized this was not much of a deal, since we would be wandering around on foot in the desert in a strange land and our pursuers would be on camels or horseback and very familiar with the territory. Well, it sounded good anyway.

Apparently at that time, there were many Bedouin tribesmen wandering the deserts who lived by their own laws and were generally very inhospitable. I also noticed from the air that the Persian Gulf had some of the biggest sharks that I have ever seen. They looked like miniature submarines from the air. I sure did not want to ditch in those waters. Neither land nor water seemed hospitable.

On my cruise to China and Japan in 1948, I was a participant in the navy's evacuation of Americans from Tsingtao, China just before the communist Chinese takeover. Our carrier was part of a task group of two carriers, several cruisers, and numerous destroyers that were providing cover for a safe withdrawal of Americans from China. We spent a couple of months conducting exercises offshore to demonstrate our firepower. We did get to spend time ashore and again I was introduced to an unbelievably strange and cruel world. Many people were dying in that communist takeover. We could watch the battle through the big binoculars on the bridge of the carrier.

Three other pilots and I almost took a last ride in rickshaws one night without understanding what was happening. Unbeknownst to us, the Chinese pulling the rickshaws were taking us into communist territory in the city apparently to rob us and kill us. The U.S. Navy Shore Patrol rescued us in some very dark alleyways of Tsingtao. The shore patrol leader told us later that we were headed to our own execution. We were pretty young and innocent.

One incident that really made an impression on me was a search off Guam for five of our aircraft that apparently got lost and went down during a gunnery training flight. We were flying our aircraft off the NAS Orote Field at the time. The missing aircraft were never heard from after takeoff in the morning. The next day, we launched a massive aerial search with about fifty aircraft assigned to various search sectors all around the island.

I was outbound in my search sector, about 50 miles offshore, when my crewman in my TBM spotted orange smoke in the ocean behind the aircraft. I turned around and flew back a couple of miles and saw the smoke and some dyemarker. It turned out to be one of the downed pilots. I notified the control tower on Guam and they in turn notified a destroyer in the general area.

We tossed out our emergency life raft, but the downed pilot did not find it. I circled the pilot for an hour or so until the destroyer got there. We did not have rescue helicopters in those days. I was really amazed at the difficulty in keeping the pilot in sight. He was floating in a life jacket but it was startling to realize how small he was in that vast ocean. The sea was choppy with 3- or 4-foot waves and I would lose sight of the pilot every once in a while. I was terrified that I would lose sight of him and not find him again. I finally unbuckled my own life raft, made a pass over him, and tossed it out to him. He did not find it in that choppy sea, but finally the destroyer arrived and picked him up.

That episode really impressed me. I had flown many, many hours and thousands of miles over the oceans in a single engine airplane, never really worried too much about having to ditch because I always believed I would be found and rescued. I always thought I would be easy to find even though I might be in a life vest. It was, therefore, a tremendous shock to see just how small a person in a life jacket really is in that huge ocean. The Lord was with that downed pilot whom I found. We never found the others and had to give up the search due to a typhoon that came through the next day. That was another shock, to realize that the navy would give up on a search. I had naively assumed that they would never give up as long as there was a chance that the pilots were still alive.

During my 3 years in the fleet, I was a torpedo bomber pilot and finally a fighter pilot. I flew TBMs and the F8F Bearcats. The Bearcat was the most impressive aircraft that I have ever flown. It was a small airplane and an outstanding performer for its day. When I flew that airplane, I really felt that it was a part of me. I was wearing the airplane instead of sitting in it. The cockpit was very small. My shoulders rubbed both canopy rails but the small cockpit gave me a very secure feeling. The airplane was literally wrapped around me. That airplane responded like no other airplane I have ever flown. It was a fighter pilot's dream.

I flew the P-51 Mustang when I first began flying for NACA/NASA. I was very disappointed with this plane after all the stories I had heard about it. To me, it was just a fast AT-6. The cockpits were very similar. It did not begin to compare to the Bearcat in my opinion. I hassled with a few P-51s while flying the Bearcat. I could wax them pretty easily. The only advantage they seemed to have was a speed advantage in a dive. They could pull away pretty fast. But when they finally had to pull up, we had them again.

I was released from active duty in the navy while on a cruise to Cuba and Haiti in the fall of 1949. The Secretary of Defense decided to get rid of all reservists on active duty to save money. Ironically, the Korean War started less than 8 months later and the navy then tried to get these same people to return to active duty. I was processed out of the navy at Jacksonville, Florida, and immediately set out by car for Seattle, Washington.

I chose to go to Seattle for several reasons. My wife Therese had been raised there and her family still lived there. Seattle also had a large university where I could finish college, and finally, it had a naval air station where I could continue to fly in the reserve. I had met my wife in San Diego after the round-the-world cruise. I had dated her for the next year, in between cruises and a transfer to the East Coast, and finally married her in June 1949. I drove from my station at Cecil Field, Florida, to Seattle, Washington, to get married and then back to Florida on my honeymoon, all in a 10-day period.

A week after we got back to Florida, the navy decided to evacuate our squadron aircraft because of an approaching hurricane. I had to leave my new bride in a strange apartment to weather out the hurricane by herself. She had never previously been exposed to any violent weather. She had never even been exposed to a real thunderstorm. When the hurricane hit, she was terrorized by the wind, thunder, and lightning. She spent a day and a night in a closet. Meanwhile, we brave pilots were sitting in a bar in the officer's club in Atlanta, Georgia, waiting out the storm. My wife never let me live that down.

I attended the University of Washington under the GI bill. I lived in the veterans' housing on the campus and paid $40.00 a month for the rent out of my $120.00 GI monthly allotment. Before I graduated, my first three children were born. All of the veteran students were having children while attending school. The veterans' housing area resembled a gigantic nursery school. Everyone was poor, but spirits were high. Scott Crossfield, who also lived in the same housing unit, managed to build an airplane among the baby cribs and diapers in his veteran's housing unit. In Seattle, you hung the diapers inside.

I usually had a part-time job while attending school to make enough extra money to survive. Between that and the money I made flying in the reserve, we managed to exist and even pay the doctor and hospital bills for each new child. Kids were cheap in those days. The doctor charged $125.00 and the hospital charged $150.00. The part-time job and the weekend flying in the reserve did take its toll. I seldom finished my homework before two or three in the morning. Engineering is notorious for the amount of homework required. The University of Washington was on the quarter system when I attended, so we had quite a few long breaks throughout the school year. On each of these quarter breaks, I would try to schedule a ferry flight so that I could go on active duty and get paid for the week or two that I was not attending classes.

Ferry flights were a real godsend. I would draw full pay for each day that I was on the road. I always managed to make the trip last as long as the break period from school in order to get paid the most money. If necessary, I could manage to spend a week ferrying an airplane from Seattle down to San Francisco. On other trips, when I was in a hurry I could fly an airplane from Seattle to the East Coast and back in three days. That was pretty good time in those old propeller fighters.

During summer vacations, I had to work full time to replenish the bank account. I got involved in forest spraying and crop dusting through one of the members of my reserve squadron. My first experience was spraying forests in Oregon to combat the spruce budworm. The first year I flew a BT-13 trainer aircraft, with 1,000 pounds of DDT spray on board, over some rugged forest south of Hepner, Oregon. Forest spraying in those early days was fairly hazardous. The first year of forest spraying in Oregon, eight out of sixteen pilots were killed. The second and third years, the statistics improved somewhat. We only lost eleven out of thirty-five pilots the second year and eight out of thirty the third year.

In my second year, I flew a navy SBD dive bomber with 6,000 pounds of spray on board—very overloaded. Forest spraying was a very unforgiving job. We were flying overloaded single engine airplanes within 100 feet of the treetops, up and down the mountains and into the canyons. If the engine sputtered, that was it. Those big forests just swallowed an airplane. You could not even tell from the air where the airplane went through the trees in a crash. The airplane did not cut up the trees, the trees cut up the airplane. Forest spraying normally lasted only a month, so we had time to do a little crop dusting for another couple of months before the fall quarter started. My first experience as a crop duster was in Mexico. I dusted cotton below the border, south of Mexicali. I really enjoyed crop dusting. One could certainly get his fill of buzzing as a crop duster. I got pretty good at it, too. I could roll the wheels on the tops of the cotton plants and come home with cotton bolls caught on the brake lines. Crop dusting has to be one of the most dangerous kinds of work that I have ever done. The chemicals that we were using in those days were the major hazard since they were unbelievably dangerous. Some of the insecticides were derivatives of poisonous gases that the Germans had developed during World War II.

We breathed and literally ate the stuff and must have developed an immunity to the various poisons, because the insecticides often killed more than they were intended to. We quite often killed livestock when the spray or dust drifted onto pastureland. The unknowing Mexican laborers who helped us load the dust and spray into the airplanes got mighty sick after being exposed to clouds of that dust during a 16-hour work day. They seldom made it back to work the second day. If they survived the second day, they built up an immunity and then they could breathe it with the best of the duster pilots.

One insecticide, Systox, was so potent we had to carry little pills along when we sprayed it. If we started to feel dizzy or if we started losing our vision we had to swallow a couple of pills. That would keep us conscious until we got the airplane on the ground. Just imagine what the Occupational Safety and Health Administration would think of that operation. I must admit, it was an awfully loose operation with few state or federal controls.

The other dangerous part of crop dusting was the danger of hitting something, like power lines, trees, telephone poles, irrigation plumbing, fences, buildings, or the ground. I had never had an accident before I began crop dusting. In two short summer seasons of crop dusting, I had two forced landings due to engine failure, one bad crash due to engine failure during takeoff over a big irrigation canal, two collisions with power lines in the early morning darkness, one collision with the ground due to a stall during pullout from a descent over a row of immense cottonwoods, and numerous inadvertent touchdowns due to being sucked into the cotton when rolling the wheels across the tops of the plants. Thank God for the indestructible landing gear on those Stearmans.

Prior to dusting or spraying, we flew around a field a time or two as we mentally cataloged all of the potentially hazardous obstacles. We tried very hard to remember them as we worked our way across the field on each succeeding pass. Invariably, though, we would forget and then all of a sudden we would be on a collision course with something that could kill us. God did not intend for airplanes to be flown down among the trees, power lines, fences, buildings, and poles. Why, then, are pilots so damn dumb?

As I mentioned earlier, I did get pretty good at crop dusting. The guy I worked for used to drive out and watch me dust a field. He was really impressed by the maneuvering involved. I have watched other duster pilots work. It is impressive, particularly when they are working a small field with trees and power lines around the edges. Under those conditions, dusting becomes an aerial ballet.

I encountered some hilarious situations crop dusting. One morning, I dusted a Mexican farmer's field about 70 miles below the border at Mexicali. When I finished at about nine in the morning, no one was there to pick me up and fly me back to Calexico where I was living while working as a duster pilot. The farmer invited me to his house and I was served an excellent breakfast.

We sat around for an hour or so waiting for my ride to show up but no one came. The farmer suggested that we go into town and have a beer. It sounded good to me, so away we went.

The town was a small one. I do not even remember its name. We pulled up and parked in front of the biggest building in town, a large two story building that looked like a hotel. I found out, once we were inside, that it was the town whorehouse. It had a huge barroom and surprisingly, there were quite a few customers in the place even though it was only 10:30 A.M. We drank beer for about 3 hours, during which time the farmer was trying to convince me that I should sample the merchandise. I begged off by telling him I did not have any money with me. He countered by offering to loan me some money. I was spared at the last minute when someone ran in the bar and said an airplane had landed on the street just outside the building. It was my boss coming to pick me up. He griped about all the trouble he had finding me, but I was too loaded and too tired to care. I did thank him for saving me, however.

While dusting in Mexico near the border, I used to fly down from the border each morning just as soon as it was light enough to see. I usually flew low because I still enjoyed buzzing. In fact I would have to pull up to go over single-story houses. One morning, I pulled up over a house and I saw a pretty young lady taking a bath in the irrigation ditch next to her house. She was naked. For the next few days, I made sure to sneak up on that house hoping to catch her bathing again. I did not catch her bathing, but on the fifth day I pulled up over the house and then shoved the nose of the airplane down to check the ditch and got a real surprise. I was looking down the twin barrels of a shotgun. The man behind the gun fired both barrels and I just about had a heart attack. I do not know if he was mad because I was an aerial peeping Tom or because I was waking him up so early with that daybreak buzz job. The airplane was riddled with buckshot holes, but he did not hit anything critical. I avoided that farm-house for the rest of the dusting season.

They played some other unusual games down there below the border. Quite often the farmhands would wave and beckon us as we were flying over. They suckered me in a couple of times. I would respond to their waving and beckoning by giving them a buzz job. That is what they wanted, but just as I was about to pass over them, they would all heave a big rock at the airplane. A big rock like that could tear right through the airplane. Luckily they never hit a vital spot. When they pulled a stunt like that, I would come back around and pull straight up over them and dump a load of whatever insecticide I had onboard. The insecticide would make a large cloud on the ground when I pumped it down on them like that. The farmhands had to do a lot of running to get to clear air—a funny but dangerous game for everyone involved. Under the right circumstances, that insecticide could be just as deadly as the rocks.

Every once in a while on the way back to the border, I would take the main highway that ran southeast from Mexicali. When I said I would take the main highway back to the border, I meant it. I would fly a couple of feet above the road all the way, forcing all the oncoming traffic to pull off the road. I was eyeball to eyeball with a lot of cars and trucks before they realized I was not going to give way. Those that waited too long to pull over ended up in the ditch, because they had to turn hard to avoid the aircraft. One could get away with that kind of flying below the border in those days. No one enforced any flight rules or regulations. It was paradise for a pilot who liked to buzz.

I had another experience crop dusting that was funny as I look back on it. At the time, it was not quite as funny. I had been dusting cotton down in Mexico this particular morning for about two hours. I was running low on fuel, so I pulled up to the fuel barrel that was sitting at the end of the small dirt strip that we were using as a runway. I shut the engine down and then climbed up on the fuselage to open the tank cap to prepare to refuel. My boss was there to help me refuel. We had a hand pump for pumping the fuel from the barrel into the airplane. My boss stuck the pump in the barrel and then handed me the hose to insert in my fuel tank.

When fuel is stored in barrels out in the field, it tends to collect water because of the heating and cooling cycles that it is subjected to each day. This water collects in the bottom of the barrel. To ensure that we did not pump this water into the tank, we did not allow the feed pipe to touch the bottom of the barrel. For some reason, my boss forgot to raise the feed pipe off the bottom this time. I did not find this out until much later.

After the airplane was refueled, we loaded it up with insecticide and then started the engine. I took off and flew over to the next field to begin dusting it. It was a relatively small field, about 40 acres, with power lines on all sides. I came in over the power lines on my first approach and then pushed over to get down on the cotton. I flew along spreading the dust until I got to the power lines at the other edge of the field. I pulled up to go over them and the engine quit. I mean it flat quit. It did not sputter or taper off in power. It just plain quit. My speed carried me up and over the power line, but then I had to dump the nose to prevent the airplane from stalling.

Ahead of me was another cotton field with mature cotton standing 4 to 5 feet high. There were irrigation ditches running through the cotton with mounds of dirt piled up a couple of feet high along the sides of each ditch. I knew if I landed in that field, the airplane was going to go right over on its back, but I had no other choice. All I could do was try to make a soft landing. The airplane descended into that cotton and all of a sudden everything turned green. The prop was still windmilling and chewing cotton up and throwing it over the airplane like confetti. After a couple of tremendous jolts, the airplane stopped. I could not see a thing because of the flying cotton leaves, stalks, bolls, and tremendous dust clouds. I did not know if I was right side up or not, so I just sat there. I did not move, because once before in a similar incident I had un-buckled my seat belt in a panic and had fallen out of the airplane.

The dust and cotton leaves finally settled and I found that I was still sitting upright out in the middle of the field. I assume the reason I had not flipped over was that I had a full load of dust that helped to counteract any overturn tendency. I noticed as I sat there that the prop was still turning. I moved the throttle and the engine responded. The son of a bitch was running again, just as though nothing had ever happened.

Apparently, the engine had quit due to a big slug of water, but then it started up again as the engine continued to turn over due to the windmilling prop. I could not believe it. I finally shut the engine down, since there was not much I could do. I could not taxi because the airplane was stuck in the soft dirt.

The farmer who owned that field came out and began raising hell. I had destroyed about 2 acres of prime cotton during that landing. He wanted someone to pay for it. My boss finally showed up and we began worrying about how to get that airplane out of there. We finally worked out a deal with the farmer to have him tow it out with his tractor. He had to take down part of his fence to get the airplane out on the road alongside his property. We proposed to fly it off the road. The problem was that the road was extremely narrow and the wings would not clear the fenceposts on either side of the road, so we had to pay him to take down another 500 feet of fence for clearance on takeoff. That little slug of water out of the fuel barrel cost us a bundle of money.

Before takeoff, we checked the airplane to make sure that it was safe to fly. We discovered that one of the engine mount bolts had broken during the landing. We did not have a spare, so my boss decided to use baling wire to attach the engine mount to the firewall. You would think a guy would learn after being bitten once. My boss had already caused me to crash before and now he was using baling wire to replace an engine mount bolt. I should have let him fly the airplane out of there. I was too naive and trusting, though. I climbed in the airplane and started the engine while my boss propped it. I got airborne without hitting anything and then climbed up to begin the flight back up to the American border about 50 miles away. We wanted to take the plane back there to thoroughly inspect and repair it.

I climbed up to 1,000 feet to have some maneuvering room just in case the engine quit again. We really did not know for sure why the engine had quit. We strongly suspected water in the gas, but we could not prove it. So just to be sure, I gave myself a little maneuvering altitude in case the problem was of a different nature.

As the flight progressed, I began thinking about that baling wire holding the engine on. I began worrying that the wire might break and the engine might fall off. If that happened, the airplane would quickly tumble out of control and crash. I decided the best thing to do to cope with that problem was to fly low, so that I might get the airplane on the ground quickly if the engine started to vibrate loose. So I descended to 50 feet and proceeded on toward the border. I was really congratulating myself on solving that potential problem when I began to start thinking again about the possibility of the engine quitting. Mentally, I began thinking that the engine seemed to be running rougher than normal.

After 5 or 10 minutes thinking about that possibility, I decided to climb back up to 1,000 feet to get some maneuvering room. For the next half hour, I alternated from flying at 1,000 feet to flying at 50 feet for 5- or 10-minute periods or until one fear would overcome the other. I made it back to the border. After I landed, one of the mechanics wanted to know why I came in on the approach under the power lines on the end of the field. I did not answer him. It was too complicated to explain simply. He would not have understood.

I spent the next summer crop dusting in the Yuma, Arizona, area. The thing I remember about that area was the tremendous cottonwood trees bordering many of the cotton fields. Getting in and out of those fields with a duster was spectacular, to say the least, especially if it were a small field. I was almost doing hammerhead maneuvers at the end of each run.

After graduation from college, I went to work full time and never had the opportunity to do any more forest spraying or crop dusting. In some ways I missed the excitement of dusting. In other ways, I felt lucky to have survived. It was definitely the most dangerous type of flying that I have ever done.

My first job after graduation was with the Boeing Airplane Company in Seattle, as I mentioned earlier. I then moved on to California to work for the NACA. In 1958, shortly after the NACA became NASA, an educational program was developed to bring the aeronautics community to the edge of space. A group of noted space experts toured each of the NACA facilities and lectured the employees about the state of knowledge in astronautics. These experts included such celebrities as Wernher von Braun, Willy Ley, Kraft Ehricke, and Clyde Tombaugh.

These experts explained the fundamentals of space flight, such as how to get into orbit initially and to transfer from earth orbit to an earth-moon orbit or a solar orbit or an escape orbit. They explained celestial mechanics, celestial navigation, the makeup of the solar system, the characteristics of the moon and the other planets. The German experts discussed rocket boosters and trips to the moon and Mars.

This was in 1958, and yet they had already calculated the thrust and weight of the required launch vehicles and had planned the trips in detail down to the number of hours it would take to get to the moon and Mars and back. The other experts told us what to expect when you did get to the moon or one of the other planets: the strength of the gravity field, the surface temperature, the kind of atmosphere, the diameter and depth of the various craters visible to the astronomer, estimates of the nature of the surface material, and the probabilities of finding any life.

To us earthbound engineers, this was heady stuff. It was fascinating. It was almost unbelievable. We all knew there were planets, stars, and galaxies out there in space, but we did not realize how much was known about them or that we could actually travel to them using technology that was currently almost in hand. These experts talked as though we were going to make the trip the next day. They were only waiting for the mundane things to get done, such as actually building the already designed rocket launch vehicles. My God, here we were struggling to get beyond Mach 3 with an airplane and these guys were talking about accelerating to escape velocities of 36,000 fps to go to the moon and the planets.

I was never so fascinated in my entire life. I wanted to follow them back to the launch port. I wanted to travel with them to see the wondrous things they had described. I wanted to be a part of the team that opened the door to space. I did eventually apply for a job as an astronaut on the Apollo program, but by that time I was over the age limit. I finally managed to get a peek into space during my altitude flights in the X-15. It was beautiful—just like they described it.

I had an earlier opportunity to apply as a candidate for the original Mercury program, but I turned it down. Our director at the time, Walt Williams, asked both Neil Armstrong and me if we would like to apply. He said he would recommend us if we did. He advised us, however, not to apply since he said the Mercury astronauts would not be flying as test pilots, but rather as biological specimens in an automatically controlled spacecraft. He convinced us that we would not be happy simply riding in a can. He felt our future was much brighter in the X-15 program. He later left to become director of flight operations for the Mercury program. When he left Dryden to join the space program, he convinced a number of engineers to go with him. He also called on a number of Dryden people as consultants to the space program. I was asked to serve as a consultant in the area of piloting and human factors.

On my first trip back to Langley to participate in a meeting of human factors experts, Walt Williams introduced me to the Mercury astronauts. His introduction was, "Now, here is a real test pilot." Walt was fiercely proud of the NACA, its personnel, and its pilots. It took me a long time to live that introduction down, but I soon became pretty good friends with most of the astronauts. I crossed paths with them many times during my assignment to the Dyna-Soar program and while flying the Rogallo Wing Parasev. I eventually checked Gus Grissom out in that vehicle.

Part of the Parasev checkout involved some instruction in sailplanes. I took Gus up to Tehachapi, where I rented a sailplane and made several flights with Gus to demonstrate towing operations and power off landings. On the way home, we stopped at an old bar in Mojave to have a couple of beers. The bar was owned by one of our former crew chiefs who had recently retired. We were warmly received and, in fact, quickly became the center of attraction when I introduced Gus as one of the Mercury astronauts.

From then on, we could not buy a drink. We also could not keep up with all the extra drinks that were thrust upon us. Every old desert rat, rancher, and prospector in the place bought us a shot of whiskey to go with our mug of beer. We finally had to sneak out after two or three hours of that kind of hospitality. We each had ten to twelve shots of whiskey sitting on the bar in front of us when we left.

That was a strange encounter—those grizzled old prospectors and desert rats drinking with an astronaut. The east meets the west. The old meets the new. The people are similar in some respects, but they are traveling at infinitely different speeds—one leading a burro through the desert and the other orbiting the earth in a spacecraft.

I sure hated to see Gus go the way he did. Gus died in a catastrophic fire in the Apollo capsule during a practice session for the first manned Apollo mission. He was one of my favorite astronauts. Wally Shirra was another favorite. He and I liked the same jokes.

My first research program as a pilot was a program to investigate the feasibility of obtaining substantial amounts of laminar flow on an airfoil at supersonic speeds. The testbed aircraft was an F-104. One wing had been covered with a fiberglass glove which served as the test section for the experiment.

The test flights were rather straightforward, involving a climbout to 35,000 feet heading eastbound out of Edwards. We continued eastbound until we reached the Colorado River at which time we reversed course and entered the Edwards supersonic corridor and then started accelerating back toward Edwards. The test condition desired was Mach 2 at the maximum altitude possible. On good days, we could maintain Mach 2 up to 60,000 feet. We would hold the maximum test condition until the low-fuel light came on and then, pull the throttle off and head for Edwards. During these research flights we were lucky to get 20 minutes of flight time. I flew over 100 research flights in the F-104 during that program and only logged 30 hours of flight time. Not a very good way to accumulate flight time.

My second research program was the ALSOR program. That was a fun program. It is not often that you can do acrobatics as part of a test program. That program was ultimately cancelled due to problems in deploying the balloon and tracking it. The objective of the program was worthwhile, but the effort required to achieve that objective was considered to be excessive. We had to resort to other sources for our atmospheric data during the X-15 program.

My next program was the Dyna-Soar program. The proposed X-20 Dyna-Soar was a small delta wing aircraft that was to be boosted into orbit and then flown back from orbit by a pilot/astronaut similar to the way the shuttle is flown back from space. The difference being that Dyna-Soar was to fly back from space in the mid-1960s rather than the early 1980s.

Dyna-Soar was well ahead of its time. At that time, no one was seriously interested in an operational vehicle similar to Dyna-Soar. In fact, no one was even serious about an operational vehicle with capabilities comparable to the X-15. Both vehicles were simply research aircraft to explore a new flight regime. We still do not have an operational Mach 6 aircraft 25 years after the X-15 achieved hypersonic speeds.

The Dyna-Soar started life as a follow-on to the X-15. It was to be a research aircraft launched on a booster rocket to explore the high hypersonic speed region. The goal was to reach speeds of Mach 16 to Mach 18. The flights were intended to be suborbital flights launched out of Cape Canaveral and recovered at one of the islands down range from the cape. The initial booster was to be the Titan I, a hypergolic fuel booster that could accelerate the proposed aircraft to the desired speeds. During the design, the weight of the X-20 increased and in order to still achieve the desired speeds, the booster had to be upgraded. We switched to the Titan II rocket, a more powerful booster. The Dyna-Soar ultimately ended up on the Titan III rocket which had the ability to boost the Dyna-Soar into orbit.

This major reorientation of the program was driven by several factors. One was the desire by the air force to compete with NASA's Project Mercury for public attention. Project Mercury and its astronauts were being glorified by the media. Dyna-Soar was being ignored. A more compelling reason for orbiting the Dyna-Soar was to sell the Titan III booster.

The air force desperately wanted a more powerful booster for classified satellite payloads and the Dyna-Soar program offered an opportunity to market the capabilities of such a booster. The marketing strategy was a success. The air force gained approval for development of the Titan III, but then lost interest in Dyna-Soar. This loss of interest involved some life and death struggles within the USAF over control of orbital spacecraft. The aeronautical part of the air force conceived and developed the Dyna-Soar, but the space side of the air force owned and operated the boosters and also believed that any space missions must be under their control. The space side of the air force won the battle by selling the Titan III booster, cancelling the X-20 Dyna-Soar, and initiating its own manned space program, the Manned Orbital Laboratory (MOL program). It is such a pity that the Dyna-Soar program, a good sound research program, fell victim to political infighting in the USAF with an assist from Robert McNamara's Department of Defense. The Dyna-Soar could have opened up space to routine operations 15 years before the shuttle. Surprisingly, however, the USAF was not seriously interested in manned space operations. They were quite happy with their unmanned satellites and still have not developed a manned space operation 25 years later.

I was assigned to the Dyna-Soar program in 1959 as a pilot-consultant. In all, seven pilots were assigned as pilot-consultants: from NASA, Neil Armstrong, Bill Dana, and I; from the Air Force Flight Test Center, Jim Wood, Russ Rogers, Hank Gordon, and Pete Knight. For the next 2 1/2 or 3 years, we had three pilots at Boeing in Seattle at all times. The AFFTC and NASA pilots rotated on a monthly basis with Jim Wood, the chief consultant pilot being permanently assigned at Boeing.

I spent every third month in Seattle participating in the design process and flying the Dyna-Soar simulator for hours and hours on second and third shift while I developed entry control techniques. We flew boost simulations at Martin-Baltimore to demonstrate that we could manually fly the Titan booster into orbit with the Dyna-Soar vehicle on top. This was a very controversial issue. The booster designers had been using automatic control and guidance systems from day one. In their minds that was the only way to go.

I attended a talk that Wernher von Braun gave to the young Society of Experimental Test Pilots in 1959. At that talk, the subject of pilot control of the manned spacecraft boosters came up. Wernher said that the pilots should not worry about flying the booster. He said his booster designers could put a spacecraft into orbit much better than any pilot. This precipitated a heated argument with the audience of macho test pilots, but Wehrner ultimately won out. To this day, all manned space flights have been automatically controlled during boost.

The Dyna-Soar pilots spent weeks at Johnsville on the centrifuge verifying that we could manually fly the booster under the g loads involved during acceleration into orbit. We traveled extensively to each of the subcontractors to participate in their design process. We were fitted with newly designed pressure suits, and were invited to observe a launch of a Titan booster similar to the one that would boost Dyna-Soar into orbit. We were the USAF's version of the Mercury astronauts. The USAF would have really eclipsed the Mercury program if it had flown Dyna-Soar, but DOD made the decision to cancel the program in 1963.

What a crime. What shortsightedness. I believe Neil Armstrong sensed that Dyna-Soar was going to be cancelled. He applied for a position as a NASA astronaut before Dyna-Soar was cancelled and was selected as a member of the second group in 1962. I was simultaneously named as the only NASA Dyna-Soar pilot out of a total of six Dyna-Soar pilots. Al Crews, another USAF pilot, replaced Bill Dana as a Dyna-Soar pilot. When Dyna-Soar was cancelled, Al Crews was assigned as the chief MOL pilot. He later transferred to NASA as an astronaut when MOL was cancelled, but he finally gave up waiting to fly into space and transferred out of the astronaut office into the flight operations division so he could at least fly airplanes. He is the only man I know who was named an astronaut on three different programs, Dyna-Soar, MOL, and Apollo. He waited over 15 years for a space flight and finally decided that it was not meant to be.

As a result of my participation in Dyna-Soar, I had the distinction of being one of the world's first unemployed astronauts. For some reason I was not able to draw unemployment compensation.

During my participation in the Dyna-Soar program, I happened to attend a briefing by Francis Rogallo on his Rogallo Parawing. He proposed that for one of its many possible uses, it could be used as an alternative to a parachute for recovery of space capsules, such as the Gemini capsule. I was quite impressed with his proposal and talked to Paul Bikle, our director after Williams left, about building one and flying it in a low-key program using part-time personnel. Bikle was not interested since we were by this time heavily committed to the X-15. I then talked to Neil Armstrong about building one at home and he expressed an interest in working with me.

We came up with a design and then began scrounging around for parts with which to build it. Bikle heard about our efforts and finally decided to approve an official effort to build a flight vehicle. I think he did this to prevent Neil and me from killing ourselves with our own marginal design. The vehicle was built in Dryden's shops using simple light aircraft construction techniques. We tried constructing our own cloth membrane for the wing, but finally contracted a sailmaker to fabricate one. We began flying the vehicle while towing it behind one of our utility trucks. We towed it up and down the taxiway between our facility and the tower for several weeks while I learned to fly it. Finally, we towed it up to 5,000 feet altitude with a Piper Supercub and I made the first free flight of a Rogallo hang glider in March 1962.

That first vehicle had a lot of problems. It was severely damaged during the checkout of another pilot shortly after its first flight. We encountered numerous problems developing a good flightworthy vehicle, including several spectacular crashes, but we finally constructed one that was successfully flown by a number of different pilots, including Neil Armstrong and Gus Grissom.

Our early efforts with the Rogallo wing demonstrated that it could indeed be flown and controlled by a pilot. We were not, however, convinced that a practical system could be developed to recover the Gemini capsule. The Gemini system would utilize an inflatable wing, which was to be deployed and inflated after the Gemini capsule had slowed to subsonic speeds.

Efforts by North American Aviation to develop a prototype system for Gemini spacecraft demonstrated the many problems associated with this concept for spacecraft recovery. The program was finally cancelled and Gemini was recovered in the water just as Mercury was—using a conventional parachute.

My next interesting research program was the lifting body program. Lifting bodies were conceived as entry spacecraft that could fly during entry rather than plunge down into the atmosphere as the space capsules were designed to do. The lifting body concept was a spinoff of work being done in wind tunnels in the mid-1950s to develop stable, survivable missile nose cones.

The early wind tunnel work indicated that blunt nose cones survived the heat of entry much better than sharp aerodynamically shaped nose cones. As a result, the early nuclear warheads were all blunt shaped cones with rounded noses. The engineers testing these shapes in the wind tunnel noted that these shapes could develop lift if they were ballasted in a certain way and they could develop even more lift if the blunt cone was slightly altered to enable it to achieve trim conditions at a positive angle of attack. Additional tailoring of the basic cone shape could produce a configuration that could actually fly almost like an airplane, if the necessary stabilizing and control surfaces were added. Several lifting body configurations were developed in the NASA wind tunnels and these shapes were proposed as candidate shapes for the Mercury spacecraft.

The Mercury program selected a more conventional nose cone shape to minimize the testing required to finalize the design and expedite the development program. The lifting body concept languished in the archives in technical reports for several years until Dale Reed, one of our engineers, expressed an interest in building a manned flight vehicle. This renewed interest in lifting bodies surfaced shortly before the cancellation of Dyna-Soar. We were grasping at straws, trying to keep some momentum going in the concept of lifting entry. We believed that flying back from orbit was a much more dignified way than coming back in a capsule under a parachute and ending up in the ocean.

I became interested in the lifting body concept and worked with the engineer who was proposing the flight vehicle to help him sell the idea. We finally convinced Bikle to build a low-cost manned vehicle to determine whether it would fly. We built the internal structure, the landing gear, and the control system in-house. We contracted the hull construction out to a local sailplane builder.

The hull was constructed of plywood, using typical glider-sailplane construction techniques. The vehicle had no propulsion system, rather it was to be towed into the air and released for free flight in the same manner as were sailplanes. A suitable tow aircraft was readily available, our venerable C-47. We were not quite sure what to use for ground tow tests. I wanted to learn to fly the vehicle during ground tow, just a few feet off the ground, before we towed it to altitude with the C-47.

We needed a vehicle that could tow the lifting body to speeds in excess of 80 MPH and, preferably, one that could tow it to over 120 MPH. Minimum takeoff speed was calculated to be 80 MPH. We eventually realized that we would need a very high performance automobile as a tow vehicle to achieve the desired speeds. Rough calculations indicated that the tow vehicle would need an extra 150 horsepower at 120 MPH to overcome the drag of the lifting body at that speed. We settled on a Pontiac Bonneville convertible as the desired tow vehicle. We bought the biggest engine that they offered.

The U.S. government does not normally buy high performance convertibles, so we needed some manipulation of government procurement regulations. After purchase, the car was immediately delivered to a Los Angeles speed shop to be fitted with all the essential high-speed, heavy-duty racing components. Walter Whiteside drove the vehicle back to Edwards. Whiteside was the NASA employee who was to drive it during towing operations.

The NASA driver was careful to stay well within the speed limits but about halfway home a California Highway Patrol vehicle began to tail him. The CHP vehicle tailed him all the way into the Antelope Valley and then turned on the red lights to pull him over. The CHP officer's curiosity had finally convinced him to check out this high performance convertible with a roll bar and U.S. government license plates. I cannot say that the officer did not really believe the story that the NASA employee gave him in explanation, but the officer continued to follow him until he turned into Edwards Air Force Base.

We tried to fly the M2-F1 lifting body while being towed by the Pontiac in the spring of 1963. I managed to get the M2-F1 airborne a few feet above the lakebed, but the roll control was too sensitive to maintain a stable roll attitude. We quickly decided to forgo any further flight attempts and instead, put the vehicle in a large wind tunnel at the Ames Research Center. We spent about a week testing the vehicle in the 40-by-80-foot tunnel at speeds up to 120 MPH. That was a very interesting series of tests. I sat in the vehicle during the tests to position the controls and expedite the testing. On completion of the testing, we made some control system modifications and then again began our ground towing operations to get the vehicle airborne. This time, the vehicle appeared to be flyable.

For the next several months, we roared up and down the lakebed at speeds over 120 MPH, ten to twenty times a day. I evaluated the controllability, the handling qualities, and the visibility on and off the towline. We measured performance and added a small rocket motor to be used if we had a problem during the landing maneuver. Finally, I ran out of excuses and had to admit that we were ready to try a flight to altitude. Bikle had not informed headquarters that we were going to build the M2-F1. We built it in a curtained-off section of the hangar to minimize the visibility of the program. Bikle was concerned that headquarters might disapprove the project. By building it covertly, he avoided any confrontation until it was completed and ready to fly. He finally informed headquarters just prior to our first ground tow. He never did tell them about buying the Pontiac. It never became an issue. When he informed them that we were planning to make a flight to altitude, their response was, "Don't kill anyone."

The test team gathered out on the south lakebed with the M2-F1 before daybreak on the morning of the scheduled flight. The C-47 was flown to the south lake in preparation for the towing operation. After checking out both the C-47 and the M2-F1, the tow-line was hooked up and we began the takeoff. Just as I rotated the M2-F1 to takeoff attitude, the towline separated from the C-47 and I quickly slowed to a stop. It was quite fortunate that the towline separated prior to liftoff, because our analysis indicated that we had a dead-man zone during towed flight extending from the ground up to at least 500 feet. We could not dump the nose of the vehicle and gain enough airspeed to flare and land if a towline broke in that altitude band. The towline and hook on the C-47 were subsequently checked and found to be binding, which prevented the hook from fully locking in the closed position. Some quick modifications were made and we were ready to try again an hour later.

This time, the takeoff was successful. We climbed up to 7,000 feet while circling the north lakebed and I released as we crossed the north end of runway one-eight on the north lakebed. The vehicle flew surprisingly well and the landing was a piece of cake. The flight was very impressive to the observers on the ground due to the extremely steep flight path (approximately 30 degrees). The flight was a complete success. We flew the vehicle a week later for the news media and then checked out several more pilots including Chuck Yeager.

We continued to fly the vehicle for another year, gathering data on its flight characteristics. We achieved our primary objective much sooner. Shortly after the first flight we got NASA headquarters' approval to build two high-performance lifting bodies to investigate the transonic and supersonic characteristics of these unusual flying machines. I flew a number of other more mundane research programs in various other aircraft, but these were the fun ones.

Having this background, I joined the X-15 program. I should not have been too impressed with the X-15. After all, it could only fly 4,000 MPH. I had been routinely flying spacecraft simulators in and out of orbit at speeds up to 18,000 MPH. My attitude quickly changed on my first flight.

The X-15 was impressive. It had awesome power compared to conventional aircraft. It could accelerate at close to 4 g just prior to burnout, or about 90

MPH faster every second. It had such tremendous power that it could quickly tear itself apart after launch if it were not pointed uphill immediately. It was, without question, the most impressive aircraft that I have ever flown.

MY FIRST FLIGHT

My first flight in the X-15 was to be a major step up in performance compared to any previous aircraft that I had flown. However, it was a step down from the X-20 that I had been scheduled to fly. I did not get a chance to fly the X-20 but now at least I would fly the X-15.

On my first X-15 flight, I was scheduled to fly a rocket airplane to Mach 4.0 and then maneuver it in a glide to an honest-to-God unpowered landing. Prior to my first X-15 flight, I had never flown a rocket airplane. I had never flown faster than Mach 2 and I had never really made a deadstick landing in a high performance jet aircraft. I had made a deadstick landing in a T-33 after shutting the engine down due to a persistent overheat light, but I was over the lakebed when I shut the engine down, so it was a piece of cake. I had also made a couple of deadstick landings in crop dusting airplanes and some glide flights in our paraglider research vehicle and the lightweight M2-F1 lifting body, but all that deadstick landing experience was child's play compared to the upcoming X-15 landing. I was graduating to the big league.

An X-15 landing was the ultimate in deadstick landings. The X-15 came down steeper and faster than any other existing aircraft and it landed a lot faster. According to the experts at Edwards, if you could deadstick the X-15, you could deadstick anything.

When I saw the flight plan for my first flight, I quickly realized it was going to be a real challenge. I was going to be dropped from a B-52 bomber 130 miles away from Edwards and I was going to have to learn to fly that airplane well enough in 6 minutes to be able to make a successful deadstick landing. Once I was dropped from that B-52, there was no turning back. I was on my own. I was going to be on the ground one way or another in less than 10 minutes. I would either make a successful landing, come down in a parachute, or wind up in a smoking hole. I could be forced to land at the launch lake due to no engine light, or I could be forced to make an emergency landing at an intermediate lake. The best I could hope for was a successful unpowered landing back at Edwards.

Where I landed depended mainly on the engine, although failures in other systems could dictate a premature landing short of Edwards. If the engine failed to light or did not develop full thrust, I would land at the launch lake. If the engine lit and developed full thrust but shutdown before I had enough energy to get to Edwards, I would probably end up at one of the intermediate lakes.

I had to consider and plan for each of these possibilities. I personally prayed that the flight would go smoothly according to plan. I did not need an emergency on my first flight. I had more than enough to worry about. It's surprising how the mind works. A landing at the launch lake or an intermediate lake was considered to be an emergency, while a landing at Edwards was considered normal. Yet the landing was a deadstick landing in any case, so why was one considered an emergency and one considered normal?

To me, there was a tremendous difference psychologically. The big difference was that Edwards was home. It was where God intended man to land rocket airplanes. It was big (13 miles long by 4 miles wide). It had many different runways. It was hard. It had no obstructions on any of the many approach paths. It had all of the essential emergency equipment. It was territory that we were intimately familiar with and it had a lot of friendly people waiting there.

It was an ideal place to land unpowered airplanes. God, in his infinite wisdom, knew that someday man would fly rocket airplanes, so he fashioned an ideal site to land them, the Edwards dry lakebed. We had many other dry lakebeds available for use, but none were as good as Edwards. All were smaller. Some were softer, some were only wide enough for one runway, some had mountains obstructing the approaches, all had limited temporary emergency equipment, and none had any friendly people. All of the launch or intermediate lakebeds were miles from civilization and were only accessible by dirt roads. The only living creatures at these other lakebeds were lizards, sidewinders, coyotes, tortoises, and jackrabbits.

The launch lakes were usually good lakebeds with 3 to 4-mile runways, whereas, the intermediate lakes were usually smaller with runways as short as 2 miles. Some of the intermediate lakes were on plateaus and others were down in valleys with steep mountains surrounding them. A couple of them were so soft, we were reluctant to land the Gooney Bird on them. Before I launched on a flight, I always said a little prayer. "Please God, don't let the engine quit halfway. Let it quit early or let it quit late, but never at such a time that I'll have to go into an intermediate lake." That prayer worked every time except once.

In the early rocket airplanes, each new pilot was given a glide flight before a powered flight. This allowed the aircraft to be launched at an optimum location for an unpowered approach and landing. It also allowed the pilot to concentrate on one task, the unpowered landing. He did not have to worry about getting home to Edwards or about any rocket engine problems. The original X-15 pilots, after Scott Crossfield, did not get to make glide flights, but they did make low-speed flights around Edwards on their first flights using the interim XLR-11 engines. This again minimized the possible emergency situations.

To me, either of these approaches made a lot of sense. I would have preferred to separate the challenges into several flights, rather than combine them all in one. But, someone smarter than I decided that a powered flight to a moderate speed was a more benign flight than a glide flight or a low-speed flight around Edwards. What that smarter person did not realize was that the program had gained a lot of experience in over ninety flights before Joe Engle and I made our first flights. Program personnel considered a Mach 4.5 flight to be very benign and to them, it actually was. To me, it was more than twice as fast as I had ever flown before and the entire operation was a whole new world. These X-15 people were routinely flying out to hypersonic speeds and into space. They had their own language and their own drummer that they were marching to and I was going to be a part of that new world if I could make a successful first flight. I was really impressed, but I was also worried. Would I qualify?

I had about 3 months to prepare for my first flight. One of the first things I had to do was to be measured for a new pressure suit. The X-15 pressure suits were custom made for each pilot by the David Clark Company located in Worcester, Massachusetts. We had to make several trips to David Clark to be measured, fitted, and checked out in the suit. Once we got the suit, we could then be fitted into the X-15 cockpit.

The X-15 ejection seat was not adjustable. Consequently, each pilot had to have his personal seat pad, back pad, and armrest pad to position him properly in the ejection seat and the cockpit with respect to the windows, the various control levers and switches, and the side arm controller. We had to reach all of these controls and switches whether the suit was pressurized or unpressurized, so we had to check their accessibility both ways. It really was tough to reach some of the controls and switches when the suit was pressurized since mobility was significantly restricted. It was, however, interesting to note that the pilots did not complain about the lack of mobility when the suit occasionally pressurized in flight. Apparently, the abundance of adrenaline flowing during a flight allowed the pilot to easily overpower the resistance of the pressure suit. This same phenomenon was evident in a pilot's evaluation of control forces. On the ground, the pilots often complained that the control forces were too high. In flight, they seldom noticed the forces. You obviously can move mountains when you have to and occasionally during a flight a mountain might get in the way in the form of an emergency.

The aeromedical doctors measured various physiological measurements on the pilots during flight such as heart rate, blood pressure, and breathing rate. They were quite amazed to find that the pilot's heart rates peaked as high as 200 beats per minute during various portions of the flight. This was some of the first medical evidence of these seemingly excessive heart rates. These high heart rates did not really surprise the pilots. We needed that high heart rate to keep the old adrenaline flowing.

After being properly fitted into the cockpit, I spent many hours sitting there memorizing the location of all the controls, switches, circuit breakers, instruments, and escape system components. We learned to identify and actuate everything blindfolded. I spent many hours learning the details of the aircraft and its systems during classroom type presentations by the experts on each portion of the aircraft. I also listened to the experts on stability and control, performance, structures, flutter, aerodynamics, aerothermal heating, and energy management. I became an instant expert in all of these disciplines.

I averaged 2 or 3 hours a day in the simulator during the 2 months before my first flight, practicing the planned flight and practicing various emergency procedures. The planned flight was just over 6 minutes in duration, so I could practice it 10 times each hour. I estimated that I practiced that flight over 500 times before I flew it. I practiced every emergency condition that the flight planner could conceive. When I had finished my simulator training, I could predict the altitude, velocity, rate of climb, and dynamic pressure for each second of the flight.

During simulation, I was also exposed to all of the unique or unusual flying characteristics of the airplane. I learned about the poor lateral-directional characteristics of the aircraft at high angles of attack in the unaugmented control modes. I learned about all of the airplane's minor handling qualities faults and abnormal response traits. I became a handling qualities expert on hypersonic airplanes.

I spent the remainder of my time before my first flight practicing unpowered approaches and landings, or "hurling myself at the ground," as Bill Dana used to say when he described X-15 landing approaches. For 2 months, I flew an F-104 at every opportunity to practice approaches to the various lakebeds involved in my first flight. My launch lake was to be Hidden Hills, a long narrow lakebed just across the Nevada border. It was 130 nautical miles from Edwards.

Hidden Hills was about 3.5 miles long and about 1 mile wide. Because of this narrow shape, there was room for only one runway. The lake was in a valley between two ridges but the ridges didn't obstruct the approach path. All in all it was a good emergency lakebed.

My intermediate lakebeds were the Three Sisters Lakes and Cuddeback Lake. Two of the Three Sisters Lakes were large enough for X-15 runways but just barely. They were round lakes about 2 miles in diameter. They were about 60 miles from Edwards. No one really wanted to put the X-15 into Three Sisters. Cuddeback was a much better lakebed. It was long and narrow like Hidden Hills, about 3.5 by 1 mile. It also had only one runway oriented north and south. It was 35 miles from Edwards. The only obstacle near Cuddeback was a small mountain to the north that partially obstructed a right-hand pattern from the northwest.

A dirt road ran across the lakebed in an east-west direction from Randsburg mining town to a bombing range on the east side of the lakebed. This road was built up slightly above the level of the lakebed to make it usable when the lake was wet. Thus, the road reduced the usable lakebed to less than 3 miles by cutting off the northern portion of the lakebed. The bombing range to the east of the lakebed was heavily used by aircraft from George AFB. We had to restrict its use during X-15 flights to eliminate any potential traffic problems if we had to use the lake in an emergency. During our practice landings, however, we had to dodge traffic just like everyone else.

Typically on an X-15 practice flight, I would head uprange to the launch lake right after takeoff. By the time I got to the launch lake, I would have burned off enough fuel to allow me to make touch and go landings as soon as I arrived. At the launch lake, I would simulate two different type approaches, no engine light approaches and premature shutdown approaches. The no engine light approaches could get a little sticky because a pilot could lose quite a bit of altitude during the initial engine light attempt and the relight attempt. Only then could he turn toward the launch lake and begin the emergency landing checklist. He would therefore be low on altitude when he started his approach. A major concern in a no engine light situation was getting rid of all the propellant. By starting the jettison late, after the relight attempt, the pilot was marginal on getting it all out before landing.

The premature shutdown approaches were also occasionally dicey since the pilot had to get the airplane turned around and headed back to the launch lake. Depending on when the engine quit, he could get back to the launch lake with a lot of energy or he could get back with just enough to make a minimum energy approach. I would normally make two or three practice approaches at the launch lake varying my initial energy conditions and then head down range to the Three Sisters lakebeds. I would make a couple of approaches at Three Sisters from different directions and then head for Cuddeback. At Cuddeback, I would make a couple more approaches, and then climb out and accelerate toward Edwards to arrive with a lot of excess energy, usually supersonic above 45,000 feet. After making the initial high energy approach at Edwards, I would use up the remainder of my gas approaching from different initial energy conditions including some straight-in approaches.

We normally used the north-south runway on the northern portion of the Edwards lakebed. This runway was our prime runway and we normally landed heading south. Our alternate runway was zero-five, two-three also on the north lakebed. We used this one when we had high winds which were usually out of the southwest. All of the other Edwards lakebed runways were usable in case of unforeseen problems, but we very rarely used any other runway. Most of the Edwards lakebed runways were a minimum of 4 miles long and one runway was over 7 miles long. Now that is a REAL runway.

At Edwards, we normally made 360-degree overhead approaches into runway one-eight. High-key altitude was nominally 35,000 feet and low-key altitude was 18,000 to 20,000 feet. Airspeed in the pattern varied with each individual pilot, but usually ranged between 240 and 300 knots. We rolled out on final at about 8,000 to 10,000 feet, ideally at 300 knots in roughly an 18- to 20-degree glide angle. We maintained the steep final approach until about 1,000 feet above the ground and then initiated the flare for landing. The aim point during the final approach was roughly half a mile short of the runway, which would result in a touchdown about a mile down the runway. The length of runway one-eight was 4.5 miles, so we had 3.5 miles remaining to slide out. I made this same practice flight at least four times a week for 2 months prior to my first flight.

On the day of my first flight I got up early and made a final practice flight before suiting up for my X-15 flight. As I remember it, the day of my first flight was a typical beautiful fall day in the desert. I felt good. I had gotten a good night's sleep and I had had a light breakfast before my practice flight in the F-104. Roger Barnicki, our personal equipment specialist, met me after my practice flight and escorted me to a carryall vehicle for the trip down to the X-15 servicing area.

The X-15 servicing area was to me a rather eerie scene particularly early in the morning. There were dozens of people moving in and out of the darkness

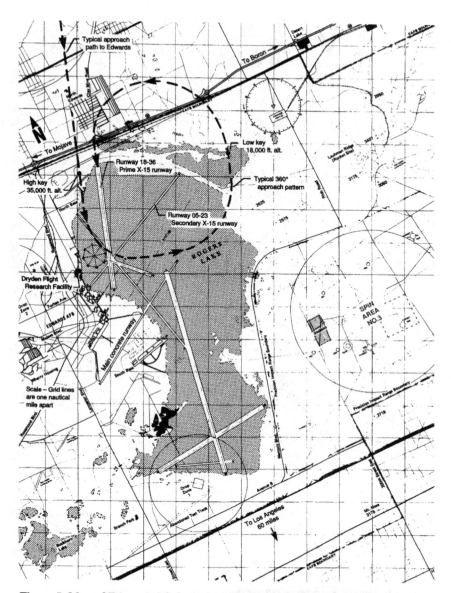

Figure 5. Map of Edwards lakebed, showing a typical approach pattern.

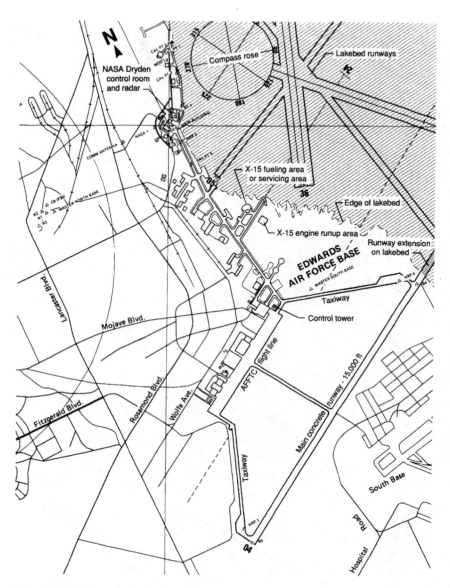

Figure 6. Map of X-15 servicing areas.

into the glare of the floodlights around the B-52 and the X-15. Numerous trailers, carts and other servicing equipment were sitting under the wing of the B-52 next to the X-15, while various liquids and gases were being pumped into tanks in the X-15. Liquid oxygen vapor was drifting all around the area like a swirling fog. A strong pungent ammonia odor permeated the air. The whole scene looked like something out of a Frankenstein movie. I would not have been surprised to see a monster walk out of the center of all that activity. In that setting, the black X-15 reminded me of some ominous creature—a menacing black bull.

After a brief glance at all that activity, I entered the suit van and immediately stripped down to my long johns to begin the suiting up process. The first items attached to me were some biomedical sensors to measure heart rate, blood pressure, and respiration rate. Next came the inner pressure suit garment which resembled a reinforced rubber body suit with many hoses, knobs, and other fittings attached to it including a big metal neck ring. Getting into that garment was a real chore. It was designed to enclose the entire body and yet, the design did not seem to provide a big enough opening to get into it without some real body contortions. I preferred to have my suit fit very tight to minimize the ballooning effect when it was pressurized. Excess ballooning severely restricted mobility. My suit fit like a full body girdle. Although my suit was extremely tight and uncomfortable in an unpressurized condition, it was worth enduring that to have good mobility in case I should lose cabin pressure and be forced to control the airplane while in an inflated suit.

Once the inner garment was all zipped up, I was then helped into the outer garment which was a silver-colored coverall made of a nylon-type material. This garment was simply intended to protect the inner garment from the effects of wind blast and aerodynamic heating in case the pilot ejected. Next came the boots, gloves, and finally, the helmet. A lengthy checkout of the suit followed. This involved pressurizing it and checking all the joints for integrity, leakage, and mobility. The whole process reminded me of movies that I have seen about warriors in ancient times being dressed for battle in their suits of armor.

The pressure suit was quite critical in X-15 flight operations since it was not uncommon to lose cabin pressure during a flight. In addition, it was the pilot's only source of oxygen because the cockpit was filled with nitrogen. The pilot could not open his faceplate to breathe. The pressure suit was to be my cocoon for the next couple of hours.

When the suit was finally checked out, I had a few minutes to relax before the aircraft was ready for pilot entry. As I sat there relaxing, my thoughts drifted back in time to an earlier era of exploration. . . .

The early morning light revealed a small ship drifting idly on the calm sea off the shore of a barren land. At the stern of the ship a group of men were gathered around a young man seated on a small bench. The men were fastening armor to the young man's body, carefully setting it in place and then adjusting the straps. They strapped other pieces of armor to his arms and legs and then some heavy leather boots on the young man's feet. Gloves were then fitted to his hands and finally a helmet was lowered down over his head and the visor closed. The men helped the young man to his feet and escorted him up the deck of the ship to the bow.

At the bow of the ship another group of men had been fitting armor to the body of a huge, black bull. They had also placed a saddle on the bull's back. The bull was restless and strained against his tethers and vapor rose from his body in the cool morning air. The young man climbed up a ladder next to the bull as the men assisted him into the saddle. They then strapped him to the saddle and fastened his feet in the stirrups. They slipped his sword into its scabbard on the saddle and handed him his shield and his spear. The crew of the ship then raised the sail and the ship began moving toward the shore.

As the ship approached the beach, an old man spoke to the young man on the bull. "We have provided you arms and armor to protect yourself. We have provided you a sturdy mount who will carry you safely on your journey. We have told you all we know about this strange land. Thus we have prepared you for this journey as thoroughly as we can. We have provided you protection from any danger that we could foresee. Now you must go and explore this strange land and then come back and tell us what you have learned. But before you go, one last word of caution: Beware of the bull. He will carry you safely anywhere that you have to go and he will protect you from any enemies. He is awesome in battle. However, if you lose control of him or fall off, he will kill you as quickly as he would kill your enemy."

As the old man finished talking, the ship slid to a gentle stop on the sandy beach. A gangplank was lowered and the young man rode the bull down onto the beach.

Like the warrior, I too had a sturdy mount, the X-15. I had also been painstakingly prepared for my journey. I had been indoctrinated into the un-explored world of hypersonics, a region of strong shock waves and intense heating. The aerodynamicists explained the rationale for the aircraft configura-tion, the benefits of the wedge-shaped vertical fins, and the theoretical perfor-mance of the aircraft. The structures engineers described the structural design philosophy and identified the critical load conditions. The aerothermodynamicists explained the effects of aerodynamic heating and the resultant temperature environment on the surface of the aircraft. The stability and control experts defined in minute detail the predicted flight characteristics of the aircraft at every conceivable flight condition.

The systems engineers inundated me with schematic drawings showing the components and the mode of operation of each subsystem. I became an expert on APUs, inertial platforms, ballistic controls, ball noses, nitrogen cooling systems, rocket engines, pressure suits, and instrumentation systems. I had huge binders full of notes taken during lectures on the aircraft, the environment, and the protection provided me in case of an unpredicted problem. I hoped not to encounter any surprises or lose control of the aircraft.

A call for pilot entry brought me quickly back to reality. Pilot entry took on the aura of a ritualistic ceremony. Two of the personal equipment specialists walked along with the pilot and carried the portable liquid oxygen cooling system and other equipment in a manner similar to the squires who served the knights and warriors of ancient times. The servicing crew and the aircraft crew were generally waiting for the pilot, standing along his pathway out to the aircraft and on the ramp up to the cockpit. It appeared as though the pilot was walking the final steps to the altar to be offered up to the gods. This very dramatic pilot entry made it tough for the pilot to back out of flying that mission. Everyone could see that he voluntarily walked out to the airplane and climbed in under his own power. He could not say that he was coerced or forced into flying the mission. He was like the Kamikaze pilot. He had drunk the wine and had accepted the sword. He could not turn back. He had to fly the mission.

Luckily, the pilot was rather busy once he got in the cockpit. He did not have a lot of time to worry about whether he was going to live or die. In fact, the tempo picked up as it got closer to launch. The pilot was, in effect, too busy to think about aborting the flight until after launch, and then it was too late. He could not turn back. He did not have a reset button like he had in the simulator to stop the flight and return him to the starting conditions. That is a nice button to have. If we saw that we were going to crash in the simulator, we just hit the reset button and we were back to our starting conditions. Every airplane should have a reset button.

The pilot had a lot of help getting into the cockpit and getting all of the lines, hoses, and straps hooked up. Following all that activity, he again went through a pressure suit checkout and then began the cockpit checkout. During this process, he went through a detailed checklist with an aircraft inspector assisting him in verifying the status of all the aircraft systems and the position of every switch, lever, and circuit breaker in the cockpit. He verified that he had good X-15 systems, as well as good system support from the B-52 bomber.

While attached to the B-52, the X-15 was supplied several expendables through various lines and an umbilical cord. One of these was liquid oxygen to top off the X-15 liquid oxygen tank. Boiloff of the liquid oxygen in the X-15 was quite rapid. The B-52 routinely transferred 600 to 800 gallons of liquid oxygen to the X-15 during captive flight before launch. The B-52 carried about 1,200 gallons of LOX for this purpose. In addition to LOX, the B-52 also provided breathing oxygen for the X-15 pilot, electrical power, radio and intercom communications, and data to align the X-15 inertial platform. The only thing they did not provide was window washing and restroom facilities. Restroom facilities would have made a tidy profit for the B-52 crew. Every once in a while, the X-15 pilot had to spend as much as 3 to 4 hours in the cockpit due to various delays on the ground or in flight before launch. It was touch and go on a number of occasions.

Once the cockpit checkout was complete, the cockpit canopy was closed, the crew chief, Larry Barnett, gave me a salute and the servicing and access equipment was cleared away from the X-15 and the B-52. Next came B-52 engine start and checkout of the various B-52 systems, and then the B-52 entry hatch was closed and we were ready to taxi. The taxi out to the runway for takeoff was another major event. A convoy of about ten vehicles trailed the B-52 out to the runway and a chase aircraft taxied out with it. A rescue helicopter took off to survey the runway before the B-52 takeoff. It then took up a hover position alongside the B-52, preparing to follow it down the runway on takeoff. Just prior to takeoff, the X-15 crew pulled the safety pins on the X-15 launch hooks. At that point we were armed and ready to go.

It was very unusual riding out on the wing of the B-52. The X-15 pilot obviously was a part of the B-52 team. He chatted and joked with them on the intercom unbeknownst to people on the ground or in the chase aircraft, but he could not get to them nor could they get to him in case of a problem. The early rocket aircraft were carried in the bomb bay of the mothership and thus, the crew of the mothership could help the rocket aircraft pilot in case of a problem. Being out on the wing, however, precluded any physical help, but the pilot could get a lot of moral support.

The ride out to the launch point was actually a pleasant ride, in some respects. The X-15 pilot could do a little sightseeing and he could critique the flying performance of the B-52 crew and make sarcastic remarks about their piloting abilities over the private intercom. They, in turn, might threaten to dump him out in the boondocks. From takeoff until 12 minutes to launch, the pilot was just doing housekeeping chores in the X-15. The checklist had very few items for the X-15 pilot to perform during this time. The B-52 crew was busy navigating out to the launch point with the assistance of ground vectoring. They were also topping off the X-15 LOX tank and aligning the inertial platform.

At 12 minutes to launch, I began activating the X-15 by initially starting the APUs. The APUs provided the essential hydraulic and electrical power to operate many of the other systems. We started them 12 minutes prior to launch to allow us to begin checking out the various other systems in the airplane to make sure they were all working properly before launch.

The radio communications illustrate the various checks performed before launch. The primary communications are between "NASA-1," which is the pilot controller in the ground control room, the "B-52," which is the B-52 pilot, "Butchart," who is Stan Butchart, a NASA pilot who flew as a launch panel operator on the B-52, and "Chase," which can be one of three different chase pilots depending on the phase of the flight. The specific chase is not always identified since it is difficult to know which chase pilot is speaking unless he calls out his number. Starting at 12 minutes to launch, the radio communications were as follows:

Thompson: "APU cooling switch going to normal."

NASA-1: "OK, Milt."

Thompson: "Pressure cooling coming on. My inertial altitude is just below 44,000, Butch and I'm reading about 1,000 foot per second on velocity."

Butchart: "OK-want to reset your altitude? I've got just a hair shy of 1,000 foot per second velocity and oh, maybe about a couple of hundred feet down."

B-52: "Eleven minutes."

Thompson: "Attitudes look good and cabin source is 3,400 and you want the precool switch off now, is that right?"

NASA-1: "Right."

Thompson: "Helium shutoff valve coming open. Hydraulic temperatures are OK. Data coming on, APUs coming on, number two."

NASA-1: "Zero-zero-eight, (the call sign number of the B-52 bomber) let's turn right 2 degrees."

B-52: "Right, three-one."

Thompson: "Number two APU is on. Pressure is 35 on hydraulics and holding. Starting number one."

B-52: "Ten minutes."

Chase-1: "Number one APU looks OK."

Thompson: "I can't get number one generator on—OK there she is.

	Engine reset. Hydraulic pressures are about 34 on number two APU and 3,500 on number one APU."
NASA-1:	"Roger, Milt."
B-52:	"Just past 9 minutes. Does 8 minutes still look good for the turn?" [The turn at 8 minutes is the turn back toward Edwards in preparation for the launch.]
NASA-1:	"Roger, Fitz. " [Fitz Fulton is the B-52 pilot].
Thompson:	"I'm on the controls and checking flap circuit breakers. Got engine reset. Data coming off."
B-52:	"Reading three-one degrees on heading."
NASA-1:	"Milt give us number two APU tank pressure."
Thompson:	"APU tank pressure is about 550 for both number one and number two. Mixing chambers temperatures are –35 and –45. Alpha [angle of attack] is about 1 degree and Beta [angle of sideslip] is about .5 degree to the left."
Chase:	"Will you try controls again, Milt?"
Thompson:	"OK, here's roll—pitch—and the rudder."
Chase:	"OK. And the flaps?"
Thompson:	"OK, flaps coming down."
Chase:	"Flaps coming down."
Thompson:	"And back up."
Chase:	"Flaps up."
Thompson:	"OK, aux cabin pressure switch is on. Inertial platform is going internal—is that OK, Butch?"
Butchart:	"Rog."
Thompson:	"OK, everything looks good. Fire extinguisher going to auto. Alternate SAS coming on."
B-52:	"Seven minutes."
NASA-1:	"That's OK, Fitz."
Thompson:	"Starting SAS check—all channels are on— going to monitor. OK, they all came off and alternate SAS shows off. SAS check complete."
NASA-1:	"Roger."
B-52:	"Six minutes."
Thompson:	"Horizontal stabilizer at 0. Going to X-15 oxygen and oxygen pressure is 2,800. Cabin altitude is 35."
NASA-1:	"Your launch lake winds are southwest at 15."
Thompson:	"Roger, Jack." [Jack McKay is the pilot controller in the control room.]
B-52:	"Five minutes to launch."
Thompson:	"OK. Data coming on. Data calibrate."
NASA-1:	"And Fitz—we will call the 4-minute point."
B-52:	"Roger."
Thompson:	"Tank handle going to pressurize. Ammonia tank pressure is 45 and LOX tank pressure is about 48."
NASA-1:	"Roger."

B-52:   "Two-one-four degrees."

NASA-1:   "Milt, check your ASAS switch on arm."

Thompson: "ASAS is armed and I've got two jettison switches on jettison. Going to jettison now."

NASA 1:   "OK, Fitz. Four minutes now."

B-52:   "Four minutes, Rog."

Thompson: "OK, Jack, intercom switch going off."

NASA-1:   "OK, Milt. And data off?"

Thompson: "OK. How do you read now, Jack?"

NASA-1:   "Five square and check your data off, Milt."

Thompson: "OK. OK, Butch, I've got slightly under 1,000 on velocity and about 45,000-feet altitude."

Butchart: "Altitude looks good in here, Milt."

NASA-1:   "OK, turn left two-one-two degrees."

Thompson: "About 80 on number two and 100 on number one."

NASA-1:   "Fitz, turn left two-one-two degrees."

B-52:   "Two-one-two degrees. Three minutes now."

NASA-1:   "Roger."

Butchart: "My inertial speed has dropped back to about 700, Milt."

Thompson: "Mine's just shy of 1,000."

NASA-1:   "Milt, did you get that 3-minute point?"

Thompson: "Affirm, Jack. I think I called everything off the checklist."

NASA-1:   "Let's turn right 2 degrees."

B-52:   "Right 2 degrees, heading two-one-five degrees, coming back 3 degrees at 1 minute to go."

Thompson: "Did you call 2 minutes yet?"

B-52:   "Two minutes, now."

Thompson: "OK, data is on. Tape to 15. Push to test ball nose. Looks good. Alpha is still about 1 degree, Beta is about .5 degree left. Cine camera going to pulse."

NASA-1:   "Calibrate, Milt?"

Thompson: "Affirm, I got a calibrate."

B-52:   "One minute to go, picking up heading two- one-two degrees."

Thompson: "OK, no head bumper. OK, we'll call that 40 seconds. Prime switch to prime. Igniter- ready light. Precool switch to precool. And igniter idle. Coming up on 10 seconds, pump idle."

NASA-1:   "Everything looks good here."

Thompson: "Manifolds and lines look good. Launch light going on. And we'll call that three, two, one, launch." (The bull and I were off on our journey.)

At this point I really got a shock. That launch was like being shot downward out of a cannon. It was a real jolt. No one warned me about the severity of the launch. This was due to the fact that the early participants in the program had flown so many flights that they had almost forgotten the early lessons learned. They, too, had been surprised by the hard launch, but they forgot to mention it to us new boys on the block.

The hard launch was primarily a result of the X-15 being trimmed for 0 *g* at launch to ensure a good clean separation from the B-52. Thus at launch, the X-15 went immediately from a stabilized 1 *g* flight condition to a 0 *g* flight condition and it remained at 0 *g* until the pilot initiated the pullup to round out and begin the climb. During the launch process, the X-15 would also roll off to the right unless the pilot applied some left roll input. This was due to the effect of the local flow field around the X-15 while on the pylon. Usually, it rolled off some even if he did apply some corrective roll control, because he never applied exactly the right amount.

In any event, I ended up in a 0 *g* trajectory with about 10 degrees of right roll. I decided the first thing to do was to try to light that engine to see if it was going to run. It lit off successfully and then I received my second surprise. The thrust of the engine forced my body back hard into the seat and headrest and effectively pinned me in that position for the duration of the powered portion of the flight. This was not a major problem, but it was a real surprise and it somewhat compounded my control task. In all my simulation practice for the flight, I had been very relaxed, smoking cigarettes, drinking coffee, and sitting in a slumped, head forward position. Now all of a sudden I was viewing the instrument panel from a completely different perspective and suffering from tunnel vision.

My instrument scan pattern that I had developed in the simulator was useless. I had to devise a new scan pattern in real time. To compound the problem, the pressure suit helmet had very little clearance in the small canopy, so when I attempted to move my head, I usually got hung up on a pad or the canopy structure. I had not used a pressure suit in any of my simulations prior to the flight, so I was surprised by a few of the minor problems associated with the suit. Again, the early pilots had practiced with the pressure suit in a simulation, but they had forgotten to recommend it to Joe Engle and me. It was not a big deal but it was another straw.

After the engine lit, I adjusted the throttle to 50 percent thrust, rolled the wings level and initiated the pullup to begin the climb. The flight plan called for a pullup to 10 degrees angle of attack which would be maintained until reaching a climb angle of +20 degrees. This pullup to 20 degrees required 26 seconds to accomplish. I was a couple of seconds late getting to 20 degrees due to the surprises and my delayed response time in getting the airplane started up hill. I was also late getting to my pushover altitude of 65,000 feet, but everything else was going according to plan.

At 83 seconds after launch, I was scheduled to extend my speed brakes to decrease my rate of acceleration. At 83 seconds, I should have accelerated to 2,800 feet per second and reached an altitude of 72,000 feet. I was a little low on both speed and altitude, so I delayed a couple of seconds before I extended the speed brakes. At 90 seconds, I had achieved the planned 3,100 feet per second, but I was about 2,000 feet low on profile. I finally peaked out at 74,400 feet at 100 seconds.

After reaching 74,000 feet altitude, I was supposed to maintain altitude while accelerating to 4,000 feet per second or about Mach 4. I unintentionally let the nose drop slightly and, as a result, I quickly built up a large rate of descent. At these high speeds a small error in nose position can produce a big altitude deviation. NASA-1 alerted me to the loss of altitude and I finally got the nose back up where it belonged. At 122 seconds after launch, I shut the engine down. I was traveling at 4,100 feet per second and I was at 73,000 feet altitude. In just over 2 minutes, I had gained about 30,000 feet of altitude and 3,200 feet per second of velocity or over three Mach numbers. This had been accomplished at half throttle and with the speed brakes extended for the last 30 seconds. That's pretty impressive. A fighter pilot would give his left nut for an airplane like that.

After shutdown, I retracted the speed brakes and began a constant altitude glide toward Edwards. Energy management on this flight was pretty straightforward since the flight was planned to be rather benign. There were no requirements for aggressive maneuvering to dissipate energy. NASA-1 vectored me to high key and guided me along the desired altitude profile.

NASA-1: "Ease it on over. Watch your nose position, Milt. We have you low on altitude. Bring it back up. Pull your nose on up, Milt."

Thompson: "OK, it's coming up."

NASA-1: "Turn left 3 degrees. Bring it left 3 degrees."

Thompson: "Roger, Jack."

NASA-1: "Make it 5, 5 degrees. Speed brakes in. Turn left 3 degrees, Milt."

Thompson: "Rog, Jack."

NASA-1: "And maintain your altitude, you're a little low, Milt."

Thompson: "Rog."

NASA-1: "OK, you're about 10 miles from your checkpoint. Hold your altitude. And you're looking very good here, Milt. Milt, delay your descent until you get over Cuddeback—we'll give you a call."

Thompson: "Rog, Jack."
NASA-1:   "And better go to land position on your test."
Thompson: "Rog."
NASA-1:   "What is your velocity, Milt?"
Thompson: "I've got about two-point-four, Jack."
NASA-1:   "OK, you can start your descent now, you're on profile. And we have you just northwest of Cuddeback. Do you have the field in sight?"
Thompson: "Affirm, Jack."
NASA-1:   "OK, we have you about Mach 2 here, Milt, and coming down through 70,000. Engine master off."
Thompson: "Rog, engine master off."
NASA-1:   "And understand you have the field in sight, is that correct?"
Thompson: "Affirm."
NASA-1:   "OK, maintain what you have there, Milt. You have a good rate of descent here. OK, you can cut it to the left just a little, Milt."
Thompson: "Rog, Jack."
NASA-1:   "180 would be a nice heading and keep your speed brakes in right now."
Thompson: "Rog."
Chase-4:   "What's your altitude, Milt?"
Thompson: "I'm coming through about 48 now."
Chase-4:   "Start your jettison, Milt."
Thompson: "OK, going to jettison."
NASA-1:   "OK, you're about 6 miles out of high key here, Milt."
Thompson: "Rog, Jack."
NASA-1:   "One-point-two on velocity and watch your angle of attack."
Thompson: "Rog."
Chase-4:   "I have a tallyho, got him in sight, he's quite a little ways away. Kind of high, Milt."
Thompson: "Rog. OK, am I about over the highway?" [The highway just north of the lakebed.]

Now came the moment of truth. The deadstick landing. I had made it back to Edwards in reasonably good shape but now I was going to have to make an honest-to-God deadstick landing. I had only one chance. If I screwed up, I lost the airplane and maybe more. I had good energy for my approach. I was approaching the high-key position with about 35,000 feet of altitude, which was the desired altitude. I had trouble determining my position over the ground due to the restricted downward vision in the X-15. As soon as I rolled into the turn to low key, I had a reasonably good view of the lakebed and the rocket site and I could judge my approach quite well.

I began to think I might really pull this off successfully. At the low-key position, I had about 20,000 feet—a little high, but I could always use some speed brake to kill off any excess altitude. The turn from low key onto final worked out well and, as I rolled out on final, I was just about right on the desired speed. I picked up my aim point on the edge of the lakebed and then I maintained speed and flight path angle until time for the landing flare.

Judging the landing flare was the final major task. A pilot did not have a lot of leeway for error, but by this time I felt pretty comfortable. As I passed through 1,000 feet above the ground, I started the flare to come level. I came level about 100 feet above the runway, lowered the flaps, and then dropped the gear. The airplane was flying very nicely now. I eased it on down to within 5 feet of the runway and just let it settle in.

The initial touchdown was very smooth, until the nose came down. The nose came down with a vengeance. For a moment, I thought the nose gear had failed as the nose slammed down on the runway. I did not realize how close the cockpit was to the ground in the landing attitude. I thought my butt was going to scrape the lakebed. It was a real jolt when the nose slammed down, about 8 *g* in the cockpit. From that point on, the pilot was just along for the ride. The airplane kind of slid out on its own. The last few seconds of radio conversation just prior to landing kind of sums up the flight:

Thompson: "Rog. Flaps coming down."
Chase-4:   "OK, flaps look good, gear looks good, let's go down. Fifty feet, ten, five, a beauty, Milt. A beauty!"
Thompson: "Where's the brake?" [I was just kidding, there is no brake.]
NASA-1:   "That little handle on the left." [NASA-1 was kidding also.]
Chase-4:   "Pull back on the stick." [Bob Rushworth in Chase 4 wasn't kidding. Pulling back on the stick did increase the sliding friction.]
Thompson: "How about that!"
NASA-1:   "Real nice show, Milt."

My first X-15 flight lasted exactly 523 seconds. The engine burned for the first 2 minutes of the flight. In those 2 minutes, I climbed to 75,000 feet altitude and accelerated up to 4,100 feet per second or 2,712 miles per hour. That is almost twice as fast as a rifle bullet. After engine shutdown, the X-15 became a hypersonic glider, gliding over 100 miles in a matter of seconds. Five minutes after launch, I was in the landing pattern over the north lakebed at Edwards. The descent from high key to landing lasted just over three and a half minutes.

In less than nine minutes after launch, I had learned to fly a new airplane well enough to make a "beautiful" deadstick landing. I guess I was now qualified to join the X-15 program.

When the airplane finally stopped, the recovery convoy converged on me like sharks on a piece of raw meat. The convoy was actually coming to help me, but I could not help but be intimidated by the intensity of their approach to the airplane. The first to arrive was the recovery helicopter. It came in over the airplane at 25 or 30 feet to check for any fire or propellant leak. Then they landed and dropped off an X-15 crew member and a personal equipment specialist. They came running over to the airplane to open the canopy and begin securing the ejection seat. Next came the fire chief in his hopped-up pickup and a series of ground crew vehicles, ground support equipment, crash and fire truck, and finally, the ground control van and the pressure suit van. In all, there were about fifteen or twenty vehicles in the recovery convoy.

It was a fantastic feeling when that canopy opened up. I had been cooped up in that cockpit for over 2 hours and had been exposed to some traumatic new experiences. You cannot believe how good the fresh air smelled. I had made a successful flight. I had climbed Mt. Everest and had made it back safely. I went through the post landing checklist, shut everything down, and then unbuckled with the assistance of the personal equipment specialists. They helped me out of the airplane and the congratulations began.

Paul Bikle, the Dryden director, was there on the lakebed, as was General "Twig" Branch. My wife and four kids were there and, as Ralph Jackson (our public affairs officer) reminded me later, so was my favorite bartender. Ralph had invited him out to watch the flight. It was a pleasant surprise to have my family waiting to greet me on the lakebed, but I could not help but think of what a traumatic experience it would have been if I had pranged the airplane on landing.

I believe I shook hands with 100 people out on the lakebed before the welcoming ceremony was over. It really was a tremendous welcome home. My flight was the ninety-third flight of the program, but the morale was so high among the project team members that it was almost treated like a first flight. In fact, every flight was treated as a significant event and was at least celebrated at Juanita's in Rosamond after working hours.

I was impressed by a couple of things during the flight. The various g forces imposed on the pilot during powered flight were very conducive to severe vertigo. The eyeballs-in g forces due to the thrust of the engine were much greater than any experienced in conventional airplanes. When these g forces were combined with the eyeballs-down forces during the pullup to the planned climbout angle after launch, the pilot sensed that he had overrotated his climb angle. This was compounded by the visual loss of the horizon out the window.

Every X-15 pilot suffered this disorientation during the climbout and many felt that they were climbing straight up or even going over on their back. The *g* forces from the engine thrust continued to increase as the aircraft became lighter due to fuel usage and ultimately achieved a level of almost 4.0 *g* just prior to burnout. This level of *g* force was not excessive by any means, but it compromised the pilot's ability to fly the airplane, it restricted his breathing and caused chest pain, and it was just plain annoying. I commented to engineers after the flight that this was the first aircraft that I had flown that I was happy to shut the engine off. The resulting deadstick landing was the lesser of two evils, in my opinion, after that long exposure to that high *g* environment. Bill Dana loved the comment about being happy to shut the engine off and quoted it in many talks for years after the program ended.

The one other thing that impressed me on this flight was the amount of physical effort required to fly the airplane. I was really exhausted after the flight. Some of that exhaustion was obviously due to the mental stress, but much of it was due to the muscular exertion required to manipulate all the controls and fly the aircraft while fighting the *g* forces and the resistance of the pressure suit. Following that flight, I immediately embarked on a physical fitness program to get back in shape. Flying the X-15 was definitely not a piece of cake. I felt like I had put in a 12-hour-day digging ditches.

Chapter 6............................

Trial by Fire and Water
(1964–1968)

My fifth flight was to be a low-speed flight in the number three aircraft to simulate the flight conditions of the proposed Supersonic Transport and to measure the heat transfer rate, the skin friction, and the boundary layer noise at this flight condition. The desired speed was about 2,800 feet per second, or just under Mach 3. In planning the flight, we were looking for the closest launch lake that would still provide some stabilized flight time at Mach 3. The only lake that seemed to fulfill the requirements was Silver Lake, which was approximately 100 miles east of Edwards. It appeared, however, that we could not keep the speed below Mach 3 coming out of Silver Lake without violating one of our basic flight safety ground rules. That rule dictated that a pilot could not retard the throttle until he had enough energy to get home to Edwards. This rule was established as a result of the unstable engine operation at low-thrust settings that was observed during ground runs. The concern was that the engine might shutdown prematurely when the throttle was retarded. This had happened during ground runs and during flight on at least one occasion.

Ed Saltzman, the research engineer who was conducting the experiment, was very adamant about the desired flight conditions. He did not want to exceed Mach 3 while recording his data. I sympathized with him. I had worked as a research engineer before I had become a pilot and I appreciated the importance of obtaining accurate flight conditions. I decided to go with him to argue for special dispensation to make the flight at the lower speed. We went to see Joe Vensel, who was the chief of flight operations. He listened to our argument and then said, "Not only no, but hell no!" He was not about to approve a flight that required a power reduction before the aircraft had enough energy to make it home to Edwards.

Saltzman did not like the decision, but he accepted defeat and went off mumbling about the lack of support for basic research. I was not as smart as Ed. I decided that I would not give up so easily. I had made four X-15 flights. I felt pretty confident in my ability to cope with any problems that might arise during a flight. In fact, I probably felt a little cocky. I kept bugging Joe Vensel to let me fly the flight at the lower speed in the interest of science and to uphold the honor of the pilot's office. It took a couple of weeks, but I finally wore him down.

The flight was scheduled for May 21, 1964. The B-52 took off at 8:58 A.M. and climbed to 25,000 feet in the immediate vicinity of Edwards before heading outbound to Silver Lake. Everything proceeded smoothly up to launch, except that when I went to pump idle at 10 seconds to launch I did not get second-stage igniter. I had to recycle the pump two times to get second-stage igniter and, as a result, I was about 15 seconds late for launch. The radio conversation at launch included the following:

Thompson:	"OK, pump idle again and we're all set. Call that three, two, one, launch."
Chase:	"No light."
NASA-1:	"OK, you got a light. OK, you're coming up on profile. Should have your theta, Milt. Standby for pushover. Get set for throttle back. We have you going just a little high, Milt. How do you read? Shutdown!"
Thompson:	"Engine shutdown. Reset, prime, reset, and throttle off."
NASA-1:	"Rog. Malfunction, reset."
Thompson:	"Throttle back."
NASA-1:	"Bring your nose up. Bring your nose up, Milt."
Thompson:	"Throttle's off."
NASA-1:	"Malfunction. Cuddeback!!"

That conversation tells it all. When I retarded the throttle at 42 seconds as called for in the revised flight plan, the engine quit just as Joe Vensel feared that it would. We did not have enough energy to get to Edwards, so the call came to go to Cuddeback Lake. I tried a couple of engine restart attempts with no luck. A small explosion had occurred in the engine when I throttled back and this precluded any engine restart.

I now had a real emergency on my hands. I was not going to make it home and I might not even make it to Cuddeback Lake. I might have to land on one of the Three Sisters Lakes and they were awfully small compared to Edwards or even Cuddeback, only 2 miles in diameter. The slideout in the X-15 was close to 2 miles long, so if I did not land accurately at the edge of the lake at Three Sisters, I was going to slide off the lake and into the boondocks. Or conversely, if I landed short at over 200 MPH in the sagebrush, I probably would not survive. It was not a nice prospect. I really did not want to land at Three Sisters.

As soon as I realized that I did not get an engine relight, I started the airplane uphill. I was traveling at about Mach 2.9 at shutdown at 55,000 feet altitude, so I had some speed that I could convert to altitude, but I had a long way to go to get to Cuddeback, over 70 miles. As I slowly climbed on up, I started jettisoning propellants to prepare for landing. I did not need that volatile stuff if I had a landing accident. NASA-1 confirmed that I had a good heading to reach Cuddeback and asked that I give them an altitude check as I approached Three Sisters. They informed me that I had to have at least 45,000 feet at Three Sisters to make it in to Cuddeback.

I decided right then that I would lie if necessary about my altitude at Three Sisters. I did not want to land there. I was going to try to make it to Cuddeback. As it turned out, I had plenty of altitude when I reached Three Sisters. I had 60,000 feet. I had to rely on NASA-1 to tell me when I arrived at Three Sisters because I could not see the lakes or Cuddeback. They were under my nose.

As I descended into Cuddeback from Three Sisters, the chase aircraft began to join up. Soon, I had all four chase aircraft on my wing. They had all caught up to me in my slow cross-country flight from Silver Lake. Bob Rushworth finally suggested that a couple of them get out of the way. As I passed over the runway at Cuddeback, I asked for an altitude check and Bob indicated that he had 32,000 feet. He was on my right wing. I was crossing the north-south runway on a westerly heading, so I had plenty of altitude for a 270-degree overhead pattern to the north-south runway. As I proceeded on past the runway to set up my pattern, NASA-1 called and said, "Bring your turn around, Milty, tighten your turn." That call was somewhat perplexing because from what I could see I had plenty of altitude to make a wide pattern. But since it was an emergency, I thought maybe they knew something that I did not know. I tightened my turn up a bit.

As I continued around the turn, I got another call from NASA-1 to "tighten my turn." Again, it looked like I was already a little too close in, but the call raised some doubt in my mind. I had never landed at Cuddeback, although I had made many practice approaches there. I really did not want to do it, but I went ahead and tightened my turn a little more. I did not get any advice from my chase to the contrary. As I came around on final, I realized I was way too high. I opened the speed brakes and dumped the nose over to kill off energy. I came down the final approach doing over 350 knots and "S-turning" to kill off more energy. I pulled the speed brakes in while I made the flare, but then put them right back out to slow down to get it on the ground.

Full speed brakes in the landing configuration significantly decreased directional stability. In fact, the airplane became directionally unstable. The nose of the aircraft started to diverge as I leveled out for the landing, but I managed to stop the divergence and finally plunk it on the ground. I was misaligned with the runway as a result of this control problem, but I managed to turn the X-15 after touchdown by applying roll control to load up one skid. This worked very well at high speeds. After the turn, the aircraft slid out right down the center of the runway.

I landed long, about a mile and a half down the runway. The runway was about 3 miles long with a road going across the north end. The road was just a graded track across the north end of the lakebed with dirt piled up on either side. Beyond the road was another half mile of usable lakebed. I had slowed to about 60 knots when I hit the dirt piled up alongside that road. The pile was about a foot and a half high, but I plowed through it like a tank. It was a good jolt, but everything stayed together and I stopped about 300 feet beyond the road. I did not see it, but the fire truck that was standing by on the lakebed for an emergency landing had pulled in behind me during my slideout. The fire truck hit the same dirt pile traveling at my same speed. According to some other observers on the lake, that entire truck flew up in the air 5 feet before coming back down. I had landed safely without any significant damage to the airplane, but now I had to go back home and face Joe Vensel. I almost wished that I had not made it.

The rescue C-130 landed immediately after I did and they flew me back to Edwards after I secured the X-15. One of my cousins and his son came up to watch that flight. They were thoroughly impressed by that flight. As I have said previously, when an emergency occurred, everyone at Edwards held their breath until the airplane was safely on the ground. The silence was deafening on the radio. My cousin witnessed that and was impressed. He never came back to watch another flight.

When I saw Joe at the postflight debriefing, he raised hell like a father would if his kid had narrowly escaped death due to some stupid action. He was mad but mainly because he had been so worried. He swore again that he would never allow the engine to be throttled before the X-15 could make it home. This time he meant it.

I found out at the postflight debriefing that NASA-1 had been misinterpreting their radar map when they were vectoring me around the pattern at Cuddeback. They were misreading the scale on the map when they were telling me to tighten up my turn. We made a decision after that flight to stop vectoring the X-15 once it got into the landing pattern. We felt the pilot could better judge the landing pattern without help from the ground. We only provided help after that if the pilot requested it. In describing the runway on Cuddeback Lake, I had to borrow a line from Jack McKay, "It was 3 miles long with a 300-foot overrun."

FIRE WARNING

My eighth flight was a flight to measure acoustic noise in the boundary layer. Acoustic noise is of interest to aircraft designers because it can cause aircraft skin panels to vibrate and ultimately to fail due to fatigue. The boundary layer is a term to describe the layer of air between the skin of the aircraft and the free stream air. A boundary layer is a natural occurring phenomenon on any object moving through the air. In a boundary layer, the velocity of the air varies from zero on the surface of the object to the speed with which that object is traveling through the air.

Thus, in a car traveling 80 MPH, the velocity of the air next to the surface of the car is zero, while the velocity of the air outside of the boundary layer is 80 MPH. The boundary layer varies in thickness from a few thousandths of an inch on the front of the car to several inches at the rear of the car. The air in a boundary layer can do strange things. It can flow in different directions and it can even move forward.

The aircraft designer is very interested in the characteristics of this boundary layer since it can impact the design of the aircraft in many ways. For example, if the boundary layer is predicted to be thick on a particular aircraft configuration at the desired operating speed, then the engine inlets may have to be moved out away from the skin of the fuselage to capture the high-speed air rather than the stagnant air next to the fuselage. If the boundary layer air is turbulent, the aerodynamic heating rate is higher and the airplane will get hotter. The designer will then have to build in some extra heat protection for the aircraft structure.

It offered the first opportunity to measure the characteristics of the airflow at hypersonic speeds. These characteristics were important to the designers of future hypersonic aircraft. The wind tunnels provided some clues as to these characteristics, but some actual flight data were needed to confirm the wind tunnel data. The X-15 provided much of the aerodynamic data needed to validate the hypersonic wind tunnels.

My eighth flight was one small step in this process. It was a rather benign flight plan calling for a climb and acceleration up to 80,000 feet at Mach 4.5. After engine shutdown, I was to make a mild 2 *g* left turn and then later a 2.5 *g* right turn while maintaining a constant dynamic pressure. After recording data in these maneuvers, I was to vector to high key at Edwards while doing some handling quality evaluations using the center stick with the roll and yaw stability augmentation system turned off. At high key, I was to terminate the research maneuvers and commence the approach to landing. This flight promised to be an easy one. I could sit back and enjoy this one.

Things went well up until 4 minutes to launch at which time NASA-1 lost telemetry data. Telemetry data was essential for flight. I asked Jack McKay, who was the controller in NASA-1, what we were going to do. He informed me that we would proceed with the checklist for the time being. I continued on down the checklist to the one minute point and got another call from NASA-1 to continue on even though they were still not receiving telemetry data.

At 1 minute, the B-52 crew armed the launch release system. At 40 seconds I began priming the rocket engine and shortly thereafter I got an igniter ready light. I turned precool on and then finally, at 20 seconds, got a call from NASA-1 that they were receiving telemetry data. We were "go" for launch. I switched tape on at 15 seconds and at 10 seconds I pushed the pump-idle button. The fuel and LOX manifold pressures rapidly increased to almost 600 psi and a quick check of the other propellant system gauges indicated that we were ready for launch. I called out that "everything looks good here." NASA-1 responded saying, "everything good down here also." I turned the launch light on and called out on the radio, "Three-two-one-launch."

At launch I rolled off to the right about 60 degrees, but that did not slow me down in getting the engine lit. Getting that engine lit was always top priority even if the airplane rolled over on its back. Once the pilot got the engine burning, he could worry about the small stuff, like getting the aircraft under control. I had to correct my heading during my pullup to my planned climb angle. I reached my planned climb angle of 20 degrees at 18 seconds after launch and then checked my velocity. I was right on 1,600 feet per second or roughly Mach 1.6.

At 28 seconds I opened the speed brakes as I passed through 50,000 feet and Mach 2. NASA-1 called, "Real nice profile" and "standby for your push-over." At 49 seconds after launch, I was exactly on profile passing through 64,000 feet at Mach 2.85. I pushed over to 0 *g* at that point and held it until I reached 80,000 feet altitude and Mach 4.5. I then shut the engine down as planned. NASA-1 called to remind me to retract the speed brakes and asked me, "How do you read NASA-1?" I had not been doing any talking and they wanted to know if I was still alive and well. I responded, "Five square, Jack."

From this point on, I set up a rate of descent to maintain a constant dynamic pressure for data purposes and then initiated a gentle left turn. I maintained that turn for about 15 seconds and then rolled out to get data in a wings level attitude. As I was about to roll into the planned right-hand turn decelerating through Mach 3.2, I noticed a second-stage ignition malfunction light flash on my left-hand instrument panel. That seemed odd because the engine had been shutdown some 50 seconds or so earlier. Then I saw the big one—the fire-warning light. That light was the biggest, brightest light on the panel and it was strategically located directly in front of the pilot's eyes to ensure that he could not overlook it. That light was blinking ominously. "FIRE," "FIRE," "FIRE."

We had had fire-warning lights before such as when Scott Crossfield had a rocket chamber blow up on the LR-11 engine early in the program, but we had not had one with the big engine. The system had not previously given any false alarms. It had been highly reliable and now it was telling me that I had a fire in the engine compartment. The first thing to pass through my mind was the image of that huge fireball when the X-15 blew up on the test stand with Crossfield in it. I could vividly see the boiling fire engulfing the airplane and see pieces flying out of the fire. I waited for the explosion, but nothing happened.

I called NASA-1 and informed them that I had a fire-warning light and that I was going to jettison peroxide. NASA-1 responded, "Roger—understand you are going to jettison. Go engine master off." I wanted to get rid of that engine peroxide because that was the type of hazardous material that could blow the whole rear end of the airplane off. I had quite a bit of peroxide remaining since

I had shut the engine down early as planned. As I jettisoned the peroxide, I noted that the automatic fire system had actuated and dumped my number two source gas into the engine compartment. Maybe that put the fire out.

But the fire-warning light kept blinking. In fact it seemed to be blinking faster. That must have been my imagination though, because an electronic system does not have any emotion. It cannot tell me to hurry like a human might if the fire were getting worse. Yet, it was blinking faster. I was still flying at over 2,500 MPH at 70,000 feet and I did not know what was happening in the back end of the airplane. What the hell can burn? The airplane was made of heat resistant steel. It should not burn, but then I realized that almost anything will burn in the presence of liquid oxygen, even steel. Was the fire burning through the hydraulic and electrical lines? Was it burning through the structure? Was it burning through the fuel tank? NASA-1 could not help me. They did not have any more data than I had. The chase could not help. They were 30,000 feet below me and 50 miles away. I quickly ticked off my options. There were not many. I could eject and hope the complicated ejection seat worked as designed or I could sit still and wait it out hoping that the airplane did not explode. If it exploded, I probably would not get a chance to eject since the explosion could either damage the ejection system or it could incapacitate me.

I could start down to let the chase join up and check for a fire, but if I did that, I might not have made it home. I could not get the airplane on the ground much quicker by slowing down sooner since the total flight only involved 8 minutes of flight time and about half of that time was utilized in the landing pattern. There were only two real options: eject, or ride it out.

Somehow though, as the seconds ticked by I seemed to gain confidence. It had not blown up yet. I could still control the aircraft, so it had not burned through the hydraulic lines or the control cables. As I gained confidence, I began to reassess the bigger picture. Was I still on profile? Was my speed and altitude still high enough to allow me to make it home? I noticed that I had let the rate of descent build up much more than planned. At those speeds, only 2 or 3 degrees change in attitude could result in a 10,000 foot per minute rate of descent. A pilot could not be distracted for long in this airplane. Five or 10 seconds of inattention could result in the loss of the airplane and possibly the pilot's life.

I finally realized that Jack was urgently calling to tell me to "bring it up— bring the nose up, Milt." I started the nose up and responded, "OK." Jack then informed me that I was about 10 miles out of Cuddeback and asked if the fire-warning light was still on. I responded, "Affirm." Jack informed me that the light would stay on once it was activated. It would not go out, even though the fire might go out. By this time, my confidence had improved significantly and I decided that the airplane was not going to blow up so I may as well try to get some more research data. In fact, I called out that I missed that second data point and Jack said, "That's all right, forget it." I had failed to make the second planned turn for data gathering purposes while I was responding to the fire-warning indication. First things first. Don't sweat the small stuff.

As I passed Cuddeback, I began setting up for the next data point and started the planned handling quality investigation while approaching high key. As I passed over high key, the fire-warning light went out. That should have made me feel better, but Jack had told me it should stay on. If that were true, then maybe the fire was real and it had finally burned through the fire-warning system and deactivated it. By now though, I could not worry about that anymore. I had to begin the approach to landing.

This airplane did not afford the luxury of a delayed approach while one attended to other concerns. It came down relentlessly. From the instant the engine quit, the airplane began losing energy and started downhill. By this time, the landing chase aircraft had joined up and after a quick inspection he informed me that there was no external evidence of a fire. The landing approach was uneventful and the landing was a "beauty" according to Joe Engle, the landing chase pilot. The emergency vehicles really swarmed around me on this landing. They thought they had a real emergency this time. Postflight inspection of the aircraft revealed no fire damage. The fire detection loop did show evidence of having been hot. It was changed prior to the next flight. All of that terror because of a faulty fire-warning system. A review of the cockpit film did indeed confirm that the fire-warning light blinked faster as the flight progressed. I was not imagining it.

Bikle informed me later that he and many others had become somewhat complacent. The flights had been progressing so smoothly and successfully that they were becoming routine. My fire call really shocked him back to reality. He suddenly realized that flying the X-15 could still be dangerous, even after flying over a hundred test flights.

Someone once said that test flying involved hours and hours of boredom punctuated by moments of stark terror. This flight included a few moments of the latter. The X-15 did not, however, offer the pleasure of hours and hours of boredom to compensate for those moments of terror since the flights were normally ten minute flights. In the case of the X-15, it appeared to be the other way around. Hours and hours of terror punctuated by moments of pure boredom.

WATER SKIING

In the winter of 1964–65, after a series of particularly heavy rain storms, the lakebed had accumulated about 6 inches of standing water. The lakebed really looked like an honest-to-goodness lake. First-time visitors to Edwards were always impressed when they saw the lakebed in that condition—a huge lake out in the middle of a barren desert. We would string them along and talk about fishing, sailing, and water skiing on the lake. On one particular occasion in the pilot's office I made the statement that I thought we really could ski on the lake if we could find a suitable tow vehicle. Several of the pilots disagreed and we ended up in a vigorous argument. One pilot finally suggested that we settle the argument by giving it a try.

The next morning the mediator pilot brought in a pair of water skis. He also volunteered to fly our small Bell helicopter as a tow vehicle. The gauntlet had been thrown down. I had to pick it up. I had to put up or shut up. I went down to the pilot's locker room, carrying the water skis on my shoulder. Joe Vensel, our director of flight operations, happened to pass me in the hallway. He looked askance at me and the water skis, but he did not say anything and neither did I. I went into the locker room and changed into my oldest flight suit and my most beat-up flight boots. That water was shallow and if I should happen to fall, I would bottom out in the mud of the lakebed. That mud was really sticky.

After I finished dressing, I picked up the skis and walked out to the flight line. The helicopter had been towed out of the hangar and the crew was finishing up the preflight inspection. Vic Horton, the lightweight lifting body project engineer, had volunteered to fly as the tow rope tender and monitor. He had even supplied some of our lifting body tow rope for the operation. We were all set to go. By this time a large crowd had gathered on the aircraft ramp and on the roof of the main office building to watch the big event. Word had gotten around. We laid out the tow rope from the helicopter to the ramp at the edge of the lakebed and then the helicopter crew started the engine.

I walked down to the ramp at the edge of the lake and began putting on the skis. I began to have second thoughts about the whole idea, but it was too late to back down now. I was committed. I got the skis on, picked up the end of the rope, and waited for the helicopter to get airborne. The more I thought about it, the more stupid this whole idea seemed. I was going to break my damn neck, and yet, my ego would not let me back down. The helicopter crew added power to begin the liftoff. Just before they broke ground, a message came over the public address system that said, "Shut that thing down." That message came from Joe Vensel.

After passing me in the hallway, he had gone to a short meeting in the front of the building. While in the meeting, he thought about me and the water skis and then remembered the argument that he had overheard in the pilot's office the day before. He decided he had better check to see what was going on. When he got back to his office overlooking the ramp and lakebed, he could hardly get in. It was filled with spectators. Our director, Paul Bikle, was also there. Joe Vensel almost had a heart attack when he saw what was happening. He immediately got on the public address system and commanded the shutdown. Paul Bikle did not say a thing. I think he would have let us try it.

All of the participants were thoroughly chewed out by Vensel. I was somewhat flabbergasted to learn that his main concern was that I might break an arm or leg and not be available to fly the X-15. I decided not to ask him if he would have been sorry if I had broken my neck. The timing somehow was not exactly right for that particular question.

The helicopter crew later admitted that they had planned to tow me out in the middle of the lake and then drop the towline. It would have been almost impossible to walk the 2 miles back to shore in that water and mud. That lakebed mud was so sticky, it would build up 2 or 3 inches thick on the bottom of your boots after walking just a few steps. I am glad I got a reprieve at the last minute.

THE BULL REARS ITS HEAD

I somehow always managed to be a little late getting to work on the days when I had an X-15 flight. I usually had just enough time to rush into the cafeteria and grab a cup of coffee and a couple pieces of toast and then rush back out to the flight line to the waiting carryall. Usually Roger Barnicki or one of his people would be waiting in the carryall to drive me the mile or so down the taxiway to the X-15 servicing area.

This particular morning I was scheduled to make a low-altitude, high-speed heating flight. It was to be my tenth flight and my eighth heating flight. On arrival at the servicing area, I immediately entered the suit van and began the suiting up process. This normally required 30 to 45 minutes to complete. Everything progressed smoothly this morning and I was ready for pilot entry 15 minutes before the airplane was ready. I had time for a last cigarette.

Once the X-15 and B-52 were fully serviced the crew called for pilot entry. It was a short walk from the suit van to the ladder leading up to the X-15 cockpit, but with the tight and constraining pressure suit on, it took some effort. The pressure suit people walked along with me carrying the portable liquid oxygen breathing and cooling unit which was hooked up to the suit. Entry into the cockpit was relatively easy from the access platform since the cockpit was quite large. The only feature of the cockpit that made it seem small was the canopy itself, which fit rather tightly around the head. It was only large enough for the helmet and I always seemed to be bumping the canopy, when the lid was down, whenever I moved my head.

Below the canopy, there was ample space. In fact, for some of the pilots, there was too much space. They had trouble reaching some of the controls and switches on the front panel. I normally flew with some slack in the left shoulder strap to ensure that I could always get to such critical controls as the throttle and landing gear handle. I remember on one flight Joe Walker could not reach the throttle to shut the engine down on schedule. He subsequently overshot his speed and altitude.

When I was settled in the cockpit, the suit people began strapping me in. Theoretically, the pilot could do this himself since he was supposed to be able to reach and release all of the restraint harness fittings for emergency egress. In reality, it was almost impossible to get in and out of the cockpit without assistance. After landing he really had to wait for someone to release all the fittings and help him out. In the ten emergency landings that were made during the course of the program, the pilot seldom managed to get out without some assistance. Pete Knight managed to do it after his Mud Lake landing, but he injured himself in the process.

During the strapping-in process, the suit people were also connecting the suit to the emergency bailout kit and the aircraft's breathing oxygen supply and the suit pressurization and cooling supply. The lower part of the suit was cooled and pressurized with nitrogen gas from a liquid nitrogen supply tank. With that type of system, the pilot never lacked for cooling. In fact, if he turned the cooling up too high, he would occasionally get a few drops of liquid nitrogen into the suit and end up with a few inches of frozen skin on his left side where the cooling hose connected to the suit. I often thought they should have connected the hose to the right side to cool the liver, considering that part of the flight day activity involved a lot of drinking the night after the flight. Some precooling of the liver might have been beneficial.

Once the suit was hooked up and checked, I began checking out the cockpit with the assistance of the crew chief, Charlie Baker, and John Reeves, an inspector who read off the items on the cockpit entry checklist. This cockpit checkout procedure required about 30 minutes to complete. During this time, the ground crew was disconnecting the many servicing carts and buttoning up the various access panels on the X-15 aircraft. When the cockpit check was complete, the cockpit entry crew closed the canopy and I was in my own little world, inaccessible to anyone except through radio contact.

In one sense, to the B-52 crew, the X-15 (including pilot!) was just a bomb hung on two bomb shackles under the wing that they dutifully hauled out to the launch area and dropped on command. In another sense, the X-15 pilot was a part of the B-52 crew. He was physically attached to the B-52. He saw the same scenery and felt the same bumps that they did during the flight. He was connected to the same intercom system so that he could converse with them without broadcasting on the air, but in many other ways he was completely isolated from them and from everyone and everything else. It was a rather lonely feeling.

The pressure suit that I was wearing did not help to relieve this sense of isolation. The pressure suit protected the pilot, but it also isolated him. He could not feel or touch anything directly. He could not remove his gloves. He could not smell anything other than the pure oxygen being piped into his suit. He could not open his faceplate and he could not hear much of anything outside of the suit due to the sound proofing effect of the crash helmet. He could see out the windows and he could hear the radio communications, but that was about it. I could relate to the boy in the plastic bubble. He was surrounded by things and people that he could see and hear, but he was still isolated. I could also relate to the Mercury astronauts sitting alone in their capsules on top of their launch vehicles.

I realized I was not the only one who experienced these feelings of isolation when I spent several months serving as a technical advisor to a motion picture crew that produced the movie, "The X-15 Story." It was not the greatest movie in the world, but it did have some good flight footage in it. It also featured a couple of rising stars—Mary Tyler Moore and Charles Bronson. One of the actors was suited up for a scene in the X-15 cockpit. We put a *g* suit on him and then a pressure suit outer garment to simulate a pressure suit. The script called for him to walk out to the X-15 which was hanging on the B-52, get into the cockpit, and close the canopy.

The actor made it up the stairs and into the cockpit. He also tolerated being strapped into the seat and closing his faceplate. When the canopy was lowered into position and locked, however, he panicked. He began pounding on the canopy windows to get out. The director eliminated that scene from the movie. In retrospect, I can understand how he felt, but I guess my incentive to endure it was higher.

I remember the glorious feeling I would get when that canopy was raised after landing and I could open the faceplate and smell the beautiful fresh air. Conversely, at the same time, there was a feeling that someone was invading my privacy when they opened the canopy. In that cockpit, I was in my own little world. I was comfortable and secure and protected from harm. I had complete control over the environment in the cockpit. I could make it hot or cold, light or dark. I could tune in or tune out the world with my radio volume control. The cockpit should have been equipped with a "Do Not Disturb" sign.

The unique carry arrangement of the X-15 on the B-52 resulted in some harsh sounding mission rules. For example, if the B-52 developed a major problem, the crew was allowed to drop the X-15, at their discretion. This sounded a little hard-hearted to the X-15 pilot at first, but then after thinking about it he could accept the fact that it would be better to save the three B-52 crew members if they could do so by getting rid of the X-15. What seemed harder to accept was that if the X-15 pilot had aircraft problems that might endanger the B-52, they could again jettison him.

During most of the captive portion of the flight, the X-15 was not ready to drop. Most of the systems were inactive, including the vital control system. X-15 systems were not activated until 12 minutes before launch, due to the limited duration of the on-board power supply. Thus, if the X-15 were dropped in an emergency, the X-15 pilot really had a bucket of worms to untangle before he had a flyable aircraft.

It was even worse if he was at low altitude or not within gliding distance of a landing site, because then he had to try to start the rocket engine from scratch to get some altitude. If possible, the B-52 crew would delay jettisoning the X-15 until the X-15 pilot could start the APUs. In the worst possible situation, however, it was every man for himself and dump the X-15. This never happened during the X-15 program. We had several emergencies during captive flight but the B-52 crew always brought the X-15 home.

A premature launch due to an emergency only happened once to my knowledge during the many rocket airplane programs. As I indicated earlier, these rules may sound cold-hearted, but on the other hand, the X-15 pilot felt he was the lucky one since he had his own lifeboat, if the B-52 developed serious problems. He could drop himself and leave the B-52 crew to handle their own difficulties. In this total scenario, regardless of whether you are an optimist or a pessimist, you are right. As a last resort, there was the ejection seat in the X-15, which could be used before or after launch.

Once the X-15 canopy was closed, the pace picked up as the access stands were removed, the B-52 engines started and the B-52 hatches and access panels closed. The B-52 was ready to taxi within 10 minutes after canopy closure. This morning, Chase-1 was standing by on the taxiway to taxi out with us. The B-52 had to taxi either 2 or 5 miles depending on whether the duty runway was two-two or zero-four. We preferred using runway zero-four since this allowed use of the entire lakebed as an overrun if we had problems on takeoff. In fact, we occasionally used the lakebed for takeoff if we had strong crosswinds. This particular morning, we were going to use runway zero-four. Eight to ten ground vehicles usually accompanied the B-52 during the taxi out to the takeoff position.

The B-52 taxi was always a rough ride, as felt in the X-15. It felt like the B-52 had square wheels and, in fact, the B-52 tires usually were out of round due to sitting for an extended period with a heavy load. At the takeoff end of the runway, the B-52 stopped to do its pretakeoff checklist. During this period, Chase-1 made its takeoff to get in position for an airborne pickup of the B-52. The crash and rescue helicopter also took off to get into position to cover the B-52 takeoff. And finally, the X-15 crew pulled the safety pin on the X-15 release hooks. Over the radio, the control tower announced, "Zero zero three, cleared for takeoff."

In the X-15, the takeoff roll was also a rough ride because the Edwards main runway is rough and uneven at both ends. The B-52 seemed to leap off the runway when it reached flying speed, rather than lift off gently like a normal aircraft. This was a characteristic peculiar to all B-52s. Once airborne, however, the ride smoothed out and the checklist procedures began.

Fitz Fulton was flying the B-52 today, so I settled back for a nice smooth ride out to the launch point. Fitz was an excellent pilot who had years of experience launching rocket aircraft. The B-52 with Chase-1 tucked in beside it, climbed around the Edwards lakebed until it reached at least 25,000 feet before heading out toward the launch point. This was done to ensure that the

X-15 had sufficient altitude to make it to a landing site if it had to be dropped in an emergency during the flight out to the launch lake.

At the 12-minute-to-launch point in the checklist, we are beginning to activate the various systems in the X-15 in preparation for launch. The first action is to start the APUs, which provide both hydraulic and electrical power.

Following APU start, we began a checkout of the Minneapolis-Honeywell Flight Control system in the X-15. This was an advanced command augmentation type control system with adaptive gain scheduling. The system checkout was automatically accomplished from the B-52 through a computer that cycles the controls while checking overall system performances.

This control check was somewhat unnerving to the pilot because some electrons were now moving the control system without any inputs from the pilot. He then realized that he was not in direct control of the aircraft with a system such as this. He was only commanding a computer that then responded with its own idea of what is necessary in terms of a control output. As a pilot, you hope the guy who designed this electronic control system knew what he was doing. In fact, you would like him to be in the airplane with you to be exposed to any adverse results.

You finally rationalized that if the control stick and control surfaces ended up back where they started after the control check, the system was probably working correctly. You were therefore rudely shaken out of your false sense of security when the controls did not return to their original position, but instead the stick ended up over in the corner of the cockpit. I do not think any of the X-15 pilots really felt comfortable with that system during the early stage of its development, even though it offered many helpful features. This system was, however, a vital step toward fly-by-wire which finally evolved in the early 1970s.

At 8 minutes to launch, the B-52 began a turn back towards Edwards. The B-52 had been proceeding outbound for 21 minutes since leaving North Base at Edwards. At 4 minutes to launch, the B-52 rolled out of the turn on a heading back to Edwards and I began to activate the propulsion system. At 1 minute to launch, I began activating the engine and at the end of that minute, I launched myself in the X-15.

At this point, let me again say a few words about the launch. It was a surprise no matter how many times I went through it. It felt as if the X-15 exploded off the hooks. In addition, the X-15 always tended to roll off at launch. To minimize the rolloff at launch, we normally put in a little bit of countering aileron.

On this flight I almost forgot to put in some aileron because it was not on the checklist. When I did finally remember, my mind momentarily went blank on which direction to put the aileron in. I finally said, "Aha, it's to the left." I applied left aileron and then hit the launch switch. The airplane rolled violently to the left at launch and then I realized I had put too much aileron in. I ended up right under the B-52 fuselage. I felt stupid, but I had to smile because I knew the B-52 crew really got a jolt out of the rocket engine starting up right under their feet. It made a big boom on initial startup.

As an X-15 pilot, if you thought you were busy before launch, you were really impressed after launch. Joe Walker used to say that they intentionally kept us busy in the cockpit before launch so that we would not have time to think about the launch and chicken out. After launch, we could not chicken out because we had to really move to get the engine lit, the wings back to level, the nose started up, and the heading corrected. All of this had to be done within the first 5 seconds after launch.

The success of the entire flight depended on how well the pilot flew the airplane in the next 80 or 90 seconds. The engine normally burned approximately 82 seconds at 100 percent thrust. It would burn longer at reduced thrust, but it was much more efficient to use 100 percent thrust to get to the desired test condition and then, if there was any propellant left over, the pilot could throttle back to sustain that test condition.

This particular flight was a heating flight. On heating flights, we went to high velocities at relatively low altitudes, 80,000 to 90,000 feet, to intentionally heat the airplane up and then measure the temperatures and heating rates on various parts of the aircraft. On this particular flight, we were planning to fly as fast as we could but still get some stabilized flight time before the engine burned out.

That meant that we had to shoot for a speed less than the maximum capability to save some fuel for the stabilized flight period. Getting to the desired flight conditions on these heating flights was like trying to thread a needle using vice-grips. The X-15 had so damn much thrust it was almost impossible to accurately hit a desired altitude.

But, back to my flight. I lit the engine while I was still in a 60-degree bank under the B-52 and then rolled wings level and pulled up to 10 degrees angle of attack. Five seconds had elapsed by the time I accomplished all this and I heard NASA-1 call, "Good light, Milt." A quick check of the rocket engine instruments indicated that it was functioning properly and putting out full thrust. NASA-1 called and said, "Should be coming up on alpha." Seven seconds, turned 3 degrees right to correct my heading. Nine seconds. Ten seconds. Checked angle of attack, angle of sideslip, roll attitude, rate of climb (it should have been positive by now). Twelve seconds, I lost the horizon now because the nose of the aircraft was 10 degrees above the horizon and the small windows cut off my downward view. Thirteen seconds, rolled the wings level to stop my turn and held my planned heading. Fifteen seconds, 16 seconds, cross-checked angle of sideslip, normal acceleration to make sure that I did not exceed 2 g and checked my pitch attitude vernier needle since it should be coming off the peg soon. Seventeen seconds, 18 seconds, the pitch attitude vernier needle is now moving toward the null position. Twenty seconds, 21 seconds, and the pitch attitude needle is now centered and I ease off on angle of attack to maintain the planned 25-degree climb angle.

NASA-1 called and said, "You should be on theta (pitch attitude) now." I then had a little time to relax. NASA-1 reported, "Track looks real good." All I had to do was lock on that pitch attitude, keep my heading constant, and cross-check altitude and velocity versus time. I should have been back above launch altitude after losing 3,000 to 4,000 feet during the roundout and my velocity should have been about 1,600 feet per second or roughly 1.6 Mach number.

The rate of climb was starting to build up rapidly. NASA-1 called, "Coming up on profile real nice." Thirty-one seconds, cross-checked altitude, velocity, and rate of climb versus time. Rechecked engine instruments, hydraulic pressures, generators, APU bearing temperatures, stabilizer position, and a few other mundane items. Thirty-five seconds, 36 seconds. Tried to get a little more comfortable in the seat because the g forces pushing me back in the seat were over 2 and building up fast. NASA-1 called and said, "Standby for pushover." Forty-one seconds, time to push over, but first checked altitude and velocity.

I should have had 62,000 feet altitude, 2,600 feet per second velocity and about 1,000 feet per second rate of climb (60,000 feet per minute). I was not quite at 62,000 so I delayed pushover a half a second and then pushed over to 0 g. I reset the trim to maintain 0 g and then, again went through a cross-check of my instrument panel. Everything still looked good. NASA-1 called, "Beautiful profile," meaning that my altitude versus time was right on schedule. Fifty-two seconds, 53 seconds. NASA-1 reported, "Right on track and profile." Fifty-seven seconds, NASA-1 called and said, "Standby for your left roll, Milt." At 61 seconds, the flight plan called for a left roll to 90 degrees bank angle and a pullup to 10 degrees angle of attack. At 60 seconds, I checked altitude and velocity. I should have had 80,000 feet altitude and 3,900 feet per second velocity and I was almost there, so I rolled over as planned and pulled up in angle of attack.

I could now see the ground and horizon again through my left window and I recognized some landmarks down below. A quick cross-check of my instruments indicated that everything was normal. NASA-1 called and said, "Nice profile." Sixty-four seconds. Sixty-five seconds and NASA-1 reported, "Stand-by for minimum thrust and speed brakes." At 71 seconds I was scheduled to reduce throttle to minimum thrust and open the speed brakes partially to slow the rate of acceleration or speed buildup. At 71 seconds I was right on speed, 4,750 feet per second or 4.75 Mach number—and on altitude—88,500 feet. I lurched forward to reach the throttle since the *g* force pushing me back in the seat was over 3 g, and I slowly retarded it to minimum thrust. You always treated a rocket respectfully, particularly when it came to throttling it down. It was very temperamental.

On a previous flight the engine had quit when I throttled back. I did not get home on that flight. On yet another flight, the engine shut down as I retarded the throttle too far and unported the fuel lines. On that flight I got home, but I did not get the planned test maneuvers at high speed.

I started the speed brakes out to reduce my longitudinal acceleration to near 0 and then concentrated on maintaining 10 degrees angle of attack and 90 degrees bank angle. At these flight conditions, my dynamic pressure should read about 600 pounds per square foot. Dynamic pressure is the pressure of the air impacting against the aircraft. If you could hold your hand out the window palm first, at 600 pounds per square foot, you would have roughly 100 pounds pushing on your hand.

Dynamic pressure was the key parameter that we wanted to control on this flight. We wanted to maintain a constant 600 pounds per square foot while we measured the rate of heating of the aircraft structure. We had made measurements of the heating rate at these conditions in a wind tunnel and we wanted to determine if the actual heating rate in flight was the same as that predicted in the wind tunnel. Verifying wind tunnel predictions is one of the primary objectives in flying research aircraft. We want to ensure that the wind tunnels accurately predict the real flight conditions when we begin to design the operational aircraft that will follow along after the research aircraft. We cannot afford to put a lot of design margin, excess structural strength, in an operational aircraft. We had a lot of design margin in the X-15, since we were not exactly sure what the real flight environment was like at hypersonic speeds, when the X-15 was designed.

In the X-15, we were probing the so called thermal barrier for the first time in a manned aircraft. Research aircraft generally were designed with a lot of structural margin. The X-1s, for example, were designed to withstand 18 g in case they went out of control and swapped ends. One X-1 did tumble on one of Chuck Yeager's flights.

Now, back to my flight again. From 71 seconds to 80 seconds, I held dynamic pressure constant while the speed gradually built up to about 5,000 feet per second. To keep dynamic pressure constant, I had to gradually increase altitude as the speed built up. At 80 seconds, my altitude was about 93,000 feet and I was scheduled to increase my angle of attack to 17 degrees and bring the speed brakes back in to maintain a slow speed buildup. This would put me in a stabilized 4 g turn.

NASA-1 called at 80 seconds and said "17 degrees, speed brakes in and check H dot." From 80 seconds to 90 seconds, I was to continue holding a constant dynamic pressure while speed and altitude slowly built up. At 83 seconds, NASA-1 called and said, "Beautiful profile." At 90 seconds, the engine should have burned all the fuel and shut down. By that time I should have reached 92,000 feet altitude and 5,100 feet per second velocity. At 87 seconds, NASA-1 said, "Standby for your burnout." Ninety seconds came and went and the engine kept burning. Ninety-one seconds, 92 seconds, 93 seconds, 94 seconds, and still no engine shutdown.

At this time I had mixed emotions. I was in a 4 g turn, turning away from Edwards. I did not want to turn too far away from Edwards, because I might have trouble getting back. On the other hand, I was getting some beautiful data. I was in a very smooth 4 g turn at exactly 600 pounds dynamic pressure— an ideal condition to get good heating rate data. So I decided to sit tight and wait for burnout. I assumed it had to burn out within another second. Ninety-five seconds, 96 seconds, 97 seconds, 98 seconds, and still no burnout. That was just too much time. I decided I had better reverse the turn to get the airplane headed back toward Edwards, and pick up the next test maneuver which was a 60-degree right bank at about 2.4 g to gather more heating data while the aircraft decelerated after burnout.

As I reversed the turn, NASA-1 called and said, "OK, shut it off, Milt." They, too, were concerned about the extra burn time. To the average person, 8 seconds of extra burn time may not seem like much, but to a rocket expert, 8 seconds of extra burn time is extremely unlikely. Burn rate does not vary that much at the same thrust level. In all our previous X-15 flights (over one hundred flights), we had never seen more than 2 or 3 seconds of variation in burn time at the most. True, I was at a reduced throttle setting and that 8 seconds was probably equivalent to 5 seconds of burn time at 100 percent throttle, but still that was an unbelievably long burn time.

One might wonder why all the fuss about 8 extra seconds of burn time. It was very significant because I was accumulating too much energy (speed) approaching Edwards. With too much energy, I could not slow down to land at Edwards and could go whizzing on by with no place to land.

When I reversed the turn, I put in a relatively large roll command and at the same time pushed the nose down to prevent the aircraft from climbing as I rolled over the top. Then, as I approached 60 degrees right bank, I put in a healthy roll command to stop the roll at 60 degrees bank. My speed at this time was close to 5,500 feet per second (approximately 3,700 MPH) and my altitude was just under 100,000 feet.

Just as I completed this maneuver, the aircraft started rolling violently back and forth. At the same time, it was pitching up and down. I was being thrown against the straps with tremendous force. I was flying at almost 4,000 MPH and the airplane was totally out of control. I happened to glance out the window during one oscillation and everything was black. At the time, I could not figure that out. It was, of course, the sky as seen from high altitudes. I had never been that high before. This wild oscillation continued for what seemed like an eternity, but was actually only 8 to 10 seconds and then the aircraft motions stopped just as quickly as they had started. That was some ride—just like being on a wild bull. I tentatively moved the control stick and the aircraft responded normally, so I rolled back to the 60 degree right bank that I was supposed to be in and pulled up to 10 degrees angle of attack which gave me about a 2.5 *g* turn to the right.

Thinking about the last few seconds, I realized that NASA-1 was unusually silent during that violent maneuver. Usually when something unplanned occurred on a flight, the experts in the flight control room were clamoring to tell you what the problem was and what action to take to correct it. In this case, nothing.

NASA-1 finally called and said, "Watch your H dot" (rate of descent) and then said, "Ninety-eight thousand, bring her down a little bit." I said, "OK." As I decelerated through 4,300 feet per second velocity, I pulled on up to 17 degrees angle of attack and rolled to 90 degrees bank angle just as NASA-1 called to say, "Bring brakes out now and come on up to 17 degrees." A few seconds later NASA-1 advised me that I was passing over Three Sisters. They were only about 40 miles northeast of Edwards.

As I discussed earlier, I was now in a real high-energy situation. I was still traveling about Mach 4 (close to 3,000 MPH) and I was only 40 miles out. I was hotter than a pistol and I really had to slow it down. I was supposed to reverse my turn at 3,800 feet per second, but I had turned too far on the first turn and I was way high on energy, so I called NASA-1 and asked what to do about the turn.

NASA-1 responded, "Hold it there in the right turn and we will want you about two-two-five degrees" (heading). The next call, a couple of seconds later, was, "Bring it around to two-four-five." A few seconds later, NASA-1 said, "You're coming up abeam Cuddeback now. Have you down to 70,000 and 3.5. Full speed brakes now."

Cuddeback, another of our emergency dry lakebeds, was only 30 miles from Edwards and I was still traveling over 2,300 MPH at 70,000 foot altitude. I said, "OK, full out." NASA-1 called again to say, "OK, keep her coming on downhill, looks real good. Field is off to about your ten o'clock, do you have it in sight?" I said, "Yep." A few more seconds and NASA-1 said, "You're about 15 (miles) out now, coming through Mach two now, real nice. Keep your brakes out." The next call from NASA-1, about 15 seconds later was, "You can bring the brakes in now, have you about 10 (miles) out. One point five Mach." My energy was now in good shape.

The next call came from Bob Rushworth, Chase-4, who was flying in the Edwards area waiting to pick me up during the landing approach. "OK, Milt, you can go to jettison anytime." We usually waited to jettison any remaining propellant until the landing chase called, since it provided the chase pilot a good visual cue to locate you. The jettisoned propellants normally came out like a white vapor trail. I responded, "OK." Chase-4 then asked, "What's your altitude?" I said, "I got 40."

NASA-1 called to tell me, "Engine Master off." I said, "OK. Am I coming across the highway?" As I mentioned earlier, the windows in the X-15 were very limiting in downward vision. NASA-1 said, "Coming across the highway now." This was the highway just north of the Edwards lakebed running between Mojave and Boron. I said, "OK." NASA-1 said, "And if you got time, give us a calibrate." I said, "OK, damper disengaging." NASA-1 then said, "OK, coming subsonic, watch your angle of attack."

Chase-4 then chimed in with a "Tallyho." He had finally spotted me. NASA-1 then called and said, "Check your flap and squat circuit breakers." I said, "They're in." NASA-1 said, "Experiment off," and I said, "Rog." NASA-1 said, "You can set in your nose down trim now if you want," and

I responded, "OK. I'm using some brakes in here." Chase-4 then said, "You can go to pressurize anytime now. I don't see any jettison at all." We always repressurized the fuel tanks after we jettisoned fuel to gain extra fuselage rigidity during the landing, to minimize the chance of the fuselage breaking as the nose slammed down.

My next call was, "Flaps," and Chase-4 called, "Flaps coming down." I then called, "Gear," and Chase-4 said, "Looks good" and finally, when I touched down, he said, "Good." I slid for about 2 miles on the lakebed before I stopped. The flight from launch to landing lasted just under 7 minutes.

During that flight, I had zipped on up to 3,750 MPH, performed a number of test maneuvers, lost control of the aircraft momentarily, traveled over 150 miles of desert and landed back home at Edwards in a 2-mile-long cloud of dust, all in less time than it it takes to smoke a king-sized cigarette. As I said before, it is a poor way to build up flight time and it is really tough to get your 4 hours minimum flight time a month.

While I was sitting in the suit van, getting out of the pressure suit, I reflected back on the flight. For 10 seconds during that flight, the airplane had been doing its own thing. That reinforced my previous thought that the X-15 was like a bull. When it decided to do something on its own, it did it. There was nothing you could do to stop it. I had momentarily lost control of the bull.

It only took a couple of days after the flight to determine why the engine burned an extra 8 seconds. Normally, in level flight, the engine burned out when the propellant level in the tank dropped below the level of the top of the propellant line leading out of the tank. At that time, pressurizing gas also began escaping and the fuel pump cavitated. In that condition we normally ended up with about 150 gallons of residual propellant left in the tanks at burnout. In my 4 g turn, the propellant was forced to the rear wall of the tank in such a manner that no pressurizing gas escaped until all the propellant went out the line. I managed to use up all the propellant and got 8 more seconds of burn time. Chase-4 confirmed this theory when he mentioned during the flight that he saw no jettison at all.

The other problem—loss of control—took about a month to solve. At first, Bob Rushworth facetiously said it was just a result of my ham-fisted flying. (Rushworth, at that time, was the senior X-15 pilot.) He implied that I had caused the aircraft to go unstable with my large control inputs just before burnout. We were all aware of the need to treat the system gently. To counter that, I dug up some of the records from one or two of Rushworth's flights and showed him where he had made similar control inputs. I really liked Bob and had tremendous respect for him, but I knew this was a unique problem that I had encountered.

After many hours on the simulator and some necessary improvements to the simulator, our control system experts were finally able to duplicate the problem. In essence, that smart control system had fooled itself into thinking that it was at a more benign flight condition. When I applied control it gave me much more control deflection than I should have gotten. The airplane then responded more than the control system thought it should, and the control system in turn fought that excessive response. A limit cycle, oscillation developed wherein the system was periodically calling for full control, first one way and then the other. The airplane was forced into a sustained violent oscillation in both pitch and roll. It was a wild ride.

After about 10 seconds of this nonsense, the system finally stabilized itself and the aircraft recovered. It did not cause any damage during this flight, but at a more severe flight condition, it could have torn the aircraft apart. We learned something new about the airplane.

I was always impressed with the philosophy used in the early days of flying in World War I. Any mechanic who worked on an aircraft could be ordered to fly with the pilot on the first flight after the repair work was done. Any parachute rigger could be ordered to jump in any of the chutes that he had packed. That really created an incentive for quality work. It also weeded out the incompetents since they did not make it back to work after a failure. I wish the control system designer had been along on this ride.

I strongly recommended that the control system be modified to prevent this from ever happening again, but modification of the control system would have been very expensive and time consuming. Program officials decided against any modification. They believed we now understood the problem and could take preventative steps to ensure that this problem would not cause the loss of the aircraft. This decision came back to haunt us.

MY ALTITUDE FLIGHTS

I flew my first altitude flight in the number one X-15. This aircraft had separate controllers for aerodynamic and reaction controls. Aerodynamic controls were on the right sidestick controller and reaction controls were on the left sidestick controller. On an altitude flight in this aircraft, the pilot was flying with both hands. The flight was planned to an altitude of 180,000 feet. The purpose of the flight was to provide an altitude buildup flight for me to obtain data with the MIT horizon photometer, and to check out the Dyna-Soar Honeywell Inertial System. (Even though I did not have the opportunity to fly Dyna-Soar, I did get to fly some of its parts.) Altitude buildup flights were normally done in 40,000- to 50,000-foot increments. In my case, my highest previous altitude was 100,000 feet, so I was taking an 80,000-foot step in maximum altitude. That is a pretty big step.

The flight was to be launched at Mud Lake on May 25, 1965. The prelaunch activities proceeded without a hitch and I was launched at 10:12:07.5. I got a good light and pulled up to 11 degrees angle of attack. I held 11 degrees alpha for approximately 24 seconds until I reached my climb attitude of 30 degrees. My speed had increased to 1,700 feet per second as I stabilized on my climb angle. When I reached a speed of 2,000 feet per second, I opened my speed brakes to slow down my rate of climb. This procedure was used during altitude buildup flights to give the pilot more opportunity to observe the transition from aerodynamic to space flight and enable him to better feel out the airplane during this transition. At 82 seconds of burn time, I shut the engine down as I passed through a speed of 4,900 feet per second. I then retracted the speed brakes and sat back for the long coast to peak altitude.

As I continued to coast up to peak altitude, I was surprised at how easy it was to fly an altitude flight compared to the exacting heating flights that I had been flying. On these altitude flights, I simply pointed the airplane uphill at the proper climb altitude and then shut the engine off at the specified velocity. There was none of this business of pushing over to 0 *g* opening speed brakes, adjusting the throttle and pulling into turns while maintaining the precise altitude and velocity that was required on heating flights. Altitude flights were easy, and fun.

Admittedly, flying two-handed was not the most simple task, but so far I was doing a pretty good job of it. I was able to hold pitch and roll attitude and compass heading within a couple degrees of the desired values. I tended to work each axis individually with the left-hand reaction controller, rather than make combined inputs. I was primarily concentrating on maintaining heading and a wings level attitude while slowly adjusting pitch attitude to correlate with flight path angle. The control technique utilized by most of the pilots with the left-hand controller was to make pulse type control inputs in one axis at a time.

These inputs were used in pitch to change the pitch attitude as required and in yaw and roll to maintain heading and a wings level attitude. The one thing the pilot did not want to do was get the airplane moving in more than one axis at a time. He wanted to keep the aircraft motions simple and slow. At these lower peak altitudes, below 200,000 feet, he was assisted in his task by small aerodynamic forces that tended to keep the airplane pointed in the right direction. Do not misunderstand. A pilot could still get in trouble and lose control at these lower peak altitudes, but he had some help from the inherent aerodynamic stability of the airplane.

Above 200,000 feet, the pilot was on his own. If something caused the aircraft to start rotating in any axis, it would continue to rotate until he put in a control pulse to stop it. The airplane could turn completely around if he did not stop it. That is why he really did not want to get the airplane moving in more than one axis at a time. If it ever did get moving in more than one axis at a time, the best control technique was to stabilize the motion in one axis before working on the other axis.

As I approached peak altitude, I concentrated on changing pitch attitude to be in the proper attitude for entry. The flight path changes quite rapidly on these high-altitude flights as we go over the top, since we come down as steeply as we go up. In just a matter of seconds, the flight path changes from +30 degrees to −30 degrees. It was very desirable to have our entry pitch attitude established as we peaked out in altitude. We actually began pushing the nose over before we reached peak altitude and ended up going over the top with the aircraft in a 10- to 20-degree nose-down attitude. As I reached a nose-level attitude before going over the top, I had my first look at the earth from high altitude. It was impressive. As Bob White replied when asked how far he could see on his maximum altitude flight, "You could see as far as you looked."

The earth was very bright below me. I could see the earth curve away in all directions and the atmosphere appeared as a band of blue haze sitting below me and just above the horizon. The sky was quite black above and to the sides. But something seemed strange. The bright earth was under the nose of the airplane. Out ahead, the earth was a darker color, a bluish grey color. All of a sudden I realized I was looking down on the Pacific Ocean. The California coastline was down under my nose at what appeared to be a 45-degree angle. I was going to reenter over the Pacific Ocean!

I could not believe it. Someone had made a horrible mistake. I was either launched too far down range or I was higher and farther down the track than my instruments and ground radar indicated. I was going to end up in the Pacific Ocean and I did not even have a life raft in my emergency bailout kit. For that matter, I did not have a life vest. I was in deep crap. There was no way I could get the airplane back down in the atmosphere and turned around before crossing the coastline.

As I sat there dumbfounded, NASA-1 continued to babble on about how nice my track and profile were. Little did they realize what was happening. I was tempted to tell NASA-1 that they did not know what the hell they were talking about. I was in real trouble. But, as I sat there subconsciously flying the airplane and wondering about the ditching characteristics of the X-15, the blue band of the atmosphere began to get thicker and thicker and all of a sudden it enveloped me. The *g* forces started to build up and the ocean seemed to recede from my view.

I began to see the desert and the mountains in a more familiar perspective. I could now look out ahead and see land, not water. In fact, there ahead was good old Rogers Lakebed at Edwards. It was still down below my nose, but now I could convince myself that I could get the airplane down to a landing on the lakebed. Somehow things had worked out. But I was still upset and I was going to raise hell with the guy who had planned that flight. He had scared the hell out of me and I had survived only through my own skill and cunning. I was going to kick his butt. He could have at least warned me about this.

I learned later that each of the pilots had been similarly surprised on their first high-altitude flight. The geometry of the flight profile was highly unusual. At peak altitude, the pilot was within 100 miles of his destination but he was close to 40 miles high on a 200,000-foot flight and almost 60 miles high on a 300,000-foot flight. Experience with normal airplanes would indicate that you could not possibly descend fast enough to remain over land from that position. But the X-15 was not a normal airplane. It was a super airplane—a cross between an airplane and a spacecraft. It was something else.

The remainder of the flight was routine and I made an uneventful landing at 10:21:09.5. Total free flight time—9 minutes, 2.5 seconds. Not quite enough to qualify for flight pay, but then we did not get flight pay anyway.

My second altitude flight was even more uneventful than the first. I went to a higher altitude, 214,000 feet, but I had no problems and again felt that altitude flights were a piece of cake. I might qualify that statement somewhat. Altitude flights were extremely easy to fly if the flight control system was working properly. If it was not, the pilot could very easily get into trouble real fast, especially during reentry. During entry he had to hold a fairly high angle of attack to accomplish the pullout. At these high angles of attack, the X-15 was not exceptionally stable and would oscillate if disturbed, particularly in the roll and yaw axes. It required stability augmentation, or artificial damping, to cope with these high-frequency aircraft oscillations. Without damping, these airplane oscillations could result in loss of control. We really did not want to lose stability augmentation during entry.

On my second altitude flight, I missed my intended peak altitude of 220,000 feet by 6,000 feet due to an improper setting of my climb indicator. I was upset by this because I had hit my intended altitude on my first flight almost right on—179,600 feet actual versus 180,000 feet planned. The 6,000-foot error on my second flight seemed huge by comparison. Bikle calmed me down though by reminding me that it was less than a 3 percent error. Our measurement accuracy was not a great deal better than that. In fact, before launch it was not uncommon to have 2,000 or 3,000 feet discrepancies between X-15 pressure altitude and inertial altitude. Radar altitude may or may not agree with either of the two. We kind of had to average everything out.

My next altitude flight was scheduled to be a flight to 265,000 feet, high enough to qualify for astronaut wings. I did not get a chance to make that flight, because I was reassigned full time to the lifting body program. I would not have gotten astronaut wings anyway. NASA did not award astronaut wings to NASA pilots.

SOME MINOR DISTRACTIONS

Joe Engle seemed to have a charmed relationship with the X-15. He flew sixteen flights without any major emergencies, or significant deviations from his planned flight conditions. He always managed to get an engine light on the first try and he made it back to Edwards for landing on every flight. Joe seemed to have more than his share of uneventful flights while other pilots reaped more than their share of emergencies to compensate for Joe's good luck.

Joe did have his share of stability augmentation system problems. On his sixth flight, a checkout flight in the number three aircraft with the MH-96 system, Joe lost all of his stability augmentation 10 seconds after launch. The flight was an altitude buildup flight for Joe in the number three aircraft to an altitude of 180,000 feet. Joe did not realize that he had lost stability augmentation until after engine burnout during the climb. He was committed to ballistic flight without the essential high-frequency damping required for safe flight outside the atmosphere.

After engine burnout, the aircraft began oscillating rapidly in all three axes reaching peak amplitudes of ± 10 degrees in pitch, ± 6 degrees in yaw and over 90 degrees in roll. It was a wild ride for 40 seconds during the climb. Joe finally managed to reengage the MH-96 system after several attempts and the oscillations stopped. The MH-96 system remained engaged and operating properly during reentry. Joe had no further problems during the flight.

On Joe's ninth flight, a checkout flight of the Dyna-Soar inertial system installed in the number one X-15, Joe lost his pitch augmentation 10 seconds after launch. The flight was a relatively low-altitude flight to 110,000 feet altitude, so pitch damping was not critical. The damper appeared to reengage when Joe reset the switch during boost but it did not seem to work properly because Joe had serious controllability problems during a planned pullup to high angle of attack after engine burnout. The remainder of the flight was uneventful.

Joe's most noteworthy flight was his fifteenth flight. The flight was a planned altitude flight to 266,000 feet, in the number three aircraft. On that flight, the yaw damper failed immediately after launch. Joe managed to reset the damper and continued flying the profile. Mission rules dictated that the pilot revert to an alternate, low altitude profile if the yaw damper failed within the first 32 seconds after launch. Joe did not feel obligated to fly the alternate profile since the damper reset satisfactorily. However, the yaw damper failed again, 19 seconds later, and again, 10 seconds later. It failed three times within the critical 32 seconds after launch. Joe managed to reset it each time, but the system was trying to tell Joe something. Joe should have reverted to the alternate profile.

During the last of these resetting attempts, he inadvertently engaged the control-stick-steering control mode. This control mode was engaged while Joe was still pulling up into his climb. The control system logic then assumed that Joe wanted to continue the pullup, so it began to apply more nose up control. During the next 49 seconds prior to engine burnout, the yaw damper failed three more times. Joe reset it each time, but now he was also having to fight the tendency of the control system to continually pull the nose up.

At burnout, he was committed to exoatmospheric flight to more than 50 miles altitude. The yaw damper was quite critical for a successful reentry from that altitude. Without it, he could lose control and tumble or spin back into the atmosphere. During exoatmospheric flight, the yaw damper failed nine more times. Joe reset the damper each time within a second and a half of the failure, indicating that he was keeping one hand on the damper switch as he flew the aircraft with the other hand. Joe managed to keep the airplane at the desired pitch attitude while fighting the nose-up command of the autopilot. All of this had to be horribly distracting, but Joe seemed to take it all in stride. He did not report each of the yaw damper failures, only the first one. He did comment on the apparent out of trim condition in pitch during exoatmospheric flight.

The control room received indications of each yaw damper failure in the telemetered data, but since Joe did not confirm the failures, they assumed that the data were erroneous.

The yaw damper failed a total of twenty-one times during the 10-minute flight. In the postflight debriefing, Joe did not consider the damper failures to be a real problem but rather a distraction. In the flight report, the flight planner enumerated and described all of the system failures and discussed the piloting problems created by the inadvertent activation of the control-stick-steering mode. He summarized his discussion by saying, "It is difficult to understand why no pilot comments were made during the flight and very few made during the postflight [de]briefing." Joe apparently did not want to abort the planned flight just because of a damper failure. He could be quite stubborn at times. For some pilots, that flight could have been very suspenseful. For Joe, it was uneventful with only minor distractions.

Joe was lucky that he encountered this kind of a problem while flying the number three aircraft. Aerodynamic and reaction controls were combined in one control stick. If he had encountered this problem in one of the other aircraft, he would have been flying with both hands and would not have had a free hand to re-engage the damper. That could have been potentially catastrophic.

On Joe's last X-15 flight, he had yaw damper failures at launch and during reentry from an altitude in excess of 50 miles. The airplane oscillated wildly in yaw during the entry, but Joe completed the pullout successfully. By this time, Joe had become an expert, by necessity, on damper off controllability. He was ready for something more challenging, like flying the space shuttle.

A SLIGHT OVERSHOOT

On the first day of November 1966, Bill Dana in the number three X-15, was carried aloft on the B-52 to make an altitude flight to 267,000 feet. The purpose of the flight was to collect micrometeorites, measure wing tip pod accelerations, measure the optical background at altitude using a dual channel radiometer, check out the precision attitude indicator, check out the Alert computer, measure sky brightness, and evaluate a new cockpit display panel. This was the 174th flight of the program. At this late stage of the program the X-15s were carrying a significant number of experiments on each flight.

The flight had been delayed over a month due to wet lakebeds, weather, lack of a C-130 support aircraft, several system problems, and having repeated aircraft and engine functional checks due to the long delay before flight. The prelaunch checklist proceeded without any major problems, and the launch occurred on schedule.

Bill got the engine lit on the first try and then pulled up to establish his climb angle of 39 degrees. He reached his climb angle slightly early, but his cross-checks seemed to indicate that he was on his planned profile. Bill was not reading NASA-1 on the radio during the early portion of the climb and thus did not receive any altitude checks for verification of his climb profile. Post-flight checks indicated that he was climbing at a steeper angle than planned due to an error in the climb attitude indicator. He was climbing at 42 degrees rather than 39 degrees.

When Bill finally began receiving NASA-1 as he climbed through 110,000 feet altitude, NASA-1 did not alert him to any error in his profile. In fact, at the time that Bill shut the engine down, NASA-1 indicated that Bill's track and profile were looking very good. Postflight analysis would indicate that Bill was high on energy at engine shutdown and would overshoot his planned peak altitude. The engine burned longer than planned, so Bill shut it down about a second later than the predicted burnout time. This extra engine burn time significantly increased the impending altitude overshoot.

As Bill climbed through 230,000 feet altitude, he got the first confirmation that he was going to go high on peak altitude. NASA-1 said, "Roger, and we have you going a little high on profile. Outside of that, it looks good." Several seconds later NASA-1 said, "Rog, we got you going through 280,000 now." Dana responded, "How about that." At this time, Dana was already 13,000 feet higher than his planned peak altitude and he was still climbing.

NASA-1 called again to say, "Right on track, Bill. Looking real good. Track is real good. We have you peaking out around 310,000 feet." Dana responded, "OK. How many alpha would you like on re-entry?" NASA-1 replied, "Twenty-three degrees." Dana said, "OK." NASA-1 then said, "Track looks real good. You're going to be in good shape for Eddy." Dana responded, "Roger," and then asked if Jack McKay was sending his congratulations. About a year earlier, Bill had been the controller in NASA-1 on one of Jack McKay's flights. Jack had overshot his planned altitude by over 30,000 feet due to an accumulation of small variations in climb angle, engine burn time, and engine thrust. Bill really bugged Jack about that overshoot in altitude. In fact, for a whole year he needled Jack about that gross altitude error. Bill was merciless at times.

Now it was Jack's turn. Bill had overshot his planned altitude by almost 40,000 feet. Forty thousand feet! Most airplanes could not even climb 40,000 feet, let alone overshoot by that much.

I could just imagine the conversation if Bill Dana had to report the altitude overshoot to an FAA controller. It would have gone something like this:

Dana:	"Las Vegas Control, this is NASA 672."
FAA:	"Roger, NASA 672, this is Las Vegas Control, go ahead."
Dana:	"This is NASA 672. I'd like to report that I overshot my altitude a little bit."
FAA:	"Roger, NASA 672. It doesn't appear to be a problem right now. We have no conflicting traffic in your area within 5,000 feet of your assigned altitude. By the way, how much did you overshoot?"
Dana:	"Forty thousand feet."
FAA:	"Oh."

On this flight, Dana established an almost unbeatable world overshoot record for an airplane. To add insult to injury, as Dana shut the engine down, he apparently bumped his kneepad with his arm and released the clip holding the checklist pages to his kneepad. All of a sudden he had twenty-two pages of checklist floating around the cockpit during the entire time that he was outside the atmosphere at 0 g. He could not see his cockpit instruments without brushing away the checklist pages. Bill commented after the flight that it was "like trying to read Shakespeare [while] sitting under a maple tree in October in a high wind."

Bill managed to make a very nice reentry and then proceeded to make an uneventful glide back to Edwards and a nice landing. He had to have some help from NASA-1 to complete the post landing checklist because he could not find the right page of his checklist. It was somewhere down on the floor of the cockpit.

This altitude overshoot did not really compromise the objectives of the flight. In fact, the overshoot actually enhanced the data obtained on some of the experiments. When precise altitude was required to achieve the flight objectives, Bill showed that he could hit the desired altitude precisely. A cold-wall experiment to measure aerodynamic heating rate required a very precise altitude and Mach number combination. Bill was scheduled to fly that experiment on his next flight.

This experiment was an attempt to measure aerodynamic heating rate at a specific Mach number. A skin panel on the upper vertical fin was instrumented to measure temperature, skin friction and static pressure at various locations on the panel. A cover was then fastened over this panel to prevent the airstream from impinging on the skin panel. This cover would keep the skin panel cool during the climb and acceleration to the desired Mach number. At the specified Mach number the panel was blown off and the instantaneous heating rate and skin friction were measured as the airstream impinged on the instrument panel.

On the first attempt to conduct this experiment, Bill had to make an emergency landing at the launch lake due to a low fuel line pressure indication. On the second attempt, Bill came within 100 feet of the desired altitude and was right on the desired Mach number. It was a beautiful data point. As mentioned earlier, these heating flights were extremely tough to fly precisely. They were a real challenge.

Bill was somewhat surprised when he shut the engine down on this flight. It was his first low altitude, heating flight. He said, "Then I got my surprise for the flight and that was that I was reading my heading indicator from a distance of 2 inches." The aircraft drag at this flight condition was extremely high and when the engine was shutdown Bill was thrown violently forward into his shoulder straps, due to the rapid deceleration. An unanticipated problem surfaced when the panel was blown off. The rudder oscillated violently for several cycles in response to the detonation of the explosive bolts.

The next flight was planned to a lower dynamic pressure to ensure that no structural damage would occur as a result of this problem. On that flight, Bill again nailed the desired flight conditions, coming within a few feet of the intended altitude. When the chips were down, Bill came through. Bill will have to work on his statistics, though. It will take a lot of precise flying to compensate for that 40,000-foot overshoot.

Chapter 7 ....

Results and Unanticipated Problems

Flight research is conducted for a number of reasons. One reason is to obtain data that cannot be obtained by any other means. The X-1 flight program was an excellent example of this. The X-1 was developed and flown to obtain data that existing wind tunnels were incapable of providing—transonic and supersonic aerodynamic data. Another reason to do flight research is to validate the results obtained from wind tunnels, computational fluid dynamics, or other predictive techniques. There have been many examples in this area. Two that come to mind are the supercritical wing and the forward swept wing programs. The wind tunnels predicted the benefits of these two new innovations but, because of their somewhat radical nature, flight was deemed necessary for confirmation.

Still another reason for flight research is to stimulate the application of new technology. In this case, a flight demonstration can be worth a thousand paper studies. A good example of this type of flight research is fly-by-wire flight controls. There was no real question that fly-by-wire controls were feasible, but no one was willing to design an airplane with such a system until a flight program verified the practicality and reliability of fly-by-wire controls. A more basic reason to do flight research is "to separate the real from the imagined problems and to make known the overlooked and the unexpected problems," according to Dr. Hugh L. Dryden.

At the time that the X-15 was developed, there were ground facilities capable of providing good hypersonic data. These facilities were lacking in some respects, but they were adequate to design a research aircraft. With this predictive design capability, the X-15 would not be probing the unknown like the X-1. It would instead be validating the results obtained from these new facilities which had a limited track record. There were some areas of great concern when the aircraft began its flight program, but there were no areas completely void of information.

The flight program provided the following results. The basic aircraft stability and control characteristics measured in flight compared quite well with predictions. There were no surprises or problems in this disciplinary area. The X-15 flight results confirmed that existing wind tunnels were capable of accurately predicting the stability and control characteristics of hypersonic flight vehicles. The excellent agreement between wind tunnel and flight results obviated the need for another, higher-speed, research aircraft since hypersonic aerodynamics do not change significantly from Mach 6 to orbital speeds of Mach 25. And, in fact, the space shuttle was designed and successfully flown based primarily on the credibility of the results obtained by the X-15.

Without the lower ventral fin, the X-15 had some limitations such as low directional stability at moderate angles of attack at subsonic speeds. Large speed brake deflections further reduced directional stability at these conditions. Overall, however, the stability and control characteristics were completely adequate throughout the flight envelope.

The augmented handling qualities of the aircraft within the atmosphere were generally very good—equivalent to those of the best fighter aircraft. A pilot-induced oscillation was encountered on the first flight due to inadequate actuator rate limits on the horizontal stabilizer, but once these rates were increased, there were no further PIO problems.

The major handling quality problem unaugmented was a lateral-directional divergence at moderate to high angles of attack at high Mach numbers. This problem was significant because it compromised the pilot's ability to make a successful atmosphere entry if the augmentation system should fail during the attempt. This problem was a result of the negative dihedral resulting from the extended lower ventral fin. Removal of the lower ventral fin eliminated this problem and the latter half of the flight program was flown without the lower ventral. Directional stability was still positive and adequate at high Mach numbers without this segment of the ventral.

Exoatmospherically, the major handling quality problem was the requirement to fly using both hands during the transition from atmospheric to exoatmospheric flight and vice versa. The X-15 had one controller, the right-hand, for aerodynamic controls and another, the left-hand, for reaction controls. This was aggravated by the fact that there was no static stability so to speak during exoatmospheric flight. The pilot had to manually counter any induced aircraft motion. There was some rate damping in the reaction control system, but it was not as crisp as it might have been to convince the pilot that the aircraft was indeed stable. The threshold at which the rate reaction control system triggered was large enough to allow the aircraft to drift off the desired attitude at a disturbing rate causing additional pilot anxiety. The solution would have been to add an attitude hold feature to the system to lock the aircraft attitude except during control inputs. This type of system was available in the MH-96 flight control system and it proved to be very good. The MH-96 system also blended both aerodynamic and reaction controls on one controller which significantly improved the exoatmospheric handling qualities. The MH-96 system also provided increased damping at low dynamic pressures due to its higher gain capability. Overall, the MH-96 system provided much better handling qualities during the transition from atmospheric to exoatmospheric flight and back again.

The MH-96 system did have some handling quality deficiencies during atmospheric flight. It lacked speed stability in the rate command mode. It also had a poor longitudinal trim system that would insidiously apply a continuous trim rate when you were not expecting it. The most serious handling quality problem of this system was a tendency to float or climb following the landing flare. This was very disturbing to the pilot because he only had a limited amount of time to get the aircraft on the ground before he ran out of airspeed. This problem was minimized by trimming in a nose-down pitching rate during landing approach. In general, the handling qualities of the aircraft were in agreement with the simulator predictions and the major discrepancies were a result of simulation deficiencies rather than real aircraft deficiencies.

The flight control systems performed as predicted with only two major exceptions. The standard SAS flight control system exhibited a structural resonance problem due to a poor choice of gyro package mounting location. Structural vibrations were transmitted into the flight control system command loop causing severe control system vibrations. This was corrected by a simple relocation of the gyro package. The MH-96 flight control system was susceptible to a self-sustaining limit cycle problem whenever abrupt control inputs were made while the control system gain was at its maximum. This subsequently resulted in a catastrophic accident.

Aerodynamically, the aircraft performed as predicted with base drag being the only significant discrepancy. Base drag was substantially higher than predicted, but this was attributed to the lack of proper compensation for the model sting which was mounted in the aft end of the model to support it in the wind tunnel. Thus the model drag was not simulated accurately. As a result of this increased base drag, the subsonic lift/drag ratio was lower than predicted.

In the structures area, there were no major discrepancies between predicted and measured loads and thus there were no structural problems except in the landing gear. The dynamic landing loads were not accurately predicted, particularly those due to aerodynamic forces, and as a result several structural failures occurred in various landing gear components. On one occasion the failure was catastrophic resulting in severe aircraft damage and injury to the pilot.

In the aerothermal structures disciplinary area, the thermal protection system consisting of high-temperature materials and a heat sink structural concept, worked as intended. The overall structural temperatures and stresses were within acceptable limits. Admittedly, the heating rates encountered at hypersonic speeds were lower than predicted, but it appears that there was enough design margin in the structure to accommodate the higher anticipated rates. The researchers were somewhat surprised that maximum-altitude flights subjected the aircraft to a larger total heat pulse or total Btu increment than a low-altitude heating flight. This may have been anticipated with a more thorough assessment of the two different missions. A typical heating flight was flown at relatively low altitudes: 80,000 to 90,000 feet. On this type of flight, the aircraft was subjected to high heating rates during the climb and acceleration phase, but the heating rate decreased abruptly after engine burnout due to the rapid deceleration of the aircraft in the denser air. Thus, although the heating rate was relatively high, the duration of the heat pulse was short.

A maximum-altitude flight subjected the aircraft to a somewhat lower heating rate during the climb, due to the higher average altitude, but it also exposed the aircraft to another long heat pulse during the lengthy entry, pullout, and deceleration phases of the mission. Little heat was dissipated while the aircraft was outside the atmosphere, so the end result was a hotter airplane at landing. This was not a major problem, but it was a surprise.

The thermal protection system concept used in the X-15 worked well for the short duration missions of the X-15. That TPS concept would not be a viable concept for vehicles such as the shuttle or the proposed National Aerospace Plane. A number of more advanced systems are being considered for future hypersonic vehicles.

For the most part, the X-15 was not probing the unknown. Rather it was validating existing design tools. In one area however, it was doing pioneer work, investigating the pilot's ability to fly an aircraft outside the atmosphere and then make a successful reentry into the atmosphere. There was no way to conduct that investigation on the ground. Existing simulators were inadequate. Flight was the only way. The answer soon became obvious as more and higher altitude flights were successfully accomplished. The maximum-altitude flight of the X-15 to 67 miles above the earth provided dramatic proof of the pilot's ability to accomplish such a mission.

Overall, the research results obtained during the flight program were very impressive. The data generally agreed with predictions. There were some surprises and some problems, but the results confirmed the validity of the existing design tools and provided the necessary confidence to proceed with the design of a lifting entry spacecraft, the space shuttle. Many of the discoveries encountered in flight were the kind that Dr. Dryden had described; the unanticipated or practical kinds of problems that should have been foreseen but were overlooked; the kind of problems that were quite obvious after the fact. Some of those are described in the following pages.

As mentioned previously, we did not have any major problems during the initial envelope expansion flights to the design speed and altitude conditions. We did not encounter major problems until we began exceeding those design conditions or until we really began stressing the airplane at the limits of the design conditions. We were courting trouble when we intentionally flew the airplane at high speed at low altitude to heat it up, but we wanted to get good heating data. We were also at risk routinely flying above 250,000 feet altitude since a damper or stability augmentation system failure could have been catastrophic but again the potential information return was considered to be worth the risk. This is not to say that we had no problems early on—we had problems beginning with the first flight.

One of the early problems we encountered was the unreliability of the inertial system. The inertial system provided aircraft attitude information, inertial velocities and inertial altitude. Inertial data were essential for flying an accurate flight profile, since barometric airspeed, altitude, and rate of climb were not measurable at the flight conditions where the X-15 normally operated. We could not use a standard flight test nose boom to obtain air data above Mach 4, because the nose boom would fail structurally due to aerodynamic heating. Instead, we utilized a cooled servo-driven ball nose to measure dynamic pressure and angles of attack and sideslip, but we could not readily convert dynamic pressure into airspeed. Thus, we were forced to rely on inertial velocity to ascertain our true speed. We were also dependent on inertial measurements for altitude and rate of climb above 80,000.

The original X-15 inertial system was very unreliable. The system would quite often fail completely or would accumulate errors of such magnitude as to render it useless. It was not uncommon to have the inertial system indicating an altitude of over 100,000 feet when you were back on the lakebed after landing.

Loss of inertial data was not a major safety of flight problem. We had radar data from the tracking radar which could be relayed to us for energy management purposes, but those data were not available quick enough to use for flight test purposes. We wasted many flights during the early part of the program because we could not get to the desired flight condition due to inertial system failures.

The inertial system failed on my second flight passing through Mach 5 at 80,000 feet. It is hard to imagine how helpless one feels climbing and accelerating at fantastic rates and not knowing how high and how fast he is going. It is very disconcerting, to say the least.

Some major modifications were made to the original inertial system to improve its accuracy and reliability. These mods improved the system significantly, but we later opted for the inertial system developed for the Dyna-Soar spacecraft and used that system for the remainder of the flight program. That system proved to be both accurate and reliable.

Analysis of wind tunnel data prior to flight predicted a serious stability and control problem at high angles of attack for the basic airplane without stability augmentation. The problem exhibited itself as a divergent lateral-directional oscillation which increased in severity with increasing angle of attack. Above 10 degrees angle of attack, the airplane became uncontrollable. The airplane was equipped with a stability augmentation system, but there was a concern about the reliability of that system. Electronic systems in aircraft were relatively new at that time. The implications of this problem were that we could not safely achieve the design altitude of 250,000 feet since a pullout from that altitude required an angle of attack greater than 10 degrees. If we attempted a design altitude mission and lost the stability augmentation system for any reason, we would lose the airplane.

This problem became a challenge to the stability and control engineers. They attacked the problem in a number of different ways. One straightforward proposed solution was to provide a redundant stability augmentation system. Another proposal was to provide stability augmentation in the reaction control system. This would not be as good a solution but it would help. A less attractive proposal was a special control technique to damp the divergent oscillations. This proposal was not highly regarded by the pilots. The most innovative proposal involved the removal of the lower segment of the lower ventral fin. Analysis and simulation indicated that this would eliminate the basic problem rather than just fix it as the other solutions would do.

An aggressive flight investigation was initiated on Flight 37 to confirm that the problem existed and to demonstrate a solution or solutions to the problem. On Flight 37, Joe Walker evaluated the controllability of the airplane at high angles of attack with the stability augmentation system deactivated. He did not like what he saw. He continued the controllability evaluation on Flights 40 and 44 and confirmed the seriousness of the problem. In this same series of flights, the special control technique to damp the divergent oscillations was evaluated and a flight was also made without the lower portion of the lower ventral. The special control technique did not appear to be a viable solution and it was not pursued any further. The results of the ventral-off flight appeared encouraging, but more data was needed to commit to removing the ventral permanently.

A redundant stability augmentation system was developed, installed in the airplane, and checked out on Flight 50. The results were encouraging enough to convince the engineers to proceed with a flight to the design altitude. On Flight 52, Walker flew to 246,700 feet, essentially achieving the 250,000 feet design altitude. Thus, in less than fifteen flights, three of the four proposed solutions had been evaluated and the flight envelope had been expanded to the design altitude.

The effort to achieve a final solution to the problem continued. A reaction augmentation sytem, the fourth solution, was installed and evaluated on Flight 66. It showed promise. On Flight 67, Joe Walker was scheduled to investigate a new reentry technique using a constant pitch attitude instead of a constant angle of attack, in a flight to 220,000 feet. During the reentry Joe inadvertently deactivated the roll stability augmentation system. The airplane began a wild roll oscillation to bank angles over 90 degrees. Joe grabbed the center stick with his left hand during this oscillation in an attempt to control the airplane. He almost lost control. He finally managed to recover by decreasing the aircraft's angle of attack. It was a wild ride, and it vividly demonstrated the severity of the controllability problem at high angles of attack without stability augmentation.

This incident expedited the decision to permanently remove the lower portion of the lower ventral. Flight 69 was the last flight flown with the lower portion of the lower ventral. This effectively eliminated the catastrophic nature of the high angle of attack problem. A pilot could still lose control, but the odds were now in his favor.

Some gutsy decisions were required during the effort to solve this serious problem. The decision to attempt a design altitude mission with a newly developed backup stability augmentation system was a bold move. Removing the lower ventral was very risky since no one was certain whether we would retain an adequate level of directional stability. We could possibly solve one problem but create another. As it turned out, the overall effort was successful—a tribute to an aggressive flight research team.

Local heating effects were another problem encountered during envelope expansion. This involved localized structural failure of the aircraft's skin or other structure due to aerodynamic heating. A good example of this problem was the buckling of the wing skin behind the wing leading edge expansion gaps. The wing leading edge was constructed in several segments with gaps to accommodate expansion of the leading edge due to aerodynamic heating.

These gaps, however, created small vortices which were like welding torch jets of hot air that overheated the skin behind the gap and caused it to buckle. This buckling resulted in popped rivets or torn wing skin. The solution involved adding covers over these gaps to prevent the creation of these vortices. These small vortices of air were extremely hot. The wing skin was made of Inconel-X material, which was capable of sustaining strength up to 1,800° F, and yet these vortices caused the material to fail.

This type of local heating caused buckling of other skin panels at high speed and, ultimately, cracking in the skin at various locations that had to be patched. This skin buckling was suspected to be the source of the popping and banging noise that the pilots noted as the airplane got hot. We referred to this phenomenon as the oil-canning effect. The airplane really popped and banged as it got hot and I noted that the airplane twitched as it popped and banged. We also observed smoke entering the cockpit. We subsequently learned that the smoke was a result of outside air entering the aircraft through small gaps in external doors or panels. The incoming air acted just like a torch at high speeds and burned electrical wiring, aluminum internal structure, metal tubing, or anything else that it impinged on.

The nose gear scoop door, a small door on the nose gear door, normally opened during the gear deployment sequence to assist the deployment of the nose gear. It opened unexpectedly on three different occasions at high speed due to structural deformation resulting from excessive heating. The air rushing into the nose wheel well through this scoop door burned the tires on the dual wheels and partially burned the wheels. The wheels stayed intact during the landing, but the rollout was extremely rough due to disintegration of the tires.

Aerodynamic heating also shattered cockpit windows on two different flights. Luckily, on each occasion only one windshield shattered. The shattered windshield was completely opaque. If both had shattered, the pilot would have had no choice other than to eject. He would not have been able to see through the shattered glass well enough to land the aircraft.

Shattered windows remind me of an incident that occurred several years after the conclusion of the X-15 program. One of our former X-15 flight planners, John Manke, had been selected as a research pilot. He happened to be flying in an F-111 on a research mission that involved a supersonic low level maneuver. These types of maneuvers were generally conducted in a designated portion of the supersonic corridor. The supersonic corridor, as the name implies, is a specified corridor running through the Edwards restricted area which is reserved for supersonic testing. The low-level portion of this corridor is relatively short and is located in an extremely remote uninhabited area to ensure that nothing will be damaged as a result of the strong sonic booms produced at low altitudes.

John entered the corridor to begin his supersonic research maneuver. It took longer than anticipated to set up the proper flight conditions for the maneuver, thus using up some precious distance in the corridor. Once he established the proper conditions, he had to maintain them for 30 seconds to obtain good stabilized data. During this stabilized period, ground control requested that he extend the maneuver for another 15 seconds. John knew that he was approaching the end of the low-level corridor and was coming up on the town of Mojave, but he felt that he could complete the extended maneuver before he boomed Mojave. He was wrong—dead wrong. He boomed hell out of Mojave. He shattered windows in a wide swath right through the heart of the city. The angry phone calls started coming in before John could get back in the landing pattern at Edwards. John was advised by radio before he landed that he was in trouble.

Some of the wags in the pilot's office, including myself, quickly located a picture of our acting center director, De Beeler. When John walked into the pilot's office, he was greeted by a picture over his desk of the center director with a stern look on his face, which we had captioned with the words, "Damn you, John Manke." The crowning touch or *coup de maître* was the shattered picture frame glass covering the picture. It was a magnificent stroke of genius, if I do say so myself.

Word got around about the picture. Later in the day, the center director happened to casually stop by the pilot's office. He had obviously heard about the picture since he did not normally visit our office. He was a very quiet, reserved individual who seldom showed any real emotion. He rather nonchalantly glanced at the picture as he walked by John's desk. A big smile came over his face as he walked back out of the office. We had scored a double coup, and in addition, had saved John from a tongue lashing.

But, back to the X-15. We also lost cabin pressure due to aerodynamic heating. The heating would cause the canopy to distort enough to allow outside air to reach the canopy seal. The outside air would burn through the seal in milliseconds. A small metal lip was installed ahead of the canopy leading edge to shield the gap from the airstream and solve this problem.

One of the things that I always worried about in the X-15 was the canopy coming off at high speed. The canopy opened from the front and hinged in the rear just like the suicide door on some cars that were built in the early 1930s. During flight, cabin pressure and aerodynamic heating caused the canopy to distort and open up a gap at the front or leading edge of the canopy. I could envision the air getting under the edge of the canopy, causing the canopy hooks to fail and the canopy to depart the airplane. If that had happened at high speed, the pilot would have been cooked to a charred mass in a matter of seconds. A complete window failure would have been just as catastrophic.

The auxiliary power units or APUs in the X-15 were, in reality, improperly named. They were not really auxiliary power units, but were the primary power units for electrical and hydraulic power, since there were no conventional engine driven pumps or generators. The X-15 had two APUs for redundancy. If these two units failed, we lost the airplane. As described earlier, these units were small steam turbines powered by steam created by the decomposition of hydrogen peroxide. These units each drove a generator and a hydraulic pump to provide electrical and hydraulic power. APU failures occurred on several flights early in the program. Joe Walker lost one APU during an altitude flight and then lost the second one just after landing. These early APU failures were finally determined to be caused by the vaporization of the lubricating oil in the APU gear case at high altitude and low atmospheric pressure. The gear box would quickly fail without lubrication. The solution to this problem was to pressurize the APU gear case.

The most startling APU failure occurred on the 184th flight. Pete Knight was scheduled to make a flight to 250,000 feet with two piggyback experiments. The prelaunch checklist procedure progressed without incident. After launch, Chase confirmed a good engine light. NASA-1 also verified this and then told Pete to "Check your alpha and watch your heading." NASA-1 then indicated that Pete's track was looking good and he was coming up on profile. At about 28 seconds after launch, NASA-1 informed Pete that they had him on theta (climb angle) and that his track and profile were good. In fact, NASA-1 said, "Beautiful track, Pete." NASA-1 called out an altitude check at 80,000 feet and then, a few seconds later, told Pete he was coming up on 104,000 feet. Almost simultaneously Pete called out, "Shutdown."

NASA-1:	"Understand shutdown, Pete."
NASA-1:	"We've got a Grapevine time here." [The premature shutdown time dictated an emergency landing at Grapevine Lake.]
NASA-1:	"Chase, we will confirm Grapevine landing."
NASA-1:	"How do you read, Pete?"
Chase-3:	"NASA-1, did you say Grapevine?"
NASA-1:	"That's affirm. How do you read me, Pete?"
NASA-1:	"Is anybody reading the X-15?"
NASA-1:	"Chase-1, NASA-1, do you read anybody?"
Chase-1:	"I don't read Pete."
Chase-3:	"Do you have a position here?"
NASA-1:	"No, we have lost TM."

When Pete called "shutdown," it was as though the X-15 had literally disappeared. The control room lost radar track, telemetry, and radio communications. All the marker pens on the plotting boards just stopped. The radar slewed around some, attempting to reacquire a lockon, but then it too stopped. Some control room personnel thought that the airplane blew up. It was as if Pete and the X-15 had flown into the Bermuda Triangle and disappeared.

In the X-15, just before engine shutdown, Pete saw a ripple of red and yellow warning lights: an inertial system gross malfunction light, all three stability augmentation system (SAS) lights, the engine vibration malfunction light, and the number two APU light. Numerous other warning lights were about to come on, but Pete was spared from further warning lights by a complete electrical failure.

All the lights went out, including the cockpit lights. Pete was now in a darkened cockpit climbing out of the atmosphere at over 2,000 feet a second.

The majority of his instruments were no longer working and he quickly noted that his aerodynamic controls were not responding to his attempted inputs. Indeed, his controls were essentially locked. He tried his ballistic controls, but they provided little noticeable response. The airplane began to wallow around as it continued up to the peak of its trajectory.

Postflight simulation indicated that the X-15 peaked out at approximately 173,000 feet altitude. In one sense, Pete was lucky. Even though he had little or no aerodynamic control, there was enough aerodynamic pressure at this altitude to keep the aircraft from swapping ends immediately. It was oscillating in roll through large bank angles. At one point, Pete noted that it was a beautiful day as he looked down on the desert. He decided about that time that he would have to eject. Then he noticed Mud Lake below him and made a decision to try to land there if he got the airplane back under control.

Pete realized that he had lost both APUs since he had neither hydraulic or electrical power. He attempted to start his number one APU with no success. He then remembered that he had to turn on his emergency battery to provide power to start his APUs. With the emergency battery on, he managed to get the number one APU started. He tried the number two APU again, but could not get it going. Then he tried resetting his number one generator to regain electrical power. The generator would not reset. During this critical period, Pete had no help from the control room or his chase aircraft because he had lost his radios. This was another example of the fallacy of assuming that ground control could always help the pilot in an emergency. If the pilot lost his radios, he was on his own. Radio failure or momentary loss of radio reception was very common during X-15 flight operations. It was hard to believe that in this age of rockets and space travel we could still have total loss of communications, but we had numerous instances of this occurring.

Pete had to give up on resetting the generator because he had to position the aircraft for the reentry. He had no indication of his angle of attack and yet he knew he had to maintain a fairly high one to successfully reenter. He resorted to flying by the seat of his pants. He pulled the nose up until it started to diverge sideways and then lowered the nose slightly. This little maneuver gave Pete a rough indication that he was at an acceptable angle of attack for the entry. He held this attitude until the g forces started building up and then, when he felt that he had made the pullout, he rolled into a steep bank to start the turn back to Mud Lake. Pete had managed to make a successful reentry without instruments and without any stability augmentation—quite a feat.

On the ground, NASA-1 was still trying to determine what happened.

Chase-3 reported, "I've looked all over Grapevine." Based on energy management calculations, Pete should have headed for Grapevine, but Grapevine was one of the smaller lakes. Pete elected to try to get back to Mud Lake, a much bigger and better lake for an emergency landing.

NASA-1:	"Chase-3, you can be looking for jettison down around Grapevine."
Chase-3:	"Roger One, I'm looking."
NASA-1:	"OK. Pete, do you read?"
Chase-3:	"Over Grapevine at 30,000 feet."
NASA-1:	"I kind of think he will be coming in from the southeast if he comes in there."
Chase-1:	"OK."
NASA-1:	"Chase-1 & -2, keep an eye around Mud."
Chase-2:	"Rog, Mike. I'm over Mud and keeping an eye peeled."
NASA-1:	"Rog."
Chase-2:	"Pete, do you read?"
Chase-3:	"Seen or heard anything?"

At this point, over 8 minutes had elapsed since Pete and the X-15 had disappeared. Again, 8 minutes does not sound like a lot of time, but it can be an eternity to those waiting to hear some word, any word. An airplane does not just disappear. Someone has to see or hear something—a Mayday call, a parachute, a dust cloud from a landing or a crash, or at least pieces of the airplane lying on the ground. Then, all of a sudden, Chase-2 called, "He is going into Mud. I think he is landing east to west." Several seconds later Chase-2 said, "He's in the center of Mud and in good shape right now." NASA-1 said, "Roger, understand." That message was almost drowned out by the noise of a couple hundred hearts beginning to beat again. "Gentlemen, start your hearts."

The cause of the APU shutdown was never proven. There was speculation that the first APU to shutdown was momentarily overloaded due to a large electrical power demand. That transient load probably stalled the APU, which in turn activated a safety circuit that shut it down. When that APU shut down, it transferred its essential electrical power demands to the other APU, as it was designed to do. The other APU was, however, already heavily loaded down with a high power demand and was unable to accept the additional power load and maintain speed. It, too, stalled and shutdown.

The APUs were generally reliable, but they required a lot of tender care and feeding. They were usually completely disassembled after each flight, refurbished, reassembled, and then test run before being reinstalled in the aircraft.

We were very conscious of the fact that APU problems could be catastrophic.

Pete was extremely lucky. The circumstances of the APU failures were such that he was able to control the aircraft using reaction controls until he was able to restart an APU. If he had been flying a low-altitude speed type flight, the airplane would probably have swapped ends and either failed structurally or crashed due to the loss of stability and control.

Paul Bikle has said on numerous occasions that Pete's recovery of the airplane on this flight was one of the most impressive events of the whole program. Pete should have been mentally prepared for this emergency. He told me about a complete electrical failure he had early in his flying career in a T-33 over Detroit, Michigan, at night in severe weather conditions. It was a hairy story—almost as hairy as this one. Pete also managed to recover that airplane.

Landing gear problems persisted throughout the flight program. The most serious problems involved the main landing gear, the two struts at the rear of the aircraft with skids instead of wheels. Landing gear failures of a minor nature occurred on a number of flights. Most of these failures were attributed to the larger than anticipated aerodynamic loads imposed by the horizontal stabilizer after the aircraft was on the ground. Aerodynamic loads caused a catastrophic landing gear failure on one of Jack McKay's flights out of Mud Lake. In that incident, the main gear failed completely and the aircraft ended up on its back after flipping over during slideout.

In an attempt to solve this problem, a squat switch was added to disable the stability augmentation system at landing and thus prevent the horizontal stabilizer from deflecting full leading edge down as the nose of the aircraft slammed down. This fix helped to relieve the aerodynamic loads, but it was not enough.

The next fix required the pilots to push forward sharply on the stick when the nose began to fall through after main gear touchdown. This procedure resulted in a leading edge up horizontal stabilizer deflection at nose gear touchdown which significantly reduced the main gear loads. On a number of occasions, the pilots actually lifted the rear end of the aircraft off the ground during the landing slideout. This procedure worked well as long as the pilot remembered to do it. Every now and then the pilot forgot to perform the maneuver and loads reached design limits.

The obvious answer to the design engineer was to design and install an automatic system to push the stick forward as the aircraft touched down. The pilots rebelled at this proposal, fearing a premature actuation of this system before landing. The engineers, however, persisted and after adding a few safeguards to prevent premature actuation, the system was implemented on the aircraft. This system worked as advertised, but the engineers finally decided to add a third skid on the lower ventral to substantially reduce the original main gear loads. This was the final mod to the landing gear, not necessarily because it was the ultimate fix, but because the program came to an end. We are now assured that the landing gear will not collapse as the aircraft sits in the museum.

The LR-99 engine was amazingly reliable if we got it lit, and if we did not move the throttle while it was running. Joe Vensel, our director of flight operations, used to say, "If you get the engine lit, leave it alone, don't screw with it." He was right.

The LR-99 had a poor starting record initially. It quite often took two attempts to start the engine and occasionally, it would not start at all or would hang up at low thrust. The starting problem appeared to be due to the instability of the engine at low thrust settings. Initially, we were trying to start the engine at minimum throttle which was about 30 percent thrust. The engine just did not want to start or run at that thrust level. We then began to start the engine with the throttle at the 100 percent thrust level. This greatly improved the start reliability. We very seldom had to make a restart attempt using that procedure.

We still had problems, though. The engine would often quit when we attempted to move it back to minimum throttle. If the pilot throttled the engine back before he gained enough energy to get home, he risked making an emergency landing at one of the intermediate lakebeds. To correct this problem, we increased the minimum throttle setting to 40 percent thrust. We also moved the throttle gently and said a quick prayer before we moved it. This procedure further improved the engine reliability, but I still had to hitchhike one time.

In all, there were eight emergency landings as a result of propulsion system problems with the LR-99 engine—one due to no light, one due to a hangup at low thrust, one due to premature shutdown at throttle reduction, two due to low fuel line pressures, one due to a turbopump case failure, one due to a fuel tank rupture, and one due to lack of fuel flow from an external tank.

On Jack McKay's twenty-fifth flight, he was scheduled to carry three experiments to high altitude. These experiments were an atmospheric density measurement, a micrometeorite collector, and a horizon scanner. The flight was the 157th flight of the program and it was launched at Delamar Lake. Jack got the engine lit right after launch and pulled up to begin the climb. He had just reached his planned climb angle when the engine quit. The engine turbopump that supplied the propellants to the thrust chamber failed due to a rupture of the case and propellants began spewing at high pressure into the engine compartment. Luckily, there was no fire, but Jack had a problem getting the airplane turned around and headed back toward the launch lake.

The engine had burned 35 seconds and during that time the airplane had accelerated to Mach 2.2 in the climb. Jack peaked out at 78,400 feet altitude during the wingover turn back to Delamar. He made a nice approach pattern, but he was high on energy. Jack was an old navy pilot like me, and we both carried an extra 5 knots of airspeed in the approach for each kid, to ensure that we did not stall the aircraft. Trouble was, Jack had eight kids. He landed long and ran off the edge of the lake about 500 feet in the sagebrush before stopping. It did not hurt the airplane and Jack did not let it effect his ego. After the postflight debriefing, someone asked Jack how long the lakebed runway was. Jack's answer was, "Three miles with a 500-foot over-run."

Jack made his third emergency landing on his twenty-ninth flight, which was his last X-15 flight. He launched at Smith Ranch Lake on September 8, 1966. Shortly after he began his climb, he noticed that his fuel line pressure was low. He throttled the engine back to 50 percent thrust on the recommendation of NASA-1 to see if the fuel line pressure would recover. When it failed to recover, he shut the engine down, turned the airplane around and made an uneventful landing at Smith Ranch. With this landing, Jack established an all time record for emergency landings. He had three. No other pilot had more than one.

For its time, the LR-99 was a very impressive engine. It was unique in its throttling capability and its restart feature. It produced almost as much thrust as the Redstone missile booster and it was reusable—another unique feature.

The X-15 made 199 flights with only eight flight engines. There were no catastrophic engine failures and no serious design deficiencies. The engine was temperamental, but so were all the other rocket engines. Twenty-five years later, rocket engines are still temperamental. They still occasionally fail to light properly and they still quit unexpectedly and they still blow up once in a while. So what's new?

As the program progressed, the airplane became somewhat safer and more reliable in some respects since most of the major problems were fixed as they were encountered. Thus, at least the variety of problems was reduced. In some cases, however, the fixes were not complete fixes and we had recurring problems after the fixes were incorporated. To some extent, this was due to a lack of money. We could not afford the luxury of a complete redesign whenever we encountered a problem. Some problems were not fixed at all. We lived with them and modified our procedures or our flight operations. As a result of these actions and inactions, we continued to have problems throughout the entire program. We also continued to have emergencies.

We encountered some new problems after 150 flights. Some of these new problems appeared to be aging or fatigue problems. An engine turbopump case failed, a bulkhead in the fuel tank failed, and yet the airplanes did not have a lot of flight time on them. In fact, they averaged 10 hours of free flight time apiece at the end of the program. They were only 10 years old at the end of the program, but they did not have a lot of miles on them. In the classified pages of the newspapers, they could have been advertised as low mileage airplanes, flown by little old ladies only on Sundays.

Total free flight time for the 199 flights in the program was 30 hours, 13 minutes, and 49 seconds. Total flight time including captive flight time on the B-52, was less than 400 hours for the three airplanes. The average total flight time per airplane including captive time was roughly 130 hours. We obviously did not wear them out flying them. We did, however, do a lot of ground testing. After each flight, we routinely disassembled each system, inspected it, reassembled it and then operated the system to ensure that it was ready for the next flight. Therefore, for each flight, we operated each system at least twice—once during checkout and once during flight. If the flight was an aborted flight, we still usually operated the systems during the captive portion of the flight, so we added another cycle to the total number of system operations. My personal opinion is that we wore the airplanes out testing them in preparation for flight.

The airplane and its systems did operate in a rather severe environment. Atmospheric pressures on the airplane ranged from over 2,000 pounds per square foot down to almost 0 in the vacuum of space. The *g* environment varied from –2.5 *g* to over 8.0 *g*. The temperatures on the various parts of the airplane varied from –245° F to 1,200° F.

Some parts of the airplane had a controlled environment. The cockpit and the equipment bay were pressurized and the temperature was regulated. In most of the airplane, however, the environment was uncontrolled and the temperatures varied widely. The hydraulic lines, for example, ran alongside the liquid oxygen tank in the side fairings. The hydraulic fluid in these lines was super-cooled such that when you started the APUs and the hydraulic pumps, the pressure went off scale over 4,000 psi. This was obviously detrimental to the integrity of the system, but the system survived this exposure. Ultimately, though, we could expect failures as a result of this environment and we did have representative failures. On the basis of our X-15 experience, the space shuttle can anticipate problems for many years to come.

PART 3 . . . .

TRIUMPH AND TRAGEDY

Chapter 8 . . . .

Toward Mach 7—The X-15A-2

This phase was the last distinct phase of the program. It began with the first flight of the modified number two aircraft on the 109th flight of the program. It came to a conclusion after twenty-one flights on the 188th flight of the program, when the airplane was damaged due to excessive heating during its maximum-speed flight.

An event that led to this phase occurred on November 9, 1962. Jack McKay was scheduled to make a ventral-off stability and control flight out of Mud Lake in the original number two X-15. The weather was good that morning and things went smoothly during the countdown to launch. During prelaunch checkout of the X-15 there were no symptoms that hinted of the dire events to follow. The launch occurred on time and Jack advanced the throttle to light the main chamber. During that phase of the program, the engine light was performed at minimum throttle setting, which was approximately 30 percent thrust. Jack got a main chamber light at 30 percent power, but when he attempted to increase power, he got no response. The engine was not going to cooperate this particular morning.

Theoretically, Jack could have made it back to Edwards at 30 percent thrust, but there was no way of knowing whether the engine would continue to run long enough at that power setting to get home to Edwards. The problem of energy management was seriously compromised by the low power since the decision times for an emergency landing at each of the various emergency lakebeds were calculated on the basis of 100 percent thrust. We had no way of recomputing those decision times in real time, so mission rules under these conditions dictated that the pilot shut the rocket engine down and make an emergency landing at the launch lakebed. Jack shut the engine down after 70.5 seconds of engine burn time and turned the aircraft back toward Mud Lake.

Mud Lake was circular, approximately 5 miles in diameter, and quite smooth and hard. It was a good lake for an emergency landing. Jack began jettisoning propellants immediately after shutting the engine down. Complete propellant jettison was never fully achieved on aborted missions and thus, Jack was destined to land with a considerable amount of residual fuel and liquid oxygen on board. On final approach, he selected flaps down, but the flaps failed to move. Jack was now unknowingly set up for a catastrophic landing. As he came across the edge of the lakebed, he was high on airspeed due to the excess weight. He touched down very gently, but at a higher than normal speed due to the inoperative flaps. Jack actually touched down at 296 MPH. We normally touched down at approximately 230 MPH.

In a normal landing, when the X-15 main gear skids touched down, they created a large drag load as they slid along the surface of the lake. This drag on the skids caused the nose of the aircraft to slam down. This slamdown caused a large load on the nose gear, but it also resulted in a large load on the main gear a fraction of a second later as the aircraft rebounded and loaded up the main gear.

To compound the problem, as the nose of the aircraft rotated down after main gear touchdown, the control system automatically tried to stop the nose from slamming down. It did this by deflecting the horizontal stabilizers to the full leading edge down position. This was a futile attempt on the part of the control system. It could never hold the nose up, due to the high drag on the skids. What it did do, however, was load up the main gear with a large aerodynamic down load. This was an undesirable effect since the main gear was now simultaneously subjected to a large rebound load and a large downward air load. The magnitude of the air load was a function of the touchdown airspeed. The higher the touchdown airspeed, the larger the aerodynamic down load. This sequence of events during a normal landing tended to load the main gear up near its design limits.

On this landing the combination of the two loads was large enough to cause the main landing gear to fail due to the higher landing speed. The left landing gear collapsed almost immediately, causing the aircraft to tilt over to the left.

As the aircraft tilted over, the left horizontal stabilizer dug into the lakebed and tore off the aircraft, taking the left main gear strut with it. The lower ventral also struck the lakebed and was torn off the aircraft in small fragments.

The aircraft continued to roll over until the left wing tip contacted the lakebed. Shortly thereafter, the nose wheels failed and came off the nose gear strut. The aircraft began sliding on the nose strut, the left wing tip, and the right main gear skid. As it did so, the aircraft began to swerve to the left. Jack realized he was in serious trouble and elected to jettison the canopy in case the aircraft should roll over. Milliseconds later, the aircraft abruptly tilted over to the right as the aircraft swerved through 90 degrees. The right wing tip dug into the lakebed and the aircraft flipped over, slamming into the lakebed on its back. Jack's helmet was one of the first things to hit the lakebed. One might say that the aircraft came down on Jack's head. It was a crushing blow.

Jack was now pinned in the cockpit, hanging upside down, while propellants and peroxide were starting to leak from the aircraft. The liquid ammonia fuel was the greatest hazard because the rescue crew could not help Jack while those potent vapors enveloped the aircraft. Their emergency breathing masks were not working properly.

The rescue helicopter pilot finally realized what the problem was and set up a hover over the cockpit area to blow the ammonia vapors away from Jack and the rescue personnel. Now the problem was getting Jack out of the cockpit. The rescue crew had no way of lifting the airplane up to get Jack out. They finally decided to dig a hole below the cockpit to allow him to slide out underneath. By this time, the C-130 with the paramedics on board had landed and, after Jack was assisted out of the X-15 cockpit, they carried him aboard and headed back to Edwards.

This emergency landing was the first to benefit from all the emergency planning and procedures. It was always a major operation to get the emergency crews and equipment in position for each flight, but in this case it all paid off and justified the expense. Within seconds after the X-15 flipped over, the X-15 ground rescue crew was at the airplane after racing across the lakebed from their standby position on the lake. The fire truck was right behind them and the helicopter was already hovering near the X-15 when they arrived. The rescue crew vehicle and the fire truck had been flown up to Mud Lake in the C-130 before daybreak to be in position for the X-15 launch. The helicopter had also flown up from Edwards in the early dawn to be on station for the launch. The C-130 had made a trip back to Edwards to pick up another fire truck and the paramedics and had flown back up range to take up its standby station halfway between Mud Lake and Edwards. It was then in position to cover an emergency landing at any one of the intermediate lakebeds. It was in position this day to assist in the rescue effort and transport Jack back to the hospital at Edwards. We only had three landings at intermediate lakebeds during the X-15 program, but the preparations paid off. I can vouch for that, because I made one of those landings at an intermediate lake.

Jack was seriously injured when his head hit the lakebed. The force of that impact squeezed the cartilage out from between the vertebrae in Jack's neck and upper back. He ended up 1 inch shorter, with a couple of cracked vertebrae. Jack recovered sufficiently to fly again, but ultimately his injuries forced him to retire on a disability.

The airplane survived Jack's Mud Lake accident in amazingly good shape. That, of course, is a testimony to the steel construction. The outer 2 feet of the right wing were bent up 90 degrees, but the remainder of the wing was perfectly straight. The airplane came to rest on the upper vertical stabilizer and the upper fuselage, just behind the cockpit. The upper vertical stabilizer was slightly crushed, but easily repairable. The left-hand horizontal stabilizer had been ripped off when the left main gear failed, but the rest of the primary empennage and fuselage structure were undamaged. The aircraft was hauled back to North American's El Segundo plant on a flatbed for repairs.

Instead of just repairing the aircraft, the program officials elected to take this opportunity to modify the aircraft for scramjet engine tests. Approximately a year after the accident, the number two X-15 emerged like a phoenix from the bowels of the North American Aviation production facility on the south side of the Los Angeles International Airport. After Jack's Mud Lake accident, the X-15 had been extensively modified to carry an experimental scramjet engine up to speeds of over 5,000 MPH.

The modifications included the addition of a 28-inch plug in the middle of the fuselage between the LOX and ammonia tanks. A spherical tank was installed in this extra space to carry the liquid hydrogen fuel for the scramjet engine. The scramjet engine was to be carried on the lower ventral fin stub, but there was not sufficient ground clearance with the standard landing gear. The solution was to increase the length of the main landing gear struts. This was the second major modification. The nose gear also had to be modified to increase the length of the oleo travel to accommodate the extra force produced by the slamdown of the longer, heavier fuselage. (An oleo is a shock strut like the shock absorbers on a car. A longer oleo is required for a higher total force.)

The major modification was the addition of two huge external tanks for

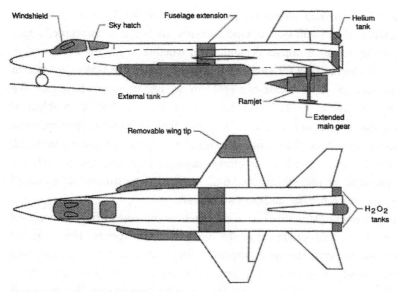

Figure 7. X-15A-2 with modifications.

additional main engine propellants. One tank contained liquid oxygen and the other, liquid ammonia. Together these tanks carried an additional 1,800 gallons of propellants which corresponded to approximately 60 seconds of engine burn time. An additional peroxide tank was added externally at the rear of the aircraft to provide more steam to drive the engine turbopump for a longer period of time. Several additional source gas tanks were added to the aircraft to provide pressurization for the extra propellant tanks.

The total propellant was almost double that carried by the standard airplane. One might assume that this would provide a big increase in maximum speed. Realistically, the actual speed increase was disappointingly small. The extra weight and tremendous increase in drag due to these tanks severely reduced the rate of rotation to achieve the desired climb angle and also reduced the rate of climb and acceleration. With full external tanks, the aircraft weighed almost 57,000 pounds compared to 33,000 pounds for the standard, fully fueled aircraft. All of the external fuel would be used up just to reach Mach 2 at 70,000 feet, where the tanks were jettisoned. The internal fuel did not provide the same total acceleration as the standard airplane, since the new airplane was heavier and had somewhat more drag, particularly with the ablative coating on the aircraft. The net result was, at most, two additional Mach numbers at the expense of a lot of additional complexity.

The tanks contained a recovery parachute system which added even more complexity to the overall system. Operationally, we had to be concerned about where the tanks might impact depending on whether or not the chute system worked. We had to plan for either case and ensure that the tanks impacted in a controlled area. Also, in case of a problem, we had to be able to jettison the tanks at any time to try and save the airplane. We thus had the problem of ensuring that we did not drop a 1,000 gallon tank of liquid oxygen on some old prospector's shack. The California desert is very barren and uninhabited, but ironically, when you have to jettison anything in an emergency, it always finds something of value to hit. The B-52 also had to be structurally modified to carry the much heavier number two aircraft.

The basic aircraft structure had to be somehow protected from the increased aerodynamic heating predicted at the higher planned speeds. The proposed solution was to cover the entire airplane with an ablative material developed to protect missile nose cones. This material acted as an insulator. More effectively, it acted as a dissipater of heat through a burning process that produced a heat resistant char layer. Variations of this ablator material were used to protect the Mercury, Gemini, and Apollo spacecraft. This material was installed on the X-15 in both premolded pieces and as a spray-on coating.

The material was pink in color. When it was first applied to the X-15, the crew called Joe Walker out to look at it just to needle him. A pink airplane did not quite fit the macho image of a test pilot. Luckily, a protective coating was required due to the material's sensitivity to liquid oxygen. The protective coating was white—an acceptable color.

The actual installation process proved to be a lengthy, tedious job involving many hours of hand finishing the coating. This coating was not applied until the aircraft was being prepared for the final high-speed flights. It would have been extremely hard to service, operate, and maintain the airplane routinely with that protective coating permanently installed. We were fortunate in some respects that the flight program was terminated after only two flights with the protective coating. It was a real pain to install it on the airplane. Several other modifications were required due to the decision to use the ablative coating.

The cockpit canopy windows were modified to an oval shape to withstand the higher aerodynamic heating anticipated at Mach 8. An eyelid was designed to cover one window during high-speed flight to prevent the window from being clouded by the residue from the protective ablative thermal protection material. This eyelid could be opened manually once the aircraft slowed down to subsonic speeds, providing good vision for landing. The other window was not covered and was used at the high speeds.

An extendable airspeed probe was also designed to be deployed at subsonic speeds to ensure that the pilot had a good, clean airspeed system for landing. It was suspected that ablator residue might plug the normal fixed external probe.

The initial justification for modifying the number two aircraft was accepted as a worthwhile research effort. It was generally agreed that the aircraft could be modified to successfully accomplish the desired objectives. It was not obvious how complex or painful the development process was going to be.

Once the number two X-15 was modified, we began a flight envelope expansion program on the basic airplane, without tanks, to determine the effects of the basic airplane modification on the aircraft's stability, control, and handling qualities. The effects were not anticipated to be significant because the external configuration of the modified basic aircraft had not changed much. However, we needed to accurately quantify the aircraft's flying characteristics before the external tanks and scramjet engine were installed on the aircraft.

The flight data would be used to update our simulator and allow the pilots to assess the predicted flying characteristics with the tanks and scramjet installed. It was known from wind tunnel tests that the tanks and the scramjet would definitely alter the flying characteristics and, in general, degrade them. This was verified in the simulator and was subsequently confirmed much later when the airplane was finally flown with external tanks.

The first envelope expansion flight was a flight out of Hidden Hills to a maximum speed of Mach 4.59. Everything worked fine and the airplane flew reasonably well. Bob Rushworth flew that flight and also the next one out of Delamar Lake. On the second flight, he achieved a maximum Mach of 5.23. As he was decelerating back through about 4.5 Mach, Bob heard a tremendous bang under his feet, almost like an explosion. Simultaneously, the aircraft pitched down, the nose yawed to the side and the aircraft rolled over on its side. Smoke began to fill the cockpit, compounding the problem. Bob had no indication of what had occurred. The control room could not tell him what had happened because data they were looking at showed no indication of a malfunction.

The chase aircraft were no help, as they were more than 10 miles below him. Bob could only guess at what might have happened. The possibilities included an explosion of some sort or a structural failure. Bob did note on reflection that the loud bang resembled somewhat the noise generated during nose gear deployment. Other evidence seemed to substantiate that possibility. Bob informed the control room that he thought the nose gear had come out. The control room still could neither confirm nor help since no one had ever anticipated that kind of problem and therefore there were no specific emergency procedures.

This, of course, is typical of experimental aircraft testing. Something violent happens, but no one has enough information or they cannot assimilate it fast enough to tell the pilot what the problem is. The pilot has to cope with it immediately on his own. The control room is not much help in real time unless they have anticipated an emergency and have practiced it.

Bob managed to regain and maintain control of the aircraft and get the nose back up to maintain altitude. His major concern now was to get the aircraft home since the nose gear added a lot of drag. He did not want to land the aircraft at one of the emergency lakes, but he was losing energy much faster than planned. NASA-1 recommended that he keep the airplane at high altitude until he slowed to subsonic speeds, and then begin his descent into the Edwards area. The control room continued to provide Bob with heading information, energy status, and position along the planned ground track. Bob requested that the chase join up as quickly as possible to inspect the aircraft and confirm that the nose gear was deployed. The chase finally spotted him as he was descending about 20 miles northeast of Edwards and climbed on up to join him.

The chase quickly confirmed that the nose gear was extended, but he had to move in close to determine the extent of the damage. He informed Bob and the control room that the tires were badly burned, but they appeared to be intact. The nose gear strut, door, and wheel well appeared to be charred but otherwise normal in appearance. There was, however, a question of whether the tires were deflated and whether the nose gear strut was damaged sufficiently to compromise the oleo function. If the oleo was badly damaged, the aircraft could break as the nose slammed down. Bob was now in the landing pattern and less than 3 minutes from touchdown. A major decision was required. Should a landing be attempted under these conditions?

This kind of potential life-and-death decision was frequently required during the X-15 program and during every other experimental flight program. Decisions were needed in real time in a matter of minutes and sometimes seconds. Luckily, we had the kind of people who could readily make such decisions. The decision was made to land the airplane. It was not a dramatic pronouncement, it was just a quiet comment to the controller, "Let's go ahead and bring it on in." The landing was a good one, but the rollout was rough. The tires failed at touchdown and rapidly disintegrated during the high-speed rollout, but the gear survived.

From flight data, we learned that the nose gear had deployed at Mach 4.4. The temperature created by the impact of the air at that speed was over 1,000° F. That obviously accounted for the burned tires and charred nose gear. During the slideout after landing, Bob was heard to comment sarcastically, "Thank you, Mr. North American."

Following the flight, the landing gear system was carefully inspected in an attempt to determine why the nose gear had deployed. There was no obvious answer. The landing gear system appeared to be properly rigged and functioning normally during ground checkout.

The landing gear deployment system then became a prime suspect. The deployment system was a relatively simple system consisting of cables attached to the various uplock hooks on the gear and nose gear door which terminate at a T-handle on the lower left side of the instrument panel. To release the gear, the pilot simply pulled the T-handle and the gear deployed by gravity, with some aerodynamic assistance. The gear release handle opened a small scoop door on the nose gear door which then pulled the nose gear door open and allowed the nose gear to fall free. The cable release system had some built-in slack to accommodate the expansion of the aircraft as it got hot.

Some of the engineers suspected that the slack allowance may not have been adequate for the longer, modified airplane. They recalculated the expansion of the aircraft and found that indeed the aircraft would expand almost three-quarters of an inch more than the available slack. Thus, as the airplane got hot, it caused the cables to tighten up and finally release one of the hooks. The landing gear cable release system was subsequently modified to increase the slack to a total of 3 1/2 inches. This would provide ample margin, but it also required a longer pull of the release handle to release all the hooks. The pilots were not too happy with the additional T-handle motion required. It almost required two hands to pull the cable all the way out. We could not really argue, though, because we really did not want the gear coming out prematurely.

The next flight was finally scheduled about 6 weeks later and Rushworth was again scheduled to fly it. The flight plan called for a flight up to Mach 5. Additional stability and control data was to be obtained at roughly 100,000 feet. The flight proceeded as planned up through burnout. As the aircraft decelerated through Mach 4.5, Bob heard another bang and the aircraft pitched down and began to oscillate in roll and yaw.

Again, Bob was not certain of what had happened, but he suspected the landing gear system had malfunctioned again. The bang was not as loud as on the previous flight, so he assumed that it might be just the nose gear scoop door opening, rather than the entire gear extending. He advised the control room of his suspicions, but again the control room could not identify the problem nor really help him other than to offer sympathy. Bob had to wrestle with the airplane to regain complete control and fly it on to Edwards.

On arrival at Edwards, the chase joined up and confirmed that the nose gear scoop door was open. As Bob came level following the landing flareout, he pulled the gear handle and nothing happened. He immediately pulled the handle again and heard the nose gear deploy. Joe Engle, who happened to be the chase pilot, noted that the nose gear was extending very slowly. He called out to Bob to, "hold it off" to allow the nose gear time to extend and lock. Bob managed to hold the airplane in the air just long enough to let the nose gear lock before the main skids touched the lakebed. The nose slammed down hard, but the tires stayed intact for the first thousand feet of the slideout and then disintegrated.

A visual inspection of the nose gear and the nose gear wheel well showed extensive heating damage. The scoop door opening allowed the hot air to enter the nose gear compartment, which burned the tires, melted some aluminum tubing and caused the nose gear to bind up during extension. This incident had the potential to be more catastrophic than the previous one. Luckily, it was not. Rushworth was beginning to have mixed emotions about the joys of flying the X-15. He was getting upset with these surprises and, was also getting gun-shy. What might happen the next time?

Postflight inspection revealed that the nose gear scoop door uplock hook was distorted, indicating excessive loads on the hook. Again, the engineers assumed that a heating problem had caused the door to open. They ultimately heated up the nose section in the hangar to simulate the in-flight heating to confirm their suspicions. As a result of this test, they redesigned the uplock mechanism and prepared the aircraft for flight.

This modification was subsequently made to each of the X-15s, since they were all susceptible to this problem. Somehow, we had only experienced it three times previously. I was elected to make a captive flight to demonstrate proper gear deployment after this modification since I was scheduled to make the next X-15 flight. The captive flight was scheduled to be made the day before my drop flight. It was late afternoon before the airplane was mated and serviced. We got airborne just before five o'clock and climbed to altitude to cold soak the airplane. By the time we completed the climb, cold soaked the airplane, and then deployed the landing gear, it was dark. That was the first and only night X-15 operation. I would have really had a problem if I had to be launched in an emergency.

The flight planners took pity on Bob and decided to give him a breather. They scheduled Jack McKay for the next flight. Jack flew an uneventful flight and then it was Bob's turn again. Bob's flight plan was very similar to his last two flights. A climb and acceleration to about 100,000 feet at slightly over Mach 5.

The flight proceeded normally until the aircraft decelerated through Mach 4.4. At that time, Bob felt, rather than heard, something let go. The airplane pitched down and then yawed violently to the right. This incident occurred at a particularly bad time since, just prior to the event, Bob had deactivated the stability augmentation system to do stability and control maneuvers. With the stability augmentation system off, the airplane was very loose and it would diverge and oscillate wildly in response to any external force.

Bob was subjected to a few seconds of terror as the aircraft oscillated violently until he could reengage the SAS. Again, there was no obvious indication of what had happened, either in the cockpit or in the control room. This time Bob could not deduce what had happened. He had to wait until the chase joined up to be informed that his right main gear was down. This caused some concern that the skid might not function properly on touchdown and would result in a failure of the gear itself. Bob made a very smooth landing and the gear remained intact. During the slideout Bob commented, "Boy, I'll tell you, I've had enough of this!" When Bob finally got out of the airplane, he turned around and kicked it.

Postflight examination revealed a bent right-hand main gear uplock hook. Further analysis indicated that aerodynamic heating caused the new longer main gear strut to bow outward more than normal, which failed the uplock hook and allowed the gear to deploy. The uplock hook was subsequently modified to compensate for the extra deflection of the longer strut.

It is amazing how easy it is to overlook something that can be catastrophic, during a major redesign of an aircraft. After this modification, we had no further incidents. Some say the fact that we had no further incidents can be attributed to an extensive re-analysis of the entire landing gear system to determine if there were any more lurking problems that had not been considered in the initial redesign of the number two airplane. Others said, we had no more landing gear incidents because the crew put a small sign above the landing gear T-handle that said, "Do not extend landing gear above Mach 4."

Jack McKay flew the next two flights to complete the modified basic airplane envelope expansion. Then the aircraft began a series of flights to evaluate a star tracker experiment. The objective of this experiment was to photograph the sky, to locate the brightest stars in the ultraviolet spectrum in preparation for the launch of the Orbital Astronomical Observatory Satellite. A camera was mounted on a gyrostabilized platform in the instrument bay behind the cockpit. As the airplane ascended above 200,000 feet altitude, two doors opened up allowing the camera to photograph the sky. Four flights were made for this purpose during the next 4-month period.

Following those four flights, the next was the first flight with external tanks. The intent of this flight was to demonstrate jettison of empty tanks at the design jettison conditions of Mach 2 at 70,000 feet. Rushworth made the flight. The flight was planned to be flown from Cuddeback Lake to Edwards. It was planned as a very benign flight to minimize the potential complications in case of malfunction.

This flight was, however, a potentially hazardous flight. The tanks were enormous compared to the airplane. They were each about half the size of the airplane and they were not aerodynamically stable. The major concern was that they might not separate cleanly and as a result might critically damage the X-15. Other possibilities included such things as one tank jettisoning and the other not jettisoning, or a hang-up of one hook on a tank and a release of the other.

The other extreme malfunction would be no release at all. It was theorized that the airplane could be landed with the tanks since they would crush as the aircraft nose slammed down and the aircraft would slide out on its gear with the tanks dragging along. All of this optimistic fantasy provided some small measure of confidence to the pilot, but there was no question that this flight was a "biggie." Fortunately, the flight went as planned. The tanks separated cleanly and Bob made an uneventful recovery at Edwards.

The next flight was a stability and control flight out of Mud Lake by Rushworth with no unusual occurrences. The following flight was the first flight with fully loaded external tanks. Bob was again the lucky pilot selected to make the flight. It was to be a launch out of Mud Lake and a flight to Edwards. The major concern on this flight was the possibility of an unplanned partially full tank jettison due to an emergency. For a number of reasons, the tank jettison analysis had only included the empty tank and full tank conditions. A partial fuel jettison scenario had an infinite number of CG (center of gravity) and inertia combinations which were not readily solvable in that era of analog computers, so they made no attempt to calculate any intermediate fuel tank jettison trajectories. You either jettisoned them full or empty or you suffered the consequences.

As you might guess, on this flight the tanks had to be jettisoned in a partially full condition. Shortly after X-15 launch and engine light, Bob could not confirm that he was using fuel out of the external tank. His propellant flow meters indicated that he was using LOX out of the external tank, but no fuel. If this were indeed true, Bob would soon have an uncontrollable airplane with a large asymmetry in internal and external fuel tank loading. Bob jettisoned the tanks at 1.6 Mach at 41,000 feet and then jettisoned his internal fuel and made an emergency landing at Mud Lake. That was Rushworth's last X-15 flight. He told me later that he was glad to finally leave the program. He wanted to try something less hazardous for a while, like going into combat in Vietnam.

Bob did an outstanding job as an X-15 pilot. He flew a total of thirty-four flights—more than any other pilot—and more than twice the average number of flights per pilot. He flew the X-15 almost 6 years. Bob Rushworth and Jack McKay were the dog soldiers of the program. They did the grunt work. Walker and White were the pioneers and received most of the glory. Bob received very little recognition in reward for his contributions, but he gained tremendous respect from his peers and coworkers. Paul Bikle felt that Bob was one of the best research pilots that he had ever been associated with, and Bikle had worked with the cream of the crop during his many years in the flight test business. I would agree with Bikle. I really liked and respected Bob. He was my hero.

Pete Knight inherited the program from Rushworth and flew all of the remaining flights in the airplane. His first three flights, without the external tanks, were high-altitude ultraviolet stellar photography flights or star tracker flights. These flights also served to familiarize Pete with the modified basic airplane. It flew somewhat differently than the other two aircraft.

The flight following the star tracker flights, his fourth in this airplane, was made to obtain data for another experiment to investigate the effects of the hypersonic flight environment on high-resolution photography. Pete also evaluated the aircraft's handling qualities on this flight.

Pete's fifth flight was his first flight with external tanks. The flight was launched at Mud Lake and flown almost exactly as planned. Pete reached a maximum Mach number of 6.33 at 97,000 feet altitude. Tank jettison was clean and both recovery chutes deployed. The tanks were slightly damaged at touchdown, but were refurbishable.

Pete did not sense a big change in aircraft handling qualities on this flight. He had to use more aileron to counteract the asymmetric lateral CG, which was a result of the difference in weight of the LOX and ammonia tanks. Overall, though, the airplane appeared to handle surprisingly well with the tanks on.

The airplane was not aesthetically pleasing with the tanks on, but apparently it flew all right. Once the tanks were gone, the airplane handled about the same as the standard airplanes.

Several experiments were conducted on this flight to obtain data for the higher-speed flights. In one experiment, ablative material was installed on the lower ventral to determine its ability to minimize the aerodynamic heating of the structure. No data was obtained on this experiment, owing to a malfunction of the thermocouple temperature measurement system. Another experiment was conducted to determine the effects of ablator residue on windshield visibility. A piece of high-temperature glass was installed on the ventral behind the ablative material to determine whether the residue would stick to the glass and compromise the transparency of the glass. The ablator residue did cloud the glass, which meant that we would have to protect the windshield with an eyelid at high speeds to ensure that the pilot could see out the window for landing. Another experiment measured the local flow conditions in the lower ventral area to define the aerodynamic flow environment for the scramjet engine. Good data was obtained on this experiment.

Due mainly to wet lakebeds resulting from the seasonal rains, the next flight, number 180, did not occur until 6 months later. On that flight, the new canopy eyelid was installed on the left windshield to protect it from ablator residue and a dummy scramjet was installed on the lower ventral. The scramjet was installed to evaluate its effect on aircraft handling qualities and to check out the scramjet jettison system. Ablative material was installed on the ventral behind the inlet spike of the dummy scramjet.

The flight was launched out of Hidden Hills and was flown as planned. The maximum Mach number of 4.75 and maximum altitude of 97,600 feet were slightly higher than planned, due to an error in the inertial system computer. However, all the flight objectives were achieved. The scramjet had no significant effect on aircraft handling qualities and the eyelid worked as advertised. One significant result of this flight was the complete erosion of the ablator material from the leading edge of the ventral behind the spike of the dummy scramjet. The temperature measuring thermocouples in the ventral failed to work properly again, so we were unable to determine how hot the ventral skin got during the flight.

Later events would indicate that we used poor judgment in proceeding to high speeds without having temperature data in this region. The missing ablator on the lower ventral was a result of much higher than expected heating in that area due to the presence of the dummy scramjet. Shock waves off the dummy scramjet were impinging on the ventral and lower fuselage and creating local hot spots of extremely high temperatures. We did not appreciate the significance of this clue because we had no thermocouple data to confirm the high heating rates and we continued to expand the flight envelope to higher speeds.

The next flight, number 186, was made with a complete ablative coating on the aircraft and the dummy scramjet. It was originally planned to be a flight to Mach 6.5 with external tanks, but was subsequently changed to a lower speed flight without tanks. This change was made to obtain more data prior to committing to a maximum-speed flight.

This flight was also accomplished as planned without any incidents or surprises. The ablative coating did not appear to affect the flight characteristics of the aircraft although there seemed to be a significant increase in drag. This was anticipated because of the roughness of the ablative coating and the resultant thicker airfoil sections. The maximum Mach number achieved was 4.94 at an altitude of 85,000 feet. The eyelid worked properly to prevent the ablator residue from clouding the windshield. The only significant result of this flight was the severe erosion of the ablator on the ventral leading edge. This duplicated the results of the previous flight and should have warned us, again, of the consequences of going to higher speeds. The heating on this flight was calculated to be only one-third of that predicted for the maximum Mach number flight, and yet we still saw severe erosion of the protective ablative coating. We even correctly deduced that the excessive heating was due to shockwaves off the dummy scramjet, but we did not fully appreciate the ultimate intensity of the heating. We simply replaced the ablator on the leading edge of the ventral and prepared the aircraft for the next flight.

Although not planned as such, the next flight was to be the last flight of the aircraft. It was planned to be a high-speed flight to Mach 6.5. The ablative coating applied for the previous flight was refurbished as necessary and the aircraft prepared for flight. This flight was the first flight with all of the elements needed for a high-speed flight. The configuration included the ablative coating, the canopy eyelid, the dummy scramjet, and external tanks.

Good flight test practice would have dictated that we do a build-up test program on the complete configuration. That would mean a first flight to a relatively low Mach number with the complete configuration and then subsequent flights to increasingly higher Mach numbers. We vigorously debated whether to do this, but finally decided that we had indeed already done a buildup test program. We had done it in bits and pieces, however. We had made a low and a high-speed flight with the tanks. We had made a Mach 4.75 and a Mach

4.94 flight with the dummy scramjet and eyelid, and we had made a Mach 4.94 flight with the ablative coating. The decision was to proceed with a high-speed flight with the all up configuration.

System preflight functional tests were initiated on Saturday, September 16, and were completed the following Wednesday. The drop tanks were installed on Monday, September 18. An APU ground run was made on September 20. No engine ground run was made, but the aircraft was serviced with a full load of LOX and ammonia to conduct leak checks and to check propellant transfer from external to internal tanks. The airplane was closed out for flight on September 22. Final ablative coating repairs were made on Saturday, September 23, and the aircraft was mated to the B-52 two days later. Rain in the Mud Lake area rendered Mud Lake unusable for the entire week, so the flight was rescheduled for Tuesday, October 3.

A problem with the radio headset in Pete's pressure suit helmet caused a delay in the Tuesday takeoff. Pete was finally fitted with a spare helmet. A second problem, a persistent ammonia leak, required that the tank be pressurized to reseat the leaking jettison value. This procedure did not completely stop the leak, but it reduced it to a small dribble which was considered acceptable. Takeoff occurred at 1,330 hours, rather than the scheduled 1,200 hours. This was a rather late takeoff time for normal X-15 flights, but this aircraft required a lot of extra servicing on the day of the flight.

The flight proceeded uneventfully during captive flight up until about 4 minutes to launch. At that time, Pete had problems hearing NASA-1, but he continued the checklist activities in preparation for launch. At 2 minutes to launch, the radio communications improved and the countdown proceeded smoothly right down to launch. At launch time, Pete hit the launch switch and started to reach for the throttle when he realized that he had not launched. He hit the launch switch again and this time the airplane launched. He got a good engine light and pulled the nose up to begin the climb. The climb went according to plan and at 60 seconds Pete pushed over to 5 degrees angle of attack and prepared to jettison the tanks. The tanks came off at 67 seconds and, according to Pete, they came off hard, very hard.

At tank separation, the airplane pitched down to a –2.5 degree angle of attack before Pete could catch it and bring it back up to a +2 degree angle of attack. He maintained that angle of attack until he came level at approximately 100,000 feet and then began increasing angle of attack to maintain level flight at that altitude. Pete continued to accelerate in level flight until he reached an indicated 6,500 feet per second, or roughly Mach 6.5. At that time, 141 seconds after launch, he shut the engine down. The thrust seemed to fall off slowly and velocity increased to 6,630 feet per second, or Mach 6.7.

After shutdown, Pete began doing control pulses in the yaw and pitch axes to obtain stability and control data. As he decelerated through Mach 5.5, Pete noticed a peroxide hot light. This light was one that really got a person's attention. Hot peroxide was like hot nitroglycerine, something one would rather not encounter. Unknown to Pete and those in the control room, the intense heat from the shock waves off the dummy scramjet was burning the ablator off and melting huge holes in the skin of the ventral.

Even if Pete had known what was happening as a result of the shock wave heating, there was nothing he could do to prevent the damage once he exceeded Mach 6. The burn through of the ventral was inevitable from that point on. He may have been able to minimize the damage by deploying speedbrakes to slow down quicker, but he could not stop the cutting torch action of the air impacting the ventral at hypersonic speeds.

The temperatures were later calculated to be over 2,700° F in this region. The flow of hot air into the ventral through the holes caused the peroxide to get hot, burned the instrumentation wiring, burned through a control gas line, and cooked off some of the explosive bolts that were used to jettison the dummy scramjet from the airplane. The burnthrough of the control gas line resulted in the loss of the tank pressurizing gas, which prevented jettison of the residual fuel.

The peroxide hot light in the cockpit distracted Pete from his planned maneuvers and his energy management. NASA-1 finally instructed him to jettison his peroxide and began vectoring him toward high key at Edwards. Pete was high on energy coming into high key due to being distracted and he came across the north edge of the lake at over 55,000 feet at Mach 2.2.

He attempted to jettison the remaining propellants during his turn to low key, but nothing came out. This lack of jettison prevented the chase from spotting him since the chase relied heavily on jettison to acquire the X-15. Jettisoned propellants created a bright vapor trail similar to a contrail which was easily seen. Pete was not going to get any help from the chase until he rolled out on final. Pete had his work cut out for him.

He was high on energy, unable to jettison propellants, and unsure of the condition of the aircraft. He finally got the airplane turned around over the south end of the lakebed but was still supersonic at 40,000 feet altitude. As he rolled out heading northbound, the dummy scramjet tore off the airplane and tumbled on down to impact on the bombing range without a recovery chute.

The chute and deployment system had been damaged by the extreme heating and the chute failed to deploy. As Pete proceeded up the east shore of the lakebed for a landing on runway one-eight, he sensed that he was losing altitude at a greater than normal rate. NASA-1 noted this also and suggested that Pete consider landing on runway two-three instead of one-eight.

Pete called for an altitude check from the chase to help him decide which runway to try for, but the chase had still not acquired him. Pete decided to press on for runway one-eight. Pete made it around the turn to final on runway one-eight and, as he rolled out, the chase finally saw him. The landing was a good one and the slideout was normal. The higher rate of descent was later confirmed and attributed to the extra drag from the charred and roughened ablative coating.

The dummy scramjet was later located and recovered as a result of some excellent investigative effort on the part of Johnny Armstrong, one of our flight planning engineers. No one was certain when the scramjet tore off the aircraft. Armstrong examined the flight records in minute detail looking for some clue. He noted a sudden increase in longitudinal acceleration at one point in the flight, and he suspected that the increase in acceleration might be due to the decrease in drag resulting from separation of the dummy scramjet. He correlated the time of the sudden increase in acceleration with the time on the radar map of the aircraft's ground track and defined a location at which he suspected the scramjet separated from the aircraft. He then estimated the free-fall trajectory of the scramjet and established a potential ground impact point which happened to be located in the Edwards bombing range. He drove out to his predicted impact point, stopped the van that he was driving, began walking, and within several minutes found the scramjet within 300 feet of his predicted impact point.

Examination of the airplane after the flight revealed extensive damage to the ventral and the lower fuselage structure. The tough nickel-steel skin was melted through like butter, creating several large holes in the ventral. The recovered dummy scramjet showed similar heating damage. Everything inside the ventral was burned, including the hydraulic lines that connected to the speed brake actuators. These lines had not burned through. If they had, we would have lost the aircraft, and possibly Pete. The damage to the aircraft was a sobering sight.

The airplane was returned to North American Aviation for repairs. A month later, Mike Adams was killed in the number three aircraft. These two events— the near loss of the number two aircraft and the loss of the number three aircraft—precipitated a reassessment of the overall X-15 program. The number two aircraft never flew again. It was repaired and then sent to the USAF museum at Wright-Patterson AFB where it is proudly displayed at this time.

It is always more dramatic to discuss the problems, malfunctions, or near disasters when telling airplane stories. The flights highlighted in the X-15A-2 program are those types of flights wherein problems occurred or there were significant elements of risk. There were many routine flights and there were some textbook flights. Even on the last X-15A-2 flight, there were many positive aspects of the flight. Pete flew a perfect flight until he was distracted by the peroxide-hot light. Even with that distraction, he brought the airplane home and made a beautiful landing.

Most of the modifications had performed as they were designed to perform. The eyelid worked well to protect the windshield. The external tank system worked well—fuel and LOX transferred into the main tanks as intended, while maintaining an allowable center of gravity position. The tanks ejected and separated cleanly, and the parachute recovery systems functioned properly with only minor anomalies. The aircraft was completely stable and controllable with the huge external tanks and the dummy scramjet installed, and the ablative coating worked well to protect the aircraft in all areas except the lower ventral area. We burned through the ventral in several areas, but we later defined the problem and developed a fix. The aircraft was quickly repaired and modified and could have been ready to fly within a couple of months. After these last modifications, the aircraft could have successfully carried the scramjet to speeds in excess of Mach 7.

The X-15A-2 development program was a success. There were a few moments of stark terror, as the saying goes, but this is to be expected in any flight test program.

Chapter 9 . . . .

Sometimes the Bull Wins

M ike Adams started his X-15 career with a bang. The bang was the noise made by the failure of the forward bulkhead of the ammonia fuel tank. As a result of that bang, Mike had to make an emergency landing on his first flight. As I have said earlier, the last thing any pilot needed on his first X-15 flight was an emergency. The mental stress level was high enough on a normal first flight. Mike handled his emergency very well.

Mike was scheduled to make his first flight out of Hidden Hills. The flight plan called for a pull-up after launch at 50 percent throttle to a climb angle of 20 degrees. At 80 seconds after launch, he was to push over to 0 g and maintain 0 g until 104 seconds, at which time he was to increase angle of attack to hold level flight at 74,000 feet altitude. He was to maintain altitude until reaching 4,000 feet per second at 129 seconds after launch, at which time he was to shut the engine down. Following engine shutdown, Mike was to perform a series of mild maneuvers to familiarize himself with the handling qualities of the airplane and then vector to high key for a landing at Edwards.

As indicated above, the flight did not go according to plan. The engine shut down 90 seconds after launch as Mike was extending the speed brakes to decrease the rate of acceleration. The engine shutdown occurred as a result of the forward bulkhead failure in the fuel tank coupled with a momentary pushover to less than 0 *g*. In the postflight debriefing, Mike said that, "Immediately after the engine shutdown, I saw two little lights below the igniter-ready light come on and say something bad."

Mike immediately attempted an engine relight, but with no luck. The engine failed to light. Pete Knight, who was the controller, asked, "Did you get a shutdown, Mike?" and Mike replied, "Rog." Then Pete said, "OK, you're going to Cuddeback." Mike was subsequently heard over the radio talking to the airplane saying, "Now what did you go and do that for?" NASA-1 said, "Say again, Mike." Mike responded with the comment, "Wonder why I picked a shutdown."

As Mike approached Cuddeback, he made the comment that, "It looks like I could make Edwards." Mike, like all the other X-15 pilots, preferred landing at "home." Pete would have none of that wishful thinking. He replied, "Let's make it Cuddeback." Mike arrived at high key at Cuddeback with ample energy and commented to Pete at NASA-1 that, "This thing is sort of fun to fly." Pete said, "Say again," and Mike said, "This thing is fun to fly even if I have to go to Cuddeback." Pete was not in the mood for frivolity in the middle of an emergency and said, "Well, let's talk about it after you get it on the ground."

Pete's reaction was quite typical of the reaction of most pilots who are serving as controller or flight director during a flight. They are generally under more stress than the pilot in the airplane because of a sense of responsibility for the safety of the pilot in the airplane. We verified this by monitoring the heart rate of each pilot when he acted as controller and when he flew the airplane. The pilot's heart rate was higher when serving as a controller than when he was actually flying the airplane. Pete was so concerned about Mike that he was attempting to give Mike a GCA (ground control approach) around the pattern at Cuddeback using radar information.

This practice of vectoring the X-15 around the approach using radar was discouraged after my emergency landing at Cuddeback. In this instance, Pete forgot the ground rules and talked him all the way around the pattern, preventing the chase from getting a word in edgewise. Mike commented after the flight that "After the restart attempt, I had all the help I needed there and WE brought it into Cuddeback."

After returning to Edwards and being debriefed, Mike had scheduled a T-38 flight in the afternoon. Even this routine flight would not go smoothly for Mike on this day. For the second time in one day, Mike got an inadvertent engine shutdown. Fortunately, the T-38 has two engines. Nevertheless, Mike now had to make another emergency landing, this time at Edwards. I never checked, but I wonder if Mike's car made it home that evening without quitting.

Mike's second flight was made in the number three X-15. Normally a new pilot was not scheduled to fly the number three X-15 until he had made at least two flights in the standard aircraft. The control system in the number three aircraft was more complex and unconventional. It had some good and some bad characteristics. The bad ones could sneak up on you if you were not forewarned. The flight planners apparently felt that Mike could handle the number three aircraft after his successful emergency landing on his first flight.

This flight was planned as another pilot checkout flight from Hidden Hills. A tip pod accelerometer experiment was also carried on this flight. This plan called for a climbout after engine light at 75 percent throttle to a climb angle of 30 degrees. Engine thrust was increased incrementally on a pilot's first three flights from 50 to 75 to 100 percent to allow the pilot to adjust to the higher acceleration levels. One hundred percent thrust was impressive, to say the least. I believe a pilot would have been overwhelmed by the g forces and the events if he had to make his first flight at 100 percent. I was thoroughly impressed by 50 percent thrust on my first flight.

Mike was to climb at 30-degrees flight path angle to 58,000 feet altitude and then push over to 0 g and hold that until reaching 77,000 feet at 80 seconds after launch. Then he was to increase angle of attack to maintain level flight until he reached 4,500 feet per second velocity, at which time he was to shut the engine down. Following shutdown, he was to perform a number of roll and yaw maneuvers to familiarize himself with the aircraft's flying characteristics and vector to high key for landing at Edwards.

On this flight, everything proceeded as planned. The only problem Mike had was with his radio just prior to launch. He had to rely on the B-52 to relay calls from NASA-1 to verify that everything was okay for launch. After launch he did not hear NASA-1 until passing Cuddeback Lake while vectoring to high-key. During the approach, just prior to landing, Mike ballooned dangerously but managed to recover and got the airplane on the lakebed before he lost all his airspeed.

This ballooning tendency was one of the bad characteristics of the MH-96 flight control system that tended to surprise every new pilot. We had developed a special trim technique to minimize this tendency, but Mike forgot to utilize it. It required two or three flights in the number three aircraft to learn the system and become proficient flying it. After that, it was a nice airplane to fly.

Mike's third flight was made in the number one aircraft. It was another pilot checkout flight to expose Mike to flight at a higher altitude. Four experiments were carried and operated on this flight. It was planned to be flown out of Mud Lake near Tonapah, Nevada. The flight plan called for a two step climb coming level initially at 100,000 feet altitude at 5,500 feet per second. The engine would then be shutdown and the pilot was to pull up to 15 degrees angle of attack and maintain that angle of attack until he peaked out in altitude at 133,000 feet at 157 seconds after launch. After reaching peak altitude, Mike was to hold 15 degrees angle of attack until he descended back through 115,000 feet and then he was to open the speed brakes and maintain a constant rate of descent while vectoring to high key at Edwards.

During the actual flight, Mike lost cabin pressure while climbing through 77,000 feet on the way up to peak altitude. This caused his pressure suit to inflate, which in turn made it more difficult to fly the airplane. As he went over the top at 133,000 feet, his inertial computer failed and he lost his cockpit readouts of rate of climb, altitude, and velocity. He made his reentry without this information. In spite of these failures, Mike managed to fly a successful flight and acquire the desired flight data. During his approach to landing, Mike commented over the radio, "I thought you said every once in a while something goes wrong, Pete." Mike was obviously getting more than his share of problems in-flight.

During the postflight debriefing, Mike indicated that he had suffered from vertigo during the climbout. He indicated that after the pushover at 60,000 feet on the way up, he thought he was going straight up. Pete had warned him that he might have this sensation during boost. Mike had indeed suffered severe vertigo on this flight. He commented, "I did not know what the hell I was doing"—an ominous pronouncement. Mike had momentarily lost control of the situation. The bull only bucked once this time.

Mike's fourth flight was another altitude buildup flight out of Delamar Lake north of Las Vegas. In addition to the altitude buildup, on this flight Mike was to operate the PMR (Pacific Missile Range) experiment to check out the system. This experiment was a very complex experiment used to monitor ballistic missile launches from the PMR with equipment installed in the X-15. This experiment required a coordinated launch of a missile and the X-15, such that both would be above the atmosphere simultaneously. This was attempted on several flights but was never accomplished due to the inability to coordinate a simultaneous launch of both vehicles.

On this flight, Mike was to extend the experiment as he climbed through

170,000 feet on the way to his planned peak altitude of 180,000 feet. The flight went off as planned except that Mike had problems controlling his climb angle due to an apparent stickiness in the indicator needle. As a result, his climb angle was 1 to 2 degrees low. He did not get high enough to safely open the experiment doors. Mike did obtain data on an MIT experiment, however. The flight back to Edwards was uneventful. Mike had finally gotten a nice peaceful flight.

Mike's fifth flight was made in the number one aircraft. It was his third altitude buildup flight. The flight was also planned to obtain data on the MIT horizon scanner experiment and to attempt to checkout the PMR experiment again. The planned maximum altitude was 220,000 feet. The flight was flown as planned, except that Mike was one second late in shutting the engine down. This resulted in an overshoot of 7,000 feet in peak altitude. Data was obtained on the MIT experiment, but a fuse failed in the PMR experiment, deactivating the video recorder.

Mike indicated in the debriefing that he had trouble maintaining precise pitch and roll attitudes and heading while going over the top and, in fact, had a slight oscillation going as he peaked out. This was not unusual in this airplane since the pilot was flying with both hands. He was controlling the aerodynamic controls with his right hand and the reaction controls with his left hand. If the aerodynamic controls were not properly positioned, the aircraft would not maintain an attitude or angle of attack, but would diverge requiring extensive reaction control usage to counteract the small aerodynamic control moments. It was relatively easy to excite an oscillation while doing this two-fisted flying. Mike did make a successful reentry and brought the aircraft home without any further problems.

Mike's sixth flight was made in the number three aircraft. It was a low-altitude flight to evaluate a boost guidance system and to obtain data on horizontal tail loads. Two other experiments were to be activated during flight—one to measure the noise in the fuselage boundary layer and another to measure the heat transfer rate on a cold wall surface. The flight was a rather benign flight to a maximum speed of 4,500 feet per second at 78,000 feet altitude. After shutdown, Mike was to perform a rapid pull-up to 15 degrees angle of attack and then push over to 0 g to vary the load on the horizontal tail for data gathering purposes. The flight plan called for this same maneuver at three other speeds while slowing down, during the approach to Edwards.

Unlike his first flight, this flight did not start out with a bang. In fact, Mike got no noise at all out of the engine when he tried to start it after launch. The engine had a vibration sensor system that monitored the vibrations during engine operation. If these vibrations exceeded a preset g level, this system shut the engine down automatically to prevent catastrophic damage to the engine, and possibly the aircraft. For some unexplained reason, this system sensed a vibration spike during the start sequence and prevented the engine from starting.

Mike had to quickly try a restart. He went through the restart sequence automatically. Each of the X-15 pilots had that sequence burned into their memory bank. "Throttle off." "Engine reset." "Prime switch on and hold until the igniter-ready light came on." This required roughly 5 seconds, but in an emergency it seemed like 5 hours. Once the igniter-ready light came on, he could move the throttle to the on position.

Mike managed to get the engine lit on his second try, sixteen seconds after launch. The airloads were quite high during his roundout to the desired climb angle, but he finally got back on his desired profile and the flight proceeded as planned. The boost guidance experiment was cancelled prior to flight due to a problem with the system computer. This boost guidance system was intended to provide the pilot with simple steering commands during boost to reduce the pilot's workload. This type of system would potentially enable a pilot or an astronaut to manually fly a spacecraft into orbit. This capability has still not been demonstrated since all manned spacecraft have relied on automatic guidance and control to achieve orbit. The astronauts do have a manual backup capability in the shuttle, but it has never been used. Mike obtained good data on the other three experiments.

Mike's seventh flight was his fourth altitude flight. It was to be made in the number three aircraft to an altitude of 250,000 feet. The aircraft carried seven different experiments on this flight—the boost guidance experiment, which was carried on Mike's previous flight, a solar spectrum measurement device, an ultraviolet plume detector, a micrometeorite collector, a tip pod deflection camera, Saturn booster ablative material, and a traversing probe in one of the wing tip pods.

The solar spectrum measurement experiment was an experiment to obtain solar spectrum data outside of the atmosphere in order to improve methods of correcting for atmospheric absorption. This experiment was a Jet Propulsion Laboratory experiment to obtain data needed before launching spacecraft to Venus or Mars. The ultraviolet exhaust plume experiment measured the ultraviolet characteristics of the X-15 rocket engine exhaust plume against an earth background and a sky background. The micrometeorite collector was a small experiment mounted in a wing tip pod. This experiment was exposed at high altitude to measure the size, velocity, and frequency of micrometeorites impacting the experiment collector. The fifth experiment, the tip pod camera, was an experiment to measure the deflection of the tip pod during flight by photographing it from a camera located in the fuselage side fairing. The Saturn booster ablative material was installed on the speed brakes to determine whether it would survive the aerodynamic and thermal loads imposed during hypersonic flight. The seventh experiment, the traversing probe, was an experiment to measure the stand-off distance of the bow shock on a blunt nose cone. In this experiment, a small needlelike probe was cycled in and out of the tip pod nose cone to measure the stand-off distance of the bow shock produced by the tip pod. The majority of those experiments were classified as scientific piggyback experiments. They were independent of the X-15 and were simply carried by the X-15 to obtain data in and out of the atmosphere.

The flight was originally scheduled to be launched out of Delamar Lake on October 31, but the flight was aborted just prior to launch because the engine would not cycle into the igniter idle mode. Following the abort, the X-15 was de-mated from the B-52 to troubleshoot the engine. The engine was finally replaced and a ground run made to check out the new engine. This new engine also had to be replaced due to a fuel leak. A successful ground run was made with the second replacement engine on November 9 and the flight was rescheduled for November 15.

Mike's wife and mother came over to NASA on the morning of the flight to monitor the flight from the viewing area outside the control room. Walter "Whitey" Whiteside escorted them up to the control room and explained the control room operation and the progress of the activity in preparation for the flight.

Takeoff was scheduled for 9:00 A.M., but actually occurred at 9:12 A.M. The weather conditions in the southern Nevada and Mojave desert region included some scattered clouds at 12,000 to 16,000 feet and some higher broken clouds with a thin overcast. The clouds initially appeared to be a problem that might force an abort, but the clouds tended to dissipate as the captive flight progressed. The captive portion of the flight was uneventful with only a minor delay due to a late takeoff by the rescue C-130 aircraft. This minor delay required Mike to reset his command pitch and roll attitudes to compensate for the change in sun position. This command attitude change would later become a significant factor.

Mike launched the X-15 at 10:30:07. The aircraft rolled off to the right about 20 degrees, but Mike immediately rolled back to wings level. He had the throttle on within a second after launch, before leveling the wings. The engine lit a half-second later and was up to full thrust within one second. The radio conversation after launch, and significant events, are listed below:

10:30:07		[Launch.]
10:30:09		[Engine light.]
10:30:12	NASA-1:	"Good light here, Mike."
10:30:14	NASA-1:	"Check alpha, heading."
10:30:21	NASA-1:	"Right on track, Mike, coming up on profile."
10:30:30	NASA-1:	"Standby for theta."
10:30:33	NASA-1:	"How do you read, Mike?"
10:30:39	NASA-1:	"Check your boost guidance null, Mike, and how do you read?"
10:30:42		[Aircraft velocity is 2,000 feet per second and altitude is 60,000 feet.]
10:30:44	NASA-1:	"OK, Mike, we have you right on track, on the profile."
10:30:45	B-52:	"You're on track and profile, Mike."
10:30:52	Adams:	"Roger." [This was Mike's first radio call since launch and was apparently in response to the B-52 radio relay of NASA-1's call.]
10:30:54	B-52:	"I'll relay, Pete." [Pete Knight was the controller in NASA-1. The B-52 copilot was offering to relay radio calls to Mike.]
10:30:56	NASA-1:	"OK."
10:31:01	NASA-1:	"Standby for 83,000 feet, Mike."
10:31:04	B-52:	"Standby for 83,000."
10:31:07		[An electrical disturbance causes a transient motion in all three control system servo actuators at this time and drives the system gain down below 50 percent, which deactivates the normal reaction controls. The electrical noise apparently emanated from the traversing probe experiment. This electrical noise would persist for two minutes and 46 seconds. While this noise persisted, it would tend to keep the normal automatic reaction controls deactivated. The electrical noise also affected the inertial system computer and the boost guidance computer causing significant errors in the inertial data displayed on the cockpit instrument panel. The reaction controls occasionally became functional fortuitously, or insidiously, when Mike had to make a special maneuver, but they were not working for a major portion of the climb to altitude. They were not available to prevent the aircraft from slowly drifting in heading during ascent. The malfunctioning of the flight control system and the inertial system computer tended to distract Mike throughout the remainder of the climb to peak altitude.]

10:31:09	NASA-1:	"Do you read us at all, Mike?"
10:31:12	NASA-1:	"OK, you're right on track."
10:31:13	B-52:	"Right on track, Mike."
10:31:19	NASA-1:	"Coming up on 110,000."
10:31:21	B-52:	"Coming up on 110,000."
10:31:22	NASA-1:	"On the profile, on the heading."
10:31:24	B-52:	"On profile, on heading."
10:31:26	NASA-1:	"Standby for shutdown."
10:31:27	B-52:	"Standby for shutdown."

10:31:28   [The inertial system computer and instrument failure lights came on at this time as a result of the electrical noise. This malfunction light would tend to be another distraction to Mike.]

10:31:30   [Engine chamber pressure starts to decrease, indicating shutdown of the engine by the pilot. Actual velocity at shutdown was 5,236 feet per second, which was higher than the planned 5,100 feet per second. This would result in a higher than planned peak altitude. The engine was shut down 4 seconds later than planned, probably as a result of the pilot waiting for the proper indicated velocity for shutdown. The electrical noise caused the computed velocity to lag the actual velocity. Actual altitude at shutdown was 150,000 feet, which was also higher than the planned 140,000 feet.]

| 10:31:33 | NASA-1: | "Precision attitudes, Mike." |
| 10:31:35 | B-52: | "Precision attitudes, Mike." |

10:31:36   [Mike attempts to reset the computer malfunction light.]

10:31:39	NASA-1:	"Alpha to zero."
10:31:40	B-52:	"Alpha to zero."
10:31:42	NASA-1:	"And rock your wings and extend your experiment, Mike."
10:31:45	B-52:	"Extend your experiment, Mike."

   [The wing rocking maneuvers were to obtain data for the ultraviolet exhaust plume experiment. The experiment to be extended was the JPL solar spectrum experiment.]

10:31:50	NASA-1:	"On the heading, on the profile."
10:31:52	NASA-1:	"Have you going a little bit high. That's all right."
10:31:54	B-52:	"On the heading, on the profile. Maybe a little bit high."

10:31:54   [The X-15 is climbing through 200,000 feet altitude.]

10:31:58	Adams:	"I am reading him now. I got a computer and instrument light now."
10:32:03	NASA-1:	"OK, Mike."
10:32:08	NASA-1:	"We'll go ahead and try computed alpha at 230, [230,000 feet altitude] Mike." [The ball nose could not sense any airflow above 230,000 feet altitude. Angle of attack and

		angle of sideslip had to be computed from inertial data at higher altitudes.]
10:32:10		[Aircraft heading begins to deviate slowly. The automatic reaction controls are inactive due to the electrical noise and do not resist this deviation. Heading drift continues to peak altitude.]
10:32:14	NASA-1:	"Check your computed alpha now."
10:32:18	NASA-1:	"And you're right on track, Mike."
10:32:27	NASA-1:	"I lost my pitch and roll dampers." [Pitch and roll stability augmentation. A severe electrical transient caused the dampers to disengage at this time.]
10:32:32	NASA-1:	"OK, Mike let's try to get them on."
10:32:32	Adams:	"They reset." [The dampers reengaged satisfactorily.]
10:32:35	NASA-1:	"Did they reset?"
10:32:35	Adams:	"Yep."
10:32:36	NASA-1:	"OK."
10:32:37	NASA-1:	"And I'll give you a peak altitude, Mike."
10:32:42	NASA-1:	"Have you coming over the top. You're looking real good. Right on the heading, Mike."
10:32:51	NASA-1:	"Over the top at about 261 [261,000 feet altitude], Mike. Check your attitudes."
10:33:00		[At this time, the aircraft actually peaks out at 266,000 feet altitude. The heading drift stops due to a momentary reactivation of the automatic reaction controls. The aircraft heading is now misaligned 15 degrees to the right of the flight path. Aircraft velocity is approximately 4,600 feet per second.]
10:33:02	NASA-1:	"You're a little bit hot, but your heading is going in the right direction, Mike. Real good."
		[The control room is unaware of the aircraft misalignment since they do not have heading displayed in the control room. Aircraft heading outside the atmosphere does not effect the ground track, so there was no deviation of the track to alert them to the heading misalignment.]
10:33:05		[At this time Mike makes three yaw reaction control inputs with the left-hand manual controller. He apparently realizes that the normal reaction controls are not working properly. The control inputs that he makes are, however, in the wrong direction to correct the heading error. They are actually in the direction to increase the heading error. A slow, steady heading drift to the right begins as a result of these control inputs.]
10:33:09	NASA-1:	"Real good. Check your attitudes. How do you read, Mike?"

10:33:14	NASA-1:	"OK, let's check your dampers, Mike."
10:33:17	Adams:	"They're still on."
		[Mike reached down and cycled his damper switches turning the dampers off, then on. This was another distraction.]
10:33:18	NASA-1:	"OK."
10:33:24	NASA-1:	"A little bit high, Mike, but real good shape."
10:33:25		[Mike makes two more right yaw control inputs that increase the heading drift rate to the right.]
10:33:28		[Mike makes right, left, and then right yaw control inputs which further increase the right heading drift. His heading is now misaligned 50 degrees to the right of the flight path.]
10:33:33	NASA-1:	"And we got you coming down hill now. Are your dampers still on?"
10:33:37	Chase-1:	"Dampers still on, Mike?"
10:33:39	Adams:	"Yeah, and it seems squirrelly."
		[At this time, the heading has deviated 90 degrees from the ground track. The aircraft is turned sideways to the flight path. Mike is apparently unaware of this gross heading misalignment.]
– –		[Squelch break.]
10:33:44	NASA-1:	"OK, have you coming back through 230 [230,000 feet altitude]. Ball nose, Mike." [The heading deviation is increasing in rate and the aircraft apparently begins to spin.]
10:33:49		[At this time, the aircraft has turned 180 degrees from its ground track. The tail of the aircraft is pointed along the ground track.]
10:33:50	NASA-1:	"Let's watch your alpha, Mike."
10:33:58	NASA-1:	"Let's not keep it as high as normal with this damper problem. Have you at 210. Alpha, beta, and check your alpha, Mike."
10:34:02	Adams:	"I'm in a spin, Pete."
		[At this time, the aircraft has turned completely around and is again heading along the flight path momentarily as it continues to spin.]
10:34:05	NASA-1:	"Let's get your experiment in and the camera on."
10:34:13	NASA-1:	"Let's watch your theta, Mike."
10:34:16	Adams:	"I'm in a spin."
10:34:18	NASA-1:	"Say again."
10:34:19	Adams:	"I'm in a spin."
10:34:21	NASA-1:	"Say again."

I was in the control room monitoring the flight when this conversation was taking place. I heard Mike say, "I'm in a spin," three times very clearly. I know that Pete heard Mike also, since almost all the witnesses in the control room mentioned those calls in their statements after the accident. The only conclusion that I can draw is that Pete subconsciously did not want to hear that call. I, too, did not want to hear that call or believe it. My mind said, "What the hell do you mean, you're in a spin. How can you spin traveling 3,500 MPH? There is no such thing as a hypersonic spin. Spin? What do you mean spin. You've got to be kidding, Mike."

Pete may also have mentally refused to acknowledge Mike's call because he knew there was nothing he could do to help Mike. There was no known spin recovery technique for a hypersonic spin, since no one had ever anticipated such a phenomenon. No one had done any wind tunnel tests or analysis to confirm or deny the existence of such a phenomenon. Pete and the other control room occupants were completely helpless.

While I was trying to convince myself that this must be a bad dream, I noticed Whitey quickly grab Mike's wife and mother and lead them out of the control room viewing area. Whitey knew we had a serious emergency in progress and he wanted to somehow spare Mike's wife and mother the brutal details, at least for a few moments.

There was a time when wives were discouraged from observing test flights. Under those conditions, the wife would learn of an accident or death sometime after the fact under more controlled conditions. The Challenger accident was an example of a very traumatic event that was observed in real time by the wives, husbands, and other family members. I am not sure that is the best way to receive the bad news.

Before the days of instant communications, soldiers would go off to war and not be heard of, or from, for months and even years in the case of the crusades. If a soldier was killed, his wife and family only heard of it after the fact—much too late to do anything about it. Conversely, in the Vietnam war, wives were watching nightly TV newscasts in an attempt to recognize their husbands during battle or among the dead or wounded. If you observe such a thing in real time, you are almost forced to try and influence the outcome and when you realize you cannot, you are even more devastated. Again, I am not sure that is the best way to receive the bad news.

| 10:34:27 | NASA-1: | "OK, Mike, you're coming through about 135 [135,000 feet altitude] now." |
| 10:34:34 | NASA-1: | "Let's get it straightened out." |

[Pete apparently finally admitted to himself that the aircraft was in a spin.]

10:34:36   [At this time, the spin apparently breaks. The angle of attack decreases to a nominal value and the yaw rate decreases to zero. Simultaneously, the aircraft horizontal stabilizers begin to oscillate ±10 degrees in a sawtooth manner. These stabilizer motions begin to force the aircraft to oscillate in pitch and roll. The aircraft motions are initially small, but begin to rapidly increase in amplitude as the aircraft continues its descent into the atmosphere. The aircraft is plunging into the atmosphere at over 3,000 feet per second. This is the same control system oscillation that I had previously encountered on one of my flights. On my flight these oscillations had become extremely violent, slamming me against my restraint harness with great force before they finally stopped.]

10:34:37 – –   [Two squelch breaks.]

10:34:42 NASA-1:   "OK, you got theta zero now. Get some angle of attack up."

10:34:50 NASA-1:   "Coming up to 80,000, Mike."

10:34:53 NASA-1:   "Let's get some alpha on it."

10:34:54   [At this time, the aircraft fuselage buckled due to excessive side loads produced by the large, violent aircraft motions. These motions were a result of the continuing horizontal tail surface oscillations which were producing higher and higher oscillatory g loads as the aircraft continued to descend. Radar altitude at this time was approximately 80,000 feet.]

10:34:57 NASA-1:   "Get some g on it, Mike."

10:34:59 NASA-1:   "Let's get some g on it."

[At this time, telemetry data ceased. Just prior to loss of telemetry data, the oscillatory g forces exceeded ±13 g Radar altitude was 62,000 feet. Velocity had decreased to less than 4,000 feet per second, or about Mach 4. The aircraft was descending at approximately 2,500 feet per second and broke into many pieces at this time.]

10:35:02 NASA-1:   "We've got it now. Let's keep it there. Coming around."

10:35:09 NASA-1:   "OK, let's keep it up, Mike."

10:35:14 NASA-1:   "Keep pulling up. Do you read, Mike?"

10:35:20 NASA-1:   "Let's keep pulling it up, Mike."

10:35:27 NASA-1:   "OK, 130 let's head down that way."

[Pete is telling the C-130 to head down toward Cuddeback Lake.]

10:35:37 NASA-1:   "He was abeam Cuddeback 130, three-five-eight."

10:35:42	NASA-1:	"Chase-4, do you have anything on him?"
10:35:44	Chase-4:	"Chase-4, negative."
10:35:47	NASA-1:	"OK, Mike, do you read?"
10:35:52	Chase-4:	"Pete, I got dust on the lake down there."
10:35:55	NASA-1:	"What lake?"

At this time, the long wait began. The forward fuselage portion of the aircraft was finally spotted by the backup Chase-4 at approximately 10:52. The landing recovery helicopter had proceeded northbound from Edwards as soon as the pilot heard Mike's call that he was in a spin. It arrived at the crash site at 10:57. Colonel Cotton, the B-52 pilot, said, "At 11:02 the unwanted announcement was heard from the helicopter that the remains of the pilot were in the cockpit."

Colonel Cotton had become an unwilling witness to a second major catastrophe. Joe Cotton had been flying chase on the B-70 when Joe Walker's plane collided with the B-70. Joe Cotton called out the fateful words on that occasion, "Midair. Midair."

Based on the accident investigation, somewhere during the climb, Mike had apparently started experiencing the symptoms of vertigo. On a previous altitude flight, Mike had experienced severe vertigo from the time he had shut the engine down until he had reentered the atmosphere. Mike's words in the debriefing on that flight were, "I didn't know what the hell I was doing."

On a subsequent altitude flight, Mike again suffered extreme vertigo. He related that information off the record to a couple of flight planning engineers during a discussion at lunch the day after the flight.

Mike apparently did not mention this to the flight surgeon, possibly for two reasons. First, all of the X-15 pilots suffered from vertigo during the climbout. It was common knowledge that the high *g* forces in the X-15 during climbout caused vertigo. Every pilot thought he was climbing straight up or was even over on his back at engine shutdown. So Mike had no reason to suspect that he was experiencing something unique. He was, however, apparently disoriented for a much longer period of time than the other pilots, based on his previous postflight comments and his unofficial conversation with the flight planning engineers. He may or may not have been aware of this.

The second possible reason that Mike may not have mentioned this to his flight surgeon is that he may have been concerned about being grounded or at least taken off the X-15 program. This was obviously a possibility. Aerospace flight surgeons were generally quite conservative in that era. If a pilot on a major aerospace program showed any abnormal symptoms of any kind, he was usually grounded or removed from the program. Two classic cases were Deke Slayton and Alan Shepard. Both were grounded for years for minor abnormalities. A severe vertigo problem would undoubtedly have been considered disqualifying and Mike may not have wanted to surface the problem.

I could personally empathize with Mike. I had participated in a research program on the human centrifuge at Johnsville, Pennsylvania, in 1959. I spent one month being whirled around in the centrifuge for several hours a day at both low and high g's. At the end of that program, I had serious disorientation problems. If I moved my head back rapidly, I would become completely disoriented and think that I was back in the centrifuge at Johnsville whirling around on a test run. The disorientation would last as long as a full minute. That problem plagued me for over 6 months before it finally cleared up. I voluntarily admitted that I had a problem. It was duly recorded in my physical record, but I was not officially grounded.

Mike was, unfortunately, the victim of ignorance. No one understood the effects of g forces on the human sensory system. They still do not. Astronauts are still suffering from space sickness. He obviously knew he had a problem. He also did not want to be grounded. He may have been subconsciously appealing for help when he discussed his problem with the flight planning engineers. Unfortunately, they had no appreciation for the problem.

Although we strongly suspected that Mike had misinterpreted his instruments due to vertigo and responded to the roll guidance error indication with yaw control inputs, to misalign the airplane with the flight path, we could not verify this without knowing what the cockpit instruments were indicating during ballistic flight. We needed the cockpit camera film to verify this. The problem was that the cockpit camera was mounted on the inside of the canopy and the canopy was missing from the forward fuselage wreckage. Apparently, the canopy had come off in flight, but where? The airplane had failed structurally while descending through 65,000 feet altitude. Whether the airplane disintegrated at that point or whether it shed parts all the way to impact, no one knew. We organized a search party to locate aircraft parts. Over half of the aircraft was missing.

The location of the structural breakup point was pinpointed on a large scale topographic map using data from our radar tracking maps. The breakup point, the aircraft track over the ground, and the forward fuselage impact point were plotted on the topographical maps. This information provided some general guidance for the search party. The terrain in the proposed search area was, however, extremely rugged—steep rock strewn hills with numerous narrow dead-ended canyons—an ideal place for prospecting, but a hell hole for a search party. The search area was just to the southwest of Death Valley, an ominous reminder of the business at hand.

The search party quickly began finding parts and identifying the location of each part on the topographic maps. We soon surmised from a master plot of the location of the various parts, that the aircraft had indeed disintegrated at the point of the initial structural failure. The parts then impacted in a pattern dictated by their individual density. Those with higher densities traveled farther along the flight path before impact. Using this information, we began to identify more fruitful search areas for the canopy. After an agonizing and frustrating search, the canopy was finally located. It was in excellent condition with no significant damage. It had apparently sailed down to a smooth landing.

The searchers were ecstatic. They had located the missing evidence. But, on examination of the canopy, they found that the cockpit camera had torn loose and was missing. What a blow. They had not found the missing evidence and worse, the part they now had to find was quite small—about the size of a Cracker Jack box. We were now literally looking for the needle in a hay stack. A small camera with a neutral color could blend in with the rocks and brown vegetation like a chameleon.

An early winter rain made the search area inaccessible for about a week. Another search party was organized after the area dried out. The search party lined up in a long line abreast and began walking up and down the hills and gullies in a precise pattern. This technique paid off handsomely. The camera was located on the second pass along the 2-mile route. Again, the searchers were quickly disappointed. The film magazine was missing from the camera. We were now forced to search for something even smaller—something the size of a pack of cigarettes. The search continued but with no further success.

By this time we gave up hope of ever finding the film magazine, but a few die hards would not give up. Another search party was organized and again, the searchers lined up in a long line abreast, 10 feet apart, and marched up and down the rugged terrain for a last, final search effort. Again, it paid off. The film magazine was found intact. It was hand carried to a photo lab back on the East Coast that specialized in salvaging damaged film. The film had been slightly damaged by the rain, but it was completely readable. That cockpit camera film provided vital information in the accident investigation.

The accident report states in the summary that:

The only unusual problem during the ascent portion of the flight was an electrical disturbance that started at an altitude of 90,000 feet and that effected the telemetered signal, the altitude and velocity computer associated with the inertial platform and the reaction controls that operate automatically in conjunction with the MH-96 adaptive control system. Although the pilot always had adequate displays and backup controls, the condition created a distraction and degraded the normal controls. As the aircraft approached the peak altitude of 266,000 feet, it began a slow turn to the right at a rate of about 0.5 degrees per second. This rate was checked by the MH-96 system which operated normally for a brief period so that at peak altitude, the aircraft was 15 degrees off heading. Then the pilot, apparently mistaking a roll indicator for a sideslip (heading) indicator drove the airplane further off in heading by using the manual reaction controls. Thus the aircraft was turned 90 degrees to the flight path as the aerodynamic forces became significant with decreasing altitude. The aircraft continued to veer and entered what appeared to be a classical spin at an altitude of about 230,000 feet and a Mach number of about 5.0.

Some combination of pilot action, the stability augmentation system, and the inherent aircraft stability caused the aircraft to recover from the spin at an altitude of about 120,000 feet and a Mach number of about 4.7. As the aircraft recovered from the spin, however, a control system oscillation developed and quickly became self-sustaining. At this time the airplane was descending at a rate of about 160,000 feet per minute and dynamic pressure was increasing at nearly 100 pounds per square foot each second. There was a corresponding rapid increase in the g forces associated with the oscillation, and structural limits were exceeded. The airplane broke into many pieces while still at high altitude probably in excess of 60,000 feet, and fell to the earth northeast of Johannesburg, California.

The pilot, probably incapacitated by the high g forces did not escape from the cockpit and was killed on ground impact. The accident board concluded that the accident was precipitated when the pilot allowed the aircraft to deviate in heading and subsequently drove it to such an extreme deviation that there was a complete loss of control. The board believes that these pilot actions were the result of some combination of display misinterpretation, distraction, and possible vertigo. The board further concludes that the destruction of the aircraft was the result of a sustained control system oscillation driven by the MH-96 adaptive control system that caused the divergent aircraft oscillations and aerodynamic loads in excess of the structural limits. The electrical disturbance was attributed to the use in one of the scientific experiments of a motor that was unsuited to very high altitude environments.

In my opinion, there was no pilot error involved. I also believe the accident board shared this opinion. I think everyone believed that Mike suffered severe vertigo during this flight. There were many malfunctions and distractions that were contributing causes which severely compromised the control task, but

Mike was an excellent pilot and under normal conditions he would have successfully coped with these problems. As we have learned from painful experience, vertigo can be extremely incapacitating. It can effect the best or the worst pilot and can strike at any time. Amazingly, the pilots of that era were not routinely subjected to any specific test for vertigo susceptibility. Vertigo tests were apparently considered passé.

My personal conclusion was that Mike was thrown off the bull, and the bull killed him.

Chapter 10 ....

The End

fter Mike's death, there was a reassessment of the program. The program had been winding down. Most of the basic research work had been accomplished and we had flown most of the proposed follow-on experiments. Support for the program was dwindling in NASA, the USAF, and in Congress. The scramjet development was several years behind schedule, and the X-15 delta wing proposal was in limbo due to lack of high-level support. There was also some trepidation about the possibility of another accident. Bikle could have taken the easy way out and shut the program down. Instead, he elected to fly for another year in the hope that the scramjet or delta wing experiments might come to fruition. Bikle was very concerned about losing a national capability to operate advanced research aircraft. By extending the program at least another year, Bikle would also be able to end the program in a more positive fashion if the program finally had to be cancelled.

The program had been an extremely productive and successful one up until Mike's accident. One hundred and ninety flights had been made without a fatality. Admittedly, there had been several accidents and Jack McKay had been injured, but considering the experimental nature of the program, the overall success record was outstanding. For every hazardous flight that I have described, there were ten good, routine ones. Even the hazardous flights produced some good data. The program and its personnel deserved an upbeat ending to the program.

In the year after Mike's death, eight more flights were made. Bill Dana and Pete Knight alternated in flying the single remaining flightworthy aircraft. All of these flights except the first were flights to high altitude to carry piggyback experiments into the space environment. There were no significant problems or incidents on any of these flights. The last attempt to fly was made on December 12, 1968. The flight was aborted after takeoff due to bad weather up-range. It was snowing on several of the planned emergency lakebeds. The program ended with a white Christmas.

The program has been described as the most successful flight research program ever conducted. It produced over 750 research papers and reports. John Becker, one of the early advocates of the program, summarized the program in a paper written in 1968. A list of the accomplishments of the X-15 program, compiled by Becker, included the following:

- Development of the first large restartable man-rated throttleable rocket engine, the LR-99.
- First application of hypersonic theory and wind tunnel work to an actual flight vehicle.
- Development of the wedge tail as a solution to hypersonic directional stability problems.
- First use of reaction controls for attitude control in space.
- First reusable superalloy structure capable of withstanding the temperatures and thermal gradients of hypersonic reentry.
- Development of new techniques for the machining, forming, welding, and heat treating of Inconel-X and titanium.
- Development of improved high temperature seals and lubricants.
- Development of the NACA Q-ball hot nose flow direction sensor for operation over an extreme range of dynamic pressure and a stagnation air temperature of 1,900° F.
- Development of the first practical full pressure suit for pilot protection in space.
- Development of nitrogen cabin conditioning.
- Development of inertial flight data systems capable of functioning in a high dynamic pressure and space environment.
- Discovery that hypersonic boundary layer flow is turbulent and not laminar.

- Discovery that turbulent heating rates are significantly lower than had been predicted by theory.
- First direct measurement of hypersonic skin friction and discovery that skin friction is lower than had been predicted.
- Discovery of hot spots generated by surface irregularities.
- Discovery of methods to correlate base drag measurements with tunnel test results so as to correct wind tunnel data.
- Development of practical boost guidance pilot displays.
- Demonstration of a pilot's ability to control a rocket boosted aerospace vehicle through atmospheric exit.
- Development of large supersonic drop tanks.
- Successful transition from aerodynamic controls to reaction controls and back again.
- Demonstration of a pilot's ability to function in a weightless environment.
- First demonstration of piloted lifting atmospheric entry.
- First application of energy management techniques.
- Studies of hypersonic acoustic measurements used to define insulation and structural design requirements for the Mercury spacecraft.
- Use of the three X-15 aircraft as testbeds carrying a wide variety of experimental packages.

There were several attractive experiments that were not accomplished in the X-15 program. One, of course, was the ramjet or scramjet demonstration program. The experimental flight engine fell way behind in its development program. It was to have been flown on the modified X-15A-2 aircraft. When that aircraft was damaged on its maximum speed flight, the momentum behind the scramjet program seemed to dissipate. Wind tunnel testing of that engine continued after the X-15 program terminated and it was successfully operated at speeds near Mach 8 in the wind tunnel. It still has not flown, however, and probably never will.

Another very challenging proposed experiment was a delta wing for the X-15. This wing was to be constructed like a hypersonic cruise vehicle wing. It was to be radiatively cooled and capable of sustained flight at speeds of Mach 8. This experiment never got beyond the conceptual design stage, but it generated a lot of interest. It would have been a very expensive project. It is too bad that it was not proposed early in the program when money and political support were available.

The X-15 flight program received very little attention or publicity. Both

NASA and the USAF were simultaneously involved in much more glamorous space programs. NASA was launching Mercury and Gemini missions and the USAF was trying to launch Dyna-Soar and later the MOL (Manned Orbital Laboratory). The X-15 program and the pilots were, as a result, completely overshadowed in the news media. The program did receive recognition from the aerospace community. Among the many awards received were the Collier Trophy, the Harmon Trophy, the Schilling Award, the John J. Montgomery Award, the Ivan C. Kinchloe Award, the James H. Wyld Award, three Distinguished Flying Crosses, three NASA Distinguished Service Medals, two Octave Chanute Awards, and numerous other NASA and USAF medals and awards. However, few people outside of the aviation community knew anything about the program.

In some respects, the X-15 was ahead of its time. Data and technology from the X-15 have still not been applied to a subsequent operational aircraft. As far as I know, there are currently no operational hypersonic aircraft. The X-15 is still the fastest aircraft in the world. The space shuttle has flown at higher speeds, but it is a spacecraft, not an aircraft. The proposed National Aerospace Plane will be the first aircraft to fly faster than the X-15 if it survives the current budget cutting exercises.

This status quo was not foreseen when the X-15 was originally conceived. The country had a much grander vision of the future of aviation. The Dyna-Soar X-20 was to immediately follow the X-15 to expand the usable flight envelope to orbital speeds. A Mach 3 bomber, the B-70, and a Mach 3 fighter, the F-108, were to follow the Mach 2 B-58 and the Mach 2 Century series fighters. In civil aviation, the airlines would soon be flying a Mach 2.7 Supersonic Transport. If the X-15 program faltered, it would be quickly overtaken by more grandiose follow-on programs. We felt we had to expedite the X-15 program to make the data available to all those who would need it to design the next generation of aircraft. We worked three shifts during the X-15 program to stay ahead of the planned advances in aviation.

Then it all stopped. Progress in aviation did not just slow down, it stopped. The X-20 Dyna-Soar program was cancelled in the spring of 1963. The F-108 was cancelled in 1965. The B-70 was cancelled in 1967. The SST hung on a little longer, but was finally terminated in 1968 by the overzealous environmentalists who prophesied the extinction of the human race if the SST took to the air.

Progress in aviation then began moving in a different direction. Instead of faster fighters, we developed more maneuverable fighters. These fighters were actually slower in top speed than the century series fighters. We believed a proposed theory that all aerial combat in the future would occur at subsonic speeds and, as a result, we designed and built new transonic fighters. We currently do not have a fighter that can catch the Russian Foxbat.

The military still has no firm plans to build an operational hypersonic combat aircraft. It is currently working with NASA to develop the National Aerospace Plane, but it is not putting a lot of priority on the program, nor is NASA. Both agencies are willing to spend the money that Congress authorizes for the program, but neither agency is willing to contribute from its own budget. With this type of support, the program appears to be questionable.

The military has been unable to define a mission for a hypersonic airplane. Until it does, there will be no operational hypersonic aircraft. The huge cost of developing an airbreathing hypersonic propulsion system will stifle the development of any research or prototype aircraft. There must be a military mission to justify that cost since only the military has sufficient funding to develop a new class of propulsion system.

An even more discouraging outlook is evident regarding a manned military space mission. There are no plans for a military presence in space, other than the military astronauts assigned to NASA. Again, the military has not defined a manned space mission. They are satisfied that they can do without a military man in space. This is awesome. Only the Russians will know what a military man can contribute in space. We have given up the high ground both in the air and in space.

Civil aviation has progressed in a similar manner. Transport aircraft have become much more efficient and generally much bigger to capitalize on the passenger miles per pound of fuel, but transports still fly at subsonic speeds and in fact fly 40 to 50 knots slower than they did in the 1960s and 1970s to conserve fuel. The Concorde is still flying but only as a status symbol. There will be no supersonic transport until the military develops an efficient supersonic airbreathing propulsion system.

Although X-15 data were not applied to follow-on aircraft, they were used in the design and operation of manned spacecraft. Alan Shepard made the nation's first suborbital space flight on May 5, 1961. During his flight, he was boosted to a maximum speed of 5,180 MPH and reached an altitude of 116 miles above the earth. His flight duration was 15 minutes and 22 seconds from launch to splashdown. He covered a distance of 302 miles during that 15- minute flight. Prior to that flight, the X-15 had flown thirty-six times. It had achieved a maximum speed of 3,074 MPH and a maximum altitude of 169,600 feet or approximately 34 miles above the earth. The X-15 flights were roughly 10 minutes long from launch to landing to cover distances up to 130 miles.

Some X-15 advocates felt that the X-15 program paved the way for the first Mercury flight and even the follow-on orbital flights. The X-15 did demonstrate a lot of technology that was critical to Mercury, such as the use of reaction controls outside the sensible atmosphere, the use of an inertial guidance system, the use of a side arm controller, the use of a full pressure suit, and the ability of a pilot to control a vehicle under high g accelerations and extended 0 g flight. The X-15 program also verified that we could fly at hypersonic speeds, that actual heating rates were lower than predicted at hypersonic speeds, and that wind tunnel predictions for flight at hypersonic speeds were accurate.

All of this X-15 experience did not really pave the way for the Mercury program, however. The Mercury spacecraft was being designed and developed before the X-15 reached hypersonic speeds or exoatmospheric flight. Thus the X-15 did not contribute from its experience to the Mercury design. There was obviously some benefit of the X-15 design to the Mercury design since the X-15 designers had to address the problems of space flight and come up with a solution before the Mercury program came into existence.

The X-15 did, however, provide the Mercury program personnel with a lot of confidence since the X-15 had successfully flown at hypersonic speeds and had also flown outside the sensible atmosphere. The X-15 proved that a spacecraft could successfully fly out of the atmosphere and then execute a controlled reentry into the atmosphere without losing control or burning up during entry.

The Mercury program quickly surpassed the X-15 flight envelope as Gus Grissom predicted it would to Joe Walker. The X-15 program was eclipsed by the Mercury program and almost totally ignored by the news media. This was a serious blow to the ego of some X-15 personnel, but it was a blessing in another sense. We were free to conduct our research program without a lot of oversight or second guessing. We produced research data instead of headlines. We were doing research 15 years ahead of its application—a good position to be in and one we are not in now.

Many of the scientific experiments flown on the X-15 were prototype systems for Apollo. Much of the X-15 experience was used in the design and operation of the space shuttle. Indeed, the shuttle is presently the prime benefactor of the X-15 program. I hope someday that there will be a conventional airplane that will cruise at hypersonic speed as a result of X-15 experience. As of now, I am one of the fastest airplane pilots in the world. I am too old for that. Someone younger should have that honor.

Surprisingly, the United States is the only country that flew a series of rocket research aircraft. The Germans flew some operational rocket aircraft near the end of World War II, but no other nation took advantage of rocket power to expand the flight envelope of manned aircraft. It was a risky and expensive operation. Several aircraft and pilots were lost, but there were some significant advances made in aeronautics as a result of this effort. I believe it was worth the gamble.

As it turned out, the X-15 was the last of the real exploratory aircraft. It was the last aircraft to probe unknown regions of flight where wind tunnel and other prediction techniques had not been verified. The X-15 probed the last major speed regime, the hypersonic speed regime, and verified the ability of the wind tunnel to accurately predict the flight characteristics of hypersonic aircraft. The space shuttle ultimately demonstrated the validity of these predictions at the high end of the hypersonic speed range.

The one single individual responsible for the success of the X-15 flight program was Paul Bikle. Bikle was the director of the Dryden Flight Research Center from September 1959 through May 1971. Richard Hoerner, the associate administrator of NASA in 1959 handpicked Bikle to succeed Walt Williams when Williams left to join the NASA Space Task Group. At the time he was selected, Bikle was the technical director of the Edwards Flight Test Center. In that position, Bikle had been involved in air force tests of many of the early jet and rocket aircraft. He came to Dryden well equipped for the job. Bikle had previously worked at Wright Field from 1940 to 1951. He flew as a flight test engineer during World War II and participated in the explosive growth of military aviation from biplanes to jets. Bikle had tried to become a pilot with the air corps during the war but he was rejected due to color blindness. He settled for the next best job, in his opinion, flight test engineer. Bikle accumulated over 3,000 flying hours as a flight test engineer and he agreed with my description of that job as the most demanding job that he ever had. He also felt it was the most satisfying job that he ever had. As a result of this experience and his experience at the Edwards Flight Test Center, Bikle was a recognized flight test expert before he came to Dryden.

He was also a record holding sailplane pilot with over 3,000 hours in sailplanes. He established a world altitude record in sailplanes of 46,620 feet in February 1961. This record remained unbroken for almost 25 years. Bikle established that record without the use of a pressure suit or pressurized cockpit. His only high-altitude equipment was a pressure breathing oxygen system. He had no cockpit heat even though the outside air temperature was –65° F. He had donned an extra pair of cotton khaki pants for the flight, but had no exotic clothing to cope with the brutal temperatures. In some respects, that flight appeared to be a foolhardy attempt by a naive pilot. Bikle's description of the flight indicated otherwise. It was well thought out and conducted in a relatively careful manner. That is not to say that all of his flights were conducted in that manner. Some of his flying stories raised the hair on the back of the neck. They were really hairy! Bikle also flew powered aircraft, accumulating over 1,100 hours in various propellor aircraft.

It was very fortuitous that Bikle was available to replace Walt Williams. He was the right man for the job. He knew the flight test business as well as any of the pilots or engineers. He was a strong leader and an excellent judge of people. He exhibited a lot of confidence with no sign of indecisiveness and he could not be intimidated by egotistic pilots, Washington bureaucrats, or pompous generals. There was no question of who was running the flight program.

Bikle was not only the center director, he was also the unofficial project manager. He did not, however, try to dominate the flight program. He encouraged individual initiative and promoted friendly competition among the aircraft crews. He stimulated morale through personal contact with every member of the team and participated in many flight parties. He was an ideal leader of the flight test effort and the results verified this.

There were many other key individuals involved in the flight program such as the project manager, the operations engineers, the flight planners, the research engineers, the instrumentation engineers, the crew chiefs, the many marvelous mechanics and technicians who kept the various systems working, the pressure suit technicians, the B-52 crew, the radar and telemetry engineers and technicians, the machinists, the sheet metal smiths, the welders, and on and on and on. I would love to list the names of these people, but that would require a second volume, and I would surely miss someone. As is the case in any major aircraft or spacecraft flight program, it is these people that make the pilot or the astronaut look good. The pilot gets the glory and the support team is lucky to hear an appreciative word. But that only seems to stimulate the team even more. It is almost unbelievable how hard these people worked to get a flight off. It was common to work overtime, paid or unpaid, to get an aircraft ready for flight the next day.

Much of the energy and enthusiasm could be attributed to the youthfulness of the overall team. Paul Bikle was only 43 years of age when the X-15 began flying. Walker, the oldest pilot was 38, while Neil Armstrong, the youngest, was only 29. Ninety percent of the team members were under 45 years of age.

The average age was less than 40, possibly as young as 35. I have not seen that level of effort or enthusiasm since the completion of the rocket aircraft program. It truly was an exciting time.

LIFE (AND DEATH) AFTER THE X-15

The number one X-15, serial number AF 5-6670, now hangs in the National Air and Space Museum at the Smithsonian Institution. It is very appropriate that it was selected for this honor since it is the only X-15 that all twelve pilots flew. The number one aircraft also had the distinction of being the first and the last X-15 to fly. It made a total of eighty-one free flights and 142 takeoffs on the B-52. It retired in its original basic configuration.

The number two X-15, serial number AF 56-6671, is at Wright-Patterson AFB in the USAF Museum. It retired with the maximum speed record of 6.7 Mach number or 4,520 MPH. It is displayed in its modified X-15A-2 configuration. It was modified following a landing accident on its thirty-first flight. The airplane made a total of fifty-three flights—thirty-one as the original number two aircraft and twenty-two as the modified X-15A-2. It had made ninety-seven flights on the B-52. Six pilots flew the original aircraft and three flew the modified aircraft. A total of seven pilots flew it. This aircraft made the second flight of the program. Its last flight was the 188th flight.

The number three X-15, serial number AF 56-6672, was destroyed during its sixty-fifth flight. It had been carried aloft on the B-52 ninety-seven times. It had made the maximum altitude flight of 354,200 feet and had been flown by ten of the X-15 pilots. It was the only X-15 with the MH-96 adaptive flight control system. Its first flight was the forty-sixth flight of the program and its last flight was the 191st. Fittingly, some of the pieces of the aircraft still rest in the vast desert graveyard just south of Death Valley, over which it soared so many times during its active career.

Scott Crossfield was the first to leave the X-15 program concluding his demonstration flights in December 1960, a year and a half after his first flight. Scott stayed with North American Aviation for several years as the director of safety, reliability, and quality assurance. He moved on to become a vice president of Eastern Airlines and then became a consultant to Congress, where he is currently working.

Forrest Petersen was the next to leave the program, in January 1962. He assumed command of a fighter squadron at NAS Miramar after leaving the program. Then Admiral Rickover selected him to attend the Nuclear Propulsion

School. Following that school, he assumed command of a navy oiler and then became executive officer of the nuclear aircraft carrier *Enterprise*. He later became captain of that ship before moving to the Pentagon as a rear admiral. He served his final tour as a vice admiral in the Pentagon as the commander of naval air systems command. After retiring from the navy he worked as a consultant and vice president of Kaman Aircraft. He died in November 1990.

Neil Armstrong was the third pilot to leave the program, in August 1962. He joined the NASA Astronaut Corps and then I lost track of him.

Bob White was the fourth pilot to leave the program, in December 1962. Bob also assumed command of a fighter squadron. He flew F-105s in Vietnam and gained a great deal of respect for his gung ho attitude. He also acquired a very distinguished combat record. Bob came back to Edwards as the commander of the flight test center in 1970 and ultimately retired as a major general. He is currently living in Germany.

Joe Walker was the next pilot to leave the program. Joe stepped aside to let some younger pilots have a crack at the X-15. Joe left the program in August 1963 and spent the next couple of years as the prime pilot on the lunar landing research vehicle helping to develop the lunar landing technique and the lunar lander control system. Joe's final flight program was the XB-70, but he never got a chance to fly it. He was killed in a midair collision with the second B-70 while flying chase.

Joe Engle left the program a couple of months after I did. Joe had been selected as a NASA astronaut prior to leaving the X-15 program and moved on to Houston to participate in the Apollo and space shuttle programs. Joe was scheduled to fly on the last Apollo flight but was bumped at the last minute to allow an astronaut with a geology specialty to go instead. Joe finally made it into space in the space shuttle and is now retired from both the U.S. Air Force and NASA. He is currently a brigadier general in the air force reserve.

Bob Rushworth left the program in July 1966. Following graduation from the National War College, Bob went to Vietnam and flew 189 combat missions. After several other assignments, Bob also came back to Edwards in 1974 as a brigadier general to assume command of the flight test center. From Edwards, he moved on to become commander of AFOTEC in Albuquerque, New Mexico, and served his last tour as vice commander of the aeronautical systems division at Wright Field in Dayton, Ohio. He retired as a major general and is currently living in California.

In September 1966, Jack McKay was the ninth pilot to leave the program.

Jack was beginning to have severe neck and back problems at that time as a result of his Mud Lake accident in the number two X-15. After Walker's death, he was moved to the chief pilot's job with the understanding that he could move into less physically demanding research aircraft. Jack's back continued to deteriorate and he finally retired on a medical disability. Jack died in 1972 as a result of complications of his accident injuries.

Mike Adams was killed in the number three X-15 on November 15, 1967. The road to the Edwards AFB Rod and Gun Club is designated Adams Way.

Bill Dana and Pete Knight were actively flying the X-15 when the program was cancelled in December 1968. Bill Dana continues to fly as a Dryden research pilot and is currently chief pilot. Bill has the longevity record at Dryden. As a research pilot, he has flown there for over 30 years. He has had an illustrious career as a research pilot and does not intend to quit flying in the near future. Pete Knight moved on to a number of special assignments in the Air Force Systems Command. He also served a tour in Vietnam. He returned to Edwards as vice commander of the flight test center and then retired as a full colonel. When last seen, Pete was vice president of Eidetics (an aerospace research firm), and mayor of Palmdale, California.

In the late summer of 1965, I had to choose between the X-15 program and the heavyweight lifting body program. I was assigned to both programs at the time. Joe Walker wanted to give some of our newer pilots an opportunity to participate in one of the bigger programs, so he suggested that I choose one or the other. I decided to go with the lifting body program. I felt that I had played a major role in selling that program and I wanted to stay with it.

I made my last X-15 flight in August and then began concentrating on my role as chief lifting body pilot. There was plenty of work to do to support the development and construction of the M2-F2 and HL-10 vehicles and prepare them for flight. I spent most of my time working with Northrop, our construction contractor, to help define the various subsystems and the cockpit layout. I also spent hundreds of hours in the NASA simulator assisting in the definition of the flight control system. My flight time was devoted to the development of an unpowered landing technique for the lifting bodies and the definition of a first flight plan.

With all of this work to do, it was obvious that I could not have continued to participate in the X-15 program. I think Joe Walker was really making me face up to reality in choosing one program or the other. We spent almost a year preparing the lifting body vehicles for their first flight. I finally made the first M2-F2 flight on July 12, 1966. I flew the next four flights and then began checking out the other lifting body pilots.

Prior to flying the M2-F2, I had told Paul Bikle, our director, that I wanted to transfer back into the research engineering organization after I had flown the M2-F2. I felt that the exciting programs were winding down, and I could not see any new challenging programs coming up in the near future. I really enjoyed the challenge of an X-15 flight or a lifting body flight, but I was getting bored with the routine proficiency flying that was required between research flights. When a pilot gets bored with flying, it is time to quit.

In January 1967, I moved into the research organization as chief of the research projects office. In this position I was responsible for all of the flight projects at Dryden, which included the X-15 and the lifting bodies as well as a number of other projects. I continued in this position until 1975, at which time I became chief engineer of the center. I have remained in that position up to the present time.

While serving as the director of research projects, I became involved with the space shuttle program. I was appointed a member of the space transportation system technology steering committee in 1970, and in this role I had the opportunity to relay our X-15 and lifting body experience to the shuttle program developers. Our flight experience was uniquely applicable to the atmospheric entry phase of their mission. I emphasized our energy management techniques and our unpowered landings. The shuttle initially was to have deployable engines for powered landings. We attempted to convince them that landing engines were an illusory benefit and instead advocated unpowered landings. We flew a number of NASA headquarters and program officials, including Bob Thompson, Roy Day, John Yardley, Mike Malkin, and George Low, in our F-104 aircraft to demonstrate the safety and simplicity of unpowered approaches. In response to a concern about whether a large aircraft like the proposed shuttle could accomplish an unpowered approach, we used our B-52 mothership to fly simulated shuttle approaches. We subsequently used the NASA Convair 990 aircraft to demonstrate shuttle approaches to other shuttle program officials and a number of astronauts. Deke Slayton was one of the astronauts who flew simulated shuttle approaches in the 990 aircraft.

We also advocated a mothership for the shuttle for ferrying it in lieu of the planned ferry engines. Our mothership proposals included twin 747 and twin C-5 configurations. Luckily, one of the JSC engineers, John Kiker, came up with the much simpler idea of using a single 747 aircraft as a mothership. We

persevered in our crusade and finally convinced shuttle management to eliminate the air-breathing engines, make unpowered landings, and use a mothership
for ferry. This decision reduced the weight of the orbiter by roughly 10,000
pounds. Thus, our X-15 and lifting body experience had a significant impact
on the design and operation of the space shuttle.

Author's Note

One might wonder why I have written this book. That role may seem more likely to some for Crossfield, who made the first flight, or one of the other pilots who participated in the early envelope expansion. It may be because none of the other pilots were involved from the beginning to end. They each participated and contributed and then moved on before the final curtain. Of the surviving pilots, Bob Rushworth was the most qualified to write the story because he was assigned to the program for almost 8 years and flew the most flights. But apparently Bob has no plans to write a book. Bill Dana joined the program late, but he was involved in a support role from the early phases of the program until he started flying as a project pilot. He could also write a book, and he may still write one someday.

For many years I assumed that someone would write a book about the X-15 flight program. It was such an exciting, challenging, and productive endeavor that someone should have been anxious to document it. As the years passed by and no book appeared, I began to worry. I was concerned that the story might not be told. I was particularly concerned that the story might not have a personal touch, that memories would fade, or that the participants would die off. The story required a participant's perspective, in my opinion, to describe the excitement and vibrancy of the program.

Twenty-seven years after the first flight, a story still had not appeared. I decided then to try and tell the story. I was, however, not particularly qualified to write the story since I was neither a professional writer nor a historian. I knew I would have trouble describing all of the emotions and other human responses so evident in the actions of the participants. It is not easy to describe in words the tremendous camaraderie, fierce pride, strong commitment, absolute dedication, and total honesty and integrity exhibited by this diverse team. I hope, however, that I have reflected some of these traits in the story. The X-15 program was to me a powerful human endeavor. The opportunity to participate in such an endeavor is not available to everyone. I was honored to have had that opportunity.

This, then, is my story of the X-15 flight program. I have done a considerable amount of research to ensure that the story is reasonably accurate, but I also know that a professional historian would have done more. I assume that someday a professional historian will also document the program and thus, if the reader waits long enough, he can gain both perspectives. I, however, have one advantage—that of being privy to the many humorous personal stories that were never documented. I hope the reader enjoys those stories. In fact one of my greatest desires in writing this account is that the reader enjoy it. I hope I have succeeded.

I also hope I have reflected some of the realism. Winston Churchill once said, "I'm confident that history will treat me well because I will write the history." I have tried to write some of the history of the X-15.

My one regret is that I could not convince the publishers to use my original title, "Don't Fall Off the Bull." To me that title reflects the pilot's primary objective during any research flight: to hang in there and successfully complete the mission.

I am still working at Dryden as the chief engineer. I think Bill Dana summed up "life after the X-15" better than anyone. He said, "Crossfield went on to become an airline vice president and a consultant to Congress. Forrest Petersen went on to become a vice admiral. White and Rushworth moved up to be major generals. Neil became an astronaut and was the first man to step out on the moon. Joe Engle became an astronaut and flew the space shuttle. Pete Knight became mayor of Palmdale. That's quite an illustrious bunch of pilots. And then," Dana said, "there is you and me."

Appendix 1

Flight Logs

KEY TO THE FLIGHT LOGS

Flight: Program flight number

Date: Date of this flight

Pilot: X-15 pilot who flew the flight

plan M: Planned Mach number

actual M: Mach number actually attained

plan h: Planned altitude in feet

actual h: Altitude actually attained

A/C Flight: Three-part designation: (Example: 2-43-75)

2 = Aircraft number (1, 2, or 3)

43 = Number of times this X-15 has flown

75 = Number of times this aircraft has been carried aloft by the B-52 (includes planned captives, aborted missions, and free flights)

Launch Lake: Dry lake, or general area, where flight was launched

Launch Time: Local California time of launch

plan Burn: Planned engine burn time in seconds

actual Burn: Actual engine burn time in seconds

Duration: Flight duration, or time, from launch to touch down (minutes and seconds)

Speed (MPH): Maximum speed attained, in miles per hour

B-52: Tail number of the B-52 used for launch (003 or 008)

B-52 Crew: Pilot and copilot of the B-52, in order

Chase: Chase pilots for the mission, in order from 1 to 3, 4, or 5

Purpose: The reasons (Studies, experiments, etc.) for the flight

Remarks: Interesting events of the flight, if any

Flight 1

Flight :	1	A/C Flight :	1-1-5	B-52 :	003
Date :	6-8-59	Launch Lake :	Rosamond	B-52 Crew :	Bock/Allavie
Pilot :	Crossfield	Launch Time :	08:38:40.0	Chase :	Maj. White
plan M :	0.80	plan Burn :	0		Capt. Wood
actual M :	0.79	actual Burn :	0		J. Roberts
plan h :	40,000	Duration :	:04:56.6		
actual h :	37,550	Speed (MPH) :	522		

Purpose :
Aircraft checkout
Pilot familiarization

Remarks :
Glide flight - No propellants aboard.
Pitch damper failed, PIO during flare and
landing.

Flight 2

Flight :	2	A/C Flight :	2-1-3	B-52 :	003
Date :	9-17-59	Launch Lake :	Rosamond	B-52 Crew :	Bock/Allavie
Pilot :	Crossfield	Launch Time :	08:08:48.0	Chase :	Al White
plan M :	2.00	plan Burn :	?		Joe Walker
actual M :	2.11	actual Burn :	224.3		Maj. White
plan h :	50,000	Duration :	:09:11.1		
actual h :	52,300	Speed (MPH) :	1,393		

Purpose :
Aircraft and systems checkout

Remarks :
Turbo pump case failed.
Fire in H202 compartment, engine
compartment, and lower ventral.
Flaps only extended 60%.

Flight 3

Flight :	3	A/C Flight :	2-2-6	B-52 :	003
Date :	10-17-59	Launch Lake :	Rosamond	B-52 Crew :	Allavie/Bock
Pilot :	Crossfield	Launch Time :	10:13:07.0	Chase :	Al White
plan M :	2.00	plan Burn :	?		Joe Walker
actual M :	2.15	actual Burn :	254.5		Maj. White
plan h :	60,000	Duration :	:09:37.7		
actual h :	61,781	Speed (MPH) :	1,419		

Purpose :
Aircraft checkout

Remarks :
Nose gear door failed on landing.
Fire in engine bay.

Flight 4

Flight :	4	A/C Flight :	2-3-9	B-52 :	003
Date :	11-5-59	Launch Lake :	Rosamond	B-52 Crew :	Fulton/Allavie
Pilot :	Crossfield	Launch Time :	09:39:28.0	Chase :	Bob Baker
plan M :	2.00	plan Burn :	255		Maj. White
actual M :	1.00	actual Burn :	11.7		Joe Walker
plan h :	80,000	Duration :	:05:28.0		
actual h :	45,462	Speed (MPH) :	660		

Purpose :
Aircraft checkout

Remarks :
Engine fire and explosion.
Fuselage structural failure on landing at
instrument bay.

Flight 5

Flight :	5	A/C Flight :	1-2-7	B-52 :	008
Date :	1-23-60	Launch Lake :	Rosamond	B-52 Crew :	Fulton/Kuyk
Pilot :	Crossfield	Launch Time :	16:17:05.0	Chase :	Bob Baker
plan M :	2.00	plan Burn :	?		Joe Walker
actual M :	2.53	actual Burn :	267.0		Maj. White
plan h :	65,000	Duration :	:09:53.8		
actual h :	66,844	Speed (MPH) :	1,670		

Purpose :
Aircraft evaluation
SAS evaluation

Remarks :
Good flight.

Flight 6

Flight :	6	A/C Flight :	2-4-11	B-52 :	008
Date :	2-11-60	Launch Lake :	Rosamond	B-52 Crew :	Allavie/Fulton
Pilot :	Crossfield	Launch Time :	10:15:04.0	Chase :	Al White
plan M :	2.00	plan Burn :	260		Joe Walker
actual M :	2.22	actual Burn :	258.6		Maj. White
plan h :	80,000	Duration :	:10:15.5		
actual h :	88,116	Speed (MPH) :	1,466		

Purpose :
Aircraft checkout

Remarks :
Good flight.

Flight :	7	A/C Flight :	2-5-12	B-52 :	008
Date :	2-17-60	Launch Lake :	Rosamond	B-52 Crew :	Fulton/Allavie
Pilot :	Crossfield	Launch Time :	09:41:32.0	Chase :	Al White
plan M :	2.00	plan Burn :	260		Joe Walker
actual M :	1.57	actual Burn :	332.0		Maj. White
plan h :	50,000	Duration :	:10:35.9		
actual h :	52,640	Speed (MPH) :	1,036		

Purpose :	Remarks :
Aircraft checkout	Premature shutdown of upper engine.
SAS checkout	
Stability and control data	

Flight :	8	A/C Flight :	2-6-13	B-52 :	008
Date :	3-17-60	Launch Lake :	Rosamond	B-52 Crew :	Allavie/Kuyk
Pilot :	Crossfield	Launch Time :	08:31:25.0	Chase :	Al White
plan M :	2.00	plan Burn :	260		Maj. White
actual M :	2.15	actual Burn :	233.5		Joe Walker
plan h :	50,000	Duration :	:08:39.5		
actual h :	52,640	Speed (MPH) :	1,419		

Purpose :	Remarks :
Aircraft rolls	360 degree roll, 6 g turn.
SAS checkout—Dampers off and on	
Stability and control data	

Flight :	9	A/C Flight :	1-3-8	B-52 :	008
Date :	3-25-60	Launch Lake :	Rosamond	B-52 Crew :	Allavie/Fulton
Pilot :	Walker	Launch Time :	15:43:23.0	Chase :	Scott Crossfield
plan M :	2.00	plan Burn :	?		Maj. White
actual M :	2.00	actual Burn :	272.0		Jack McKay
plan h :	50,000	Duration :	:09:08.0		
actual h :	48,630	Speed (MPH) :	1,320		

Purpose :	Remarks :
Pilot familiarization	Roll damper and stable platform failed.
	First NASA flight.

Flight 10

Flight :	10	A/C Flight :	2-7-15	B-52 : 008
Date :	3-29-60	Launch Lake :	Rosamond	B-52 Crew : Fulton/Allavie
Pilot :	Crossfield	Launch Time :	09:59:28.0	Chase : Maj. White
plan M :	2.00	plan Burn :	267	Capt. Knight
actual M :	1.96	actual Burn :	244.2	Capt. Rushworth
plan h :	50,000	Duration :	:09:10.5	
actual h :	49,982	Speed (MPH) :	1,293	

Purpose :	Remarks :
Minus 2 g pushover Full throw rudder step	Good flight.

Flight 11

Flight :	11	A/C Flight :	2-8-16	B-52 : 008
Date :	3-31-60	Launch Lake :	Rosamond	B-52 Crew : Allavie/Fulton
Pilot :	Crossfield	Launch Time :	08:42:05.0	Chase : Maj. White
plan M :	2.00	plan Burn :	267	Capt. Rushworth
actual M :	2.03	actual Burn :	254.5	Capt. Knight
plan h :	50,000	Duration :	:08:56.5	
actual h :	51,356	Speed (MPH) :	1,340	

Purpose :	Remarks :
High *g* maneuvers SAS gains checkout	Good flight.

Flight 12

Flight :	12	A/C Flight :	1-4-9	B-52 : 003
Date :	4-13-60	Launch Lake :	Rosamond	B-52 Crew : Allavie/Kuyk
Pilot :	White	Launch Time :	09:15:11.0	Chase : Al White
plan M :	2.00	plan Burn :	?	Crossfield
actual M :	1.90	actual Burn :	253.7	Joe Walker
plan h :	50,000	Duration :	:08:52.7	Capt. Rushworth
actual h :	48,000	Speed (MPH) :	1,254	

Purpose :	Remarks :
Pilot familiarization	First air force flight. Flown on the center stick.

Flight :	13	A/C Flight :	1-5-10	B-52 :	003
Date :	4-19-60	Launch Lake :	Rosamond	B-52 Crew :	Fulton/Allavie
Pilot :	Walker	Launch Time :	08:51:44.0	Chase :	Capt. Rushworth
plan M :	2.35	plan Burn :	?		Jack McKay
actual M :	2.56	actual Burn :	260.6		Capt. Knight
plan h :	60,000	Duration :	:09:58.6		
actual h :	59,496	Speed (MPH) :	1,690		

Purpose :
Performance buildup
Stability and control buildup

Remarks :
Good flight.

Flight :	14	A/C Flight :	1-6-11	B-52 :	003
Date :	5-6-60	Launch Lake :	Rosamond	B-52 Crew :	Fulton/Allavie
Pilot :	White	Launch Time :	09:53:19.0	Chase :	Capt. Knight
plan M :	2.50	plan Burn :	?		Jack McKay
actual M :	2.20	actual Burn :	246.5		Capt. Rushworth
plan h :	60,000	Duration :	:09:23.2		
actual h :	60,938	Speed (MPH) :	1,452		

Purpose :
Performance buildup
Stability and control buildup
Pilot familiarization

Remarks :
Roll damper failed (reset).
Normal ventral jettison failed.

Flight :	15	A/C Flight :	1-7-12	B-52 :	003
Date :	5-12-60	Launch Lake :	Silver	B-52 Crew :	Bock/Allavie
Pilot :	Walker	Launch Time :	08:47:37.0	Chase :	Maj. White
plan M :	3.00	plan Burn :	?		Capt. Rushworth
actual M :	3.19	actual Burn :	256.3		Capt. Knight
plan h :	73,000	Duration :	:10:10.3		Jack McKay
actual h :	77,882	Speed (MPH) :	2,110		

Purpose :
Performance buildup
Stability and control buildup

Remarks :
First remote site launch.
First M=3 flight.
Stable platform inoperative.

Flight 16

Flight :	16	A/C Flight :	1-8-13	B-52 :	003
Date :	5-19-60	Launch Lake :	Silver	B-52 Crew :	Allavie/Bock
Pilot :	White	Launch Time :	08:46:47.0	Chase :	Capt. Knight
plan M :	2.20	plan Burn :	?		Capt. Rushworth
actual M :	2.31	actual Burn :	274.6		Jack McKay
plan h :	110,000	Duration :	:11:24.6		
actual h :	108,997	Speed (MPH) :	1,590		

Purpose :
Altitude buildup

Remarks :
First X-15 flight above 100,000 feet.

Flight 17

Flight :	17	A/C Flight :	2-9-18	B-52 :	008
Date :	5-26-60	Launch Lake :	Rosamond	B-52 Crew :	Bock/Allavie
Pilot :	Crossfield	Launch Time :	09:08:36.0	Chase :	Al White
plan M :	2.30	plan Burn :	255		Maj. White
actual M :	2.20	actual Burn :	243.4		Cmdr. Petersen
plan h :	78,000	Duration :	:09:14.4		
actual h :	51,282	Speed (MPH) :	1,452		

Purpose :
High *g* maneuvers
SAS gains checkout
High alpha stability and control data
BCS checkout

Remarks :
Good flight.

Flight 18

Flight :	18	A/C Flight :	1-9-17	B-52 :	003
Date :	8-4-60	Launch Lake :	Silver	B-52 Crew :	Allavie/Fulton
Pilot :	Walker	Launch Time :	08:59:13.0	Chase :	Maj. White
plan M :	3.30	plan Burn :	260		Capt. Rushworth
actual M :	3.31	actual Burn :	264.2		Cmdr. Petersen
plan h :	75,000	Duration :	:10:22.6		Capt. Knight
actual h :	78,112	Speed (MPH) :	2,195		

Purpose :
Maximum speed
Stability and control data
Aero heating data

Remarks :
Good flight.

Flight 19

	Flight :	19	A/C Flight :	1-10-19	B-52 :		003
	Date :	8-12-60	Launch Lake :	Silver	B-52 Crew :		Fulton/Allavie
	Pilot :	White	Launch Time :	08:48:43.0	Chase :		Capt. Rushworth
plan	M :	2.50	plan Burn :	?			Cmdr. Petersen
actual	M :	2.52	actual Burn :	256.2			Capt. Looney
plan	h :	133,000	Duration :	:11:39.1			
actual	h :	136,500	Speed (MPH) :	1,773			

Purpose :
Maximum altitude
Stability and control data

Remarks :
Good flight

Flight 20

	Flight :	20	A/C Flight :	1-11-21	B-52 :		003
	Date :	8-19-60	Launch Lake :	Silver	B-52 Crew :		Allavie/Cole
	Pilot :	Walker	Launch Time :	08:34:22.0	Chase :		Maj. White
plan	M :	3.00	plan Burn :	?			Capt. Rushworth
actual	M :	3.13	actual Burn :	251.6			Cmdr. Petersen
plan	h :	70,000	Duration :	:09:42.4			Capt. Looney
actual	h :	75,982	Speed (MPH) :	1,985			

Purpose :
Aerodynamic heating data
Stability and control data
Performance data

Remarks :
Alpha cross-pointer hooked up backwards.

Flight 21

	Flight :	21	A/C Flight :	1-12-23	B-52 :		008
	Date :	9-10-60	Launch Lake :	Silver	B-52 Crew :		Kirk/Allavie
	Pilot :	White	Launch Time :	11:45:10.0	Chase :		Capt. Looney
plan	M :	3.20	plan Burn :	?			Neil Armstrong
actual	M :	3.23	actual Burn :	264.3			Capt. Rushworth
plan	h :	80,000	Duration :	:10:00.0			Capt. Knight
actual	h :	79,864	Speed (MPH) :	2,182			

Purpose :
Stability and control data
Performance data

Remarks :
Good flight.

Flight 22

Flight :	22	A/C Flight :	1-13-25	B-52 :	008
Date :	9-23-60	Launch Lake :	Palmdale	B-52 Crew :	Allavie/Fulton
Pilot :	Petersen	Launch Time :	09:52:06.0	Chase :	Capt. Looney
plan M :	2.00	plan Burn :	?		Joe Walker
actual M :	1.68	actual Burn :	146.4		Capt. Rushworth
plan h :	50,000	Duration :	:07:09.6		
actual h :	53,043	Speed (MPH) :	1,109		

Purpose :	Remarks :
Pilot checkout	Engines shut down early, failed to restart.

Flight 23

Flight :	23	A/C Flight :	1-14-27	B-52 :	008
Date :	10-20-60	Launch Lake :	Palmdale	B-52 Crew :	Fulton/Kuyk
Pilot :	Petersen	Launch Time :	09:30:27.0	Chase :	Maj. White
plan M :	2.00	plan Burn :	?		Capt. Rushworth
actual M :	1.94	actual Burn :	285.4		Neil Armstrong
plan h :	50,000	Duration :	:09:26.1		
actual h :	53,800	Speed (MPH) :	1,280		

Purpose :	Remarks :
Alternate airspeed calibration	Good flight.
Stability and control data	
Performance data	
Pilot familiarization	

Flight 24

Flight :	24	A/C Flight :	1-15-28	B-52 :	008
Date :	10-28-60	Launch Lake :	Palmdale	B-52 Crew :	Fulton/Cole
Pilot :	Mc Kay	Launch Time :	09:43:56.0	Chase :	Capt. Looney
plan M :	2.00	plan Burn :	?		Maj. White
actual M :	2.02	actual Burn :	267.5		Cmdr. Petersen
plan h :	50,000	Duration :	:09:05.3		
actual h :	50,700	Speed (MPH) :	1,334		

Purpose :	Remarks :
Pilot familiarization	Ventral chute didn't open.
Alternate airspeed calibration	
Stability and control data	
Performance data	

Flight :	25	A/C Flight :	1-16-29	B-52 :	008
Date :	11-4-60	Launch Lake :	Palmdale	B-52 Crew :	Fulton/Cole
Pilot :	Rushworth	Launch Time :	12:43:33.0	Chase :	Capt. Looney
plan M :	2.00	plan Burn :	?		Maj. White
actual M :	1.95	actual Burn :	271.0		Neil Armstrong
plan h :	50,000	Duration :	:08:46.3		
actual h :	48,900	Speed (MPH) :	1,287		

Purpose :
Pilot familiarization
Alternate airspeed calibration
Stability and control data
Performance data

Remarks :
Good flight.

Flight :	26	A/C Flight :	2-10-21	B-52 :	003
Date :	11-15-60	Launch Lake :	Rosamond	B-52 Crew :	Allavie/Kuyk
Pilot :	Crossfield	Launch Time :	09:59:00.0	Chase :	Al White
plan M :	2.70	plan Burn :	155		Joe Walker
actual M :	2.97	actual Burn :	137.3		Maj. White
plan h :	60,000	Duration :	:08:28.4		
actual h :	81,200	Speed (MPH) :	1,960		

Purpose :
XLR-99 first flight checkout

Remarks :
First XLR-99 flight.

Flight :	27	A/C Flight :	1-17-30	B-52 :	003
Date :	11-17-60	Launch Lake :	Palmdale	B-52 Crew :	Fulton/Allavie
Pilot :	Rushworth	Launch Time :	12:43:07.0	Chase :	Capt. Looney
plan M :	2.20	plan Burn :	?		Joe Walker
actual M :	1.90	actual Burn :	260.4		Capt. Knight
plan h :	55,000	Duration :	:08:58.2		
actual h :	54,750	Speed (MPH) :	1,254		

Purpose :
Additional pilot familiarization
Aero data

Remarks :
Lower engine shutdown and restarted.

Flight :	28	A/C Flight :	2-11-22	B-52 :	003
Date :	11-22-60	Launch Lake :	Rosamond	B-52 Crew :	Allavie/Fulton
Pilot :	Crossfield	Launch Time :	13:25:55.0	Chase :	Al White
plan M :	2.30	plan Burn :	134		Joe Walker
actual M :	2.51	actual Burn :	125.1		Maj. White
plan h :	54,000	Duration :	:07:31.7		
actual h :	61,900	Speed (MPH) :	1,657		

Purpose :
XLR-99 checkout
Restarts and throttle changes
BCS checkout

Remarks :
Throttled and restarted LR-99 engine in-flight.

Flight :	29	A/C Flight :	1-18-31	B-52 :	008
Date :	11-30-60	Launch Lake :	Palmdale	B-52 Crew :	Cole/Fulton
Pilot :	Armstrong	Launch Time :	10:42:43.0	Chase :	Capt. Looney
plan M :	2.00	plan Burn :	?		Cmdr. Petersen
actual M :	1.75	actual Burn :	309.1		Joe Walker
plan h :	50,000	Duration :	:09:53.8		
actual h :	48,840	Speed (MPH) :	1,155		

Purpose :
Pilot familiarization

Remarks :
Upper number 3 chamber did not start.
Inertial attitudes incorrect.

Flight :	30	A/C Flight :	2-12-23	B-52 :	003
Date :	12-6-60	Launch Lake :	Rosamond	B-52 Crew :	Allavie/Cole
Pilot :	Crossfield	Launch Time :	15:29:30.0	Chase :	Al White
plan M :	2.30	plan Burn :	121		Cmdr. Petersen
actual M :	2.85	actual Burn :	128.9		Maj. White
plan h :	54,000	Duration :	:08:07.2		
actual h :	53,374	Speed (MPH) :	1,881		

Purpose :
XLR-99 checkout
Restarts and high *g* maneuvers
BCS checkout

Remarks :
Crossfield's last flight.

Flight 31

Flight :	31	A/C Flight :	1-19-32	B-52 :	008
Date :	12-9-60	Launch Lake :	Palmdale	B-52 Crew :	Allavie/Cole
Pilot :	Armstrong	Launch Time :	11:52:40.0	Chase :	Maj. Daniel
plan M :	1.90	plan Burn :	?		Cmdr. Petersen
actual M :	1.80	actual Burn :	270.1		Maj. White
plan h :	50,000	Duration :	:10:49.0		
actual h :	50,095	Speed (MPH) :	1,188		

Purpose :	Remarks :
Ball nose evaluation	First ball nose flight.
Stability and control data	

Flight 32

Flight :	32	A/C Flight :	1-20-35	B-52 :	008
Date :	2-1-61	Launch Lake :	Palmdale	B-52 Crew :	Fulton/Lewis
Pilot :	Mc Kay	Launch Time :	10:47:32.0	Chase :	Maj. White
plan M :	2.00	plan Burn :	?		Cmdr. Petersen
actual M :	1.88	actual Burn :	263.5		Maj. Wood
plan h :	50,000	Duration :	:10:47.7		
actual h :	49,780	Speed (MPH) :	1,212		

Purpose :	Remarks :
Ball nose evaluation	Good flight.
Inertial velocity indicator checkout	
Sidearm controller evaluation	

Flight 33

Flight :	33	A/C Flight :	1-21-36	B-52 :	008
Date :	2-7-61	Launch Lake :	Silver	B-52 Crew :	Fulton/Mosley
Pilot :	White	Launch Time :	12:56:10.0	Chase :	Maj. Daniel
plan M :	3.10	plan Burn :	?		Capt. Knight
actual M :	3.50	actual Burn :	276.1		Cmdr. Petersen
plan h :	75,000	Duration :	:10:27.8		Capt. Rushworth
actual h :	78,150	Speed (MPH) :	2,275		

Purpose :	Remarks :
Stability and control data	Last XLR-11 flight (in the X-15).
Performance data	
Flight systems evaluation	

Flight 34

Flight :	34	A/C Flight :	2-13-26	B-52 :	008
Date :	3-7-61	Launch Lake :	Silver	B-52 Crew :	Kuyk/Cole
Pilot :	White	Launch Time :	10:28:33.0	Chase :	Capt. Rushworth
plan M :	4.00	plan Burn :	116		Joe Walker
actual M :	4.43	actual Burn :	127.0		Cmdr. Petersen
plan h :	84,000	Duration :	:08:34.1		Capt. Looney
actual h :	77,450	Speed (MPH) :	2,905		

Purpose :
Envelope expansion
Temperature data
Stability and control data
Performance data

Remarks :
First M=4 flight (for any aircraft).
First ball nose flight on ship number 2.

Flight 35

Flight :	35	A/C Flight :	2-14-28	B-52 :	008
Date :	3-30-61	Launch Lake :	Hidden Hills	B-52 Crew :	Kuyk/Fulton
Pilot :	Walker	Launch Time :	10:05:00.0	Chase :	Maj. White
plan M :	3.70	plan Burn :	79		Capt. Knight
actual M :	3.95	actual Burn :	81.9		Cmdr. Petersen
plan h :	150,000	Duration :	:10:16.5		Capt. Rushworth
actual h :	169,600	Speed (MPH) :	2,761		

Purpose :
Altitude buildup
Thermostructural data
BCS checkout
Aero data

Remarks :
Relight required.
SAS limit cycled.
First Hidden Hills launch.

Flight 36

Flight :	36	A/C Flight :	2-15-29	B-52 :	003
Date :	4-21-61	Launch Lake :	Hidden Hills	B-52 Crew :	Allavie/Mosley
Pilot :	White	Launch Time :	10:05:17.0	Chase :	Capt. Looney
plan M :	4.60	plan Burn :	67		Joe Walker
actual M :	4.62	actual Burn :	71.6		Capt. Rogers
plan h :	105,000	Duration :	:10:03.4		Maj. Wood
actual h :	105,000	Speed (MPH) :	3,075		

Purpose :
Velocity buildup
Aero heating data
Stability and control data
Performance data

Remarks :
Relight required.
Pitch damper dropout at shutdown, reset.
Cabin pressure rose to 46K feet.

Flight 37

Flight :	37	A/C Flight :	2-16-31	B-52 :	003
Date :	5-25-61	Launch Lake :	Mud	B-52 Crew :	Allavie/Fulton
Pilot :	Walker	Launch Time :	12:16:35.0	Chase :	Capt. Looney
plan M :	5.00	plan Burn :	73		Maj. Daniel
actual M :	4.95	actual Burn :	74.3		Cmdr. Petersen
plan h :	117,000	Duration :	:12:08.1		Capt. Rushworth
actual h :	107,500	Speed (MPH) :	3,307		

Purpose :	Remarks :
Velocity buildup	First launch from Mud Lake.
SAS residual oscillation study	SAS dropout at launch.
Aero heating data	Cabin altitude went to 50K feet.
Stability and control data	
Performance data	

Flight 38

Flight :	38	A/C Flight :	2-17-33	B-52 :	003
Date :	6-23-61	Launch Lake :	Mud	B-52 Crew :	Allavie/Fulton
Pilot :	White	Launch Time :	14:00:05.0	Chase :	Capt. Looney
plan M :	5.30	plan Burn :	75		Maj. Daniel
actual M :	5.27	actual Burn :	78.7		Maj. Crews
plan h :	115,000	Duration :	:10:05.7		Joe Walker
actual h :	107,700	Speed (MPH) :	3,603		

Purpose :	Remarks :
Velocity buildup	Cabin altitude rose to 56K feet, suit inflated.
Aero heating data	First M=5 flight (of any aircraft).
Stability and control data	
Performance data	

Flight 39

Flight :	39	A/C Flight :	1-22-37	B-52 :	003
Date :	8-10-61	Launch Lake :	Silver	B-52 Crew :	Allavie/Archer
Pilot :	Petersen	Launch Time :	10:27:05.0	Chase :	Maj. White
plan M :	3.70	plan Burn :	115		Capt. Rushworth
actual M :	4.11	actual Burn :	117.7		Joe Walker
plan h :	75,000	Duration :	:09:24.4		
actual h :	78,200	Speed (MPH) :	2,734		

Purpose :	Remarks :
XLR-99 systems checkout	First XLR-99 flight for ship number 1.
Pilot familiarization	
Beta-dot control technique	

Flight 40

Flight :	40	A/C Flight :	2-18-34	B-52 :	008
Date :	9-12-61	Launch Lake :	Mud	B-52 Crew :	Archer/Allavie
Pilot :	Walker	Launch Time :	14:40:17.0	Chase :	Maj. White
plan M :	5.60	plan Burn :	79		Cmdr. Petersen
actual M :	5.21	actual Burn :	115.0		Maj. Daniel
plan h :	120,000	Duration :	:08:43.9		Maj. Rushworth
actual h :	114,300	Speed (MPH) :	3,620		

Purpose :
Velocity buildup
Aero heating data
Stability and control data
Performance data

Remarks :
Fuel line low light at launch.

Flight 41

Flight :	41	A/C Flight :	2-19-35	B-52 :	008
Date :	9-28-61	Launch Lake :	Hidden Hills	B-52 Crew :	Allavie/Archer
Pilot :	Petersen	Launch Time :	09:50:25.0	Chase :	Maj. Daniel
plan M :	5.00	plan Burn :	90		Jack McKay
actual M :	5.30	actual Burn :	87.1		Maj. Rogers
plan h :	80,000	Duration :	:08:41.6		
actual h :	101,800	Speed (MPH) :	3,600		

Purpose :
Heat transfer data
Thermostructural data
Stability and control data
Performance data

Remarks :
Good flight.

Flight 42

Flight :	42	A/C Flight :	1-23-39	B-52 :	003
Date :	10-3-61	Launch Lake :	Silver	B-52 Crew :	Allavie/Archer
Pilot :	Rushworth	Launch Time :	10:40:50.0	Chase :	Maj. Daniel
plan M :	3.70	plan Burn :	120		Jack McKay
actual M :	4.30	actual Burn :	122.0		Maj. White
plan h :	80,000	Duration :	:08:31.3		
actual h :	78,000	Speed (MPH) :	2,830		

Purpose :
Ventral off handling qualities
Ventral off stability data

Remarks :
First ventral off flight.

Flight :	43	A/C Flight :	2-20-36	B-52 :	003
Date :	10-11-61	Launch Lake :	Mud	B-52 Crew :	Allavie/Fulton
Pilot :	White	Launch Time :	12:20:00.0	Chase :	Maj. Daniel
plan M :	5.00	plan Burn :	79		Jack McKay
actual M :	5.21	actual Burn :	82.5		Maj. Wood
plan h :	200,000	Duration :	:10:14.7		Maj. Rushworth
actual h :	217,000	Speed (MPH) :	3,644		

Purpose :
Altitude buildup
Aero heating data during reentry
Stability and control data during
reentry, with speed brakes open
Controllability data at low "q"

Remarks :
First aircraft flight above 200,000 feet.
Left windshield shattered during reentry.

Flight :	44	A/C Flight :	1-24-40	B-52 :	003
Date :	10-17-61	Launch Lake :	Mud	B-52 Crew :	Allavie/Archer
Pilot :	Walker	Launch Time :	10:57:33.0	Chase :	Maj. White
plan M :	5.70	plan Burn :	80		Maj. Daniel
actual M :	5.74	actual Burn :	84.6		Capt. Knight
plan h :	113,000	Duration :	:10:11.7		
actual h :	108,600	Speed (MPH) :	3,900		

Purpose :
Velocity buildup
Aero heating data
Stability and control data
Performance data

Remarks :
Good flight.

Flight :	45	A/C Flight :	2-21-37	B-52 :	008
Date :	11-9-61	Launch Lake :	Mud	B-52 Crew :	Allavie/Archer
Pilot :	White	Launch Time :	09:57:17.0	Chase :	Maj. Rushworth
plan M :	6.00	plan Burn :	83		Joe Walker
actual M :	6.04	actual Burn :	86.9		Maj. Gordon
plan h :	110,000	Duration :	:09:31.2		Maj. Daniel
actual h :	101,600	Speed (MPH) :	4,094		

Purpose :
Maximum velocity
Aero heating data
Stability and control data
Performance data

Remarks :
First flight above M=6 for any aircraft.
Right outer windshield shattered at about
M=2.7 during deceleration.

Flight 46

Flight :	46	A/C Flight :	3-1-2	B-52 :	003
Date :	12-20-61	Launch Lake :	Silver	B-52 Crew :	Allavie/Bement
Pilot :	Armstrong	Launch Time :	14:45:50.0	Chase :	Maj. Daniel
plan M :	3.50	plan Burn :	104		Cmdr. Petersen
actual M :	3.76	actual Burn :	106.3		Maj. Rushworth
plan h :	75,000	Duration :	:10:25.4		
actual h :	81,000	Speed (MPH) :	2,502		

Purpose :

MH-96 evaluation

Checkout flight of the number 3 aircraft

Remarks :

All three SAS axes disengaged at launch, reset.
Yaw limit cycle caused downmode to fixed gain.

Flight 47

Flight :	47	A/C Flight :	1-25-44	B-52 :	003
Date :	1-10-62	Launch Lake :	Mud	B-52 Crew :	Allavie/Bement
Pilot :	Petersen	Launch Time :	12:28:16.0	Chase :	Maj. Daniel
plan M :	5.70	plan Burn :	95		Joe Walker
actual M :	0.97	actual Burn :	3.3		Maj. McDivitt
plan h :	117,000	Duration :	:03:45.7		Maj. Rushworth
actual h :	44,750	Speed (MPH) :	645		

Purpose :

High alpha stability & control data

Aero heating data

Remarks :

Two engine malfunction shutdowns.
Emergency landing at Mud Lake.
First uprange landing.

Flight 48

Flight :	48	A/C Flight :	3-2-3	B-52 :	003
Date :	1-17-62	Launch Lake :	Mud	B-52 Crew :	Allavie/Bement
Pilot :	Armstrong	Launch Time :	12:00:34.0	Chase :	Capt. Gordon
plan M :	5.00	plan Burn :	100		Cmdr. Petersen
actual M :	5.51	actual Burn :	97.4		Maj. McDivitt
plan h :	100,000	Duration :	:10:27.7		Maj. Rushworth
actual h :	133,500	Speed (MPH) :	3,765		

Purpose :

MH-96 evaluation

Remarks

Good flight.

Flight 49

Flight :	49	A/C Flight :	3-3-7	B-52 :	003
Date :	4-5-62	Launch Lake :	Hidden Hills	B-52 Crew :	Allavie/Fulton
Pilot :	Armstrong	Launch Time :	10:04:25.0	Chase :	Maj. Daniel
plan M :	4.00	plan Burn :	70		Jack McKay
actual M :	4.12	actual Burn :	79.2		Maj. Rushworth
plan h :	170,000	Duration :	:11:17.0		
actual h :	180,000	Speed (MPH) :	2,850		

Purpose :	Remarks :
MH-96 evaluation at high and low "q"	Required a relight.

Flight 50

Flight :	50	A/C Flight :	1-26-46	B-52 :	003
Date :	4-19-62	Launch Lake :	Mud	B-52 Crew :	Allavie/Archer
Pilot :	Walker	Launch Time :	10:02:20.0	Chase :	Bill Dana
plan M :	5.90	plan Burn :	83		Maj. Rushworth
actual M :	5.69	actual Burn :	84.3		Maj. Daniel
plan h :	153,000	Duration :	:08:58.9		Capt. Knight
actual h :	154,000	Speed (MPH) :	3,866		

Purpose :	Remarks :
ASAS evaluation 20 degree alpha evaluation	Beta cross-pointer wired backwards.

Flight 51

Flight :	51	A/C Flight :	3-4-8	B-52 :	008
Date :	4-20-62	Launch Lake :	Mud	B-52 Crew :	Allavie/Bement
Pilot :	Armstrong	Launch Time :	11:26:58.0	Chase :	Maj. White
plan M :	5.35	plan Burn :	81		Jack McKay
actual M :	5.31	actual Burn :	82.4		Maj. Gordon
plan h :	205,000	Duration :	:12:28.7		Maj. Rushworth
actual h :	207,500	Speed (MPH) :	3,789		

Purpose :	Remarks :
MH-96 evaluation	Overshot (bounced) during reentry and ended up about 45 miles south of Edwards. Used max L/D glide to get back (just barely!). Longest flight in the X-15 program.

Flight :	52	A/C Flight :	1-27-48	B-52 :	008
Date :	4-30-62	Launch Lake :	Mud	B-52 Crew :	Allavie/Bement
Pilot :	Walker	Launch Time :	10:23:20.0	Chase :	Maj. Daniel
plan M :	5.35	plan Burn :	81		Maj. White
actual M :	4.94	actual Burn :	81.6		Bill Dana
plan h :	255,000	Duration :	:09:46.2		Maj. Rushworth
actual h :	246,700	Speed (MPH) :	3,489		

Purpose :
Altitude buildup
Low "q" controllability
Aero heating data
Performance and stability data with
speed brakes extended

Remarks :
Good flight.

Flight :	53	A/C Flight :	2-22-40	B-52 :	008
Date :	5-8-62	Launch Lake :	Hidden Hills	B-52 Crew :	Allavie/Bement
Pilot :	Rushworth	Launch Time :	10:01:28.0	Chase :	Maj. Daniel
plan M :	5.00	plan Burn :	103		Jack McKay
actual M :	5.34	actual Burn :	97.9		Maj. Rogers
plan h :	73,000	Duration :	:08:50.4		
actual h :	70,400	Speed (MPH) :	3,524		

Purpose :
Heat transfer
ASAS checkout
Stability at high alpha with
partial speed brakes

Remarks :
First X-15 flight above q=2,000 psf.

Flight :	54	A/C Flight :	1-28-49	B-52 :	003
Date :	5-22-62	Launch Lake :	Hidden Hills	B-52 Crew :	Allavie/Campbell
Pilot :	Rushworth	Launch Time :	10:04:46.0	Chase :	Maj. Daniel
plan M :	5.20	plan Burn :	77		Bill Dana
actual M :	5.03	actual Burn :	75.3		Maj. Rogers
plan h :	90,000	Duration :	:09:16.2		
actual h :	100,400	Speed (MPH) :	3,450		

Purpose :
Local flow investigation

Remarks :
Premature shutdown.
Left roll out-of-trim.

Flight 55

Flight :	55	A/C Flight :	2-23-43	B-52 :	008
Date :	6-1-62	Launch Lake :	Delamar	B-52 Crew :	Fulton/Bement
Pilot :	White	Launch Time :	10:51:15.0	Chase :	Maj. Daniel
plan M :	5.80	plan Burn :	93		Bill Dana
actual M :	5.42	actual Burn :	86.0		Maj. Rogers
plan h :	162,000	Duration :	:10:01.9		Maj. Collins
actual h :	132,600	Speed (MPH) :	3,675		

Purpose :	Remarks :
ASAS checkout	First launch from Delamar.
Stability data at 23 degree alpha	Vibrations noted at 30% thrust.

Flight 56

Flight :	56	A/C Flight :	1-29-50	B-52 :	003
Date :	6-7-62	Launch Lake :	Hidden Hills	B-52 Crew :	Allavie/Bement
Pilot :	Walker	Launch Time :	10:29:20.0	Chase :	Maj. Daniel
plan M :	5.60	plan Burn :	80		Jack McKay
actual M :	5.39	actual Burn :	81.5		Maj. White
plan h :	100,000	Duration :	:08:24.2		
actual h :	103,600	Speed (MPH) :	3,672		

Purpose :	Remarks :
Local flow investigation at high	Engine vibrations during boost.
alpha	

Flight 57

Flight :	57	A/C Flight :	3-5-9	B-52 :	008
Date :	6-12-62	Launch Lake :	Delamar	B-52 Crew :	Allavie/Fulton
Pilot :	White	Launch Time :	12:04:00.0	Chase :	Capt. McDivitt
plan M :	5.15	plan Burn :	77		Jack McKay
actual M :	5.02	actual Burn :	81.9		Capt. Collins
plan h :	206,000	Duration :	:09:33.9		Capt. Gordon
actual h :	184,600	Speed (MPH) :	3,517		

Purpose :	Remarks :
Pilot checkout	Good flight.
Reaction control system checkout	

Flight 58

Flight :	58	A/C Flight :	3-6-10	B-52 :	008	
Date :	6-21-62	Launch Lake :	Delamar	B-52 Crew :	Allavie/Lewis	
Pilot :	White	Launch Time :	09:47:05.0	Chase :	Maj. Daniel	
plan M :	5.40	plan Burn :	80		Jack McKay	
actual M :	5.08	actual Burn :	82.3		Neil Armstrong	
plan h :	250,000	Duration :	:09:33.6		Capt. Collins	
actual h :	246,700	Speed (MPH) :	3,641			

Purpose :
MH-96 contractural demo

Remarks :
Good flight.

Flight 59

Flight :	59	A/C Flight :	1-30-51	B-52 :	003	
Date :	6-27-62	Launch Lake :	Mud	B-52 Crew :	Allavie/Townsend	
Pilot :	Walker	Launch Time :	13:08:10.0	Chase :	Maj. Rushworth	
plan M :	6.00	plan Burn :	84		Jack McKay	
actual M :	5.92	actual Burn :	88.6		Capt. Knight	
plan h :	107,000	Duration :	:09:32.4		Maj. Daniel	
actual h :	123,700	Speed (MPH) :	4,105			

Purpose :
High alpha stability

Remarks :
Unofficial world absolute speed record to date.
Ventral chute lost during flight.
Pitch damper tripped during pullup.

Flight 60

Flight :	60	A/C Flight :	2-24-44	B-52 :	008	
Date :	6-29-62	Launch Lake :	Hidden Hills	B-52 Crew :	Allavie/Archer	
Pilot :	McKay	Launch Time :	10:41:47.0	Chase :	Maj. Rushworth	
plan M :	4.20	plan Burn :	122		Neil Armstrong	
actual M :	4.95	actual Burn :	112.4		Maj. Daniel	
plan h :	84,000	Duration :	:08:53.6			
actual h :	83,200	Speed (MPH) :	3,280			

Purpose :
Heating rates at low alpha and Mach
Notch filter evaluation

Remarks :
Good flight.

Flight 61

Flight :	61	A/C Flight :	1-31-52	B-52 :	008
Date :	7-16-62	Launch Lake :	Mud	B-52 Crew :	Allavie/Archer
Pilot :	Walker	Launch Time :	14:09:25.0	Chase :	Maj. Daniel
plan M :	5.40	plan Burn :	80		Bill Dana
actual M :	5.37	actual Burn :	83.9		Capt. Engle
plan h :	105,000	Duration :	:09:37.8		Maj. Rushworth
actual h :	107,200	Speed (MPH) :	3,674		

Purpose :
Notch filter evaluation at high "q"
ASAS stability investigation
Aero drag data

Remarks :
Numerous pitch and roll trip-outs.
Ventral chute malfunctioned.
Number 2 generator tripped out during flight.

Flight 62

Flight :	62	A/C Flight :	3-7-14	B-52 :	003
Date :	7-17-62	Launch Lake :	Delamar	B-52 Crew :	Allavie/Archer
Pilot :	White	Launch Time :	09:31:10.0	Chase :	Jack McKay
plan M :	5.15	plan Burn :	80		Bill Dana
actual M :	5.45	actual Burn :	82.0		Milt Thompson
plan h :	282,000	Duration :	:10:20.7		Capt. McDivitt
actual h :	314,750	Speed (MPH) :	3,832		

Purpose :
MH-96 contractural demo

Remarks :
FAI world altitude record for class.
First aircraft flight above 300,000 feet.
First flight above 50 miles.
First astronaut qualification flight.

Flight 63

Flight :	63	A/C Flight :	2-25-45	B-52 :	008
Date :	7-19-62	Launch Lake :	Hidden Hills	B-52 Crew :	Fulton/Bement
Pilot :	McKay	Launch Time :	09:53:45.0	Chase :	Maj. Rogers
plan M :	4.60	plan Burn :	120		Bill Dana
actual M :	5.18	actual Burn :	106.2		Maj. Rushworth
plan h :	73,000	Duration :	:08:23.8		
actual h :	85,250	Speed (MPH) :	3,474		

Purpose :
Heating rates at low alpha and Mach
Aero drag data
Handling qualities data
Wing pressure distribution

Remarks :
Ventral chute failed.

	Flight :	64	A/C Flight :	1-32-53	B-52 :	003
	Date :	7-26-62	Launch Lake :	Mud	B-52 Crew :	Fulton/Bement
	Pilot :	Armstrong	Launch Time :	11:22:30.0	Chase :	Maj. Rushworth
plan	M :	5.70	plan Burn :	83		Capt. Collins
actual	M :	5.74	actual Burn :	82.8		Maj. Daniel
plan	h :	111,000	Duration :	:10:21.6		Maj. White
actual	h :	98,900	Speed (MPH) :	3,989		

Purpose :
Aero stability and drag data
Handling qualities data

Remarks :
Smoke in the cockpit.
Full back trim only gave 16 degree of stabilizer.
Armstrong's last flight.

	Flight :	65	A/C Flight :	3-8-16	B-52 :	003
	Date :	8-2-62	Launch Lake :	Mud	B-52 Crew :	Fulton/Bement
	Pilot :	Walker	Launch Time :	09:56:15.0	Chase :	Maj. Daniel
plan	M :	5.10	plan Burn :	78		Jack McKay
actual	M :	5.07	actual Burn :	80.0		Maj. Collins
plan	h :	160,000	Duration :	:09:14.0		Maj. Rushworth
actual	h :	144,500	Speed (MPH) :	3,428		

Purpose :
Evaluation of MH-96 fixed gain mode

Remarks :
Good flight.

	Flight :	66	A/C Flight :	2-26-46	B-52 :	008
	Date :	8-8-62	Launch Lake :	Hidden Hills	B-52 Crew :	Fulton/Sturmthal
	Pilot :	Rushworth	Launch Time :	10:08:35.0	Chase :	Maj. McDivitt
plan	M :	4.00	plan Burn :	98		Jack McKay
actual	M :	4.40	actual Burn :	95.8		Capt. Engle
plan	h :	84,000	Duration :	:07:42.8		Capt. Collins
actual	h :	90,877	Speed (MPH) :	2,943		

Purpose :
Heating rates at high alpha, low Mach
Aero drag data
RAS checkout

Remarks :
ASAS engaged with pilot induced yaw damper
trip-out.

Flight :	67	A/C Flight :	3-9-18	B-52 :	003
Date :	8-14-62	Launch Lake :	Delamar	B-52 Crew :	Fulton/Crews
Pilot :	Walker	Launch Time :	10:41:35.0	Chase :	Maj. Rushworth
plan M :	5.80	plan Burn :	83		Bill Dana
actual M :	5.25	actual Burn :	84.2		Capt. Engle
plan h :	220,000	Duration :	:09:04.9		Maj. White
actual h :	193,600	Speed (MPH) :	3,747		

Purpose :	Remarks :
Constant theta entry	Roll damper inadvertantly turned off during
Stability at minimum yaw gain	reentry.
	Diverging motion rated as a 9.

Flight :	68	A/C Flight :	2-27-47	B-52 :	008
Date :	8-20-62	Launch Lake :	Hidden Hills	B-52 Crew :	Fulton/Andonian
Pilot :	Rushworth	Launch Time :	10:08:40.0	Chase :	Maj. Gordon
plan M :	4.90	plan Burn :	92		Jack McKay
actual M :	5.24	actual Burn :	86.5		Capt. Engle
plan h :	85,000	Duration :	:08:38.2		Maj. Daniel
actual h :	88,900	Speed (MPH) :	3,535		

Purpose :	Remarks :
Heating rates at moderate alpha and	Roll failed to ASAS at launch, would not
high Mach	reengage.
Aero drag and stability data	
ASAS checkout	

Flight :	69	A/C Flight :	2-28-48	B-52 :	008
Date :	8-29-62	Launch Lake :	Hidden Hills	B-52 Crew :	Fulton/Bement
Pilot :	Rushworth	Launch Time :	10:36:03.0	Chase :	Maj. White
plan M :	4.80	plan Burn :	91		Joe Walker
actual M :	5.12	actual Burn :	92.0		Maj. McDivitt
plan h :	87,000	Duration :	:08:47.1		Capt. Knight
actual h :	97,200	Speed (MPH) :	3,447		

Purpose :	Remarks :
Heating rates at high alpha and Mach	Intermittent roll SAS trip-outs.
	Some speed brake vibrations.

Flight 70

Flight :	70	A/C Flight :	2-29-50	B-52 :	008
Date :	9-28-62	Launch Lake :	Hidden Hills	B-52 Crew :	Bement/Sturmthal
Pilot :	McKay	Launch Time :	10:04:55.0	Chase :	Maj. White
plan M :	4.20	plan Burn :	124		Joe Walker
actual M :	4.22	actual Burn :	128.2		Capt. Engle
plan h :	87,000	Duration :	:09:27.5		Maj. Rushworth
actual h :	68,200	Speed (MPH) :	2,765		

Purpose :
Heating rates at low alpha and Mach
Ventral off stability data

Remarks :
Flew on ASAS entire flight, no attempt to reengage SAS.

Flight 71

Flight :	71	A/C Flight :	3-10-19	B-52 :	008
Date :	10-4-62	Launch Lake :	Delamar	B-52 Crew :	Fulton/Lewis
Pilot :	Rushworth	Launch Time :	10:10:11.0	Chase :	Maj. Rogers
plan M :	5.00	plan Burn :	108		Joe Walker
actual M :	5.17	actual Burn :	103.2		Maj. Collins
plan h :	103,000	Duration :	:09:50.5		Maj. Gordon
actual h :	112,200	Speed (MPH) :	3,493		

Purpose :
Pilot checkout
Ventral off stability data

Remarks :
APU number 1 failed about 5 minutes after launch.
Lost ball nose and yaw damper.

Flight 72

Flight :	72	A/C Flight :	2-30-51	B-52 :	003
Date :	10-9-62	Launch Lake :	Delamar	B-52 Crew :	Fulton/Lewis
Pilot :	McKay	Launch Time :	10:58:32.0	Chase :	Maj. White
plan M :	5.30	plan Burn :	81		Bill Dana
actual M :	5.46	actual Burn :	79.5		Maj. Rushworth
plan h :	125,000	Duration :	:09:40.3		Maj. Rogers
actual h :	130,200	Speed (MPH) :	3,716		

Purpose :
Ventral off stability data

Remarks :
Roll failed to ASAS at launch, reengaged.

Flight 73

Flight :	73	A/C Flight :	3-11-20	B-52 :	008
Date :	10-23-62	Launch Lake :	Mud	B-52 Crew :	Bement/Cross
Pilot :	Rushworth	Launch Time :	11:30:40.0	Chase :	Maj. Rogers
plan M :	5.50	plan Burn :	79		Bill Dana
actual M :	5.47	actual Burn :	78.0		Milt Thompson
plan h :	125,000	Duration :	:09:46.3		Capt. Knight
actual h :	134,500	Speed (MPH) :	3,764		

Purpose :	Remarks :
Ventral off stability data	Popped circuit breaker required B-52 to launch the X-15.

Flight 74

Flight :	74	A/C Flight :	2-31-52	B-52 :	008
Date :	11-9-62	Launch Lake :	Mud	B-52 Crew :	Bement/Lewis
Pilot :	McKay	Launch Time :	10:23:07.0	Chase :	Maj. White
plan M :	5.55	plan Burn :	79		Joe Walker
actual M :	1.49	actual Burn :	70.5		Capt. Evenson
plan h :	125,000	Duration :	:06:31.1		Maj. Daniel
actual h :	53,950	Speed (MPH) :	1,019		

Purpose :	Remarks :
Ventral off stability data Aerodynamic boundary layer investigations	Engine stuck at 30% requiring shutdown, jettison and landing at the launch lake. Higher than normal landing speed due to nonextension of the flaps caused excessive loads on the skids, buckling the landing gear and causing the aircraft to roll over. McKay jettisoned the canopy prior to roll-over, suffered crushed vertebrae, but returned to flight status. Aircraft was ultimately rebuilt into X-15-A2 configuration for carrying the proposed ramjet.

Flight 75

			A/C Flight :	3-12-22	B-52 :	008
	Flight :	75	Launch Lake :	Mud	B-52 Crew :	Bement/Cross
	Date :	12-14-62	Launch Time :	10:44:07.0	Chase :	Maj. Rogers
	Pilot :	White	plan Burn :	79		Bill Dana
plan	M :	5.40	actual Burn :	77.7		Capt. Evenson
actual	M :	5.65	Duration :	:09:37.1		Capt. Knight
plan	h :	153,000	Speed (MPH) :	3,742		
actual	h :	141,400				

Purpose :
Ventral off stability data
Ultraviolet photometer checkout
Heading vernier checkout

Remarks :
White's last flight.

Flight 76

			A/C Flight :	3-13-23	B-52 :	008
	Flight :	76	Launch Lake :	Mud	B-52 Crew :	Bement/Fulton
	Date :	12-20-62	Launch Time :	11:25:04.0	Chase :	Maj. Rushworth
	Pilot :	Walker	plan Burn :	80		Maj. White
plan	M :	5.56	actual Burn :	81.0		Maj. Daniel
actual	M :	5.73	Duration :	:08:54.3		Maj. Gordon
plan	h :	173,000	Speed (MPH) :	3,793		
actual	h :	160,400				

Purpose :
Ventral off stability data
MH-96 limit cycle investigation

Remarks :
Good flight.

Flight 77

			A/C Flight :	3-14-24	B-52 :	008
	Flight :	77	Launch Lake :	Delamar	B-52 Crew :	Bement/Archer
	Date :	1-17-63	Launch Time :	10:59:37.0	Chase :	Maj. White
	Pilot :	Walker	plan Burn :	77		Bill Dana
plan	M :	5.22	actual Burn :	81.2		Maj. Gordon
actual	M :	5.47	Duration :	:09:44.0		Maj. Daniel
plan	h :	250,000	Speed (MPH) :	3,677		
actual	h :	271,700				

Purpose :
Ventral off altitude buildup
Infrared experiment

Remarks :
APU number 1 failed about 4 minutes after
launch, lost ball nose and rudder servo.
First astronaut qualification flight for Walker.

Flight 78

Flight :	78	A/C Flight :	1-33-54	B-52 :	008
Date :	4-11-63	Launch Lake :	Hidden Hills	B-52 Crew :	Bement/Archer
Pilot :	Rushworth	Launch Time :	10:03:20.0	Chase :	Maj. Rogers
plan M :	4.00	plan Burn :	121		Jack McKay
actual M :	4.25	actual Burn :	120.4		Capt. Crews
plan h :	74,000	Duration :	:08:56.7		
actual h :	74,400	Speed (MPH) :	2,864		

Purpose :	Remarks :
KC-1 camera tests	Roll SAS disengaged at launch, reengaged.
APU checkout	

Flight 79

Flight :	79	A/C Flight :	3-15-25	B-52 :	008
Date :	4-18-63	Launch Lake :	Hidden Hills	B-52 Crew :	Fulton/Archer
Pilot :	Walker	Launch Time :	12:16:17.6	Chase :	Maj. White
plan M :	5.05	plan Burn :	86		Bill Dana
actual M :	5.51	actual Burn :	79.0		Maj. Sorlie
plan h :	75,000	Duration :	:07:13.2		Maj. Rogers
actual h :	92,500	Speed (MPH) :	3,770		

Purpose :	Remarks :
Heat transfer at high Mach and	Nose gear scoop door opened at about 55K feet
low alpha	and M=3.4.
Local flow at high Mach and	
low alpha	
Infrared experiment	
Checkout of new "q" meter	

Flight 80

Flight :	80	A/C Flight :	1-34-55	B-52 :	008
Date :	4-25-63	Launch Lake :	Delamar	B-52 Crew :	Bement/Fulton
Pilot :	McKay	Launch Time :	14:04:19.0	Chase :	Maj. White
plan M :	5.05	plan Burn :	80		Milt Thompson
actual M :	5.32	actual Burn :	86.1		Maj. Wood
plan h :	98,000	Duration :	:10:32.3		Capt. Knight
actual h :	105,500	Speed (MPH) :	3,655		

Purpose :	Remarks :
KC-1 camera tests	Roll SAS tripped at launch.

Flight :	81	A/C Flight :	3-16-26	B-52 :	008
Date :	5-2-63	Launch Lake :	Mud	B-52 Crew :	Bement/Archer
Pilot :	Walker	Launch Time :	09:59:54.0	Chase :	Maj. White
plan M :	4.97	plan Burn :	78		Bill Dana
actual M :	4.73	actual Burn :	79.2		Maj. Rogers
plan h :	206,000	Duration :	:09:17.2		Capt. Knight
actual h :	209,400	Speed (MPH) :	3,488		

Purpose :
APU altitude checkout
Ultraviolet photometer
Infrared experiment
High alpha aero flow investigation

Remarks :
Good flight.

Flight :	82	A/C Flight :	3-17-28	B-52 :	008
Date :	5-14-63	Launch Lake :	Hidden Hills	B-52 Crew :	Bement/Archer
Pilot :	Rushworth	Launch Time :	12:11:56.0	Chase :	Maj. Sorlie
plan M :	4.80	plan Burn :	84		Bill Dana
actual M :	5.20	actual Burn :	86.9		Maj. Daniel
plan h :	90,000	Duration :	:07:33.1		
actual h :	95,600	Speed (MPH) :	3,600		

Purpose :
Aero heating rates at high Mach and
high alpha
Ultraviolet photometer
Infrared experiment

Remarks :
Good flight.

Flight :	83	A/C Flight :	1-35-56	B-52 :	003
Date :	5-15-63	Launch Lake :	Delamar	B-52 Crew :	Bement/Archer
Pilot :	McKay	Launch Time :	10:50:46.0	Chase :	Maj. Rushworth
plan M :	5.53	plan Burn :	81		Bill Dana
actual M :	5.57	actual Burn :	84.1		Capt. Evenson
plan h :	98,000	Duration :	:10:20.5		Maj. Daniel
actual h :	124,200	Speed (MPH) :	3,856		

Purpose :
Optical degradation experiment
Traversing probe development

Remarks :
Nose gear scoop door opened at about M=5.2,
causing yaw transients and roll SAS tripout.
Tires blew at landing.

Flight :	84	A/C Flight :	3-18-29	B-52 :	008
Date :	5-29-63	Launch Lake :	Delamar	B-52 Crew :	Bement/Fulton
Pilot :	Walker	Launch Time :	10:43:22.0	Chase :	Maj. White
plan M :	5.60	plan Burn :	86		Bill Dana
actual M :	5.52	actual Burn :	84.3		Capt. Knight
plan h :	90,000	Duration :	:11:42.5		Maj. Rogers
actual h :	92,000	Speed (MPH) :	3,858		

Purpose :
Aero heating rates at high Mach and
low alpha
Ventral off stability investigation

Remarks :
Inner left window shattered at burnout.

Flight :	85	A/C Flight :	3-19-30	B-52 :	008
Date :	6-18-63	Launch Lake :	Delamar	B-52 Crew :	Bement/Archer
Pilot :	Rushworth	Launch Time :	10:34:21.0	Chase :	Maj. Gordon
plan M :	5.20	plan Burn :	78		Bill Dana
actual M :	4.97	actual Burn :	79.3		Maj. Ward
plan h :	220,000	Duration :	:09:40.3		Maj. Rogers
actual h :	223,700	Speed (MPH) :	3,539		

Purpose :
Altitude buildup
Ultraviolet photometer
Vertical tail pressure distribution
investigation

Remarks :
Inertial altitude and altitude rate failed before
launch.

Flight :	86	A/C Flight :	1-36-57	B-52 :	003
Date :	6-25-63	Launch Lake :	Delamar	B-52 Crew :	Bement/Archer
Pilot :	Walker	Launch Time :	09:53:50.0	Chase :	Maj. Daniel
plan M :	5.50	plan Burn :	83		Jack McKay
actual M :	5.51	actual Burn :	92.8		Maj. Wood
plan h :	102,000	Duration :	:09:59.3		Maj. Rogers
actual h :	111,800	Speed (MPH) :	3,911		

Purpose :
Optical degradation experiment
Traversing probe development

Remarks :
Good flight.

Flight 87

Flight :	87	A/C Flight :	3-20-31	B-52 :	008
Date :	6-27-63	Launch Lake :	Delamar	B-52 Crew :	Bement/Archer
Pilot :	Rushworth	Launch Time :	09:56:03.0	Chase :	Maj. Daniel
plan M :	5.10	plan Burn :	79		Jack McKay
actual M :	4.89	actual Burn :	80.1		Maj. Wood
plan h :	278,000	Duration :	:10:28.0		Maj. Rogers
actual h :	285,000	Speed (MPH) :	3,425		

Purpose :	Remarks :
Altitude buildup Ultraviolet photometer InfraRed experiment Horizon scanner	Rushworth's astronaut qualification flight.

Flight 88

Flight :	88	A/C Flight :	1-37-59	B-52 :	008
Date :	7-9-63	Launch Lake :	Delamar	B-52 Crew :	Archer/Bement
Pilot :	Walker	Launch Time :	12:12:12.0	Chase :	Maj. Daniel
plan M :	5.20	plan Burn :	81		Jack McKay
actual M :	5.07	actual Burn :	83.6		Maj. Rogers
plan h :	220,000	Duration :	:08:58.0		Maj. Wood
actual h :	226,400	Speed (MPH) :	3,631		

Purpose :	Remarks :
Optical degradation experiment Traversing probe development RAS checkout	Good flight.

Flight 89

Flight :	89	A/C Flight :	1-38-61	B-52 :	003
Date :	7-18-63	Launch Lake :	Mud	B-52 Crew :	Fulton/Bock
Pilot :	Rushworth	Launch Time :	10:07:20.0	Chase :	Maj. Rogers
plan M :	5.60	plan Burn :	84		Bill Dana
actual M :	5.63	actual Burn :	84.1		Capt. Evenson
plan h :	112,000	Duration :	:09:24.1		Maj. Gordon
actual h :	104,800	Speed (MPH) :	3,925		

Purpose :	Remarks :
Ventral off stability	Good flight.

Flight :	90	A/C Flight :	3-21-32	B-52 :	008
Date :	7-19-63	Launch Lake :	Smith Ranch	B-52 Crew :	Fulton/Bement
Pilot :	Walker	Launch Time :	10:20:05.0	Chase :	Maj. Crews
plan M :	5.40	plan Burn :	83		Bill Dana
actual M :	5.50	actual Burn :	84.6		Maj. Rogers
plan h :	315,000	Duration :	:11:24.1		Maj. Daniel
actual h :	347,800	Speed (MPH) :	3,714		Maj. Wood

Purpose :
Expansion of ventral off reentry
investigation
Ultraviolet photometer
Infrared experiment
Towed balloon experiment
Horizon scanner
Photometer

Remarks :
First Smith Ranch launch.
Instrumentation failed on balloon experiment.

Flight :	91	A/C Flight :	3-22-36	B-52 :	003
Date :	8-22-63	Launch Lake :	Smith Ranch	B-52 Crew :	Bement/Lewis
Pilot :	Walker	Launch Time :	10:05:57.0	Chase :	Maj. Wood
plan M :	5.38	plan Burn :	84.5		Bill Dana
actual M :	5.58	actual Burn :	85.8		Maj. Gordon
plan h :	360,000	Duration :	:11:08.6		Maj. Rogers
actual h :	354,200	Speed (MPH) :	3,794		

Purpose :
Expansion of ventral off reentry
investigation
Altitude predictor checkout
Barnes spectrometer
Photometer

Remarks :
Unofficial world altitude record.
Highest X-15 flight.
Walker's last flight.

Flight 92

Flight :	92	A/C Flight :	1-39-63	B-52 :	008
Date :	10-7-63	Launch Lake :	Hidden Hills	B-52 Crew :	Bement/Jones
Pilot :	Engle	Launch Time :	12:22:56.0	Chase :	Maj. Sorlie
plan M :	4.00	plan Burn :	122		Milt Thompson
actual M :	4.21	actual Burn :	118.6		Maj. Rogers
plan h :	74,000	Duration :	:07:37.0		
actual h :	77,800	Speed (MPH) :	2,834		

Purpose :	Remarks :
Pilot checkout	360 degree roll (unauthorized) performed
Optical degradation Phase II	during glide to Edwards.
checkout	Delta cross-range indicator checkout

Flight 93

Flight :	93	A/C Flight :	1-40-64	B-52 :	008
Date :	10-29-63	Launch Lake :	Hidden Hills	B-52 Crew :	Fulton/Jones
Pilot :	Thompson	Launch Time :	12:42:34.0	Chase :	Maj. Sorlie
plan M :	4.00	plan Burn :	122		Joe Walker
actual M :	4.10	actual Burn :	126.1		Maj. Rushworth
plan h :	74,000	Duration :	:08:43.0		
actual h :	74,400	Speed (MPH) :	2,712		

Purpose :	Remarks :
Pilot checkout	Good flight.
Delta cross-range indicator checkout	

Flight 94

Flight :	94	A/C Flight :	3-23-39	B-52 :	008
Date :	11-7-63	Launch Lake :	Hidden Hills	B-52 Crew :	Bement/Jones
Pilot :	Rushworth	Launch Time :	10:11:14.0	Chase :	Maj. Gordon
plan M :	4.05	plan Burn :	115		Milt Thompson
actual M :	4.40	actual Burn :	108.2		Maj. Sorlie
plan h :	79,000	Duration :	:08:51.7		
actual h :	82,300	Speed (MPH) :	2,925		

Purpose :	Remarks :
Heat transfer with sharp upper	First flight with sharp leading edge on
vertical fin	vertical tail.
Damper off controlability	

Flight 95

Flight :	95	A/C Flight :	1-41-65	B-52 :	008
Date :	11-14-63	Launch Lake :	Hidden Hills	B-52 Crew :	Bement/Jones
Pilot :	Engle	Launch Time :	11:19:21.0	Chase :	Maj. Rushworth
plan M :	4.50	plan Burn :	82		Bill Dana
actual M :	4.75	actual Burn :	83.1		Maj. Rogers
plan h :	92,000	Duration :	:07:46.8		
actual h :	90,800	Speed (MPH) :	3,286		

Purpose :
Pilot checkout
Optical degradation Phase II
checkout
Delta cross-range indicator checkout

Remarks :
Good flight.

Flight 96

Flight :	96	A/C Flight :	3-24-41	B-52 :	008
Date :	11-27-63	Launch Lake :	Hidden Hills	B-52 Crew :	Fulton/Lewis
Pilot :	Thompson	Launch Time :	12:17:40.0	Chase :	Maj. Rushworth
plan M :	4.50	plan Burn :	86		Bill Dana
actual M :	4.94	actual Burn :	87.5		Maj. Sorlie
plan h :	92,000	Duration :	:07:04.3		
actual h :	89,800	Speed (MPH) :	3,310		

Purpose :
Pilot checkout

Remarks :
Inertials failed at launch.

Flight 97

Flight :	97	A/C Flight :	1-42-67	B-52 :	008
Date :	12-5-63	Launch Lake :	Delamar	B-52 Crew :	Bement/Jones
Pilot :	Rushworth	Launch Time :	11:04:36.0	Chase :	Maj. Wood
plan M :	5.70	plan Burn :	78		Maj. Sorlie
actual M :	6.06	actual Burn :	81.2		Bill Dana
plan h :	104,000	Duration :	:09:34.0		Capt. Engle
actual h :	101,000	Speed (MPH) :	4018		

Purpose :
Optical degradation Phase II checkout
Delta cross-range indicator checkout

Remarks :
Highest Mach for unmodified aircraft.
Right inner windshield cracked during the
pattern.

Flight :	98	A/C Flight :	1-43-69	B-52 :	008
Date :	1-8-64	Launch Lake :	Mud	B-52 Crew :	Fulton/Lewis
Pilot :	Engle	Launch Time :	12:10:31.0	Chase :	Maj. Rushworth
plan M :	5.20	plan Burn :	74		Bill Dana
actual M :	5.32	actual Burn :	74.4		Maj. Wood
plan h :	130,000	Duration :	:08:50.7		Maj. Sorlie
actual h :	139,900	Speed (MPH) :	3,616		

Purpose :
Pilot evaluation of damper-off
stability

Remarks :
Inertials failed at peak altitude.

Flight :	99	A/C Flight :	3-25-42	B-52 :	008
Date :	1-16-64	Launch Lake :	Hidden Hills	B-52 Crew :	Fulton/Lewis
Pilot :	Thompson	Launch Time :	10:03:30.0	Chase :	Maj. Gordon
plan M :	4.65	plan Burn :	104		Bruce Peterson
actual M :	4.92	actual Burn :	90.5		Maj. Crews
plan h :	72,000	Duration :	:08:17.0		
actual h :	71,000	Speed (MPH) :	3,242		

Purpose :
Heat transfer with sharp upper
vertical fin
Damper off controllability

Remarks :
Speed brakes extremely hard to open during
high heat phase.

Flight :	100	A/C Flight :	1-44-70	B-52 :	008
Date :	1-28-64	Launch Lake :	Delamar	B-52 Crew :	Bement/
					Gen. Branch
Pilot :	Rushworth	Launch Time :	12:11:36.0	Chase :	Capt. Engle
plan M :	5.50	plan Burn :	76		Bill Dana
actual M :	5.34	actual Burn :	76.2		Capt. Crews
plan h :	102,000	Duration :	:10:25.5		Maj. Wood
actual h :	107,400	Speed (MPH) :	3,618		

Purpose :
Stability evaluation with upper
speed brakes only

Remarks :
100th X-15 flight.
Evaluated upper speed brakes only.
Roll SAS failed repeatedly.

Flight :	101	A/C Flight :	3-26-43	B-52 :	003
Date :	2-19-64	Launch Lake :	Hidden Hills	B-52 Crew :	Fulton/Jones
Pilot :	Thompson	Launch Time :	09:57:24.0	Chase :	Maj. Rushworth
plan M :	5.05	plan Burn :	93		Bruce Peterson
actual M :	5.29	actual Burn :	83.3		Bill Dana
plan h :	75,000	Duration :	:07:03.1		
actual h :	78,600	Speed (MPH) :	3,519		

Purpose :
Heat transfer with sharp upper
vertical fin
Boundary layer noise data

Remarks :
Premature burnout, LOX line unported.

Flight :	102	A/C Flight :	3-27-44	B-52 :	003
Date :	3-13-64	Launch Lake :	Hidden Hills	B-52 Crew :	Bement/Lewis
Pilot :	McKay	Launch Time :	09:46:27.0	Chase :	Maj. Rogers
plan M :	4.20	plan Burn :	107		Bruce Peterson
actual M :	5.11	actual Burn :	105.0		Capt. Engle
plan h :	71,000	Duration :	:07:29.0		
actual h :	76,000	Speed (MPH) :	3,392		

Purpose :
Heat transfer and skin friction with
sharp upper vertical fin
Boundary layer noise data
MH-96 pilot checkout

Remarks :
Good flight.

Flight :	103	A/C Flight :	1-45-72	B-52 :	003
Date :	3-27-64	Launch Lake :	Delamar	B-52 Crew :	Bement/Lewis
Pilot :	Rushworth	Launch Time :	10:10:18.0	Chase :	Maj. Gordon
plan M :	5.70	plan Burn :	81		Bruce Peterson
actual M :	5.63	actual Burn :	82.7		Maj. Adams
plan h :	103,000	Duration :	:09:52.4		Capt. Engle
actual h :	101,500	Speed (MPH) :	3,827		

Purpose :
Phase II optical degradation experiment

Remarks :
Good flight.

Flight 104

Flight :	104	A/C Flight :	1-46-73	B-52 :	003
Date :	4-8-64	Launch Lake :	Delamar	B-52 Crew :	Bement/Fulton
Pilot :	Engle	Launch Time :	10:02:27.0	Chase :	Maj. Gordon
plan M :	5.20	plan Burn :	78		Milt Thompson
actual M :	5.01	actual Burn :	79.6		Maj. Crews
plan h :	180,000	Duration :	:09:45.7		Maj. Rogers
actual h :	175,000	Speed (MPH) :	3,468		

Purpose :	Remarks :
Phase II optical degradation experiment Pilot altitude buildup	Good flight.

Flight 105

Flight :	105	A/C Flight :	1-47-74	B-52 :	81.3
Date :	4-29-64	Launch Lake :	Delamar	B-52 Crew :	003
Pilot :	Rushworth	Launch Time :	10:00:27.0	Chase :	Fulton/Bock
plan M :	5.70	plan Burn :	84		Maj. Sorlie
actual M :	5.72	actual Burn :	81.3		Bill Dana
plan h :	102,000	Duration :	:09:34.6		Capt. Crews
actual h :	101,600	Speed (MPH) :	3,907		Maj. Rogers

Purpose :	Remarks :
Phase II optical degradation experiment Optical attitude indicator checkout	Right hand inner windshield cracked.

Flight 106

Flight :	106	A/C Flight :	3-28-47	B-52 :	003
Date :	5-12-64	Launch Lake :	Hidden Hills	B-52 Crew :	Bement/Jones
Pilot :	McKay	Launch Time :	09:51:46.0	Chase :	Maj. Sorlie
plan M :	4.07	plan Burn :	110		Bruce Peterson
actual M :	4.66	actual Burn :	108.6		Capt. Engle
plan h :	69,000	Duration :	:08:11.3		
actual h :	72,800	Speed (MPH) :	3,084		

Purpose :	Remarks :
Heat transfer and skin friction data with sharp upper vertical fin Boundary layer noise data	Inertial velocities failed at launch, attitudes degraded. Pitch and roll SAS failed twice during boost.

Flight 107

Flight :	107	A/C Flight :	1-48-75	B-52 :	003
Date :	5-19-64	Launch Lake :	Delamar	B-52 Crew :	Fulton/Jones
Pilot :	Engle	Launch Time :	10:26:28.0	Chase :	Maj. Sorlie
plan M :	5.20	plan Burn :	81		Maj. Gordon
actual M :	5.02	actual Burn :	78.0		Bill Dana
plan h :	200,000	Duration :	:09:01.2		Maj. Daniel
actual h :	195,800	Speed (MPH) :	3,494		

Purpose :
Phase II optical degradation experiment
Pilot altitude buildup

Remarks :
Good flight.

Flight 108

Flight :	108	A/C Flight :	3-29-48	B-52 :	003
Date :	5-21-64	Launch Lake :	Silver	B-52 Crew :	Fulton/Jones
Pilot :	Thompson	Launch Time :	09:39:34.0	Chase :	Maj. Rushworth
plan M :	3.35	plan Burn :	120		Bill Dana
actual M :	2.90	actual Burn :	41.0		Maj. Sorlie
plan h :	66,000	Duration :	:07:56.5		
actual h :	64,200	Speed (MPH) :	1,865		

Purpose :
Heat transfer and skin friction data
with sharp upper vertical fin
Boundary layer noise data

Remarks :
Engine shut down at throttle-back.
First Cuddeback landing.

Flight 109

Flight :	109	A/C Flight :	2-32-55	B-52 :	003
Date :	6-25-64	Launch Lake :	Hidden Hills	B-52 Crew :	Fulton/Bement
Pilot :	Rushworth	Launch Time :	09:34:47.0	Chase :	Capt. Engle
plan M :	4.50	plan Burn :	78		Bruce Peterson
actual M :	4.59	actual Burn :	77.0		Maj. Rogers
plan h :	80,000	Duration :	:08:54.7		Maj. Sorlie
actual h :	83,300	Speed (MPH) :	3,104		

Purpose :
Modified A/C and systems checkout
Stability at low angles of attack

Remarks :
Good flight.

Flight 110

Flight :	110	A/C Flight :	1-49-77	B-52 :	003
Date :	6-30-64	Launch Lake :	Delamar	B-52 Crew :	Fulton/Lewis
Pilot :	McKay	Launch Time :	09:49:40.0	Chase :	Capt. Engle
plan M :	5.20	plan Burn :	80		Bruce Peterson
actual M :	4.96	actual Burn :	83.4		Maj. Sorlie
plan h :	182,000	Duration :	:11:27.0		Maj. Rogers
actual h :	99,600	Speed (MPH) :	3,334		

Purpose :
Phase II optical degradation experiment
Pilot altitude buildup

Remarks :
Inertial platform lost at launch, alternate
profile flown.

Flight 111

Flight :	111	A/C Flight :	3-30-50	B-52 :	003
Date :	7-8-64	Launch Lake :	Delamar	B-52 Crew :	Bement/Lewis
Pilot :	Engle	Launch Time :	13:02:52.0	Chase :	Maj. Sorlie
plan M :	5.20	plan Burn :	77.5		Bill Dana
actual M :	5.05	actual Burn :	78.3		Capt. Smith
plan h :	180,000	Duration :	:10:03.6		Maj. Rogers
actual h :	170,400	Speed (MPH) :	3,520		

Purpose :
Horizon scanner experiment
MH-96 pilot checkout

Remarks :
Dampers disengaged after launch, reengaged
after shutdown.
Had to shut off MH-96 to reengage, flew left
hand BCS.

Flight 112

Flight :	112	A/C Flight :	3-31-52	B-52 :	003
Date :	7-29-64	Launch Lake :	Hidden Hills	B-52 Crew :	Bement/Fulton
Pilot :	Engle	Launch Time :	11:55:19.0	Chase :	Maj. Sorlie
plan M :	5.05	plan Burn :	90		Jack McKay
actual M :	5.38	actual Burn :	93.6		Maj. Rogers
plan h :	78,000	Duration :	:07:49.0		
actual h :	78,000	Speed (MPH) :	3,623		

Purpose :
Heat transfer data with surface
distortion panels
Local flow experiment

Remarks :
Good flight.

Flight :	113	A/C Flight :	3-32-53	B-52 :	003
Date :	8-12-64	Launch Lake :	Hidden Hills	B-52 Crew :	Bement/Fulton
Pilot :	Thompson	Launch Time :	10:12:33.2	Chase :	Maj. Rushworth
plan M :	5.02	plan Burn :	90		Jack McKay
actual M :	5.24	actual Burn :	82.1		Maj. Sorlie
plan h :	75,000	Duration :	:06:42.8		
actual h :	81,200	Speed (MPH) :	3,535		

Purpose :	Remarks :
Heat transfer data with surface	Good flight.
distortion panels	
Local flow experiment	
Boundary layer noise data	

Flight :	114	A/C Flight :	2-33-56	B-52 :	003
Date :	8-14-64	Launch Lake :	Delamar	B-52 Crew :	Fulton/Bement
Pilot :	Rushworth	Launch Time :	09:54:19.0	Chase :	Capt. Knight
plan M :	5.20	plan Burn :	82		Bill Dana
actual M :	5.23	actual Burn :	80.3		Capt. Engle
plan h :	96,000	Duration :	:12:06.3		Maj. Sorlie
actual h :	103,300	Speed (MPH) :	3,590		

Purpose :	Remarks :
Stability and control evaluation	Nose gear extended at about
	M=4.2 during descent,
	tires failed at landing.

Flight :	115	A/C Flight :	3-33-54	B-52 :	003
Date :	8-26-64	Launch Lake :	Hidden Hills	B-52 Crew :	Fulton/Bement
Pilot :	McKay	Launch Time :	10:42:07.0	Chase :	Maj. Sorlie
plan M :	5.02	plan Burn :	90		Bruce Peterson
actual M :	5.65	actual Burn :	94.4		Capt. Knight
plan h :	75,000	Duration :	:07:19.7		
actual h :	91,000	Speed (MPH) :	3,863		

Purpose :	Remarks :
Heat transfer data with surface	Good flight
distortion panels	
Local flow experiment	
Boundary layer noise data	

Flight 116

Flight :	116	A/C Flight :	3-34-55	B-52 :	003
Date :	9-3-64	Launch Lake :	Hidden Hills	B-52 Crew :	Bement/Jones
Pilot :	Thompson	Launch Time :	09:54:54.0	Chase :	Capt. Knight
plan M :	5.05	plan Burn :	92		Joe Walker
actual M :	5.35	actual Burn :	91.0		Maj. Rogers
plan h :	75,000	Duration :	:06:20.0		
actual h :	78,600	Speed (MPH) :	3,615		

Purpose :	Remarks :
Surface distortion heat transfer test Boundary layer noise data Shear-layer rakes data Center stick controller evaluation	U-2 took off across the path of the X-15 during approach to runway.

Flight 117

Flight :	117	A/C Flight :	3-35-57	B-52 :	003
Date :	9-23-64	Launch Lake :	Delamar	B-52 Crew :	Fulton/Lewis
Pilot :	Engle	Launch Time :	13:16:00.0	Chase :	Maj. Rogers
plan M :	5.65	plan Burn :	82		Jack McKay
actual M :	5.59	actual Burn :	80.3		Maj. Parsons
plan h :	98,000	Duration :	:09:34.3		Capt. Knight
actual h :	97,000	Speed (MPH) :	3,888		

Purpose :	Remarks :
Martin MA-45R ablative material test Boundary layer noise data	Smoke in the cockpit after burnout. Inertial velocity failed.

Flight 118

Flight :	118	A/C Flight :	2-34-57	B-52 :	008
Date :	9-29-64	Launch Lake :	Mud	B-52 Crew :	Fulton/Townsend
Pilot :	Rushworth	Launch Time :	13:00:13.0	Chase :	Maj. Sorlie
plan M :	5.20	plan Burn :	81		Milt Thompson
actual M :	5.20	actual Burn :	79.7		Maj. Parsons
plan h :	96,000	Duration :	:09:51.0		Capt. Engle
actual h :	97,800	Speed (MPH) :	3,542		

Purpose :	Remarks :
Stability and control evaluation Star tracker checkout Advanced X-15 landing dynamics	Nose gear scoop door came open about M=4.5 and 88K. Aircraft handled worse than with full nose gear extended.

Flight :	119	A/C Flight :	1-50-79	B-52 :	008
Date :	10-15-64	Launch Lake :	Hidden Hills	B-52 Crew :	Fulton/Cotton
Pilot :	McKay	Launch Time :	13:15:40.0	Chase :	Maj. Rogers
plan M :	4.30	plan Burn :	73		Bruce Peterson
actual M :	4.56	actual Burn :	72.9		Capt. Knight
plan h :	80,000	Duration :	:08:40.9		
actual h :	84,900	Speed (MPH) :	3,048		

Purpose :
Honeywell inertial system checkout
Tip-pod dynamic stability data
Air density and sky brightness
experiments checkout
Investigation of tip-pod shock
impingement on the wing

Remarks :
First wing tip-pod flight.
Micrometeorite experiment opened while
going transonic at high-key.

Flight :	120	A/C Flight :	3-36-59	B-52 :	008
Date :	10-30-64	Launch Lake :	Hidden Hills	B-52 Crew :	Bement/Lewis
Pilot :	Thompson	Launch Time :	09:51:52.2	Chase :	Maj. Rushworth
plan M :	4.50	plan Burn :	74		Bruce Peterson
actual M :	4.66	actual Burn :	74.4		Capt. Engle
plan h :	81,000	Duration :	:07:10.8		
actual h :	84,600	Speed (MPH) :	3,113		

Purpose :
Landing gear door mod checkout
Boundary layer noise data
Shear layer experiment checkout
Center stick controller evaluation

Remarks :
Fire warning lite about 54 seconds after
shutdown.

Flight :	121	A/C Flight :	2-35-60	B-52 :	008
Date :	11-30-64	Launch Lake :	Hidden Hills	B-52 Crew :	Bement/Bock
Pilot :	McKay	Launch Time :	12:09:32.0	Chase :	Maj. Sorlie
plan M :	4.50	plan Burn :	80		Don Mallick
actual M :	4.66	actual Burn :	75.3		Maj. Rogers
plan h :	80,000	Duration :	:08:34.8		Capt. Knight
actual h :	87,200	Speed (MPH) :	3,089		Maj. Twinting

Purpose :
Landing gear door mod checkout
Stability and control data
Star tracker partial checkout

Remarks :
Good flight.

	Flight :	122	A/C Flight :	3-37-60	B-52 :	008
	Date :	12-9-64	Launch Lake :	Hidden Hills	B-52 Crew :	Fulton/Lewis
	Pilot :	Thompson	Launch Time :	10:36:17.0	Chase :	Maj. Rushworth
plan	M :	5.20	plan Burn :	104		Bruce Peterson
actual	M :	5.42	actual Burn :	101.4		Maj. Sorlie
plan	h :	85,000	Duration :	:06:25.7		Maj. Twinting
actual	h :	92,400	Speed (MPH) :	3,723		

Purpose :
Non-uniform 3-dimensional flow
field measurements
Skin friction data
Ablative tests
Boundary layer noise data
Landing gear door mod checkout

Remarks :
Shutdown purposely with negative g (An=-1.2).

	Flight :	123	A/C Flight :	1-51-81	B-52 :	003
	Date :	12-10-64	Launch Lake :	Delamar	B-52 Crew :	Fulton/Bock
	Pilot :	Engle	Launch Time :	11:10:26.0	Chase :	Maj. Sorlie
plan	M :	5.20	plan Burn :	78		Jack McKay
actual	M :	5.35	actual Burn :	80.5		Maj. Parsons
plan	h :	112,000	Duration :	:09:44.7		Maj. Rogers
actual	h :	113,200	Speed (MPH) :	3,675		

Purpose :
Honeywell inertial system checkout
Tip-pod dynamic stability data
Center stick controller evaluation
Air density instrument checkout
MIT horizon photometer
Effects of tip-pod shock impingement
on the wing
Scoop door hook data

Remarks :
Pitch SAS tripout after launch, reset but did not
operate properly.

Flight :	124	A/C Flight :	3-38-61	B-52 :	003
Date :	12-22-64	Launch Lake :	Hidden Hills	B-52 Crew :	Fulton/Bock
Pilot :	Rushworth	Launch Time :	10:44:52.0	Chase :	Maj. Twinting
plan M :	5.18	plan Burn :	101		Don Mallick
actual M :	5.55	actual Burn :	88.0		Capt. Knight
plan h :	81,000	Duration :	:07:51.0		
actual h :	81,200	Speed (MPH) :	3,593		

Purpose :
Skin friction measurements
GE ablative tests
Non-uniform 3-dimensional flow
field measurements
Landing gear door mod checkout
Boundary layer noise

Remarks :
High gear loads due to crosswind landing.

Flight :	125	A/C Flight :	3-39-62	B-52 :	003
Date :	1-13-65	Launch Lake :	Hidden Hills	B-52 Crew :	Bement/Fulton
Pilot :	Thompson	Launch Time :	10:51:06.7	Chase :	Maj. Smith
plan M :	5.10	plan Burn :	90		Bill Dana
actual M :	5.48	actual Burn :	98.5		Maj. Rushworth
plan h :	92,000	Duration :	:06:47.6		
actual h :	99,400	Speed (MPH) :	3,713		

Purpose :
Non-uniform 3-dimensional flow
field measurements
Discontinuity heat transfer test
Skin friction measurements
Boundary layer noise data
Landing gear door mod checkout

Remarks :
Rate limiting and loss of pitch and roll damping
experienced during pullup/roll maneuver after
burnout.
Temporarily out of control.

Flight 126

Flight :	126	A/C Flight :	3-40-63	B-52 :	008
Date :	2-2-65	Launch Lake :	Delamar	B-52 Crew :	Fulton/Bement
Pilot :	Engle	Launch Time :	12:50:14.6	Chase :	Maj. Sorlie
plan M :	5.64	plan Burn :	82.5		Bruce Peterson
actual M :	5.71	actual Burn :	81.4		Capt. Stroface
plan h :	94,000	Duration :	:09:58.4		Maj. Rushworth
actual h :	98,200	Speed (MPH) :	3,885		

Purpose :	Remarks :
Martin 25S ablative material on ventral and nose panel	Good flight.
Skin friction measurements	
MH-96 fixed gain evaluation	
Nose gear mod checkout	
Boundary layer noise data	

Flight 127

Flight :	127	A/C Flight :	2-36-63	B-52 :	008
Date :	2-17-65	Launch Lake :	Mud	B-52 Crew :	Fulton/Bement
Pilot :	Rushworth	Launch Time :	10:44:59.6	Chase :	Maj. Sorlie
plan M :	5.20	plan Burn :	81.5		Bill Dana
actual M :	5.27	actual Burn :	79.8		Milt Thompson
plan h :	96,000	Duration :	:09:20.3		Capt. Engle
actual h :	95,100	Speed (MPH) :	3,539		

Purpose :	Remarks :
Stability and control evaluation	Right main gear extended at about M=4.3 and 85K.
Star tracker checkout	Inertial altitude failed.
Advanced X-15 landing dynamics	Engine momentarily lost power at 23 seconds.

Flight 128

Flight :	128	A/C Flight :	1-52-85	B-52 :	008
Date :	2-26-65	Launch Lake :	Delamar	B-52 Crew :	Fulton/Bock
Pilot :	McKay	Launch Time :	11:45:55.0	Chase :	Capt. Knight
plan M :	5.20	plan Burn :	83		Bruce Peterson
actual M :	5.40	actual Burn :	83.2		Capt. Stroface
plan h :	180,000	Duration :	:09:24.7		Capt. Engle
actual h :	153,600	Speed (MPH) :	3,702		

Purpose :
Honeywell inertial system checkout
MIT horizon photometer
Air density measurement
Sky brightness experiment
RAS mod checkout
Pilot altitude buildup

Remarks :
Computer malfunction at launch.

Flight 129

Flight :	129	A/C Flight :	1-53-86	B-52 :	008
Date :	3-26-65	Launch Lake :	Delamar	B-52 Crew :	Fulton/Bock
Pilot :	Rushworth	Launch Time :	11:01:59.2	Chase :	Capt. Engle
plan M :	5.15	plan Burn :	75.5		Bill Dana
actual M :	5.17	actual Burn :	79.6		Capt. Gentry
plan h :	104,000	Duration :	:11:24.3		Capt. Knight
actual h :	101,900	Speed (MPH) :	3,580		

Purpose :
I.R. scanner experiment
Honeywell inertial system checkout

Remarks :
Alpha-crosspointer did not work properly.

Flight 130

Flight :	130	A/C Flight :	3-41-64	B-52 :	008
Date :	4-23-65	Launch Lake :	Hidden Hills	B-52 Crew :	Fulton/Cotton
Pilot :	Engle	Launch Time :	09:44:16.7	Chase :	Maj. Rushworth
plan M :	5.20	plan Burn :	93		Jack McKay
actual M :	5.48	actual Burn :	91.4		Capt. Knight
plan h :	78,000	Duration :	:07:42.1		
actual h :	79,700	Speed (MPH) :	3,657		

Purpose :
Heat transfer data with surface
distortion panels
Ablative tests
Handling qualities data
Boundary layer noise data

Remarks :
Good flight.

Flight 131

Flight :	131	A/C Flight :	2-37-64	B-52 :	008
Date :	4-28-65	Launch Lake :	Hidden Hills	B-52 Crew :	Bock/Townsend
Pilot :	McKay	Launch Time :	12:26:20.9	Chase :	Maj. Sorlie
plan M :	4.70	plan Burn :	83		Milt Thompson
actual M :	4.80	actual Burn :	78.9		Capt. Engle
plan h :	84,000	Duration :	:08:02.6		
actual h :	92,600	Speed (MPH) :	3,260		

Purpose :
Landing gear loads data
Landing dynamics data
Stability and control evaluation
Star tracker functional checkout

Remarks :
Highest q for damper off flight during
program (1200-1500 psf).
Inertial altitude rate failed.

Flight 132

Flight :	132	A/C Flight :	2-38-66	B-52 :	008
Date :	5-18-65	Launch Lake :	Mud	B-52 Crew :	Fulton/Jones
Pilot :	McKay	Launch Time :	09:56:38.0	Chase :	Maj. Sorlie
plan M :	5.20	plan Burn :	81.5		Don Mallick
actual M :	5.17	actual Burn :	78.9		Capt. Gentry
plan h :	96,000	Duration :	:09:42.0		Capt. Engle
actual h :	102,100	Speed (MPH) :	3,541		

Purpose :
Stability and control evaluation
Star tracker checkout
Advanced X-15 landing dynamics
Landing gear mod checkout

Remarks :
Engine shutdown during idle, reset and worked
after launch.

Flight 133

Flight :	133	A/C Flight :	1-54-88	B-52 :	008
Date :	5-25-65	Launch Lake :	Mud	B-52 Crew :	Fulton/Jones
Pilot :	Thompson	Launch Time :	10:12:07.5	Chase :	Maj. Rushworth
plan M :	4.90	plan Burn :	82		Bruce Peterson
actual M :	4.87	actual Burn :	81.1		Capt. Stroface
plan h :	180,000	Duration :	:09:02.0		Capt. Knight
actual h :	179,800	Speed (MPH) :	3,418		

Purpose :
Honeywell inertial system checkout
MIT horizon photometer
Pace transducer checkout
RAS mod checkout
Pilot altitude buildup

Remarks :
Squat switch never armed.

Flight :	134	A/C Flight :	3-42-65	B-52 :	008
Date :	5-28-65	Launch Lake :	Delamar	B-52 Crew :	Fulton/Jones
Pilot :	Engle	Launch Time :	09:43:51.0	Chase :	Maj. Sorlie
plan M :	5.40	plan Burn :	82		Fred Haise
actual M :	5.17	actual Burn :	82.5		Maj. Parsons
plan h :	200,000	Duration :	:09:35.1		Capt. Knight
actual h :	209,600	Speed (MPH) :	3,754		

Purpose :	Remarks :
Radiometer experiment	Good flight.
Langley scanner	
Boundary layer noise data	

Flight :	135	A/C Flight :	3-43-66	B-52 :	003
Date :	6-16-65	Launch Lake :	Delamar	B-52 Crew :	Fulton/Cretney
Pilot :	Engle	Launch Time :	10:26:33.0	Chase :	Maj. Wood
plan M :	5.00	plan Burn :	79		Don Mallick
actual M :	4.69	actual Burn :	77.8		Maj. Sorlie
plan h :	240,000	Duration :	:09:45.0		Maj. Twinting
actual h :	244,700	Speed (MPH) :	3,404		

Purpose :	Remarks :
Radiometer experiment	Good flight.
Boundary layer noise data	

Flight :	136	A/C Flight :	1-55-89	B-52 :	008
Date :	6-17-65	Launch Lake :	Delamar	B-52 Crew :	Fulton/Cotton
Pilot :	Thompson	Launch Time :	09:40:31.2	Chase :	Maj. Twinting
plan M :	5.15	plan Burn :	81.5		Jack McKay
actual M :	5.14	actual Burn :	82.2		Capt. Stroface
plan h :	104,000	Duration :	:08:54.0		Capt. Engle
actual h :	108,500	Speed (MPH) :	3,541		

Purpose :	Remarks :
Infrared scanner	Two pitchroll tripouts to ASAS, reset once.
Inertial system checkout	
Cross track vernier checkout	

	Flight :	137	A/C Flight :	2-39-70	B-52 :	008
	Date :	6-22-65	Launch Lake :	Delamar	B-52 Crew :	Fulton/Bock
	Pilot :	McKay	Launch Time :	09:44:43.9	Chase :	Maj. Rushworth
plan	M :	5.40	plan Burn :	83		Bruce Peterson
actual	M :	5.64	actual Burn :	85.3		Capt. Gentry
plan	h :	160,000	Duration :	:09:47.7		Capt. Knight
actual	h :	155,900	Speed (MPH) :	3,938		

Purpose :
Star tracker checkout
Landing gear mod checkout
Stability and control data
Advanced X-15 landing dynamics
data

Remarks :
Good flight.

	Flight :	138	A/C Flight :	3-44-67	B-52 :	008
	Date :	6-29-65	Launch Lake :	Delamar	B-52 Crew :	Fulton/Andonian
	Pilot :	Engle	Launch Time :	10:21:17.6	Chase :	Maj. Wood
plan	M :	5.10	plan Burn :	82		Jack McKay
actual	M :	4.94	actual Burn :	81.0		Capt. Gentry
plan	h :	283,000	Duration :	:10:32.4		Maj. Parsons
actual	h :	280,600	Speed (MPH) :	3,432		

Purpose :
Langley scanner
Radiometer experiment
Boundary layer noise data
Reentry maneuver techniques

Remarks :
Engle's astronaut qualification flight.

	Flight :	139	A/C Flight :	2-40-72	B-52 :	003
	Date :	7-8-65	Launch Lake :	Delamar	B-52 Crew :	Fulton/Cotton
	Pilot :	McKay	Launch Time :	09:16:55.8	Chase :	Maj. Adams
plan	M :	5.20	plan Burn :	82.5		Bruce Peterson
actual	M :	5.19	actual Burn :	82.9		Capt. Gentry
plan	h :	200,000	Duration :	:09:33.4		Capt. Knight
actual	h :	212,600	Speed (MPH) :	3,659		

Purpose :
Star tracker experiment
Advanced X-15 landing dynamics
Altitude buildup

Remarks :
RAS failed to operate.

Flight 140

Flight :	140	A/C Flight :	3-45-69	B-52 :	008
Date :	7-20-65	Launch Lake :	Delamar	B-52 Crew :	Jones/Andonian
Pilot :	Rushworth	Launch Time :	09:59:28.8	Chase :	Capt. Knight
plan M :	5.50	plan Burn :	80		Bill Dana
actual M :	5.40	actual Burn :	79.5		Capt. Whelon
plan h :	92,000	Duration :	:10:34.5		Capt. Gentry
actual h :	105,400	Speed (MPH) :	3,706		

Purpose :	Remarks :
Boundary layer noise data	Good flight.

Flight 141

Flight :	141	A/C Flight :	2-41-73	B-52 :	008
Date :	8-3-65	Launch Lake :	Delamar	B-52 Crew :	Bock/Andonian
Pilot :	Rushworth	Launch Time :	12:40:05.7	Chase :	Maj. Sorlie
plan M :	5.15	plan Burn :	82		Bill Dana
actual M :	5.16	actual Burn :	82.4		Capt. Whelen
plan h :	200,000	Duration :	:09:32.0		Capt. Stroface
actual h :	208,700	Speed (MPH) :	3,602		

Purpose :	Remarks :
RAS system checkout	Right roll out-of-trim.
Star tracker	
Advanced X-15 landing dynamics	
Pilot altitude buildup	

Flight 142

Flight :	142	A/C Flight :	1-56-93	B-52 :	008
Date :	8-6-65	Launch Lake :	Delamar	B-52 Crew :	Fulton/Andonian
Pilot :	Thompson	Launch Time :	09:41:46.7	Chase :	Maj. Rushworth
plan M :	5.15	plan Burn :	81		Fred Haise
actual M :	5.15	actual Burn :	83.0		Capt. Livingston
plan h :	104,000	Duration :	:10:13.0		Capt. Engle
actual h :	103,200	Speed (MPH) :	3,534		

Purpose :	Remarks :
Infrared scanner	Engine timer did not start.
Stability and control data	

Flight 143

Flight :	143	A/C Flight :	3-46-70	B-52 :	003
Date :	8-10-65	Launch Lake :	Delamar	B-52 Crew :	Jones/Andonian
Pilot :	Engle	Launch Time :	11:24:21.7	Chase :	Maj. Sorlie
plan M :	5.20	plan Burn :	81		Bill Dana
actual M :	5.20	actual Burn :	82.1		Capt. Gentry
plan h :	266,000	Duration :	:09:52.1		Capt. Stroface
actual h :	271,000	Speed (MPH) :	3,550		

Purpose :	Remarks :
Northrop scanner	Yaw damper failed and reset over 20 times
Boundary layer noise data	during flight, but alternate profile was not
Reentry maneuver techniques	flown.

Flight 144

Flight :	144	A/C Flight :	1-57-96	B-52 :	003
Date :	8-25-65	Launch Lake :	Delamar	B-52 Crew :	Fulton/Cotton
Pilot :	Thompson	Launch Time :	09:54:46.8	Chase :	Maj. Rushworth
plan M :	5.20	plan Burn :	81		Jack McKay
actual M :	5.11	actual Burn :	84.5		Capt. Merrett
plan h :	222,000	Duration :	:08:51.7		Maj. Parsons
actual h :	214,100	Speed (MPH) :	3,604		

Purpose :	Remarks :
MIT scanner	Poor pitch control during landing due to aft
Stability and control data	center of gravity location.
Pace transducer	Thompson's last X-15 flight.

Flight 145

Flight :	145	A/C Flight :	3-47-71	B-52 :	008
Date :	8-26-65	Launch Lake :	Delamar	B-52 Crew :	Cotton/Bock
Pilot :	Rushworth	Launch Time :	09:52:12.1	Chase :	Maj. Sorlie
plan M :	5.00	plan Burn :	79		Fred Haise
actual M :	4.79	actual Burn :	78.6		Capt. Livingston
plan h :	240,000	Duration :	:10:27.5		Maj. Parsons
actual h :	239,600	Speed (MPH) :	3,372		

Purpose :	Remarks :
Northrop radiometer	Experienced limit cycle 4-5 times during flight.
Boundary layer noise data	

Flight 146

Flight :	146	A/C Flight :	2-42-74	B-52 :	008
Date :	9-2-65	Launch Lake :	Delamar	B-52 Crew :	Bock/Jones
Pilot :	McKay	Launch Time :	09:40:05.6	Chase :	Maj. Rushworth
plan M :	5.00	plan Burn :	82		Bruce Peterson
actual M :	5.16	actual Burn :	84.0		Capt. Stroface
plan h :	228,000	Duration :	:09:12.8		Capt. Knight
actual h :	239,800	Speed (MPH) :	3,570		

Purpose :
RAS checkout
Star tracker
Advanced X-15 landing dynamics
Pilot altitude buildup

Remarks :
Good flight.

Flight 147

Flight :	147	A/C Flight :	1-58-97	B-52 :	008
Date :	9-9-65	Launch Lake :	Delamar	B-52 Crew :	Bock/Fulton
Pilot :	Rushworth	Launch Time :	09:55:50.7	Chase :	Maj. Wood
plan M :	5.15	plan Burn :	80		Bruce Peterson
actual M :	5.25	actual Burn :	82.1		Capt. Livingston
plan h :	104,000	Duration :	:11:10.2		Maj. Parsons
actual h :	97,200	Speed (MPH) :	3,534		

Purpose :
Infrared scanner
Ablative test

Remarks :
Alpha indicator failed.
Unexplained buffet during flight.

Flight 148

Flight :	148	A/C Flight :	3-48-72	B-52 :	008
Date :	9-14-65	Launch Lake :	Delamar	B-52 Crew :	Bock/Jones
Pilot :	McKay	Launch Time :	10:01:06.0	Chase :	LCol Rushworth
plan M :	5.10	plan Burn :	80		Fred Haise
actual M :	5.03	actual Burn :	80.9		Capt. Evenson
plan h :	230,000	Duration :	:09:58.0		Capt. Knight
actual h :	239,000	Speed (MPH) :	3,519		

Purpose :
Northrop radiometer
Boundary layer noise data

Remarks :
Auto-BCS affected adversely by servo
transients.

Flight 149

	Flight :	149	A/C Flight :	1-59-98	B-52 :		003
	Date :	9-22-65	Launch Lake :	Delamar	B-52 Crew :		Bock/Jones
	Pilot :	Rushworth	Launch Time :	10:58:39.7	Chase :		Maj. Sorlie
plan	M :	5.15	plan Burn :	80			Bill Dana
actual	M :	5.18	actual Burn :	82.0			Maj. Adams
plan	h :	104,000	Duration :	:10:54.3			Capt. Engle
actual	h :	100,300	Speed (MPH) :	3,550			

Purpose :
Infrared scanner

Remarks :
Good flight.

Flight 150

	Flight :	150	A/C Flight :	3-49-73	B-52 :		003
	Date :	9-28-65	Launch Lake :	Delamar	B-52 Crew :	Bock/Andonian	
	Pilot :	McKay	Launch Time :	10:07:37.6	Chase :	LCol Rushworth	
plan	M :	5.15	plan Burn :	79		Bruce Peterson	
actual	M :	5.33	actual Burn :	80.8		Fred Haise	
plan	h :	260,000	Duration :	:11:56.0		Capt. Engle	
actual	h :	295,600	Speed (MPH) :	3,732			

Purpose :
Northrop scanner
Boundary layer noise data
Horizontal tail loads data

Remarks :
Roll-hold drop-out at launch.

Flight 151

	Flight :	151	A/C Flight :	1-60-99	B-52 :		003
	Date :	9-30-65	Launch Lake :	Hidden Hills	B-52 Crew :		Bock/Fulton
	Pilot :	Knight	Launch Time :	09:43:55.3	Chase :		LCol Sorlie
plan	M :	4.00	plan Burn :	126			Bruce Peterson
actual	M :	4.06	actual Burn :	127.4			Capt. Engle
plan	h :	74,000	Duration :	:08:22.6			
actual	h :	76,600	Speed (MPH) :	2,718			

Purpose :
Pilot checkout
Infrared scanner

Remarks :
Good flight.

334   APPENDIX 1

Flight :	152	A/C Flight :	3-50-74	B-52 :	008
Date :	10-12-65	Launch Lake :	Hidden Hills	B-52 Crew :	Jones/Fulton
Pilot :	Knight	Launch Time :	09:43:13.2	Chase :	LCol Sorlie
plan M :	4.50	plan Burn :	93		Fred Haise
actual M :	4.62	actual Burn :	86.2		Capt. Engle
plan h :	91,000	Duration :	:07:06.1		
actual h :	94,400	Speed (MPH) :	3,116		

Purpose :
Pilot checkout

Remarks :
APU number 2 shutdown at 1.5 seconds after launch.
Pitch/roll SAS servos locked up for 5 seconds.
APU restarted after shutdown (90 seconds).

Flight :	153	A/C Flight :	1-61-101	B-52 :	003
Date :	10-14-65	Launch Lake :	Delamar	B-52 Crew :	Bock/Jones
Pilot :	Engle	Launch Time :	12:46:32.6	Chase :	LCol Sorlie
plan M :	5.15	plan Burn :	83		Jack McKay
actual M :	5.08	actual Burn :	84.8		Maj. Parsons
plan h :	250,000	Duration :	:09:27.7		Capt. Knight
actual h :	266,500	Speed (MPH) :	3,554		

Purpose :
MIT horizon photometer
Pace transducer

Remarks :
Engle's third flight above 50 miles.
Engle's last X-15 flight.
Yaw damper tripped twice, reset.

Flight :	154	A/C Flight :	3-51-75	B-52 :	003
Date :	10-27-65	Launch Lake :	Delamar	B-52 Crew :	Fulton/Jones
Pilot :	McKay	Launch Time :	10:49:10.3	Chase :	LCol Sorlie
plan M :	5.15	plan Burn :	79		Bruce Peterson
actual M :	5.06	actual Burn :	75.6		Capt. Stroface
plan h :	260,000	Duration :	:11:51.2		Capt. Engle
actual h :	236,900	Speed (MPH) :	3,545		

Purpose :
Northrop scanner
Boundary layer noise data
Horizontal stabilizer loads data

Remarks :
Roll-hold engaged 8 degrees off heading at launch.

	Flight :	155	A/C Flight :	2-43-75	B-52 :	003
	Date :	11-3-65	Launch Lake :	Cuddeback	B-52 Crew :	Bock/Doryland
	Pilot :	Rushworth	Launch Time :	09:09:10.7	Chase :	Capt. Knight
plan	M :	2.20	plan Burn :	80		Fred Haise
actual	M :	2.31	actual Burn :	84.1		Capt. Engle
plan	h :	70,000	Duration :	:05:01.6		
actual	h :	70,600	Speed (MPH) :	1,514		

Purpose :
Handling qualities with external tanks
Tank separation characteristics
Tank trajectory evaluation

Remarks :
First flight with external fuel tanks (empty).
First, and only, launch from Cuddeback.
LOX tank chute did not deploy, not repairable.
Ventral chute did not deploy.
Inertial velocity malfunctioned.
Inertial h dot wired backwards.
Tank ejection and handling qualities were quite satisfactory.

	Flight :	156	A/C Flight :	1-62-103	B-52 :	008
	Date :	11-4-65	Launch Lake :	Hidden Hills	B-52 Crew :	Bock/Doryland
	Pilot :	Dana	Launch Time :	09:11:31.0	Chase :	LCol Sorlie
plan	M :	4.00	plan Burn :	123		Bruce Peterson
actual	M :	4.22	actual Burn :	124.2		Capt. Knight
plan	h :	74,000	Duration :	:08:45.2		
actual	h :	80,200	Speed (MPH) :	2,765		

Purpose :
Pilot checkout

Remarks :
Two relights required.

Flight :	157	A/C Flight :	1-63-104	B-52 :	003
Date :	5-6-66	Launch Lake :	Delamar	B-52 Crew :	Fulton/Doryland
Pilot :	McKay	Launch Time :	13:30:12.8	Chase :	Maj. Knight
plan M :	5.30	plan Burn :	82		Capt. Curtis
actual M :	2.21	actual Burn :	35.4		Bruce Peterson
plan h :	199,000	Duration :	:06:02.7		Capt. Gentry
actual h :	68,400	Speed (MPH) :	1,452		Capt. Stroface

Purpose :
Atmospheric density measurements
Micrometeorite collection
Horizon scanner
Electrical loads survey
Nonglare glass evaluation
Stick-kicker evaluation
Sky brightness experiment

Remarks :
Pump failure required a premature shutdown
and landing at Delamar.
Canopy jettisoned before sliding off the
lakebed, little damage.
Micrometeorite experiment opened.

Flight :	158	A/C Flight :	2-44-79	B-52 :	003
Date :	5-18-66	Launch Lake :	Mud	B-52 Crew :	Fulton/Doryland
Pilot :	Rushworth	Launch Time :	10:24:00.3	Chase :	LCol Sorlie
plan M :	5.38	plan Burn :	84		Dana/Manke
actual M :	5.43	actual Burn :	81.9		Bruce Peterson
plan h :	100,000	Duration :	:08:56.8		Capt. Gentry
actual h :	99,000	Speed (MPH) :	3,702		

Purpose :
Ventral-on stability and control data

Remarks :
Good flight.

Flight :	159	A/C Flight :	2-45-81	B-52 :	008
Date :	7-1-66	Launch Lake :	Mud	B-52 Crew :	Fulton/Doryland
Pilot :	Rushworth	Launch Time :	11:02:36.1	Chase :	Maj. Knight
plan M :	6.00	plan Burn :	132		Bruce Peterson
actual M :	1.70	actual Burn :	33.2		Capt. Curtis
plan h :	100,000	Duration :	:04:28.6		LCol Sorlie
actual h :	44,800	Speed (MPH) :	1,128		

Purpose :
A/C handling characteristics with
full external tanks
Tank separation characteristics
Martin ablative tests
Local flow conditions in ramjet area
Evaluation of alternate pitot-static
measurement system
Canopy hook loads

Remarks :
TM indication of no NH3 flow caused pilot to
throttleback, eject the external tanks, and land
at Mud (Faulty TM signal).
X-15 stripped the top off a camper on the ride
back home.
Rushworth's last X-15 flight.

Flight :	160	A/C Flight :	1-64-107	B-52 :	003
Date :	7-12-66	Launch Lake :	Mud	B-52 Crew :	Fulton/Bowline
Pilot :	Knight	Launch Time :	11:32:15.7	Chase :	Capt. Curtis
plan M :	5.30	plan Burn :	80		Bill Dana
actual M :	5.34	actual Burn :	83.2		Capt. Hoag
plan h :	130,000	Duration :	:08:36.0		Capt. Gentry
actual h :	130,000	Speed (MPH) :	3,661		

Purpose :
Pilot checkout
Electrical loads survey
Nonglare glass evaluation
Stick-kicker checkout
Window shade checkout
Inertial system checkout

Remarks :
Good flight.

Flight 161

Flight :	161	A/C Flight :	3-52-78	B-52 :	003
Date :	7-18-66	Launch Lake :	Hidden Hills	B-52 Crew :	Fulton/Doryland
Pilot :	Dana	Launch Time :	11:38:24.1	Chase :	Capt. Curtis
plan M :	4.50	plan Burn :	98		John Manke
actual M :	4.71	actual Burn :	95.5		Capt. Gentry
plan h :	94,000	Duration :	:07:30.0		
actual h :	96,100	Speed (MPH) :	3,205		

Purpose :
Pilot checkout
First flight with Lear Panel cockpit
display, MH Inertial system, third
skid, and sunshade.
Inertial system checkout
Cockpit display checkout
Horizontal tail loads data
Stick-kicker checkout

Remarks :
Could not see through the sunshade during
90-degree left bank, replaced for next flight.

Flight 162

Flight :	162	A/C Flight :	2-46-83	B-52 :	003
Date :	7-21-66	Launch Lake :	Delamar	B-52 Crew :	Doryland/Bowline
Pilot :	Knight	Launch Time :	12:02:03.1	Chase :	John Manke
plan M :	5.10	plan Burn :	81		LCol Sorlie
actual M :	5.12	actual Burn :	81.3		Capt. Gentry
plan h :	180,000	Duration :	:08:51.0		Bruce Peterson
actual h :	192,300	Speed (MPH) :	3,568		

Purpose :
Pilot altitude buildup
Star tracker checkout
Alternate pitot-static system ckout
Martin ablative test
Base drag study

Remarks :
Had a right-roll out-of-trim.

Flight 163

Flight :	163	A/C Flight :	1-65-108	B-52 :	008
Date :	7-28-66	Launch Lake :	Delamar	B-52 Crew :	Fulton/Bowline
Pilot :	McKay	Launch Time :	10:01:12.1	Chase :	Capt. Curtis
plan M :	5.20	plan Burn :	83		Bruce Peterson
actual M :	5.19	actual Burn :	85.4		Sorlie/Adams
plan h :	220,000	Duration :	:09:43.0		Capt. Gentry
actual h :	241,800	Speed (MPH) :	3,702		

Purpose :
Pace transducer
Micrometeorite collection
Horizon scanner
Electrical loads survey
Non-glare glass evaluation
Sky brightness
Stick-kicker evaluation
Rarefied gas experiment
RAS checkout

Remarks :
Computer malfunction and pitch trip-out during boost, inertials degraded after the malfunction. H dot failed prelaunch.

Flight 164

Flight :	164	A/C Flight :	2-47-84	B-52 :	008
Date :	8-3-66	Launch Lake :	Delamar	B-52 Crew :	Doryland/Bowline
Pilot :	Knight	Launch Time :	08:45:26.3	Chase :	Capt. Curtis
plan M :	5.02	plan Burn :	81.8		John Manke
actual M :	5.03	actual Burn :	81.8		Maj. Parsons
plan h :	230,000	Duration :	:09:05.5		LCol Sorlie
actual h :	249,000	Speed (MPH) :	3,477		

Purpose :
Star tracker
Pilot altitude buildup
Alternate pitot-static system ckout
Base drag study

Remarks :
Inertial altitude read wrong most of the flight.

Flight :	165	A/C Flight :	3-53-79	B-52 :	008
Date :	8-4-66	Launch Lake :	Mud	B-52 Crew :	Doryland/Bowline
Pilot :	Dana	Launch Time :	09:54:43.7	Chase :	Capt. Curtis
plan M :	5.50	plan Burn :	79.5		John Manke
actual M :	5.34	actual Burn :	78.9		Maj. Parsons
plan h :	130,000	Duration :	:08:27.6		Capt. Gentry
actual h :	132,700	Speed (MPH) :	3,693		

Purpose :	Remarks :
Pilot checkout	Tape 'q' read about 50 psf higher than the gauge.
Heat transfer panels data	
Cockpit display evaluation	
Horizontal tail loads data	
Boundary layer noise data	
Optical background experiment	

Flight :	166	A/C Flight :	1-66-111	B-52 :	003
Date :	8-11-66	Launch Lake :	Delamar	B-52 Crew :	Doryland/Bowline
Pilot :	McKay	Launch Time :	09:44:13.1	Chase :	LCol Sorlie
plan M :	5.15	plan Burn :	84.5		John Manke
actual M :	5.21	actual Burn :	84.8		Capt. Evenson
plan h :	250,000	Duration :	:09:22.2		Capt. Gentry
actual h :	251,000	Speed (MPH) :	3,590		

Purpose :	Remarks :
Horizon scanner	Highest dynamic pressure (2202 psf) for any
Micrometeorite collection	X-15 flight.
Sky brightness	Computer malfunction and pitch-roll trip-out
Rarefied gas experiment	during boost, reset, inertials degraded thereafter.
Electrical loads survey	
Wing tip-pod flutter investigation	

Flight :	167	A/C Flight :	2-48-85	B-52 :	003
Date :	8-12-66	Launch Lake :	Delamar	B-52 Crew :	Doryland/Bowline
Pilot :	Knight	Launch Time :	10:25:33.0	Chase :	LCol Sorlie
plan M :	5.02	plan Burn :	81.8		Don Mallick
actual M :	5.02	actual Burn :	81.7		Capt. Smith
plan h :	230,000	Duration :	:08:39.4		Maj. Adams
actual h :	231,100	Speed (MPH) :	3,473		

Purpose :
Star tracker
Alternate pitot-static system ckout
Base drag study

Remarks :
Good flight.

Flight :	168	A/C Flight :	3-54-80	B-52 :	003
Date :	8-19-66	Launch Lake :	Delamar	B-52 Crew :	Fulton/Bowline
Pilot :	Dana	Launch Time :	10:04:35.7	Chase :	LCol Sorlie
plan M :	5.20	plan Burn :	80		John Manke
actual M :	5.20	actual Burn :	75.8		Capt. Smith
plan h :	180,000	Duration :	:09:32.7		Maj. Adams
actual h :	178,000	Speed (MPH) :	3,607		

Purpose :
Altitude buildup
Boundary layer noise data
Horizontal tail loads data
Optical background experiment
Heat transfer panels data
Cockpit display checkout

Remarks :
Tape 'q' read about 80 psf higher than gauge.
Landed with the center stick.

Flight :	169	A/C Flight :	1-67-112	B-52 :	003
Date :	8-25-66	Launch Lake :	Delamar	B-52 Crew :Doryland/Bowline	
Pilot :	McKay	Launch Time :	09:49:11.2	Chase :	Maj. Adams
plan M :	5.15	plan Burn :	84.5		John Manke
actual M :	5.11	actual Burn :	83.4		Capt. Smith
plan h :	250,000	Duration :	:10:16.2		Maj. Knight
actual h :	257,500	Speed (MPH) :	3,543		

Purpose :	Remarks :
Horizon scanner	Telemetry lost after launch.
Micrometeorite collection	Pilot momentarily hit propellant jettison handle
Rarefied gas experiment	before the throttle.
Electrical loads	Inertial malfunction during entry.
Wing pod flutter	

Flight :	170	A/C Flight :	2-49-86	B-52 :	008
Date :	8-30-66	Launch Lake :	Mud	B-52 Crew :	Doryland/Cotton
Pilot :	Knight	Launch Time :	09:51:37.2	Chase :	Capt. Curtis
plan M :	5.30	plan Burn :	81.8		John Manke
actual M :	5.21	actual Burn :	80.5		Capt. Hover
plan h :	102,000	Duration :	:08:49.9		Capt. Stroface
actual h :	102,200	Speed (MPH) :	3,543		

Purpose :	Remarks :
Ventral-on stability and control data	Pitch and roll SAS dropouts.
Maurer camera checkout	Ventral chute deployed prematurely, H2O2 fire
Ablative tests	burned the risers, jettisoned late in the pattern.
Simulated canopy glass/canopy	Camera gimbal malfunctioned.
temperature test	
Base drag study	
M=8 computer checkout	

Flight 171

Flight :	171	A/C Flight :	1-68-113	B-52 :	008
Date :	9-8-66	Launch Lake :	Smith Ranch	B-52 Crew :	Doryland/Cotton
Pilot :	McKay	Launch Time :	10:39:16.8	Chase :	Capt. Curtis
plan M :	5.42	plan Burn :	85.5		John Manke
actual M :	2.44	actual Burn :	45.5		Capt. Stroface
plan h :	243,000	Duration :	:06:24.5		Capt. Gentry
actual h :	73,200	Speed (MPH) :	1,606		

Purpose :
Horizon scanner
Electrical loads survey
Horizontal stabilizer angle of attack
study

Remarks :
Fuel line low light caused a throttleback,
shutdown, and landing at Smith Ranch.
McKay's last X-15 flight.

Flight 172

Flight :	172	A/C Flight :	3-55-82	B-52 :	003
Date :	9-14-66	Launch Lake :	Delamar	B-52 Crew :	Doryland/Cotton
Pilot :	Dana	Launch Time :	12:01:29.5	Chase :	Capt. Curtis
plan M :	5.10	plan Burn :	77		John Manke
actual M :	5.12	actual Burn :	79.3		Capt. Hover
plan h :	250,000	Duration :	:08:57.5		Capt. Stroface
actual h :	254,200	Speed (MPH) :	3,593		

Purpose :
Altitude buildup
Micrometeorite collection
Solar spectrum analysis
Dual channel radiometer
Pace transducer
Tip-pod accelerometer data
Cockpit display evaluation

Remarks :
Alert computer would not turn on (too cold).
Third skid did not deploy.
Tape 'g' was erratic.

Flight 173

Flight :	173	A/C Flight :	1-69-116	B-52 :	003
Date :	10-6-66	Launch Lake :	Hidden Hills	B-52 Crew :	Doryland/Cotton
Pilot :	Adams	Launch Time :	12:16:59.8	Chase :	LCol. Sorlie
plan M :	4.00	plan Burn :	129		Bill Dana
actual M :	3.00	actual Burn :	89.9		Capt. Gentry
plan h :	74,000	Duration :	:08:26.4		
actual h :	75,400	Speed (MPH) :	1,977		

Purpose :
Pilot checkout

Remarks :
Ruptured fuel tank caused a premature
shutdown and landing at Cuddeback.

Flight :	174	A/C Flight :	3-56-83	B-52 :		003
Date :	11-1-66	Launch Lake :	Smith Ranch	B-52 Crew :	Doryland/Reschke
Pilot :	Dana	Launch Time :	13:24:12.8	Chase :	Maj. Adams
plan M :	5.27	plan Burn :	81		Bruce Peterson
actual M :	5.46	actual Burn :	82.8		Capt. Stroface
plan h :	267,000	Duration :	:10:43.5		Capt. Gentry
actual h :	306,900	Speed (MPH) :	3,784		

Purpose :	Remarks :
Micrometeorite collection	Dana's astronaut qualification flight.
Dual channel radiometer	Last X-15 flight above 300,000 feet.
Tip-pod accelerometer data	Micrometeorite collector did not cycle.
Precision attitude checkout	Theta read high during boost.
Alert computer checkout	Check list knocked loose during 0 *g* flight.
Sky brightness experiment	Two computer malfunction lights.
Cockpit display evaluation	

Flight :	175	A/C Flight :	2-50-89	B-52 :	008
Date :	11-18-66	Launch Lake :	Mud	B-52 Crew :	Fulton/Cotton
Pilot :	Knight	Launch Time :	13:24:07.2	Chase :	Maj. Adams
plan M :	6.00	plan Burn :	132		Bruce Peterson
actual M :	6.33	actual Burn :	136.4		Capt. Curtis
plan h :	100,000	Duration :	:08:26.8		Jack McKay
actual h :	98,900	Speed (MPH) :	4261		Capt. Gentry

Purpose :	Remarks :
Aircraft handling characteristics	Got a fuel line low light, throttled back, then
with full external tanks	proceeded at full thrust.
External tank separation	Tanks separated well and were recovered.
characteristics	Two flights tried today, Ship number 3 aborted.
Martin ablative test	
Maurer camera test	
Local flow conditions in	
ramjet area	
Base drag study	
Simulated canopy glass/ablative test	
Canopy hook loads	
Thermocouple checkout	

Flight 176

Flight :	176	A/C Flight :	3-57-86	B-52 :	003
Date :	11-29-66	Launch Lake :	Hidden Hills	B-52 Crew :	Fulton/Cotton
Pilot :	Adams	Launch Time :	11:38:32.6	Chase :	Maj. Knight
plan M :	4.50	plan Burn :	98		John Manke
actual M :	4.65	actual Burn :	97.9		Capt. Gentry
plan h :	95,000	Duration :	:07:55.9		
actual h :	92,100	Speed (MPH) :	3,120		

Purpose :
Pilot checkout
Tip-pod accelerometer data

Remarks :
No radio from launch to Cuddeback.

Flight 177

Flight :	177	A/C Flight :	1-70-119	B-52 :	003
Date :	3-22-67	Launch Lake :	Mud	B-52 Crew :	Cotton/Reschke
Pilot :	Adams	Launch Time :	09:52:04.5	Chase :	Capt. Gentry
plan M :	5.50	plan Burn :	82.5		Bruce Peterson
actual M :	5.59	actual Burn :	79.7		Capt. Evenson
plan h :	130,000	Duration :	:09:27.9		Maj. Knight
actual h :	133,100	Speed (MPH) :	3,822		

Purpose :
Pilot buildup
Stabilizer angle of attack
Electrical loads survey
Third skid checkout
Stabilizer ablatives
Yaw ASAS
Sonic boom study
Precision attitude indicator checkout

Remarks :
Cockpit pressure lost during boost.
Roll out-of-trim (stabilizer ablative?).
Inertials failed after shutdown.

Flight :	178	A/C Flight :	3-58-87	B-52 :	008
Date :	4-26-67	Launch Lake :	Silver	B-52 Crew :	Cotton/Bowline
Pilot :	Dana	Launch Time :	11:20:17.3	Chase :	Capt. Gentry
plan M :	4.65	plan Burn :	103		John Manke
actual M :	1.80	actual Burn :	23.2		Maj. Knight
plan h :	71,000	Duration :	:05:16.7		
actual h :	53,400	Speed (MPH) :	1,190		

Purpose :	Remarks :
PCM system checkout	Frozen ball-nose required a ten-minute turn
Coldwall heat transfer data	before launch.
Step panel heat transfer data	Fuel line low light caused an early shutdown
Boost guidance checkout	and landing at Silver Lake.
Energy management checkout	Blow-off panel was not ejected.
Tip-pod accelerometer data	
Sonic boom study	
Horizontal tail loads data	

Flight :	179	A/C Flight :	1-71-121	B-52 :	003
Date :	4-28-67	Launch Lake :	Delamar	B-52 Crew :	Cotton/Bowline
Pilot :	Adams	Launch Time :	09:23:32.6	Chase :	LCol Sorlie
plan M :	5.20	plan Burn :	81		John Manke
actual M :	5.44	actual Burn :	82.0		Capt. Evenson
plan h :	180,000	Duration :	:09:16.0		Maj. Cuthill
actual h :	167,200	Speed (MPH) :	3,733		

Purpose :	Remarks :
Altitude buildup	Pitch attitude malfunctioned.
WTR experiment checkout	Inertial velocity was erratic.
Horizon scanner checkout	
Horizontal stabilizer alpha data	
Third skid checkout	
Electrical loads survey	
IRIG timer checkout	

Flight :	180	A/C Flight :	2-51-92	B-52 :	008
Date :	5-8-67	Launch Lake :	Hidden Hills	B-52 Crew :	Cotton/Reschke
Pilot :	Knight	Launch Time :	12:27:38.8	Chase :	LCol Sorlie
plan M :	4.50	plan Burn :	74		Capt. Evenson
actual M :	4.75	actual Burn :	76.9		Bill Dana
plan h :	90,000	Duration :	:08:31.5		Maj. Adams
actual h :	97,600	Speed (MPH) :	3,205		

Purpose :
Stability and control data with
dummy ramjet on
Thermocouple checkout
Canopy eyelid checkout
Ramjet local flow data
Modified nose gear door checkout
Yaw ASAS checkout
Canopy hook loads data
Ablative test
Wing tip accelerometer data
Ramjet separation evalation
Alternate airspeed source checkout

Remarks :
Three-axis transients when eyelid was opened.
Ramjet chute came off but ramjet was
refurbishable.
Left window fogged up in the pattern after
eyelid was opened.

Flight :	181	A/C Flight :	3-59-89	B-52 :	003
Date :	5-17-67	Launch Lake :	Silver	B-52 Crew :	Reschke/Cotton
Pilot :	Dana	Launch Time :	10:45:48.0	Chase :	LCol Sorlie
plan M :	4.65	plan Burn :	103		John Manke
actual M :	4.80	actual Burn :	96.1		Capt. Evenson
plan h :	71,000	Duration :	:06:55.6		Maj. Cuthill
actual h :	71,100	Speed (MPH) :	3,177		

Purpose :
PCM system checkout
Coldwall heat transfer data
Step panel heat transfer data
Boost guidance checkout
Energy management checkout
Tip-pod accelerometer data
Sonic boom study
Horizontal tail loads data

Remarks :
Panel ejection at 1,500 psf caused severe
oscillation in upper vertical.tail.

Flight 182

Flight :	182	A/C Flight :	1-72-125	B-52 :	003
Date :	6-15-67	Launch Lake :	Delamar	B-52 Crew :	Cotton/Reschke
Pilot :	Adams	Launch Time :	11:09:28.3	Chase :	Capt. Gentry
plan M :	5.15	plan Burn :	81		John Manke
actual M :	5.14	actual Burn :	81.4		Capt. Davey
plan h :	220,000	Duration :	:09:11.0		Capt. Hoag
actual h :	229,300	Speed (MPH) :	3,606		

Purpose :	Remarks :
Pilot altitude buildup	Stick-kicker did not operate.
Horizon scanner	
Horizontal stabilizer alpha data	
IRIG timer checkout	
WTR experiment checkout	

Flight 183

Flight :	183	A/C Flight :	3-60-90	B-52 :	008
Date :	6-22-67	Launch Lake :	Hidden Hills	B-52 Crew :	Cotton/Sturmthal
Pilot :	Dana	Launch Time :	14:57:17.1	Chase :	Maj. Knight
plan M :	5.30	plan Burn :	95		John Manke
actual M :	5.34	actual Burn :	93.2		Gary Krier
plan h :	82,000	Duration :	:07:06.5		Capt. Gentry
actual h :	82,200	Speed (MPH) :	3,611		

Purpose :	Remarks :
Cold wall heat transfer data	Panel ejected at 1200 psf, severe oscillations
Step panel heat transfer data	again.
PCM checkout	Window shade would not retract.
	Buffet at 10 degrees pullup (at M=3).

Flight 184

Flight :	184	A/C Flight :	1-73-126	B-52 :	008
Date :	6-29-67	Launch Lake :	Smith Ranch	B-52 Crew :	Reschke/Sturmthal
Pilot :	Knight	Launch Time :	11:27:51.2	Chase :	Maj. Cuthill
plan M :	5.70	plan Burn :	87		Bill Dana
actual M :	4.23	actual Burn :	67.6		Hugh Jackson
plan h :	250,000	Duration :	:10:07.0		Capt. Evenson
actual h :	173,000	Speed (MPH) :	2,870		Maj. Hoag/Davey

Purpose :	Remarks :
WTR experiment	Total power failure going through 107,000 feet.
Horizon scanner	One APU restarted and an emergency landing
Horizontal stabilizer alpha data	was made at Mud Lake. (Energy vs Time
Yaw ASAS checkout	would have indicated Grapevine landing.)
	Headrest blown inside canopy after landing.

	Flight :	185	A/C Flight :	3-61-91	B-52 :	008
	Date :	7-20-67	Launch Lake :	Hidden Hills	B-52 Crew :	Cotton/Fulton
	Pilot :	Dana	Launch Time :	10:11:00.8	Chase :	Maj. Adams
plan	M :	5.30	plan Burn :	95		Gary Krier
actual	M :	5.44	actual Burn :	92.1		Capt. Davey
plan	h :	82,000	Duration :	:07:36.5		
actual	h :	84,300	Speed (MPH) :	3,693		

Purpose :

Cold wall heat transfer data
Wavey panel heat transfer data
Boost guidance checkout
PCM system checkout
Horizontal tail loads data
Nose gear loads data
Tip-pod accelerometer data

Remarks :

Alert computer did not operate.
Panel ejected at 1,000 psf.

	Flight :	186	A/C Flight :	2-52-96	B-52 :	008
	Date :	8-21-67	Launch Lake :	Hidden Hills	B-52 Crew :	Cotton/Reschke
	Pilot :	Knight	Launch Time :	10:59:16.0	Chase :	Maj. Cuthill
plan	M :	5.10	plan Burn :	85		Capt. Evenson
actual	M :	4.94	actual Burn :	82.2		John Manke
plan	h :	90,000	Duration :	:07:40.0		Maj. Adams/Davey
actual	h :	91,000	Speed (MPH) :	3,368		

Purpose :

Stability and control with dummy
ramjet and ablatives
Martin ablative test
Hycon phase II camera
Ramjet local flow test
Ramjet separation characteristics
Wing tip accelerometer data

Remarks :

First flight with full ablative coating, no tanks,
ramjet on.
Forward quarter of right window fogged due
to the ablator (unusable).
Ramjet ejected too close to the ground,
parachute did not deploy.
Camera mount failed.

Flight :	187	A/C Flight :	3-62-92	B-52 :	003
Date :	8-25-67	Launch Lake :	Hidden Hills	B-52 Crew :	Bowline/Reschke
Pilot :	Adams	Launch Time :	13:27:28.0	Chase :	Capt. Gentry
plan M :	4.50	plan Burn :	67		Hugh Jackson
actual M :	4.63	actual Burn :	71.3		Maj. Knight
plan h :	85,000	Duration :	:07:37.0		
actual h :	84,400	Speed (MPH) :	3,115		

Purpose :
Boost guidance
Phase II tail loads data
Cold wall heat transfer data
Tip-pod accelerometer data
Boundary layer noise data

Remarks :
Engine relight required (16 sec).
Inertials and ball nose failed just prior to
touchdown.

Flight :	188	A/C Flight :	2-53-97	B-52 :	008
Date :	10-3-67	Launch Lake :	Mud	B-52 Crew :	Cotton/Reschke
Pilot :	Knight	Launch Time :	14:31:50.9	Chase :	Maj. Cuthill
plan M :	6.50	plan Burn :	141		Maj. Twinting
actual M :	6.70	actual Burn :	140.7		Gary Krier
plan h :	100,000	Duration :	:08:17.0		Maj. Adams
actual h :	102,100	Speed (MPH) :	4520		

Purpose :
Martin ablative test (full coat)
Stability and control data with
dummy ramjet
Ramjet local flow test
External tank separation data
Wing tip accelerometer data
Fluidic temperature probe data

Remarks :
Ball nose temporarily froze at high temperature.
Ramjet separated prematurely over the
bombing range.
Extensive heat damage (burnthrough) to the
pylon and ramjet.
Heating failed a control-gas line so residual
propellant could not be jettisoned.
One-half of the right window fogged.
Pitch axis was sensitive at high Mach numbers.
Unofficial speed record for its class.
Fastest flight of the X-15 program.
Last flight of X-15A-2 aircraft.
Aircraft is on permanent display at the Air Force
Museum at Wright-Patterson Air Force Base.

Flight :	189	A/C Flight :	3-63-94	B-52 :	003
Date :	10-4-67	Launch Lake :	Smith Ranch	B-52 Crew :	Cotton/Reschke
Pilot :	Dana	Launch Time :	10:16:54.0	Chase :	Maj. Cuthill
plan M :	5.68	plan Burn :	84.3		Gary Krier
actual M :	5.53	actual Burn :	84.7		Capt. Gentry
plan h :	250,000	Duration :	:10:46.0		John Manke
actual h :	251,100	Speed (MPH) :	3,910		

Purpose :	Remarks :
Ultraviolet exhaust plume	Pilot's O2 light came on in pattern.
Solar spectrum measurements	Micrometeorite collector did not fully
Micrometeorite collection	retract for reentry.
Air density measurement	
X-ray air density experiment	
Ames boost guidance	
Tip-pod camera	

Flight :	190	A/C Flight :	3-64-95	B-52 :	008
Date :	10-17-67	Launch Lake :	Smith Ranch	B-52 Crew :	Reschke/Miller
Pilot :	Knight	Launch Time :	09:40:23.0	Chase :	Maj. Cuthill
plan M :	5.60	plan Burn :	84.4		Maj. Twinting
actual M :	5.53	actual Burn :	84.2		Capt. Gentry
plan h :	273,000	Duration :	:10:06.3		Maj. Adams
actual h :	280,500	Speed (MPH) :	3,869		

Purpose :	Remarks :
Ultraviolet exhaust plume	Third skid didn't deploy.
Solar spectrum measurements	Knight's astronaut qualification flight.
Micrometeorite collection	
Ames boost guidance	
Tip-pod camera	

Flight :	191	A/C Flight :	3-65-97	B-52 :	008	
Date :	11-15-67	Launch Lake :	Delamar	B-52 Crew :	Cotton/Miller	
Pilot :	Adams	Launch Time :	10:30:07.4	Chase :	Maj. Cuthill	
plan M :	5.10	plan Burn :	79		Hugh Jackson	
actual M :	5.20	actual Burn :	82.3		Bill Dana	
plan h :	250,000	Duration :	:04:51.4		Maj. Twinting	
actual h :	266,000	Speed (MPH) :	3,617			

Purpose :
Ultraviolet exhaust plume
Solar spectrum measurements
Micrometeorite collection
Traversing probe
Saturn ablative test
Ames boost guidance
Tip-pod camera
Nose gear loads

Remarks :
Lack of proper response to heading error
caused high Mach (hypersonic) spin.
Flight control system malfunction during
reentry caused uncontrollable pitch
oscillations, breaking up the aircraft.
Major Adams was posthumously awarded
astronaut wings for this flight.

Flight :	192	A/C Flight :	1-74-130	B-52 :	008
Date :	3-1-68	Launch Lake :	Hidden Hills	B-52 Crew :	Cotton/Stroup
Pilot :	Dana	Launch Time :	11:28:11.0	Chase :	Maj. Twinting
plan M :	4.10	plan Burn :	66		Gary Krier
actual M :	4.36	actual Burn :	65.6		Maj. Knight
plan h :	106,000	Duration :	:07:35.1		Hugh Jackson
actual h :	104,500	Speed (MPH) :	2,877		

Purpose :
Aircraft checkout
Yaw ASAS checkout

Remarks :
g suit "grabbed" at 1.5 g during pattern.

Flight 193

Flight :	193	A/C Flight :	1-75-133	B-52 :	008
Date :	4-4-68	Launch Lake :	Delamar	B-52 Crew :	Cotton/Sturmthal
Pilot :	Dana	Launch Time :	10:02:17.1	Chase :	LCol Cuthill
plan M :	5.00	plan Burn :	79		Hugh Jackson
actual M :	5.27	actual Burn :	78.8		Capt. Smith
plan h :	180,000	Duration :	:09:22.8		Capt. Hoag
actual h :	187,500	Speed (MPH) :	3,634		Fitz Fulton

Purpose :
Aircraft systems checkout
WTR experiment
Saturn ablatives
Tip-pod camera
Fixed alpha ball evaluation

Remarks :
PMR experiment required the use of the
emergency retract system.

Flight 194

Flight :	194	A/C Flight :	1-76-134	B-52 :	008
Date :	4-26-68	Launch Lake :	Delamar	B-52 Crew :	Sturmthal/Reschke
Pilot :	Knight	Launch Time :	11:51:49.8	Chase :	John Manke
plan M :	5.10	plan Burn :	80		Gary Krier
actual M :	5.05	actual Burn :	81.5		Capt. Livingston
plan h :	200,000	Duration :	:09:17.1		Maj. Gentry
actual h :	209,600	Speed (MPH) :	3,545		Fitz Fulton

Purpose :
Saturn insulation
Horizon scanner
Fixed ball nose

Remarks :
Low-alpha, high-q rotation performed with
10 degrees of speed brake for the Saturn
insulation experiment.

Flight 195

Flight :	195	A/C Flight :	1-77-136	B-52 :	008
Date :	6-12-68	Launch Lake :	Smith Ranch	B-52 Crew :	Cotton/Reschke
Pilot :	Dana	Launch Time :	08:31:01.0	Chase :	Maj. Gentry
plan M :	5.40	plan Burn :	84.6		John Manke
actual M :	5.15	actual Burn :	83.4		Hugh Jackson
plan h :	222,000	Duration :	:11:28.0		Capt. Hoag
actual h :	220,100	Speed (MPH) :	3,566		Fitz Fulton

Purpose :
WTR experiment
Saturn insulation
Horizon scanner
Fixed ball nose

Remarks :
Emergency retract used for WTR experiment.

Flight :	196	A/C Flight :	1-78-138	B-52 :	003
Date :	7-16-68	Launch Lake :	Railroad Vly	B-52 Crew :Sturmthal/Reschke	
Pilot :	Knight	Launch Time :	15:23:06.7	Chase :	Maj. Gentry
plan M :	4.95	plan Burn :	83		John Manke
actual M :	4.79	actual Burn :	80.5		LCol Cuthill
plan h :	250,000	Duration :	:09:42.3		Maj. Davey
actual h :	221,500	Speed (MPH) :	3,361		Gary Krier

Purpose :	Remarks :
WTR experiment	First launch out of Railroad Valley.
Horizon scanner	Hydraulic gauge malfunction during boost
Sky brightness	required pushover to alternate profile.
Fluidic probe	Experienced shaking and vibrations during
Fixed alpha ball	glide back to Edwards.
	WTR experiment not extended due to above
	problems.

Flight :	197	A/C Flight :	1-79-139	B-52 :	003
Date :	8-21-68	Launch Lake :	Railroad Vly	B-52 Crew :	Sturmthal/Fulton
Pilot :	Dana	Launch Time :	09:04:48.0	Chase :	LCol Cuthill
plan M :	4.95	plan Burn :	82.5		Gary Krier
actual M :	5.01	actual Burn :	82.9		Capt. Hoag
plan h :	250,000	Duration :	:09:23.0		Maj. Gentry
actual h :	267,500	Speed (MPH) :	3,443		Capt. Schawler

Purpose :	Remarks :
WTR experiment	WTR retracted on timer due to altitude
Horizon scanner	overshoot.
Sky brightness	Last X-15 flight over 50 miles high.
Fluidic probe	
Fixed alpha ball	

Flight 198

Flight :	198	A/C Flight :	1-80-140	B-52 :	003
Date :	9-13-68	Launch Lake :	Smith Ranch	B-52 Crew :	Sturmthal/Miller
Pilot :	Knight	Launch Time :	11:19:23.2	Chase :	Maj. Twinting
plan M :	5.47	plan Burn :	88		John Manke
actual M :	5.37	actual Burn :	84.3		Capt. Schawler
plan h :	250,000	Duration :	:10:55.5		Maj. Gentry
actual h :	254,100	Speed (MPH) :	3,723		Gary Krier

Purpose :	Remarks :
WTR experiment	WTR experiment required emergency retract.
Horizon scanner	Knight's last flight in the X-15.
Sky brightness	
Fluidic probe	
Fixed alpha ball	

Flight 199

Flight :	199	A/C Flight :	1-81-141	B-52 :	003
Date :	10-24-68	Launch Lake :	Smith Ranch	B-52 Crew :	Sturmthal/Miller
Pilot :	Dana	Launch Time :	10:02:47.3	Chase :	LCol Cuthill
plan M :	5.45	plan Burn :	84		Gary Krier
actual M :	5.38	actual Burn :	83.8		Einar Enevoldsen
plan h :	250,000	Duration :	:11:28.3		Capt. Evenson
actual h :	255,000	Speed (MPH) :	3,716		Maj. Hoag/J. Manke

Purpose :	Remarks :
WTR experiment	Good target coordination.
Fixed alpha cone	WTR experiment extended but lost power.
Fluidic probe	Number 2 BCS never turned on.
	Last flight of the X-15 program.
	Aircraft number 1 now resides in the National
	Air and Space Museum in Washington, D.C.

DESCRIPTION OF FLIGHT DESIGNATIONS

The flight records of the X-15 mention captive flights, cancelled flights, aborted flights, and free flights. Some explanation of this nomenclature is warranted.

A "captive flight" was a planned mated flight of the B-52 and X-15. On a captive flight, there was no plan to launch the X-15. The plan called for the B-52 to take off and land with the X-15 still attached. This type of flight was utilized to check out the operation of some X-15 system or component in the real flight environment if there was some question whether that system would actually operate properly in the flight environment. We could, in this manner, ensure that the system or component would work properly without jeopardizing the X-15. All captive flights are noted in the flight logs.

A "cancelled flight" was a planned free flight of the X-15 that was cancelled before takeoff of the B-52 and X-15 combination. No formal records were kept of cancelled flights. Flights were cancelled for a wide variety of reasons, including weather, wet lakebeds, schedule slips, lack of support, schedule conflicts.

An "aborted flight" was a planned free flight of the X-15 that was cancelled, or aborted, after takeoff of the B-52 and X-15 combination. The X-15 came back still attached to the B-52. Aborted flights are noted in the flight logs. Flights were generally aborted due to failure of some component or system in the X-15 during checkout prior to launch. Flights were occasionally aborted for other reasons, such as rapid changes in weather or lack of chase support, but this was unusual.

During the X-15 program there were a total of 336 flights of the B-52 and X-15 combination. The X-15 was launched on 199 of these flights. Twelve of these flights were planned captive flights and the remaining 137 were aborted flights.

In the flight logs, a "C" designates a captive flight and an "A" designates an aborted flight. Each individual flight is defined by three numbers or a number, a letter, and a number. The first number is the aircraft number. The second number is the free flight number and the third number is the total number of times it was carried aloft, consisting of the total of free flights, captive flights, and aborted flights. If a flight is defined by a number, a letter, and a number, the first number is again the aircraft number, the letter designates the type of flight other than a free flight, and the last number is again the total number of free flights, captive flights, and aborted flights for that aircraft.

Flight number 3-7-14, for example, was made by the number three aircraft. It was the seventh free flight of that aircraft and it was the fourteenth time that the aircraft/B-52 combination had been airborne. The fourteen total flights included seven free flights and seven aborted or captive flights. The previous flight on that aircraft was designated 3-A-13. It was an aborted flight. Flight number 2-C-53 was made by the number two aircraft. It was a captive flight and it was the fifty-third time that the aircraft/B-52 combination had been airborne. The fifty-three flights included thirty-one free flights, twenty aborted flights, and two captive flights.

The program flight number included only the free flights. There were a total of

199 free flights. The number one aircraft made eighty-one of these flights, the number two aircraft made fifty-three of these flights, and the number three aircraft made sixty-five of these flights.

The program flight number is simply the free flight number of the combination of all three aircraft in chronological order. Flight number 1-1-5 was the first flight of the program made by the number one aircraft on June 8, 1959. Flight number 2-1-3 was the second flight of the program made by the number two aircraft on September 17, 1959. Flight number 2-2-6 was the third flight of the program made by the number two aircraft on October 17, 1959.

Appendix 2

Pilot Statistics

SCOTT CROSSFIELD

Flew for 18 months from June 8, 1959 to December 6, 1960.
Made 14 flights:
      1 glide flight
      10 flights with LR-11 engine
      3 flights with LR-99 engine
Achieved: Maximum Mach number of 2.97
      Maximum speed of 1,960 MPH
      Maximum altitude of 88,116 feet
Flew Phases I & IV (contractor demonstration phase and LR-99 engine demonstration
      phase)
Made first X-15 flight.
Made first flight using LR-11 engine.
Made first flight using LR-99 engine.
Made emergency landing on Rosamond Lake due to engine fire.
Survived aircraft explosion during LR-99 engine run.
First pilot to leave program.
Flew flights 1, 2, 3, 4, 5, 6, 7, 8, 10, 11, 17, 26, 28, 30

JOE WALKER

Flew for 41 months from March 25, 1960 to August 22, 1963.
Made 25 flights:
    5 flights with LR-11
    20 flights with LR-99
Achieved: Maximum Mach number of 5.92
    Maximum speed of 4,104 MPH
    Maximum altitude of 354,200 feet
Flew in Phases II, V, & VII (flight envelope expansion phase with LR-11 engine, flight
    envelope expansion phase with LR-99 engine and research phase).
Made first government X-15 flight.
Made maximum altitude flight.
Made maximum speed flight in standard X-15 (4,104 MPH).
Second pilot to fly X-15.
Fifth pilot to leave program.
Flew flights 9, 13, 15, 18, 20, 35, 37, 40, 44, 50, 52, 56, 59, 61, 65, 67, 76, 77, 79,
    81, 84, 86, 88, 90, 91.

BOB WHITE

Flew for 32 months from April 13, 1960 to December 14, 1962.
Made 16 flights:
    6 flights with LR-11 engine
    10 flights with LR-99 engine
Achieved: Maximum Mach number of 6.04
    Maximum speed of 4,093 MPH
    Maximum altitude of 314,750 feet
Flew in Phases II, V, & VII (flight envelope expansion phase with LR-11 engine, flight
    envelope expansion phase with LR-99 engine, and research phase).
Made maximum Mach number flight with LR-11 engine (Mach 3.50).
Made maximum altitude flight with LR-11 engine (136,000 feet).
Made FAI record altitude flight of 314,750 feet.
Third pilot to fly X-15.
Fourth pilot to leave program.
Flew flights 12, 14, 16, 19, 21, 33, 34, 36, 38, 43, 45, 55, 57, 58, 62, 75

FORREST PETERSEN

Flew for 15 1/2 months from September 23, 1960 to January 10, 1962.
Made 5 flights:
    2 flights with LR-11 engine

3 flights with LR-99 engine
Achieved: Maximum Mach number of 5.30
Maximum speed of 3,600 MPH
Maximum altitude of 101,800 feet
Flew in Phases III & V (pilot checkout phase with LR-11 engine and flight envelope expansion phase with LR-99 engine).
Made emergency landing at Mud Lake due to failure of engine to light.
Fourth pilot to fly X-15.
Second pilot to leave program.
Flew flights 22, 23, 39, 41, 47.

JACK McKAY

Flew for 70 1/2 months from October 28, 1960 to September 8, 1966.
Made 29 flights:
2 flights with LR-ll engine
27 flights with LR-99 engine
Achieved: Maximum Mach number of 5.65
Maximum speed of 3,863 MPH
Maximum altitude of 295,600 feet
Flew in Phases III, VII, VIII, & IX (pilot checkout with LR-11 engine, research phase, research and scientific experiment phase and X-15A-2 envelope expansion phase).
Made emergency landing at Mud Lake due to low engine thrust.
Survived major accident on landing.
Made emergency landing at Delamar Lake due to failure of engine propellant pump.
Made emergency landing at Smith Ranch due to low fuel line pressure.
Fifth pilot to fly X-15.
Ninth pilot to leave program.
Flew flights 24, 32, 60, 63, 70, 72, 74, 80, 83, 102, 106, 110, 115, 119, 121, 128, 131, 132, 137, 139, 146, 148, 150, 154, 157, 163, 166, 169, 171.

BOB RUSHWORTH

Flew for 68 months from November 4, 1960 to July 1, 1966.
Made 34 flights:
2 flights with LR-11 engine
32 flights with LR-99 engine
Achieved: Maximum Mach number of 6.06
Maximum speed of 4,018 MPH
Maximum altitude of 285,000 feet
Flew in Phases III, VII, VIII, & IX (pilot checkout with LR-11, research phase, research & scientific experiment phase, & X-15A-2 envelope expansion phase).

Made first ventral off flight.
Made maximum dynamic pressure and temperature flight.
Made maximum Mach number flight in standard X-15 (Mach 6.06).
Made first flight of X-15A-2.
Made first flight of X-15A-2 with external tanks.
Sixth pilot to fly X-15.
Eighth pilot to leave program.
Flew flights 25, 27, 42, 53, 54, 66, 68, 69, 71, 73, 78, 82, 85, 87, 89, 94, 97, 100, 103, 105, 109, 114, 118, 124, 127, 129, 140, 141, 145, 147, 149, 155, 158, 159.

NEIL ARMSTRONG

Flew for 20 months from November 30, 1960 to July 26, 1962.
Made 7 flights:
    2 flights with LR-11 engine
    5 flights with LR-99 engine
Achieved: Maximum Mach number of 5.74
    Maximum speed of 3,989 MPH
    Maximum altitude of 207,500 feet
Flew in Phases III, VI, & VII (pilot checkout with LR-11 engine, demonstration of MH-96 flight control system, & research phase).
Made first flight with ball nose.
Made first flight with MH-96 flight control system.
Seventh pilot to fly X-15.
Third pilot to leave program.
Flew flights 29, 31, 46, 48, 49, 51, 64.

JOE ENGLE

Flew for 24 months from October 7, 1963 to October 14, 1965.
Made 16 flights:
    All flights with LR-99 engine
Achieved: Maximum Mach number of 5.71
    Maximum speed of 3,888 MPH
    Maximum altitude of 280,600 feet
Flew Phases VII & VIII (research phase and research and scientific experiment phase).
Eighth pilot to fly X-15.
Seventh pilot to leave program.
Flew flights 92, 95, 98, 104, 107, 111, 112, 117, 123, 126, 130, 134, 135, 138, 143, 153.

MILT THOMPSON

Flew for 22 months from October 29, 1963 to August 25,1965.
Made 14 flights:
      All flights with LR-99 engine
Achieved: Maximum Mach number of 5.48
           Maximum speed of 3,724 MPH
           Maximum altitude of 214,100 feet
Flew in Phases VII & VIII (research phase and research and scientific experiment phase)
Made an emergency landing at Cuddeback Lake due to premature engine shutdown.
Ninth pilot to fly X-15.
Sixth pilot to leave program.
Flew flights 93, 96, 99, 101, 108, 113, 116, 120, 122, 125, 133, 136, 142, 144

"PETE" KNIGHT

Flew for 35 1/2 months from September 30, 1965 to September 13, 1968.
Made 16 flights:
      All flights with LR-99 engine
Achieved: Maximum Mach number of 6.70
           Maximum speed of 4520 MPH
           Maximum altitude of 280,500 feet
Flew in Phase VIII & IX (research and scientific experiment phase and X-15A-2 envelope
        expansion phase).
Made first flight with dummy scramjet.
Made first flight with ablative coating.
Made first flight with complete high-speed configuration.
Made emergency landing at Mud Lake due to failure of both APUs.
Tenth pilot to fly X-15.
Still flying at program termination.
Flew flights 151, 152, 160, 162, 164, 167, 170, 175, 180, 184, 186, 188, 190, 194,
        196, 198.

BILL DANA

Flew for 35 1/2 months from November 4, 1965 to October 24, 1968.
Made 16 flights:
      All flights were made with the LR-99 engine
Achieved: Maximum Mach number of 5.53
           Maximum speed of 3,897 MPH
           Maximum altitude of 306,900 feet
Flew in Phase VIII (research and scientific experiment phase).

Made last flight in X-15.
Made emergency landing at Silver Lake due to low fuel line pressure.
Eleventh pilot to fly X-15.
Last pilot to fly X-15.
Flew flights 156, 161, 165, 168, 172, 174, 178, 181, 183, 185, 189, 192, 193, 195, 197, 199.

MIKE ADAMS

Flew for 13 months from October 6, 1966 to November 15, 1967.
Made 7 flights:
   All flights made with LR-99 engine
Achieved: Maximum Mach number of 5.59
         Maximum speed of 3,822 MPH
         Maximum altitude of 266,000 feet
Flew in Phase VIII (research and scientific experiment phase).
Made emergency landing at Cuddeback Lake due to rupture of bulkhead in liquid oxygen tank.
Twelfth pilot to fly X-15.
Tenth pilot to leave program.
Flew flights 173, 176, 177, 179, 182, 187, 191.

Appendix 3

Aircraft Availability

Only two aircraft, the number one and the number two, were flying during the first forty-five flights. The number three aircraft was extensively damaged in an explosion during an engine ground run prior to its first flight. It was rebuilt and it made the forty-sixth flight of the program on its first flight. All three aircraft were flying from the forty-sixth flight through the seventy-fourth flight when the number two aircraft was extensively damaged in a landing accident at Mud Lake.

The number one and number three aircraft made the next thirty-three flights (75–109), while the number two aircraft was being rebuilt and modified. The number two made the 109th flight and then all three aircraft continued to fly until the 188th flight. The number two aircraft was damaged during the 188th flight by the excessive heating generated by shock waves off the dummy scramjet. Although the aircraft was repaired, it never flew again. Three flights later, the 191st, the number three aircraft was destroyed in flight due to excessive *g* loads following recovery from a hypersonic spin. The number one aircraft flew the last eight flights of the program (192–199).

Appendix 4..........................

Typical X-15 Flight Plan

Flight No.: 3-39-62   Scheduled Date: Jan. 13, 1965
Pilot: Milton O. Thompson

Purpose: To obtain data for the following programs.
  1. Non-uniform, 3 dimensional flow field measurements—(Bob Quinn & Murray Palitz)
  2. Surface discontinuity heat transfer test—c.g. compartment—(Joe Watts)
  3. Skin friction—(Darwin Garringer)
  4. Boundary-layer noise—(Tom Lewis)
  5. Landing Gear Door modification checkout—(Dick Rosecrans)

  Instrumentation Engineer—Febo Bartoli

Launch: Hidden Hills on magnetic heading 235°, MH-96 Adaptive, R.C. "OFF", BCS "OFF" heading vernier "Standby," ventral off. Launch Point Coordinates: 35° 55′ N; 115° 39′ W.

Item	Time	Alt.	Vel.	α	$\bar{q}$	Event
1.	0	45	790	2	145	Launch, light engine, increase to 100%T. Rotate at 10° α until θ = 25°.
2.	21	46	1550	10°	530	θ = 25°, maintain θ = 25°.
3.	41	62	2600	3°	700	Pushover to O g. ($\dot{H} \approx$ +950 fps).

Flight No.: 3-39-62   Scheduled Date: Jan. 13, 1965

Item	Time	Alt.	Vel.	α	$\bar{q}$	Event
4.	61	80	3900	0	660	Roll left to $\emptyset$ = 90°, then increase α to 10°.
5.	70	86	4500	10	630	α = 10°. Maintain α = 10°.
6.	71	88.5	4650	10	600	Reduce to minimum thrust. Modulate speed brakes ($\approx$ 10°–15°) to maintain slow longitudinal acceleration. Maintain $\bar{q}$ constant at $\approx$ 600 psf.
7.	80	91	4950	10	600	Increase α to 17°, retract speed brakes. Maintain α = 17°.
8.	90	92	5100	17	600	Burnout, pushover to $\approx$ 5° α. Roll to $\approx$ 60° right bank, set up rate of descent of $\approx$ 200 fps to maintain $\bar{q}$ constant at $\approx$ 600 psf.
9.	102	91	4900	10	600	Increase α to 10°, maintain α = 10°.
10.	128	85	4300	10	600	Increase α to 17°. Increase bank angle to $\approx$ 90° to maintain constant $\bar{q}$.
11.	138	81	3800	5	600	Pushover to $\approx$ 5° α, Roll to $\approx$ 60° left bank, increase to 10° α and vector to high key ($\psi \approx$ 225°).
12.	170	69	2800	3	600	Abeam Cuddeback, speed brakes as required. Engine Master "OFF."
13.						High-key—check flap and "Squat" circuit breakers in. Exp. switch "OFF."
14.						Before APU shutdown, cycle flaps, set stabilizer trim to zero, data "OFF."

Notes:
1. θ vernier will be set at 25°, α crosspointer will null at 4.5°.
2. Emergency Lake: Cuddeback.
3. Flight duration: Approximately 8 minutes.
4. Flight plan based on 59,500# thrust—Engine #103.
    Minimum thrust = 31,500#.
    Total burn time at 100% = 82 sec.
    Launch wt. = 33,750#
    Burnout Wt. = 15,550#.

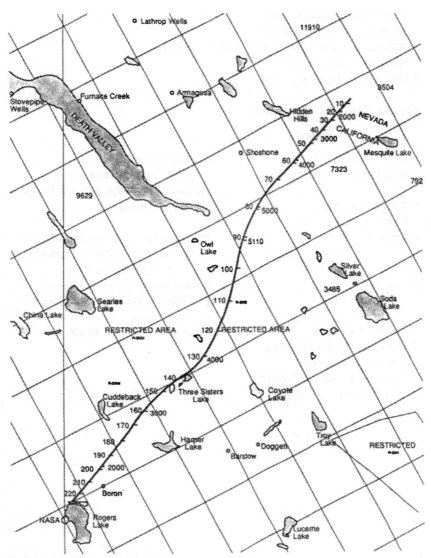

Figure 8. Map for Flight 3-39-62

Ground Rules for No Launch:
1. Radio, Radar, or TM malfunction.
2. FCS malfunctions as indicated on Analyzer check list.
3. Malfunction of ball nose.
4. Malfunction of inertial platform.

Alternate Situations After Launch:

Failure	*Action*
1. Radio, Radar	Proceed as planned.
2. Total Pitch/Roll Damper	Turn Yaw OFF, maintain $\alpha > 0$. Shutdown at 4500 fps, vector to High Key.
3. Total Yaw Damper Fixed Gain in any axis	Proceed as planned.
4. Attitude	Proceed as planned except use 4.5° α in place of 25° θ at 23 seconds. Perform roll maneuvers at pilot's discretion.
5. Ball nose	Heading vernier to $\Delta\psi$ proceed, use 1.6 g for rotation. Perform roll maneuvers at pilot's discretion.
6. Delayed engine light	Pushover to 0 g at H = 59,000 ft.
7. Inadvertent Engine shutdown: 0–45 sec. Hidden Hills 45–51 sec. Cuddeback (2800 fps) 51–UP Edwards (3200 fps)	

Index